Handbook of Communication Audits for Organisations

Why are some organisations highly successful, while others perish in the marketplace? Evidence is growing to suggest that a key part of the answer is communication. How people interact with each other, or fail to do so, often determines an organisation's overall prospects of success. Accordingly, there is growing interest in techniques which can be employed to measure current communication effectiveness and enable targets to be set for improvements.

The Handbook of Communication Audits for Organisations equips readers with the vital analytic tools required to conduct assessments. Owen Hargie, Dennis Tourish and distinguished contributors drawn from both industry and academia:

- review the main options confronting organisations embarking on audit,
- discuss the merits and demerits of the approaches available,
- provide case studies of the communication audit process in action,
- discuss how audit findings can be interpreted so suitable recommendations are framed,
- and outline how reports emanating from such audits should be constructed.

The *Handbook* will be invaluable to students of organisational communication, as well as the growing number of communications managers in the business world.

Owen Hargie is Professor of Communication at the University of Ulster. His previous publications include *The Handbook of Communication Skills* and *Social Skills in Interpersonal Communication*. **Dennis Tourish** is a senior lecturer in communications management at the University of Queensland, Australia. He is, with Owen Hargie and David Dickson, the co-author of *Communication in Management*.

International Series on Communication Skills
Series editor: Owen Hargie

Handbook of Communication Audits for Organisations

Edited by Owen Hargie
and Dennis Tourish

First published 2000 by Routledge
11 New Fetter Lane, London EC4P 4EE

Simultaneously published in the USA and Canada
by Routledge
29 West 35th Street, New York, NY 10001

Routledge is an imprint of the Taylor and Francis Group

© 2000 Owen Hargie and Dennis Tourish, selection and editorial
matter; individual chapters, the contributors

Typeset in Times by Graphicraft Limited, Hong Kong
Printed and bound in Great Britain by Biddles Ltd, Guildford and King's Lynn

British Library Cataloguing in Publication Data
A catalogue record for this book is available from the British Library

Library of Congress Cataloging in Publication Data
A catalogue record for this book has been requested

ISBN 0-415-18641-2 (hbk)
ISBN 0-415-18642-0 (pbk)

This book is dedicated to Patricia and Julie. Their love, insight, and attitude to life are a source of inspiration, and their ability to put things in perspective keeps us grounded in reality.

Contents

Illustrations

FIGURES

TABLES

CHARTS

EXHIBITS

BOXES

Contributors

Allyson D. Adrian is Assistant Professor of Business, McDonough School of Business, Georgetown University.

Laurey Berk is Senior Lecturer at the University of Wisconsin-Green Bay, and is a senior partner with MetaComm, a communications consulting firm.

Phillip G. Clampitt is Professor of Information Sciences at the University of Wisconsin-Green Bay, and a senior partner with MetaComm, a communications consulting firm.

David Dickson is Senior Lecturer and Head of the Communication Skills Training Centre, University of Ulster, Newtownabbey, Northern Ireland.

Cal W. Downs is Professor of Organizational Communication, University of Kansas.

Mary Gallagher is Lecturer in Communication at the University of Ulster, Magee Campus, Northern Ireland.

Owen Hargie is Professor of Communication at the University of Ulster, Newtownabbey, Northern Ireland.

Albert Hydeman is President of Albert Hydeman Associates, Los Angeles, California.

Mark Lount was Lecturer in Communication at the University of Ulster. Tragically, Dr Lount died just after contributing to this book.

Bernard McKenna is Lecturer in Communication in the School of Communication, Queensland University of Technology, Brisbane, Queensland, Australia.

Rob Millar is Senior Lecturer in Communication at the University of Ulster, Magee Campus, Northern Ireland.

Charles H. Patti is Professor and Head, School of Communication, Queensland University of Technology, Brisbane, Queensland, Australia.

William Renforth is Professor and Head, School of Marketing and International Business, Queensland University of Technology, Brisbane, Australia.

Myra Skipper is a Speech and Language Therapist at Belfast City Hospital, Belfast, Northern Ireland.

Glen J. Thomas is Associate Lecturer in Communication in the School of Communication, Queensland University of Technology, Brisbane, Queensland, Australia.

Dennis Tourish is Senior Lecturer in Communications Management, University of Queensland, Brisbane, Australia.

Introduction

The central purpose of this book is to explore how organisations can evaluate their internal and external communications, in order to improve their effectiveness. A core belief which animates the text is that high quality communication inside organisations, and between them and their external publics, produces many tangible benefits. These include a saner internal atmosphere, more satisfied employees and customers, greater levels of productivity and innovation, and sustained competitive advantage. As Lawrence Bossidy, CEO of the multi-billion dollar company Allied Signal, has put it: 'The day when you could yell and scream and beat people into good performance is over.' If this is true, the question is raised: what's left? It is our belief that the tools of communication are an organisation's most vital resource in the daily battle for organisational survival. This book is dedicated to establishing how their use can become as much of a reflex as barking orders often was in the past.

Yet, until now, communication has been seriously neglected. Many organisations acknowledge the need for improvements, but continue to repeat the well learnt mistakes of yesterday. Evidently, good intentions are not enough. Merely declaring the need for a new dawn does not bring it any nearer. We do not believe that these problems demonstrate bad faith on the part of the organisations and managers concerned. Most genuinely wish to move forward. But they have encountered many apparently insurmountable problems, in the attempt to turn aspiration into accomplishment. The difficulties faced include:

- accurately diagnosing current communication practices. How do you measure what seems to be invisible?
- tracking the impact of particular measures designed to improve communication. How do we know what works, and what doesn't?
- evaluating the overall contribution which communication makes to business success. How do we know that any of it matters?
- learning how to inculcate different behaviours at all levels of the organisation. It isn't that people necessarily face the new challenges with indifference. It is just that, like a drunk driver, they often do the wrong things very, very carefully.

These difficulties can be overcome. We have produced this book in the belief that communication audits build bridges between managers' aspirations and reality. What gets measured, gets done. Auditing communication involves the assessment of current practice (*diagnosis*) in order to determine what steps are required to secure improvements (*prescription*). This book offers a series of methodologies which are commonly employed to evaluate communication effectiveness. The purpose is to equip readers with vital analytic tools, enabling them to benchmark performance and effect significant improvements.

The book is, accordingly, structured in four parts: review, methods, case studies and overview. In Part I, a range of issues involved in auditing communication are reviewed. Chapter 1 provides an overall theoretical underpinning for the approaches explored. In particular, we discuss the contribution which communication makes to securing business success. It is increasingly clear that positive human resources policies are a prime determinant of organisational effectiveness. However, within this category, it is our conviction that how information is produced, exchanged and processed between people is a vital binding ingredient, holding together all the working parts of the organisation. We also look at the benefits of good communication with customers, and the costs incurred when it goes wrong. Managers are busy people and the change agenda for most of them is already stretched to breaking point. We can only justify devoting time and other resources to improving communication if it is clear that tangible, substantial and measurable benefits will accrue. In Chapter 2 the specific contribution which audits can make to the assessment of communication practices is discussed. The origins of the process in the academic and business literature are also explored.

Part II provides a detailed analysis of a range of audit methodologies, and discusses the advantages and disadvantages of each. The approaches discussed include questionnaires, focus groups, interviews, diary and log analysis, the 'mystery shopper', and techniques which may be less well known, such as constitutive ethnography and Delphi analysis. No one method works for every organisation. The intention, here, is to equip managers and researchers with a fuller understanding of the available alternatives, and so help them to decide on the most appropriate approach for whatever communication challenges they are facing.

This section also contains a chapter on auditing the communications revolution – i.e. the Intranet, e-mail, the Internet and telephones. There have been huge developments in each of these areas, and they therefore present new challenges which auditors must be ready to explore. In addition, Part II contains a chapter on writing an audit report. This chapter raises issues other than the nuts and bolts of report writing, such as breaking bad news to senior managers, devising recommendations in response to particular findings, and how to persuade key change agents within the organisation to respond positively to audit findings.

Throughout the book, it is our intention to intimately connect theory with practice. Part III therefore illuminates the approaches discussed through a range of carefully chosen case studies, derived from work in the UK, the United States and Australia. The studies here have been selected to show what a variety of methods discussed in this book look like when applied in action. They also encompass internal and external communications, in both the public and private sectors, and in the not-for-profit worlds of the Catholic priesthood and the National Health Service in Britain. It has not been possible, because of space limitations, to illustrate every available method in this way. Nevertheless, within these inevitable constraints, our aim is to explore audits in action, by illustrating how they have been employed to solve genuine problems in the real world. Each case study outlines the general context in which the audit occurred, the precise problems of the organisation concerned, the audit methodology employed (and why it was selected), and the recommendations and changes to which the intervention gave rise. These chapters provide further examples of tools and techniques which should be of enormous help to those readers undertaking audits of their own. Examples of particular audit tools which have been especially useful are also contained in the Appendix.

Finally, we conclude the book in Part IV by outlining a framework for the development of communication strategies, which integrates the implementation of audits into the strategic planning process. In this context, we discuss the criteria which should be employed in choosing between the multifarious audit tools available. This chapter also looks at the potential role of audits as a research tool, and in the teaching of management communication.

In what follows, we and our fellow contributors generally do not distinguish between audits of internal or external communication. However, Chapter 15 outlines a number of the traits which most distinguish external audits from those conducted internally. It must be acknowledged that most research in this area has been concerned with audits of internal communication. A number of the most standard instruments reflect this bias. Other approaches, such as the mystery shopper, are more widely used in audits of external communications. However, in principle, most of the approaches discussed here can be adapted to meet both situations. We refer to this issue at various points in the text which follows. Overall, we would encourage readers to be creative in their approach. There is no need to feel imprisoned by precedent. The deciding factor in what techniques to use must be the needs and resources of the organisations and researchers concerned. However, it is always useful to remember that when a conflict flares up between the ideal and the possible, it is generally wise to side with the latter. Like a battle plan, most research designs have to be changed when they engage with the real world.

Overall, this text offers a unique blend of theory, research and practice in the field of communication auditing. The communication side of organisational life looks set to attract even greater interest as we enter the new millennium. The present book will be essential for managers, communications practitioners and researchers concerned with organisational communication. Communication breakdowns are always a barometer of greater storms and mishaps ahead. Equipped with the tools discussed here, organisations will be in a better position to identify icebergs in advance of collisions (one Titanic was enough), and so chart a safe passage through the turbulent oceans of the twenty-first century marketplace.

Owen Hargie and Dennis Tourish
January 2000

Acknowledgements

We would like to acknowledge the assistance of a number of people in producing this text. Professor John Wilson, Head of the School of Psychology and Communication at the University of Ulster, has been an inexhaustible source of enthusiasm and support for research over a number of years. His assistance with sabbatical leave, and on other fronts, is much appreciated. Noel Wilson, Principal Computing Officer at the University of Ulster, greatly assisted us with statistical analysis in relation to the audit questionnaire produced in the Appendix. Technical staff at the University, particularly Philip Burch, David Pettigrew and Richard Fox, have also been unfailingly helpful in assisting us with the figures, exhibits and charts which feature at various points in the book. Finally, we acknowledge Viv Ward and Alison Dixon at Routledge for their patience and support as we wrestled with the task of welding many themes into a coherent whole.

We are grateful to the International Communication Association for giving us permission to develop and adapt their Audit Questionnaire, and for allowing us to publish the revised version in this text.

Part I

Audits in context

Chapter 1

Communication and organisational success

Dennis Tourish and Owen Hargie

INTRODUCTION

The central purpose of this book is to explore how audits provide a clear picture of the communication climate which organisations face, internally and externally. However, this approach has to be anchored within a wider context, which establishes why anyone should bother to investigate the effectiveness of their communications programmes in the first place. Managers already face a surfeit of challenges. This chapter explores the benefits derived from treating organisational communication with the same diligence normally reserved for such functions as finance. A manager's intuitive feel for whether the company's books show a profit, or are splashed in red ink, is not normally regarded as sufficient. Only communication problems are expected to correct themselves, while the organisation flails around in the marketplace, buffeted by competition from every side. This book takes a different perspective. It offers a systematic approach to the construction of a seaworthy communications strategy, and the rigorous evaluation of all steps taken along the way.

It is our contention that many business problems are the product of poor communications policies. Early action could avert shipwreck later in the day. For example, customers often take their business elsewhere because they receive inadequate information about company products; staff seek new jobs where they will have a better opportunity to contribute their ideas; levels of innovation are low because key players in rival departments are barely on speaking terms with each other. Communication audits can be used to identify and reward good practice, prepare for storms sooner rather than later, and improve business performance.

In this chapter, we review:

- the central importance of communication in the day to day work of managers;
- the growing evidence to show that internal communication helps determine an organisation's prospects of success. In the process, we review examples of good practice from leading companies. These suggest steps which other organisations should consider taking in the drive to reach world class levels of performance;

- the role of communication in maintaining customer loyalty, and the importance of such loyalty in ensuring business success;
- the implications of these issues for our general conception of the communication function.

A recurrent theme in what follows is the importance of accurately appraising what we now do, in order to establish what we must do tomorrow. Traditionally, a ship's captain was always the last person to find out that his crew intended to mutiny. Communication audits identify the symptoms of discontent, before either customers or employees storm the bridge. They are an organisation's early warning system. What follows shows why they are necessary, and how they can help.

COMMUNICATION IN MANAGEMENT

Management is about crafting a strategic vision to enhance organisational effectiveness. Turning this lofty aspiration into reality means creating and sustaining a unifying sense of purpose, on the part of many people. Organisations are increasingly becoming viewed as partnership arrangements, in which the principles of coalition building are the key to success (Tourish, 1998). But employees cannot buy into ideas which they neither know nor understand. There is a growing body of evidence to the effect that if people are excluded from the decision-making process it becomes more difficult to secure their commitment to whatever decisions have been reached by the top management team (Anderson *et al.*, 1992). In turn, if they are not committed, they are less likely to deal with customers in the manner necessary to secure repeat business.

For these reasons, communication is the most fundamental and pervasive of all management activities. Management involves an overwhelming focus on sharing information with others; seeking feedback on either the manager's ideas or those of other staff, customers, outside suppliers or franchise holders; making decisions (often in groups); commenting on proposals; and attending meetings. Information exchange, in all its multi-faceted forms, is central to the effective performance of the management function.

The pivotal role of communication in what managers actually do, as opposed to what old textbooks taught they ought to be doing, has been reinforced by the findings of many research investigations. For example, Luthans and Larsen (1986) found that managers typically spend between 60 per cent and 80 per cent of their time communicating. One study of 60 front line supervisors at a Midwest US steel manufacturing plant found that 70 per cent of them spent 8–14 hours per week in writing-related activities alone (Mabrito, 1997). These involved producing disciplinary action reports, clarifying job procedures, dealing with formal grievances, writing memos, producing instructional documents to subordinates, drafting incident reports and writing external letters or reports to customers.

It has been suggested that effective managers are particularly inclined to spend a great deal of their time in communication based activities. Kotter's landmark study into the role of general managers (1982) challenged the notion that effective executives spend their time holed up in offices where they plan, organise and motivate by manipulating pieces of paper. Kotter followed 15 chief executives through the day to day routines of their companies. He concluded that the most successful executives used a variety of influencing techniques in predominantly face to face interaction, as their primary method of persuading people and effecting successful change.

In an earlier study, Mintzberg (1973) also demonstrated the ubiquitous nature of interpersonal communication in management activity. Half the interactions engaged in by the managers in his study lasted less than nine minutes, while only 10 per cent exceeded one hour. Furthermore, around 93 per cent of the verbal contacts made by these chief executives occurred on an *ad hoc* basis. This pattern, of frequent, brief, unplanned and interrupted interactions, is rampant. A diary study of 160 British middle and top managers found that they only had the opportunity to work for a half hour or more, without interruptions, about once every two days (Stewart, 1967). More recent studies of leadership in management reaffirm the point – effective leadership in the workplace requires a constant use of the tools of communication to create meaning, share visions and build a common focus on the agenda for change (Sims and Lorenzi, 1992).

These activities are embedded in dense networks of relationships between managers and employees. The research literature generally suggests that supervisors spend between one-third and two-thirds of their time interacting with what are sometimes still termed 'subordinates' (Zorn, 1995). Most such communication is face to face, and task related rather than personal in content. Managers spend their day communicating with many people, in brief interactions which are nevertheless of enormous significance in determining the communication and cultural climate of their organisations. Effective management depends on open communication, and requires an interpersonal style characterised by warmth, candour, supportiveness and a commitment to dialogue rather than monologue. No wonder that Mintzberg (1989, p. 18), having surveyed a wide range of evidence, drew the following conclusion: 'The manager does not leave meetings or hang up the telephone in order to get back to work. In large part, communication *is* his or her work.'

Many surveys have shown that most people in organisations, from top to bottom, are keen to secure improved communications (e.g. Hargie and Tourish, 1996a; Tourish and Hargie, 1996b; Tourish and Tourish, 1997), and that such improvements are correlated with job satisfaction and commitment. These could be considered worthwhile gains in their own right. There is also now a considerable research literature to indicate that increased commitment is positively associated with improved organisational functioning (Meyer and Allen, 1997), and that even small changes in employee performance often have a significant impact on the bottom line (Cascio, 1982). These issues are of fundamental importance. As

Argyris (998) has argued, questions such as morale, satisfaction and commitment need to be viewed as a vital concern in human relations policies – but they are not decisive. That pole position is reserved for business performance. The evidence, on this issue, strongly suggests that positive communications programmes improve overall performance – a further justification for utilising communication audit methodologies as the first stage towards benchmarking and then securing further improvements. It is to a detailed consideration of this evidence that we now turn.

COMMUNICATION AND ORGANISATIONAL EFFECTIVENESS

Research findings clearly indicate that improved communication brings large scale organisational benefits. For example, Hanson (1986) found that the presence of good interpersonal relationships between managers and staff was three times more powerful in predicting profitability in 40 major companies over a five-year period than the four next most powerful variables combined – market share, capital intensity, firm size and sales growth rate. In a much wider review of the research, Clampitt and Downs (1993) concluded that the benefits obtained from quality internal communications include:

- improved productivity;
- reduced absenteeism;
- higher quality (of services and products);
- increased levels of innovation;
- fewer strikes, and;
- reduced costs.

In like vein, Snyder and Morris (1984) found that the quality of supervisory communication and information exchange within teams was significantly related to revenue and other measures of workload performance. They also found positive correlations between employee perceptions of communication and job satisfaction, which was in turn correlated with overall organisational effectiveness.

Summarising a great deal of research on this issue, Tjosvold (1991) concluded that:

> Communication within and between groups is needed for innovation in organisations. Continuous improvement occurs when people within teams and across them are identifying issues, sharing information, influencing each other, and putting ideas together.
>
> (Tjosvold, 1991, p. 81)

Similarly, Kanter (1988) argued that communication within and between organisations and sections of organisations stimulates higher levels of innovation.

When groups work in isolation, with people sharing minimal informa on across inflexible boundaries, the locomotive of change slows to a crawl. Communication audits conducted by us suggest one contributing factor to this. We have found that poor inter-departmental communication generates considerable feelings of isolation and dissatisfaction, and is in turn correlated with low levels of involvement in the decision-making process. Thus, poor information exchange exacerbates uncertainty, increases alienation and produces a segmented attitude to work which is inimical to the spirit of innovation. Kanter's conclusion is that contact at as many levels as possible is vital to wholehearted, widespread involvement in the achievement of organisational goals and the creation of a supportive climate for innovation.

Similar views have since been propounded in a series of anecdotal management books written by successful managers. One of the most interesting of such autobiographical accounts is provided by Semler (1989, 1994). He described how he turned around Brazil's largest marine and food processing machinery manufacturer. Facing ruin in 1980, by 1989 productivity and profits were rising at an annual rate of 40 per cent. Semler identified a strong focus on communications as a crucial part of the package that ensured his company's survival. The efforts made and results obtained included the following:

- Factory workers set their own production quotas.
- Employees set their own salaries, with no strings attached.
- Before people are hired or promoted into management positions they are interviewed and approved by those they will be managing.
- Managers are reviewed on their performance every six months, by those who work under them.
- Semco has grown sixfold, despite buffeting recessions.
- Productivity has increased sevenfold.
- Profits have risen fivefold.

Sheridan *et al.* (1992), in a survey of 530 nursing staff in 25 nursing homes, found a positive correlation between a healthy organisational climate and corporate success (defined as quality of care), and negative organisational climate and corporate failure. Yet the main dimensions of climate would, typically, be regarded as dealing with the soft underbelly of the management function, and as much less tangible than issues of resources, monetary reward and performance evaluation. As Mintzberg (1989) argued, there has long been a bias in management education in favour of concentrating on those variables which can be most readily quantified, often to the neglect of other issues which are of at least equal importance in determining organisational success. Consequently, whole organisations have been constructed without the mortar of communication. They risk collapse at the faintest subterranean tremor.

Participation is also emerging as a major issue in the research literature. A survey of 179 employees in one organisation suggested that employee commitment is positively correlated with what staff perceive as legitimate modes of participation, and the existence of incentives to encourage maximum participation (Brewer, 1996). Moreover, it is generally agreed that 'participation will continue to expand as part of the search for viable new forms of production organisation in contemporary global markets' (Turner, 1997, p. 312). Participative forms of management inevitably assume that many people within the organisation, outside the ranks of management, need to be kept informed of key corporate issues and that they in turn feel keen to contribute to building the organisation's success. A much more open flow of information is indispensable to the effective management of such programmes. As the requirement of participation is further extended, the communication challenges can only grow.

How does improved participation impact on organisational outcomes? Miller *et al.* (1990) surveyed over 700 people in one large organisation. They found that participation in decision-making and the existence of social support reduced workplace stress and burnout, while raising levels of satisfaction and commitment. This is connected to productivity. One meta-analysis of 43 studies concluded that profit-sharing, worker ownership and worker participation in decision-making were all positively associated with increased productivity (Doucouliagos, 1995).

In like vein, a report produced by the Institute of Directors in Britain suggested that of those companies with employee communications policies, 65.1 per cent credited them with improving productivity, 68.1 per cent with fewer industrial disputes, and 80.3 per cent with achieving improvements in loyalty (Dawson-Sheperd and White, 1994). There appears to be a correlation between high performance and the existence of internal communications programmes. A survey of 293 communications professionals in UK companies classified their organisations into well performing and poorly performing categories (Stewart, 1999). The former were defined as companies which had excellent or good financial performance for all of the three preceding years, whereas those whose financial performance had been poor or very poor for all three years were classified as poorly performing organisations. Over half those in the former category had formal communications programmes. This compared to only 25 per cent of their poorly performing counterparts.

A study has also been conducted into 135 high performing US companies (Towers-Perrin, 1993). In these, there was a strong tendency to seek suggestions from front line employees, delegate, develop two-way communications and seek suggestions. Seventy-four per cent of employees in such organisations felt that their manager or supervisor asked them for ideas on improving efficiency – in another study of poorer performing organisations this figure was only 41 per cent. In this tradition, some organisations use the information gained in surveys of employee opinion to decide on executive compensation packages. AES Inc. is a highly profitable power-generating company, committed to producing what it sees as non-nuclear and socially responsible power. Top managers' bonuses are cut in half if surveys show that its staff are not having fun (Colville *et al.*, 1999)!

The evidence on these issues is by now extensive. One of the most detailed, and therefore most interesting, accounts available concerns General Motors (GM). Few organisations have tracked exactly what they have done and its effects so precisely. It is therefore worth recounting the nature of GM's communications programme and the results in some detail. These have been recounted in depth by McKeans (1990) and Smith (1991).

The communications programme began in 1982 in one division, led by a senior manager who wished to transform the division's communication and performance. His first move was to motivate senior colleagues, by getting them to read widely into the basics of effective internal communications. He then upgraded the division's newsletter, increased the frequency of its publication and included much more key business information. A variety of other publications was also produced, including one jointly written and funded with trade union organisations.

A communications review group was set up, which met monthly, and evaluated the range of publications being issued. This group involved top management and institutionalised their personal involvement in the programme. Other steps were as follows:

- A quarterly video news magazine was produced, allowing management to present detailed business information – if not in person then at least on camera. This was shown during working hours in scheduled meetings, and served as a launch pad for face to face discussions between supervisors and staff.
- Face to face meetings were held. General managers met with randomly selected small groups of staff, with the express purpose of facilitating open discussion on highly sensitive issues.
- Regular audits, video surveys and quality culture surveys were conducted to track the impact of the programme. Thus, follow up audits were conducted every two years.

It is noteworthy that none of these steps is enormously radical. Indeed, as Arnott (1987) observed, internal communications programmes which effect significant improvements are often characterised by their simplicity. However, in their totality they can be summed up as the adoption of a creative approach to ensuring the maximum amount of interaction between as many groups of people as possible, and a new openness in the sharing of information. The results, for GM at any rate, can be evaluated in terms of both the quality of communication, and bottom line business performance:

- Less than 50 per cent of GM employees said they believed the information supplied by management in 1982. By 1986 this had risen to over 80 per cent.
- Budget savings amounted to 2.8 per cent for the first year, 4.9 per cent in the second, then 3.2 per cent, 3.7 per cent and 2.2 per cent.
- Sales doubled over a seven-year period.

- By 1988 delays in delivering service parts were eliminated.
- Suggestion scheme savings per employee were $864 in 1981, $1220 in 1982, $1306 the following year, followed by $1741, $1547, and $5748 in 1987.

A number of factors stand out in this case study. First, top management commitment is reaffirmed as necessary. This is partly because communications take time and effort – simply holding regular meetings is a big commitment, and there is a temptation on the part of managers to regard it as 'dead time'. Second, the steps involved in effective communications are in themselves simple, and involve taking imaginative steps to increase the general flow of information through more face to face and informal communications. Third, it is impossible from these data to definitively establish a causal link between the programme discussed and the resulting outcomes. However, it appears that a correlation of some kind exists. It is unlikely that the benefits which GM executives observed were unconnected with the communications efforts they initiated. Wider longitudinal studies into the effect of similar programmes, particularly in split site workforces, are necessary to resolve the full extent of this issue.

Some studies of the kind discussed in regard to GM have also been conducted in healthcare settings. Arnold (1993) reported on the quality improvement programme that he initiated as President of the largest for-profit medical centre in the United States. His paper argued that communication was central to the programme adopted. Arnold literally implemented an 'open door policy', by having his office door taken from its hinges; he moved the nearest coffee machine into his office, so that people had little option but to interact with him; department leaders received an organisation-wide monthly financial report once a month; open forums were held once a month, and the questions and answers raised at them were distributed in written form throughout the organisation. Bottom line results from the management effort, reported by Arnold, included:

- a staff turnover rate of 30 per cent in 1989 down to 12 per cent by 1991;
- accounts receivable running at 71 days in 1989, down to 44 days;
- bad debt percentage down from 3.2 per cent to an average of 0.4 per cent per month.

It is notable that this account of quality focuses on the benefits of communication, rather than the formal apparatus of quality improvement (e.g. certification) on which many organisations choose to concentrate. Such measures clearly help to reduce status differentials among organisational members – differentials which experimental studies have suggested reduce people's level of involvement in problem solving (Messe et al., 1992).

From all of this, a general agreement exists in the literature concerning the nature of the activities which characterise proactive and effective communications policies. An example, provided by Berger (1994), examined the best practice of leading companies such as Federal Express, Milliken, Xerox, AT & T,

Box 1.1 Best communication practices by leading companies

1 Clear accountabilities and objectives for communication are set company wide. (Federal Express establishes communication requirements and measurable communication objectives for each level of supervision and management.)
2 Regular employee climate surveys are conducted and communicated, and visible results, based on action plans, are achieved. (Xerox lists 'employee satisfaction' as one of its four permanent corporate priorities.)
3 Senior management maintains a high profile among all employees. (Federal Express CEO Dave Rebholtz spends 20 per cent of his time interacting directly with employees.)
4 Publications have a clear architecture, and each has a specific purpose, goal and audience.
5 Extensive face to face and two-way communication processes are practised, including permanent channels enabling employees to communicate proactively with management. (At Milliken, each employee averaged 39 improvement suggestions in one year, a figure that is tracked by management and targeted for improvement to the Japanese average of 100 suggestions per employee per year.)
6 There is a significant use of technology, with heavy emphasis on video communication, in order to speed communication and shorten cycle time for understanding and change.
7 Management bonus compensation is tied, at least in part, to employee evaluation of communication performance and effectiveness.
8 Communication training is an ongoing activity for both communicators and management personnel.

Source: B. Berger, Revolution at Whirlpool, *Internal Communication*, November 1994, p. 11. Reproduced with permission.

and IBM Rochester. The results are summarised in Box 1.1. Regular evaluation, rewards and an intense desire to secure two-way involvement are the recurrent themes.

COMMUNICATION AND THE MOTIVATION OF STAFF

We have, above, identified significant gains from a management focus on improving communication. The question arises: why should an emphasis on relationships have such a profound impact on people's ability to perform the tasks for which they are hired, and on organisational outcomes?

The explanation is that people do not set aside their normal human needs during working hours. We therefore need to stop viewing organisations through the distorting lens of positivist inspired machine metaphors. Such metaphors tend as a matter of course to assume a watertight division between thinking and feeling, and conceptualise organisations as impersonal systems, to be manipulated into new forms exclusively at management's will. This is far from the case. Organisations are chiefly systems of human interaction. People carry their emotions and wider social needs into work with them. They also then discuss and share these in groups. Such needs must be addressed, or they will become a source of dysfunctional dissatisfaction.

The implications of this become clear when we consider the issue of change management. Increasingly, communications programmes are dominated by the management of change (Stewart, 1999). Her study of UK communications professionals, cited above, found that of the organisations surveyed about their performance over the previous two years:

- 76 per cent had reorganised;
- 49 per cent had reduced staff;
- 38 per cent had engaged in mergers or acquisitions;
- a paltry 14 per cent had experienced no major changes;
- over 80 per cent anticipated that, over the following twelve months, their internal communication activities would be dominated by organisational change issues.

Yet how is such change, and the consequent communication challenges, normally managed? Lewis (1992) pointed out that when managers are introducing change and a new culture they frequently regard resistance primarily as something to be overcome. *Star Trek* has regularly featured a marauding group of intergalactic aliens called the Borg, who solemnly inform everyone they meet that 'resistance is futile'. Their goal is to 'assimilate' all new species, so that they lose their individuality and become part of 'the Borg collective'. Likewise, management inspired changes which treat resistance (or even questions) as a futile gesture risk producing the sort of monolithic cultures, stifling norms and organisational frameworks which are incompatible with innovation, and which therefore undermine competitive advantage (Tourish, 1998). As Lewis (1992) pointed out, resistance is also feedback, and that is always useful. Such feedback must be institutionalised into organisational decision-making, in order to avoid the emergence of a 'collective' consciousness characterised by drab uniformity – and profits which sink in tandem with staff morale. 'Uniform thinking', in any event, is an oxymoron. Some researchers have found that, in many cases, it is the manner in which change is introduced rather than change *per se* which alienates people (Turnbull and Wass, 1998). A lack of consultation and communication is particularly prone to spark resistance. The problem of managing change is therefore, to a very large extent, a problem of managing communication (Lewis and Seibold, 1998).

This perspective is reinforced if we consider the issue of motivation. It is clear that the quality of relationships with co-workers is a crucial factor in determining levels of job satisfaction. Yet this is far removed from the primary task-focused rationale which is generally the original spur for the creation of most organisations. Summarising a number of research investigations, Argyle (1987) concluded that job satisfaction correlated highly with popularity or acceptance by group members in many studies. In a later text, Argyle (1994) cited a study which found that while 34 per cent of respondents regarded their job primarily as a means of earning a living, 66 per cent thought that it was more than that, and placed a particular value on sociability with colleagues and their use of skills. In line with this research, one study involving 302 employees at two manufacturing firms found a strong relationship between positive communication (such as accurate information, high levels of trust and a desire for interaction) and levels of job satisfaction (Petit *et al.*, 1997). However, the same study found only a weak to moderate relationship between satisfaction with communication and job performance, indicating the need for further research into this issue.

Plainly, co-workers provide material and social rewards. If, as appears to be the case, the exchange of rewards is essential to the smooth functioning of most relationships (Dickson *et al.*, 1993), the expectation of rewards must operate within peer groups at work and become translated into generalised feelings about the entire job. Hence, Argyle (1994) reported that job satisfaction is higher for those who are accepted by co-workers and who belong to what are described as cohesive groups. If this is true, it suggests that job satisfaction cannot be achieved by an exclusive emphasis on tasks. In short, we would argue that effective organisations must be aware of their members' personal needs, and take care to nurture relationships at all levels. Communication is a vital means of furthering this objective. Through opening the channels of communication people can articulate their needs, reduce uncertainty by gaining access to information, develop opportunities to influence the decision-making process and satisfy the fundamental human need to make a difference. The alternative is a policy of exclusion, which threatens well-being on all fundamental levels and produces a workforce so preoccupied with its own unmet needs that it is incapable of responding to the needs of clients or customers.

There is a clear suggestion here that effective communication promotes organisational cohesion and effectiveness because it answers to people's basic motivational impulses. Arnott (1987) suggested that employees are preoccupied by six basic questions. These were divided into two parts. Thus:

Part One	*Part Two*
What's my job?	How are we doing?
How am I doing?	How do we fit in to the whole?
Does anybody give a damn?	How can I help?

These form two categories – the WIIFME questions (*What's In It For Me?*), and the WIIFU questions (*What's In It For Us?*). Many programmes address only the issues in Part Two. However, it appears that unless the first set are accorded equal significance people will simply be unable to hear what comes next. It is also clear that real involvement only occurs when employees ask the final question (How can I help?), and that corporate communications programmes are ultimately designed to get the maximum number of employees thinking at this level.

Business success rests on serving a need at a profit. However, people are not intrinsically motivated by the knowledge that a sound business plan underwrites their activities, that shareholders have received an adequate return on their investment, or that the CEO has met all his or her performance targets for the year (and perhaps received handsome stock options in return). It appears that the commitment of employees to the enterprise is primarily engaged, in the first instance, by the amount of attention which is paid to their perceived needs.

Thus, people are not fundamentally rational creatures. In the long term, business success is vital for individual as well as societal well being. However, the evidence reviewed here suggests that, in order to grasp this wider picture, the fundamental human needs which people bring into the workplace with them must be addressed. This is certainly a messy picture, and makes the management task even more difficult than it already is. There is an inherent ambiguity to the job of management, which sometimes makes the task feel akin to one of juggling with breeze-blocks. It also suggests that communication should be regarded as a competence of core management, underpinning the many people management skills which organisations are now battling to develop (Hart, 1996). Unless such realities are faced head-on it is unlikely that organisations will be able to achieve anything like their full competitive potential. The costs will be incalculable.

CUSTOMERS, EMPLOYEES AND COMMUNICATION

Communication with clients and customers is also, of course, a vital ingredient of overall success. A positive corporate image greatly helps in gaining sales, contracts, employees and shareholders (Rossiter and Perry, 1987). In particular, an organisation's perceived trustworthiness, competence and attractiveness have a particular potency to influence such decisions (O'Keefe, 1990). For this reason, corporate reputation is increasingly regarded as a vital barometer of health (Dowling, 1994). It has also been found that customers welcome communication from the businesses they deal with. The Henley Centre for Forecasting found that 68 per cent of customers actively wanted information from such companies and 60 per cent were more likely to buy from suppliers who kept in touch (Jones, 1997). A recognition of such factors has led to the growth of what has been defined as 'relationship marketing', in which primary importance is attached to the quality of relationships between customers and the companies they deal with (Day et al., 1998).

There appears to be a direct correlation between the willingness of organisations to address their external customer relations on the one hand, and their management of internal communication issues on the other. For example, Hartline and Ferrell (1996) found that managers who were committed to the quality of customer services were more inclined to empower employees and use behaviour based evaluations.

In turn, a recognition of such links is one means of achieving competitive advantage, by differentiating the organisation from its rivals. Hutton (1996) discusses what is called a 'culture-to-customer' philosophy, which recognises the importance of what employees believe and do, and how this is perceived by customers. The assumption is that the organisation should first define its own culture, then communicate its basic tenets internally, and finally ensure that these values are made visible to customers, via the behaviour and attitude of employees. As Hutton (1996, p. 40) expressed it: 'Customers are then able to identify and "connect" or "associate" with the organisation, with a particular product class, that best matches their own values or aspirations.' A number of key companies and the guiding values which help them to stand out in the marketplace are identified. These include:

- IBM (service);
- Ben and Jerry's/Body Shop (social conscience);
- Apple/Saturn/Benetton (non-conformity/new attitude);
- Pepsi (youth);
- 3M/General Electric (innovative products which make life more enjoyable).

Market pressures are likely to strengthen these links in the future. Many companies already highlight those aspects of their culture which they believe will most impress customers. The Body Shop regularly publishes what it calls a Values Report, an independently audited account of their record on the environment, animal protection and human relationships (Kent, 1996). There is, indeed, growing evidence to suggest that customers are influenced in their purchase decisions by these and other criteria. Scott (1996) reported one survey which found that 84 per cent of consumers were prepared to pay more for goods when manufacturers paid employees a reasonable wage. All of us are increasingly bombarded with information which enables us to base our purchase decisions on such criteria, if we so choose. The media pay enormous attention to 'organisational secrets' – the bigger, the better. Believing that news is what someone doesn't want known, and anything else is advertising, it has a tendency to focus on stories critical of business practice. We picked an edition of the UK's leading weekend broadsheet, *The Sunday Times* (17 January 1999) at random, and found that the first five pages contained the following stories:

- One of the largest drug companies in the world had hired former intelligence agents and members of the Special Air Services (SAS) to conduct industrial espionage against rivals in the pharmaceuticals market. The offices of at least one London solicitor had also been broken into, while those who carried out the operations claimed they were offered £50,000 each to stay silent. This story made the front page, under the flattering headline: 'Drugs giant "burgled and bugged" rivals'.

- The expenses of a senior government minister ('New Labour') were under the spotlight. Documents suggested that he regularly flew to America by Concorde, when cheaper alternatives were readily available; attempted to use a private jet, until restrained by colleagues and civil servants; occupied a suite rather than a room in a five star hotel when visiting Brussels; and drank expensive whiskey, which he then claimed on expenses.
- A member of the International Olympic Committee (IOC) was accused of asking cities bidding to hold the Olympics to provide college places for some of his eight children. Another received £30,000 from the leader of the Salt Lake City bid, had a free operation, and received assistance in the purchase of land for luxury homes, which was then sold at a £40,000 profit. Overall, nine IOC members were under consideration for expulsion.
- Senior staff at the Bank of England were reported to have benefited from cheap loans, to the tune of £1 million. This was used to fund private education for their children and the purchase of new cars and houses. The loans were part of a perks package, which included the use of a 40-foot yacht. The Bank's Governor was on a salary of £227,000. He was one of the most regular users of the yacht.

One study into the impact of bad news found that perceived levels of trustworthiness was the first and biggest casualty of negative publicity (Renkema and Hoeken, 1998). Like money, trust is hard to acquire but is easily squandered. Thus, customers who defect because of poor service or communication, and staff who blow the whistle on management malpractice or publicise a mood of imminent insurrection, can follow a well-trodden pathway to the air-waves. The conclusion is that best practice companies should see internal and external communications as part of a seamless whole, and devote considerable resources to monitoring their effectiveness.

However, the evidence suggests that most businesses underestimate the importance of evaluating their communications with customers. Reichfield (1996a) found that US companies lose 50 per cent of their customers every five years, and that most of them make little effort to find out why. The costs are enormous. Research has shown that it costs about six times more to get a new customer than to keep an existing one (Hargie et al., 1999). A significant body of evidence, covering organisations such as MBNA, BancOne, Southwest Airlines and Taco Bell, also shows that even small increases in customer retention lead to large increases in profitability (Bowen et al., 1999). In some cases, 5 per cent increases in the former have led to 75–100 per cent gains in the latter. This is because retention is associated with higher levels of satisfaction and a series of related commercial benefits. For example, customers in the retail sector who report that they are 'very satisfied' as opposed to merely 'satisfied' are four times more likely to come back, are more likely to make recommendations to others, and spend more money when they do visit the retail outlet (Buckingham and Cowe, 1999). With this in mind, Reichfield argued that tools should be employed to learn from customer defections, and turn the data into a strategy for reducing their loss. In our view, communication audits constitute an important part of the tool kit of businesses anxious to focus on this area.

When attention is paid to these issues the returns are substantial. For example, Sears, Roebuck and Company (a leading US retailer) spent much of the 1990s redesigning itself around what it characterised as an employee–customer–profit chain (Rucci et al., 1998). As these authors comment:

> Any person with even a limited experience in retailing understands intuitively that there is a chain of cause and effect running from employee behaviour to customer behaviour to profits, and it's not hard to see that behaviour depends primarily on attitudes.
>
> (Rucci et al., 1998, p. 84)

They go on to point out that the biggest problem with these variables is measurement, ensuring that 'many companies do not have a realistic grasp of what their customers and employees actually think and do' (p. 84). Sears, Roebuck has tackled the problem by developing a process of data collection, analysis, modelling and experimentation around a series of Total Performance Indicators. A crucial stage in their development was intense communication within the ranks of senior management, with employees and with customers. The basis for long term executive compensation has now been changed, so that it relies one-third on employee measures, one-third on customer measures and one-third on traditional investor returns. The result is that a company which recorded a mind-boggling $3.9 billion loss in 1992 ended the decade by, once again, turning in a healthy profit.

Overall, good relationships and communication with customers is essential to business success. Customer loyalty hinges on innumerable communicative episodes that have been termed 'Moments of Truth' (Ryder, 1998). One indifferent, unmotivated or surly employee is often enough to poison a relationship and lose valuable customers. Management's job is to create numerous positive Moments of Truth, which make the customer experience unforgettable for all the right rather than all the wrong reasons. Accordingly, Caywood (1998) has suggested that customer communications should be guided by the following questions:

1. Does the company employ many different methods (including readership surveys, e-mail response/tracking mechanisms, focus groups, etc.) for gathering feedback from stakeholders and other audiences?
2. What is the degree to which the company solicits and utilises input from various communication audiences in the determination of corporate and communications goals?

3. To what extent does the company segment its communications audiences in order to deliver more tailored, meaningful communications messages?
4. Is every 'brand contact point' between the company and its audiences considered a communications opportunity?

(Caywood, 1998, p. 21)

Previously, organisations have underestimated the importance of these issues, but are now coming under pressure to be more proactive. In particular, audit tools have been used infrequently, despite their utility. They represent a valuable means of providing managers with the data which can then inform action plans. As this discussion shows, insight into what is happening now prepares the ground for a wider understanding of what must happen tomorrow. The pressure of the marketplace is now such that communication with customers cannot be treated in the cack-handed way which sufficed in the past.

THE CHANGING ROLE OF COMMUNICATIONS

Given this context, communications practitioners have been attempting to delineate the impact of new thinking and recent practice on their approach. Quirke (1995), in particular, acknowledged that the role of internal communications has been transformed over the past decade, with greater changes looming in the years ahead. He summarised the traditional role of internal organisational communication as:

- The announcement of management conclusions.
- The working of management thinking into messages which are then efficiently distributed via communication channels.
- Ensuring consistency of information, and making messages easily comprehensible, and easy to disseminate.

(Quirke, 1995, p. 76)

Such a role is primarily concerned with one way communications, the regulation of the behaviour of employees and ensuring compliance with centrally decreed instructions. Much of it is also still necessary. When decisions have been made centrally it is imperative that they are disseminated widely within the organisation, as quickly as possible, and that people understand the response that is required from them. However, as this chapter has made clear, organisations are increasingly attempting to unleash the creative involvement and participation of people as well. This suggests, argued Quirke, that additional communication objectives should now include:

- The stimulation of thinking, participation and ideas.
- The networking of know how and learning across the organisation.

- The involvement of all employees in improving processes.
- The identification of ways of providing additional value to customers.
- The expansion of what all employees believe is possible.

(Quirke, 1995, p. 77)

In short, Quirke summarised this new emphasis as follows:

> The role of communication becomes not the top-down dissemination of management thinking, but the bottom-up means of connecting those who know what needs to change to those who have authority to make change happen.

(Quirke, 1995, p. 78)

Given this, it has been argued (Tourish, 1998) that the success of leadership should be measured by the extent to which it promotes open communication, involvement, participation and power-sharing, rather than in the number of visionary strategies emanating from the Chief Executive's office (Total Quality Management (TQM), re-engineering, downsizing, delayering, Investors in People, 'just in time'). It is, therefore, impossible to sustain the argument that people only need to know whatever the organisation decides they need to know in order to do their jobs. It is worth pointing out that if managers treat staff on a 'need to know' basis, what is known as 'the norm of reciprocity' suggests that this attitude will be returned in spades from the shop floor. When someone is hit, their first instinct is to strike back. This will further inflame the already difficult problem of securing accurate upward feedback. As we have seen, improving communication with customers may be one of the most important steps which companies can take to increase their profits. In addition, coherent internal communications enables the organisation to present a consistent and clear image to its external publics: absolutely vital to any prospect of sustaining internal cohesion and marketplace advantage (Treadwell and Harrison, 1994).

The underlying perspective on organisations advocated in this chapter is integrative – i.e. the organisation is viewed as an interconnected whole, which needs to be focused on agreed objectives and go through organisational transformation without collapsing into internal strife. Within this framework, a spirit of collaboration has been seen as a primary integrative force (Charns and Tewksbury, 1993). The objective is to increase employees' level of involvement in the organisation, so that they are prepared to exceed the effort required to perform narrowly defined job tasks – in short, the promotion of what has been termed organisational citizenship behaviour (Tang and Ibrahim, 1998). In this model, employees have rights in terms of information exchange, but they also have corresponding responsibilities to contribute to the achievement of important business goals. Issues of involvement, participation, democracy and power-sharing are also inevitably raised. Nevertheless, it has been noted that 'seldom has the vast literature on forms and practices of leadership been brought into direct dialogue with research on employee participation and workplace democracy' (Cheney, et al., 1998, p. 40). This is a serious weakness.

Management clearly has the biggest responsibilities to rectify this situation. We view auditing communication as part of an overall package designed to evaluate effectiveness, identify best practice within and without the organisation, and create a climate within which such practices can become more widely applied.

CONCLUSION

This chapter has identified what can be gained from a proactive focus on communications, both internally and externally. To do so is to put a greater premium on relationships with staff, business suppliers and customers. However, how can this perspective be reconciled with the self-evident fact that staff are often treated as a dispensable liability, customers as little more than a damned nuisance, and suppliers as potential industrial spies? For example, increasing employee commitment has been one of the central thrusts of human resources management in recent years (Morris et al., 1993). Yet the desire for such commitment is at odds with the downsizing and delayering process characteristic of re-engineering. Delayering has been described as 'the process by which people who barely know what's going on get rid of those who do' (Mintzberg, 1996, p. 62). It is not without significance that practitioners of the noble art of firing people generally seek refuge behind a dense and ever expanding smoke-screen of euphemisms. No one is ever fired – they are 'let go', a process which sounds almost pleasant. We know of one top executive who announced a wave of redundancies by telling those affected that he was giving them 'the opportunity to fulfil your potential elsewhere'. People are not over-worked – they are 'empowered', and so choose to do more. Employees in some organisations have even taken to joking that management jargon has acquired the status of a new language, known as 'Desperanto'. The results are predictable, if depressing. Cynicism has grown, while loyalty has declined. One study of over two thousand people in the US found that 60 per cent felt less loyal to their companies than they did five years earlier (Shapiro, 1995). Another study of human resources professionals in the United States found that 84 per cent felt their firms were experiencing increased hostility from their workforce, while 64 per cent said their firms had not been as employee friendly as they had promised (Flynn, 1998). People reason, quite understandably, that there is no point showing concern for the organisation's welfare, when it shows so little for theirs.

In the present competitive economic climate such a cynical view is unsustainable. The evidence reviewed here suggests that organisations employing positive communication policies will reap significant competitive benefits. The corollary is also true: poor communications programmes will contribute to lost competitive edge.

Thus, hierarchical and autocratic models of management run counter to what the available evidence suggests is most effective. Nor do the data suggest that practices such as 'downsizing' yields returns on bottom line financial indicators. A major study of 3628 US companies over a 15-year period concluded that companies which downsized saw their return on assets (ROA) *decline* in the year of downsizing and in the year after. It recovered slightly in the following year, but not to the levels which existed before the lay-offs occurred (Morris *et al.*, 1999). The fact that such fads are widely practised is no recommendation. Popular support for an opinion (e.g. 'women are inferior to men', and, more recently, 'men are inferior to women') does not constitute evidence that it is correct. Alternative courses of action are both possible and necessary. In the final analysis, competitive advantage is gained from doing something different to everyone else, rather than from enthusiastically emulating their mistakes.

Having identified internal and external communication as vital ingredients of organisational success the issue arises: what should be done about it? This book argues that by auditing what currently happens the ground is prepared for substantial improvements. Further chapters explore the tools and techniques which will assist organisations to achieve this objective.

Chapter 2

Auditing communication to maximise performance

Dennis Tourish and Owen Hargie

INTRODUCTION

Organisations that communicate badly can be likened to a theatrical production in which no one knows which part they are playing and constantly speak the wrong lines, often interrupting other performers to do so. Meanwhile, the audience is either ignored or insulted. A focused communication strategy helps to avert such chaos. It provides the opportunity for organisations to enjoy a long running performance in the marketplace. Such a strategy must be based on accurate information about current practices. Few managers would dispute the notion that businesses must have an accurate impression of how they are viewed externally, and what staff think of how they receive and transmit information. To achieve this key questions must be addressed:

- Is the right message getting through?
- Do people feel informed, or merely patronised?
- Has the communications programme really addressed the issues which most concern people, or has it missed the moving target of public opinion?

To answer these questions, accurate information about how both internal and external customers perceive the communication climate is vital. Illusions, hopes and pretence have to give way to an appraisal of what is. This constitutes the fundamental rationale for auditing communication.

In this chapter, we define the term 'communication audit', outline its origins in the academic and management literature, and propose an implementation framework which can be applied to the auditing of both internal and external communication. A word of caution is in order at the outset. As many other scholars have recognised, there is no one 'right' method for auditing communication. This book does not seek to become a 'cookbook' of audits, in which recipes for every contingency can be found. Each method has its strengths and limitations, and each organisation has its own unique needs, culture and problems in the marketplace. There is no perfect recipe, guaranteeing a meal to satisfy all tastes. However, we believe that it is possible to specify some ingredients which, in our experience, consistently characterise good practice. Within this framework, subsequent chapters explore a variety of auditing tools in more depth, from which readers are encouraged to select those most appropriate to their needs.

THE NATURE OF AUDIT

The term 'audit' has by now been applied to an enormous range of activities. Its very ubiquity often generates confusion (Baker, 1999). Indeed, the *Concise Oxford Dictionary* notes the existence of an audit ale, a special beer once brewed in English colleges for consumption on the day an audit was undertaken. (It is questionable whether the critical acumen of auditors was sharpened by the imbibing of such liquids.) Historically, the practice of auditing is most commonly associated with scrutinies of an organisation's financial health, and the principle is clearly derived from this area.

At its most basic, an audit is simply an evaluation of a designated process. In this connection, Frank and Brownell (1989, p. 290) characterise the communication audit as:

> an objective report of an organisation's internal communication.

A communication audit can be defined as:

> a comprehensive and thorough study of communication philosophy, concepts, structure, flow and practice within an organisation.
>
> (Emmanuel, 1985, p. 50)

It assists managers by

> providing an objective picture of what is happening compared with what senior executives think (or have been told) is happening.
>
> (Hurst, 1991, p. 24)

The term first emerged in the general academic literature in the early 1950s (Odiorne, 1954), and its use has since been frequently urged on business, human resources and public relations practitioners (e.g. Campbell, 1982; Kopec, 1982; Stanton, 1981; Strenski, 1984). Researchers have drawn attention to its role in not-for-profit organisations (Lauer, 1996), and as an important ingredient of strategic marketing in the healthcare sector (Stone, 1995). Its utility as a pedagogic instrument in the teaching of management communication has been asserted (Conaway, 1994; Shelby and Reinsch, 1996), while communication audits have been recognised as a valuable ingredient of employee relations audits in general (Jennings *et al.*, 1990). Audits can also be readily employed to assess communication with customers, suppliers and other businesses outside the organisation. As we argue in Chapter 8, they will also make an increasingly important contribution to assessing the effects of the communications revolution now taking place.

Communication audits share a number of characteristics with more established audit practices in such spheres as finance, medicine and accounting (Hargie and Tourish, 1993). These include:

1 *The accumulation of information.* In the case of finance, the goal is to check the efficacy of financial accounting procedures by sampling a representative cross-section of transactions within the organisation. In communication terms, a similar goal is to assess a sample of communication episodes, in order to determine key trends. This might be termed the *diagnostic* phase of the auditing process.
2 *The creation of management systems.* Systems are developed to control the flow of information and resources over a given period. This is the *prescriptive* phase of the audit process.
3 *The comparison of communication practices with publicly declared standards.* A finance audit ensures that funds are appropriately managed and that efficient methods of financial management are being applied (Amernic, 1992). Clinical audits monitor the effectiveness and efficiency of medical activity, and contrast both with national and international benchmarks (Shapiro, 1999). Communication audits provide similar performance benchmarks, generating a much enhanced ability to measure both performance and the impact of specific measures designed to improve it. This is the *accountability* phase of the audit process.

Organisations require all three of these strands to be applied to their internal and external communication systems. Given the propensity of communications to break down, at untold cost, a strong case can be made for ascertaining their general level of effectiveness. Managers need to know who they are communicating with, through what channels and with what effect. Proper procedures must be developed to achieve these goals. There should also be some accountability for the flow of information within the organisation. At a practical level, this means that if vital information is not getting through to its key target audiences the blockages in the channels of communication must be identified and dealt with.

Thus, Haywood (1991) argued that audits

> should cover these points; this is how the organisation is perceived, this is how we would like to be seen, this is the activity we will undertake to achieve this change in attitude and, finally, this is how we will assess our success in achieving this objective.
>
> (Haywood, 1991, p. 41)

Considerable attention was devoted to the issue of communication audits by the International Communication Association during the 1970s (Goldhaber and Krivonos, 1977), while the issue also attracted the attention of a number of prominent communication scholars (e.g. Greenbaum and White, 1976). A seminal text was published from the work of the ICA towards the end of the decade (Goldhaber and Rogers, 1979). This identified the following key objectives to be achieved by implementing a communication audit:

1. Determine the amount of information underload or overload associated with the major *topics, sources and channels* of communication.
2. Evaluate the *quality of information* communicated from and/or to these sources.
3. Evaluate the *quality of communication relationships*, specifically measuring the extent of interpersonal trust, supportiveness sociability and overall job satisfaction.
4. Identify the *operational communication networks* (for rumors, social and job related messages), comparing them with planned or formal networks (prescribed by organizational charts).
5. Determine *potential bottlenecks and gatekeepers of information* by comparing actual communication roles of key personnel . . . with expected roles . . .
6. Identify categories and examples of commonly occurring positive and negative *communication experiences and incidents.*
7. Describe individual, group and organizational patterns of *actual communication behaviors* related to sources, channels, topics, length and quality of interactions.
8. Provide general recommendations, derived from the Audit, which call for changes or improvements in attitudes, behaviors, practices and skills.

(Goldhaber and Rogers, 1979, p. 8)

Other suggestions have been made of what should constitute reasonable audit objectives in most organisations. Thus, Wynne (1990) proposed that audits should normally address the following issues:

Why communicate? What objectives should be set?
What is communicated and to whom?
Do people receive the communications? Do they understand them?
Of all the range of media used which is the most effective?
Is the right information being communicated in an understandable and digestible format?
Are briefing groups held? Have the managers been trained? Do the groups work?
What about lateral communications? Does it happen? Is it effective? Do managers feel informed?
What about upward communication? Does it get through or is it blocked off? Are senior managers aware of the views of people lower down the organisation?

(Wynne, 1990, p. 28)

Hargie and Tourish (1996b) argued that audits tell managers and organisations:

- Who they are talking to
- Who they should be talking to
- What issues people are talking about
- From which sources most people get their information
- Whether information reaches people through the media, face to face discussions with managers, internal publications or other communication channels
- The impact of all this on working relationships

In short, a communication audit strips away myths, fears and illusions about the communication climate within organisations, and about the wider culture within which the organisation works. In their place, it provides an accurate diagnosis of the organisation's communicative health.

Gildea and Rosenberg (1979, p. 7) compared communication audits to 'an annual physical', viewing it as 'a sound diagnostic procedure that can pinpoint functions and dysfunctions in organisational communication'. As Bedien (1980) noted, this approach means that audits allow organisations to determine whether communication problems are interrelated, and facilitates the implementation of solutions on a company wide basis. Thus, audit measures typically focus on issues such as:

- who is communicating with whom;
- which issues receive the most attention and arouse the most anxiety;
- how much information people are receiving and sending on crucial issues;
- how much interpersonal trust exists; and
- how the overall quality of working relationships can be characterised.

Such issues are among the core concerns of efforts to establish what has been termed 'organisational climate' (Lammers, 1994). Falcione *et al.* (1987) noted that the whole notion of organisational climate had attracted enormous attention over the preceding thirty years. In an earlier study, Redding (1972) attempted to clarify the nature of an ideal communication climate. He identified the following five dimensions as being of particular importance:

- supportiveness;
- participative decision-making;
- trust, confidence and credibility;
- openness and candour; and
- high performance goals.

Dennis (1975) then proposed an organisational climate instrument based on these dimensions, which examined:

- superior–subordinate communication;
- perceived quality and accuracy of downward communication;
- perceived openness of the superior–subordinate relationship;
- ppportunities and degree of influence of upward communication; and
- perceived reliability of information from subordinates and co-workers.

In one sense audits amount to an investigation of organisational climate, which helps managers recognise whether storms, earthquakes or sunshine lies ahead. In this way, major improvements in communication can be effected.

When such evaluations are turned into quantitative and qualitative data managers acquire a clear, comprehensive picture of how things actually are. This subverts both their own natural tendency towards self-aggrandisement, and the traditional reluctance of staff and customers to provide honest feedback to those perceived as having a higher status than they do (Odom, 1993) – in this case, top executives. In turn, this provides managers with the opportunity to develop a compelling sense of direction, indispensable for success in a crowded marketplace. Communication audits therefore perform a useful diagnostic and prescriptive role in strategic management. The various tools which can be used in this connection are discussed in separate chapters in this book.

IMPLEMENTING COMMUNICATION AUDITS: A STRATEGIC FRAMEWORK

Overall, this chapter is intended to provide a rationale for the use of communication audits as a management tool. It is also necessary to suggest a sequence of practical steps that auditors should follow to operationalise the process. It has been argued that audits of various kinds go through at least five stages (Baker, 1999). These are:

- the selection of a topic;
- the specification of desired performance in terms of criteria and standards;
- the collection of objective data to determine whether the standards are met;
- the implementation of appropriate changes to improve performance;
- the collection of data for a second time, to check whether any changes introduced have affected performance.

In reality, the audit process does not proceed in the straightforward linear sequence which might easily be assumed. For example, the specification of desired performance *should* occur at the beginning of the whole exercise. However, it will also occur *afterwards*, when the audit team uses its data to help establish what standards of performance are most appropriate to the organisation concerned. It may be that the audit itself reveals previously exalted standards as impractical, or discloses that people's sights have been set too low.

The topic under investigation in this book is obviously communication. Our experience as practising auditors suggests that management teams frequently give the whole issue little thought, and have only the haziest idea of what questions should be explored during an audit. For example, many assume that communication is concerned exclusively with the transmission of messages from managers to staff. In reality, it also encompasses the *exchange* of information vertically, horizontally and diagonally. To be effective, communication therefore needs to be two-way, and hence dialogic, in nature (Deetz, 1995).

The case study chapters in this book discuss different approaches to implementing an audit. Given that the each organisation has unique needs, there is no absolutely cut and dried process which will apply everywhere, irrespective of local circumstances. As we warned at the outset, it is not our intention to prescribe one allegedly best method for auditing communication. Nevertheless, we can extract the most pertinent themes from the research, in order to identify a number of stages which are normally followed, irrespective of the underlying method of data collection. We would suggest that the following sequence is a summary of the best general practice available. It takes account of the need to integrate auditing into the process of strategy development – a theme to which we return in the final chapter of this book. Auditors who depart from it should have compelling reasons for doing so. Thus, the process of audit implementation should generally encompass the following stages:

Engage senior management commitment

A variety of studies has suggested that unless senior managers are actively involved in any change process, and passionately committed to its success, it will fail (e.g. Spurgeon and Barwell, 1991; Pettigrew *et al.*, 1992). New tools designed to assist organisational development inevitably appear threatening to some. They require an intense level of senior management involvement, if their use is to yield positive dividends. At the outset of the audit process a problem focused workshop between senior management and the auditors should be held. Such an event serves to:

1 *Clarify in-depth the value of audits, their role in this particular organisation and the commitment required from management if maximum advantage is to be obtained.* For example, the following issues should be addressed:

- What timescale best ties in with the business planning cycle?
- Will other organisational development issues need to be rescheduled?
- How can evaluating communication channels with customers support the marketing strategy?
- What plans can be made to circulate the audit results as widely as possible?

2 *Identify the top half dozen issues on which people should be receiving and sending information.* An audit cannot examine every conceivable issue, in-depth.

Our own research has generally found that information flow on a few key issues tends to be typical of the overall communication climate (Tourish and Hargie, 1998). Restricting the number of issues to be explored in this way is sufficient to provide valid data, while ensuring that the audit remains practicable. For example, if the audit is concerned with external communication, what are the most important issues which the company wants its customers to be aware of? Conversely, what does it want to hear from its customers about? These data can then be incorporated into the materials being used during the audit exercise. If questionnaires are being employed, a section should explore information flow on the key issues identified. (See, for example, the questionnaire in the Appendix).

This also offers a good opportunity to delineate the extent of the audit exercise, and therefore clarify managers' conception of the communication process. It is essential, at this stage, to establish both what audits can and cannot do. Managers must have realistic expectations about what can be achieved. When too much (or too little) is envisioned the audit will be less likely to achieve its full potential as a tool for facilitating organisational development. For example, it is difficult to use data obtained from focus groups to set statistical benchmarks (see Chapter 5). If the focus group is the only tool which the organisation can use, and there are many circumstances under which this is the case, it is unrealistic to think that future audits will be able to measure precisely the extent of any progress that has been made. Novice auditors may be inclined to promise more than they can deliver, thereby undermining the credibility of the whole process.

3 *Discuss the communication standards the management team believes they should adopt and live up to.* For example, in the UK, the National Health Service Management Executive published standards for communication in 1995, and circulated them throughout the main management tiers of the organisation. This was a summary of best general practice, recommending that commitments be made to:

• board level discussions;
• regular audits;
• upward appraisal;
• training for effective communications;
• the consideration of communication during the business planning cycle; and
• the identification and reward of good practice.

Having established standards, answers must then be formulated to a number of key questions:

• What do they mean in practice?
• How will every organisational unit be transformed if they are implemented?
• What has stopped such implementation in the past?
• How much can be agreed and how much will remain in dispute for the foreseeable future?

- How quickly can change begin?
- What training needs arise?

The audit can then reveal the extent to which the standards are being implemented; stimulate further discussion on the gap between current practice and the characteristics of a world class communication system; and encourage overt commitments to the key publics concerned, internally and/or externally.

4 *The identification of a senior person or persons prepared to act as link between the organisation and the external audit team.* If the audit is being conducted in-house, a link between those handling the project and top management is still vital. This is not to suggest that auditors should surrender their independence. However, ongoing contact with key people is vital to keep doors open; prevent sabotage or obstruction; ensure that the audit timescale remains on track; and provide essential information on the organisation's structure, history, internal politics, business challenges, main priorities and climate.

Prepare the organisation for the audit

Usually, a simple letter is sufficient to inform staff of the nature of the audit process, and the timescale which is envisaged. We would generally recommend that it be issued by the Chief Executive, thus putting the authority of this office behind the audit. This helps to ensure that managers facilitate access to audit participants, and generally engage with what is going on. It also binds the top management team into the audit exercise, by publicly identifying them with it. This makes it more likely that the results of the audit will be taken seriously and used to effect improvements in performance. In the case of external audits, a sample of customers or supply businesses can be addressed in a similar manner. Alternatively, internal or external newsletters, videos or team briefing mechanisms can be employed.

Recurring worries which tend to arise at this point include confidentiality, how widely available the results will be, and the time commitment required of audit respondents (Tourish and Tourish, 1996). The most difficult of these issues is confidentiality. Respondents are often wary of honestly expressing their views, in case what they say will be used against them at a later stage. It may be necessary to address these issues during initial communications with audit participants. The following general rules help:

- *Participants should be assured, orally and in writing, that their responses will be treated confidentially.* Research shows that the more often a message is repeated the more likely people are to accept that it is true (Cialdini, 1993). Accordingly, these assurances should be reiterated on a number of occasions – the more publicly, the better. The steps proposed to ensure confidentiality should be explained in detail.

- *Wherever possible, participants should be selected randomly.* This reinforces the message that the aim of the exercise is not to single people out with a view to imposing sanctions. There are hazards to this. When administering questionnaires to a group during one of our audits, one of the people present approached us to remark that it was the third time in six months he had been 'randomly selected' to complete questionnaires dealing with a variety of organisational development issues. Intense persuasion was required to convince him that we were not part of a management plot against him!
- *Only the audit team should have access to questionnaires, tape recordings or anything else which might identify individual respondents.* All such materials should be destroyed at the conclusion of the audit.
- *Care should be taken, in writing the report, to ensure that it does not inadvertently enable readers to identify particular respondents.* For example, if only one person works in the payroll department the report should not cite comments, good or bad, from 'a payroll respondent'.
- *Audit instruments should be administered well away from the gaze of managers.* Again, during one of our audits, we had just spent some time explaining the confidential nature of the exercise to a group of questionnaire respondents when a member of the senior management team dropped by simply to see how many people had turned up. Unfortunately, the effect was to discredit our assurances of confidentiality with the people concerned.

Normally, these procedures are sufficient to ensure that this problem is eased. However, it remains one of the strongest arguments in favour of using external rather than internal auditors. If a top manager turns up to administer questionnaires or conduct interviews, or if the person concerned is viewed as being close to managers, confidentiality assurances have low credibility.

Data gathering

This normally proceeds in two phases. A small number of preliminary first-round interviews familiarise the audit team with staff or customer views, as well as management concerns. Typically, respondents will be randomly selected. Feedback obtained by this approach helps in the design of final questionnaires, if this is the main method to be used. A number of typical issues have been suggested which should be explored in preliminary interviews (Tourish and Tourish, 1996). The bulk of these are applicable to both internal and external audits:

- how decisions are made;
- communication channels;
- communication relationships;
- communication obstacles;
- organisational structure;
- responsiveness (e.g. the quality of information flow during a crisis).

Finally, the main audit exercise is embarked upon. A pilot test is vital. This makes it possible to detect shortcomings in the design and implementation of questionnaires (Emory and Cooper, 1991), or other approaches being employed. However, as Remenyi *et al.* (1998, p. 174) pointed out, 'in business and management research there is usually time and considerable financial pressure to get the project started'. Pilots are therefore often selected opportunistically, on grounds of convenience, availability, proximity or cost. We do not view this as a major problem. A pilot is a test case, undertaken to double check the viability of the approach chosen. It should not, even under ideal circumstances, become so elaborate that it develops into a main study in its own right. However, once the pilot is complete, the main study can proceed.

Analysis and action phase

A report is now prepared, which comprehensively describes and evaluates communication practices. It should be noted that this period presents both opportunities and dangers. Audits arouse increased interest and expectations. As a general rule, people recognise that everyone likes to sing loudly about their successes, while remaining mute about their mistakes. Thus, if an audit is followed by silence it will be widely assumed that managers are busy burying dreadful secrets in the basement. A key principle when confronted with bad news, if this is what emerges, is that it should be shared openly and quickly, thereby enabling those involved to at least gain credit for their honesty (Payne, 1996).

The results of the audit are, in the first instance, presented to the top management team, orally and in writing. Later chapters in this book explore the challenges and difficulties which also abound during this phase of the audit process – e.g. in terms of how 'bad news' should be presented, to both senior managers and the wider organisation. The results then need to be circulated widely, by whatever means are most appropriate. Action plans should also be publicised. In this way, the process of audit, as well as whatever changes to which it gives rise, helps achieve significant strides forward in open and clear communication.

THE UTILITY OF COMMUNICATION AUDITS

Based on this review, it can be concluded that communication audits have the following methodological strengths:

1 They permit auditors to identify the subjective interpretations of reality held by all important actors in organisational life. This extends to customers and clients, increasingly recognised as having a vital contribution to make to the business planning process.
2 Depending upon the method utilised, people are permitted to voice their views and feelings in their own words, while also recording on objective measurement

scales their responses to communication issues which can be analysed extensively. By one means or another, audits explore individual perceptions of communication. Such perceptions may be at odds with the conclusions of outside observers, however well trained in observational methods they happen to be (Hopfl, 1992). In other words, various people might be engaged in some excellent communication practices, but find that they are still perceived in a negative light. This is particularly likely when the organisation is being subjected to strong pressure from the marketplace, or has a history of internal strife. However, in the long run, organisational effectiveness is impossible without positive feelings towards the communication processes within the organisation concerned, and with the external publics it serves. Audits bring the reality of how people feel to the fore. In many cases, this will be overwhelmingly concerned with acknowledging the existence of excellent communication. Where problems are revealed, managers will have the advantage of knowing what obstacles they must overcome to move the situation forward.

3 Common understandings of organisational life are identified. Despite the fact that audit participants will inevitably have many different perceptions, they will also agree on enough issues to facilitate the development of a strategy which will lead to improvements in communication climate.

4 The understanding that participants have of communication episodes can be compared to formal organisational channels and systems, to explore the gaps that exist between imagined and real practice.

Having said this, the extent to which communication audits have been employed has been somewhat limited. Some work utilising this approach was conducted within the UK during the 1980s (Booth, 1986, 1988), but, overall, they have yet to enter fully into mainstream management practice. Even within the United States, it has been pointed out that 'until recently organisations have expended surprisingly little effort in the preventive maintenance that a regular communication audit would offer' (Goldhaber, 1993, p. 348). Smeltzer (1993) also noted that since 1977 no paper on communication audits had been published in the US *Journal of Business Communication*, where much of the original research on this approach appeared, and argued that this constituted an example of a useful approach to research being unjustly neglected. (Nor has any paper on audits been published in this journal during the period between Smeltzer's observation and the writing of this book.) Ellis *et al.* (1993) claimed that the general literature on communication auditing was what they termed 'sparse' (p. 143). This suggests that audit tools have not been extensively used by researchers, either to gather empirical data or to contribute towards the development of organisational and communication theory.

One possible reason for this is that communication audits deal with highly sensitive human relationships and therefore with issues of power dynamics. Pfeffer (1992, p. 302) pointed out that: 'To be in power is to be watched more closely, and this surveillance affords one the luxury of few mistakes.' More precisely, managers frequently feel that either (a) they must not make mistakes; or (b) if they do, it is essential that no one notices. This creates an atmosphere calculated to induce paranoia. Paranoia renders people wary of opening themselves to critical feedback, an issue we discuss later in this chapter.

This means that the results of communication audits may be political in ways that financial audits rarely are. Badaracco (1988) argued that the identification of communication problems sometimes leads to a shooting of the messenger rather than a focus on the cure. Thus, it is not surprising that both practitioners and researchers have sometimes been hesitant to utilise diagnostic methods which could lead to unpleasant feedback. We discuss below some of the attitudes commonly found to underlie these problems, and consider how they might best be addressed.

RESISTANCE TO THE AUDIT PROCESS

Managers often feel that their agenda is already overcrowded. They are reluctant to burden it further with issues which are widely regarded as too intangible to be measured, let alone transformed (Tourish, 1996). A war can only be fought on so many fronts before exhaustion and despair claim victory over the main protagonists. In today's marketplace enormous demands are already made on managers' time and energies. Many simply feel that they do not have the space to examine communication issues. The key, here, is to make an irresistibly convincing case in favour of the benefits obtained through the audit process, while selecting an approach which will not make unrealistic demands on people's time.

Time concerns are reinforced by fear. Once communication has broken down, the fires of rumour, uncertainty and discontent are ignited. Managers have a natural reluctance to get close to such a conflagration, fearful that they may be singed by the flames. The result is that many of them attempt to ignore a crisis, hoping that when the worst of it is over they will be able to salvage something from the debris left behind. Others send in communications experts, who often have insufficient back-up at corporate headquarters to be effective. Again, it is necessary to show how audits function like smoke detectors, alerting organisations to the first whiffs of trouble, when something can still be done about it.

Attitudinal obstacles

Tourish (1997), in discussing such resistance to the audit process, has identified the following attitudes from managers, which have been widely encountered. In each case, they represent an obstacle to the serious investigation of communication practice. Practitioners need to be aware of them, and consider their likely impact on proposals to audit communication:

1 *'Too much information is commercially sensitive, and if we let it out our competitors will benefit.'*

Accordingly, managers may be suspicious of anything which seems to promise a more open flow of information than what has prevailed in the past. Within this perspective, supply businesses are seen as competitors rather than partners. Customers are noisy, demanding and never satisfied. Employees don't know what they want, but know that they want more of it.

Our argument is that an organisation's most important assets are its staff, its suppliers and its customers. Research suggests that loyalty (on the part of employees, investors and customers) is more important in securing profitable growth than market share, scale, cost position or other key business variables (Reichfield, 1996b). However, enduring and productive relationships are only possible if people feel valued. They only feel valued if they feel informed. Secretiveness destroys trust, self-confidence and involvement (Arnott, 1987). Customers and employees, when kept in the dark, may begin to panic, and then flee.

Within organisations it has been found that most staff have a deep curiosity about the general management issues which animate those further up the hierarchy (Tourish and Hargie, 1996b; Tourish and Mulholland, 1997). People are not just interested in how they do their job. They are passionately concerned with the broader environmental context in which that job occurs. The more uncertain the external environment, the more true this becomes. Managers can and should turn this to their advantage.

However, a failure to be open results in a loss of confidence in senior managers. They are assumed to be concealing destructive hidden agendas. Such views are almost invariably exaggerated. However, their impact on relationships, cohesion and commitment is explosive. In any event, the notion that the decision-making process can be quarantined is a fantasy. As Payne (1996, p. 81) noted: 'There are few secrets in large organisations, and it is rarely possible to contain bad news.' Fax machines spring leaks. Support staff gossip with each other. Offices adjoin corridors, and people listen at doors. In consequence, much of what managers imagine to be top secret is actually routine gossip in the staff canteen. It is also probably being talked of much more negatively than is justified by the facts. Research suggests that negative information about something influences us much more than positive information, thereby enhancing the destructive impact of tittle-tattle and innuendo (Hargie *et al.*, 1999). Further, if people hear about important issues through the grapevine it means that managers have simply exchanged the opportunity to be seen as open for an image of being out of touch. This must rank as one of the worst trades in business!

2 *'Communication might be bad in most organisations, but I communicate very well and things are fine in my organisation.'*

Most managers are poor at evaluating their effectiveness as communicators (Quirke, 1996). There is widespread evidence (Sutherland, 1992) that most of us believe:

- we are more effective in our jobs than the average score of all people doing it (a statistical impossibility);
- our opinions are more correct than they are;
- more people agree with us than actually do;
- we contribute more to group decision-making than most other people involved; and
- we are better listeners than is really the case.

Furthermore, most people rate themselves as more intelligent, skilled, ethical, honest, persistent, original, friendly, reliable, attractive, fair-minded and even better drivers than others (Myers, 1996). We possess Olympian 'reflexes of self justification', which cause us to recognise weaknesses in the performance of others, but to imagine that we ourselves are doing better than we are. It is therefore hardly surprising that one national survey in the US found 60 per cent of top management respondents saying they communicated 'frequently' with their employees, while only 30 per cent of non-management staff agreed (Crampton *et al.*, 1998).

In addition, it is well known that people try to influence us through ingratiation – in particular, through flattery (Jones, 1990). When we attempt to ingratiate ourselves with people who have higher status than us we often tell them what we think they want to hear, rather than what we really feel (Rosenfeld *et al.*, 1995). Unfortunately, the research also suggests that most managers take this distorted feedback at face value. They believe it is genuinely meant, and accurate. They are not alone in being possessed by this happy conviction. Most dictators, as they are hustled off the stage of history, can be heard protesting 'but my people love me'. Psychologists have termed this perceptual myopia 'the boss's illusion' (Odom, 1993).

Thus, if we seriously want to find out how well our organisations are communicating internally and externally we must employ an objective system of measurement, rather than rely on our own intuitions, contaminated as they are by self-interest. Knowledge is virtue. A communication audit provides managers with an objective account of how well they are doing, and so bypasses those self-serving biases which may have distorted their understanding in the past. It can also inform detailed plans for change within the organisation.

3 *'Why do I need to examine my performance in detail? Can't I simply implement examples of good practice from elsewhere?'*

Finding out how well you are doing remains an essential first step towards improvement. Communication programmes need to focus on real problems, rather than on imaginary aches and pains. No one suggests that we should routinely swallow pills for every medical contingency, whether we are ill or not. Indeed, it is not advisable to take someone else's tablets – a practice which may prove fatal. Likewise, it is foolhardy to launch into an all-embracing communication programme without a thorough examination of how well existing systems are functioning. Careful diagnosis is essential, leading to a carefully targeted treatment regime.

4 *'Why should I do something (e.g. ask people how well I am doing as a communicator) that means I will get kicked in the teeth?'*

First, examining current practice focuses the minds of senior management teams on the crucial issues:

• What sort of culture do we want to create?
• What is our management style?
• What behaviours do we pursue which are inimical to our philosophy, and which we can and must change?
• What are the key issues which we should be communicating about?
• How are we communicating on these issues?

Clarity on these issues is essential for communication and business success.

Second, negative feedback is not inevitable. Many examinations of communication performance have found extremely positive evaluations towards immediate managers, positive attitudes towards the organisation, a strong desire to be involved, and in many cases an appreciation of the extremely difficult job which senior managers perform (e.g. Tourish and Hargie, 1996b). These strengths should be publicised, celebrated and built upon. However, every organisation has weaknesses. The job of management is not to preside over complacency and inertia. It is to improve the organisation's efficiency and effectiveness. This means seizing every opportunity to identify those areas where it is possible for everyone, including top managers, to do better.

Third, a communication review reveals what the dominant mood of the organisation or its external publics actually is. This might be news to some managers, but it will not be news to those who have provided feedback. If communication is really poor then most people are already well aware of it, suffer its consequences, talk about it constantly, and are eager for initiatives designed to improve it. An audit merely allows the organisation to measure the extent of their dissatisfaction. To think otherwise is akin to believing that drivers improve their prospects of avoiding collisions by closing their eyes and plugging their ears. Measures to review and transform communication also bring therapeutic benefits, by enabling people to ventilate views they are ordinarily compelled to repress. In the process, organisations gain valuable information, and can plan more effectively for the future.

5 *'Perhaps people feel alienated and uninvolved, and think that senior managers don't communicate with them sufficiently. Isn't this to be expected when large organisations have so many people to communicate with? Can I really do anything about it?'*

Such a view suggests chronically low, and disabling, expectations. We have, on occasion, also heard senior managers express the opinion that 'Communication is like the weather. We would all like it to be fine, but there's not much any of us can do to change it.' The reality is that no organisation achieves high quality outcomes over an extended period of time if staff or customers feel uninvolved and alienated. People want to feed ideas into the organisations in which they work, and with whom they do business. But our audits, in a variety of organisations, have found that many of them have largely given up on this, feeling that the system is too hierarchical and disrespectful of what those at the coal face have to say and contribute. In terms of communication, if not the weather, organisations tend to get the climate which they expect. Research suggests that high expectations are more likely to lead to quality outcomes (Eden, 1993). Low expectations become self-fulfilling prophecies, as the nightmare takes physical form, and the organisation is eventually punished in the marketplace.

Structural barriers to implementation

More generally, the issue of what stops organisations implementing high performance work practices is attracting increased attention in the research literature. A thorough discussion of this topic is presented by Pfeffer (1998). In an earlier text, the following main barriers to implementation were discussed (Pfeffer, 1996). We would suggest that they also underpin the attitudinal obstacles outlined above, and discuss them in this context:

1 *Strategy and financial barriers*

Managers have been schooled to pay more attention to strategy formulation and financial issues, rather than employee or customer relations. In many cases, strategic planning has become ludicrously complex, all-absorbing and self-defeating. One result is that over 90 per cent of strategic plans are never implemented (Mintzberg, 1993). Nevertheless, those trained in number crunching have a tendency to devote their attention to what can be most easily quantified, rather than to such apparently intangible issues as how employees and customers feel about communication. A central argument of this book is that it is much more possible to measure communication effectiveness than most managers realise.

2 *Social barriers (or 'the follow the herd' instinct)*

Many managers have been influenced by macho notions of business leadership, popularised in the anecdotal management literature. The epitome of this was the Gordon Gecko character as portrayed by Michael Douglas in the film *Wall Street*. In this world, CEOs are invariably pictured with bulging biceps rather than brilliant brains. The Arnold Schwarzenegger School of Management, world renowned for the low premium it puts on communication skills, has been swamped by star-struck recruits. (*'How many people have you terminated today?'*) The impression is created that everyone behaves this way, in 'the real world'. Thus, managers are influenced by what they think the majority of their rivals are doing. When re-engineering and other fads acquire large numbers of enthusiastic disciples, the unconverted are more likely to conclude that there must be something in them. Celluloid fantasies become reality. We have pointed to the fallacy of regarding mass support for an opinion as evidence of its correctness in Chapter 1. Paradoxically, this means that when competitors disregard the subtleties of communication other companies become inclined to do likewise, rather than seek competitive advantage from behaving differently to their rivals. Thus, if most companies do not audit communication it is more difficult to convince managers that they should buck the trend.

3 *Power and political barriers*

Once people are used to managing in a particular way, precedent, habit, inertia and a reluctance to admit to mistakes make it more likely they will continue to behave as they have always done. In management, what has already happened (rather than feedback from the marketplace) often determines what happens next. Furthermore, a great deal of experimental research suggests that 'management centralisation and involvement . . . lead to an overvaluation of the work produced under tighter managerial control' (Pfeffer and Cialdini, 1998, p. 17). In other words, once we feel that we have had responsibility for a task or a process we exaggerate the success of what has been achieved. Illusions of indispensability and infallibility then take root. (*'I know I am an excellent communicator.'*) This makes it more difficult to reconsider communication practices, particularly if critical feedback is involved and the sharing of power has been proposed. Why change something when you believe that your opinion is more important, and certainly more correct, than anyone else's?

4 *Hierarchical barriers*

Most people attempt to minimise the possibility of critical feedback, fearing that it will lead to a loss of status. For this reason, performance appraisal is fraught with difficulties (Hargie *et al.*, 1999). Managers asked to evaluate their organisation's communication effectiveness can feel threatened, and respond by challenging the necessity for doing so. Combined with this, human resources in general, and communications in particular, rarely has a status equivalent to that of other key departments.

Each, or all, of these barriers may have to be confronted before organisations can implement audits successfully. A consistent focus on the following themes is helpful:

- *Show how the audit will assist the organisation with its current business needs and priorities.* What concrete problems, internally and externally, will it help to solve?

- *Demonstrate the non-judgemental nature of the audit process.* It should be made clear at the outset that feedback, in the form of final reports, will avoid the 'naming and shaming' of individuals or groups. (This may require strong diplomatic skills, at the report writing stage.)
- *Emphasise the involvement of key decision-makers in the audit process.* (We have discussed some steps to accomplish this earlier in the chapter.) This will overcome many of the obstacles discussed here, and ensure a more receptive context for the final audit report.
- *Highlight the attitudinal and structural barriers discussed above.* An awareness that bear traps lie ahead helps managers to avoid stumbling around in the dark, and then falling into them.
- *Use the audit to celebrate what the organisation does well, as well as discuss where it has problems.* This is more likely to embed the principle of audit in the organisation's psyche, and increases the prospects that it will be employed on an ongoing basis.

Audits can effect profound improvements in communication, internally and externally. This potential will only be realised if the organisation is convinced of its potential, and managers show determination to overcome the obstacles which stand in the way. The good news is that the measures necessary to achieve this are quite straightforward. The key is to aim high, start with small steps, and grow bolder with experience.

CONCLUSION

Prioritising the quality of communication between managers and staff, and between organisations and their customers, yields business dividends. However, new ideas are often turned into planning marathons which produce long, unreadable documents, and an infestation of committees rather than action plans. Many organisations are paralysed by 'working parties' which do no work, 'project teams' which can do nothing until they report to 'project boards' (who are always too busy to meet), and 'briefing sessions' in which nothing is ever brief.

This chapter locates communication audits within a radically different approach. Audits are a means of assessing current performance, in order to devise improvements. Ideally, these should be designed to take account of the communication practices of the best performing businesses in the world. These represent a gold standard, against which the performance of the organisation conducting the audit may be compared. In turn, the audit process is an ongoing cycle. The results from one audit can be contrasted with those gained from future audits. In this way, it forms an internal benchmark. These are generally regarded as easier to maintain, and usually consist of more reliable data, than those derived externally (Cox and Thompson, 1998). If meaningful recommendations have been devised and implemented, the measurement indices should show a pattern of continuous improvement. Organisations can then rejoice over real rather than fictitious triumphs.

Communication audits render the intangible tangible, move communication issues further up the management agenda, and, ultimately, improve efficiency and effectiveness in an increasingly competitive marketplace. Subsequent chapters in this book explore the different techniques available in more detail, and offer case studies where they can be seen in action. The final chapter then explores how the audit process fits into the development of a comprehensive communication strategy, which we argue is essential for organisational success.

Part II

Audit methodologies

Chapter 3

The questionnaire approach

Phillip G. Clampitt

INTRODUCTION

Most organisations are enchanted with questionnaires. The lure of a survey lies in the seeming simplicity of the methodology, the ostensive ease of administration and the apparent directness of interpretation. Yet these are merely illusions based more on the ubiquity of surveys rather than their actual utility. For instance, researchers have shown that what survey respondents say they will purchase is often very different from what they actually buy (Morwitz *et al.*, 1997). Mothers will not readily admit to spending more on dog food than baby food. But, in fact, many do (Macht, 1998).

Methodological issues are largely a matter of the proper use of well-established scientific procedures. Administering a questionnaire and interpreting the results requires scientific understanding tempered with an artful consideration of organisational politics. The purpose of this chapter is to discuss both the art and science of developing, administering, analysing and interpreting surveys.

DEVELOPING A QUESTIONNAIRE

There is no magic formula for developing an effective questionnaire. It requires both a respect for social scientific conventions and sound judgement. The discussion below is presented as a linear step-by-step procedure. Generally, this is a useful way to proceed, but bear in mind that auditors may have to loop back and revisit a previous step.

Step 1: Research the organisational background

Having at least a minimal understanding of the organisation is essential to developing a useful survey. Why? It allows auditors to make reasonable judgements about the inevitable tradeoffs involved in the survey process. For instance, learning that the general education level of employees is low implies that adjustments are necessary in the length and complexity of the questionnaire. Indeed with

---

Box 3.1 100 'facts': some examples

1 Demographic information about employees
2 Layers of management
3 Communication tools frequently used
4 Dates of previous surveys
5 Locations of employees
6 Departmental structure

---

millions of adults considered functionally illiterate, there are limits on the utility of written surveys. The organisational background also allows auditors to ascertain the best ways to administer the survey. For instance, e-mail might be a good administrative tool for employees who frequently use the corporate Intranet.

Finally, the organisational background will aid in the proper interpretation of the data. One audacious student auditor became enamoured with data indicating that none of the employees had worked for the organisation for more than four years. He proceeded to 'illuminate' the company president with the following observation: 'If you can't retain employees for more than four years, you've got a turnover problem of major proportions. This fact alone tells me that employees can't be satisfied with your communication practices.' The president calmly replied that the 'company is only four years old'. Then he thanked the audit team for their efforts and quickly ushered them out of the door.

'The 100 facts' exercise is one way to gather this background information. The objective is simple; develop a list of 100 facts about the organisation. This is merely an exploratory procedure, so the order and level of specificity of the facts is not really important. In a way, this is like a detective doing an initial scan of a crime scene looking for any kind of information that might provide a useful lead. Box 3.1 provides some examples of the type of facts that might be useful. This information can be gathered in all sorts of ways, including interviews with key personnel, observations of organisational practices, and examination of corporate documents (employee handbooks, newsletters, annual reports, etc.). Once the facts are gathered, it is important for the audit team to discuss the implications of their findings: What tradeoffs will we need to make? What are the constraints we will be working under? What are employee expectations regarding the survey? Preliminary answers to questions of this sort provide valuable insights later in the process.

Step 2: Ascertain the purpose

This step may appear to be easy and straightforward. Years of experience suggest that it is not. In fact, it may be the most difficult step of all. The critical question is: After the survey is completed what does the organisation want to happen? Or, as I have asked CEOs, 'How will you assess the effectiveness of this process?' Sometimes organisations only have a vague notion about how they will use the results. Auditors need to help them clarify their desires. There is a variety of objectives, including assessing:

- the communication competence of employees;
- the conflict management style of employees;
- the effectiveness of communication channels (newsletters, e-mail, etc.);
- the adequacy of information dissemination;
- the quality of organisational relationships;
- the employee satisfaction with communication;
- the effectiveness of the entire communication system.

Each of these may imply a different type of survey or even methodology. Sometimes various parts of the organisation have different objectives in mind. The senior management may only want to 'get the pulse' of the organisation, while some managers will use the data to drive specific changes in their departments. Reconciling these often conflicting objectives needs to be done in the planning stages. For example, if managers are not convinced they will receive some benefit from the process they will not readily encourage their employees to participate.

Step 3: Determine the proper instrument to use

Questionnaires are often referred to as 'instruments', and with good reason. They are the tools of the trade. Like all tools they are designed for a specific purpose; hammers are for nails and screwdrivers for screws. Unfortunately, there are times when apprentices hammer in the screws. It may work but it is not particularly elegant or effective. For instance, asking employees in a survey about how often they use internal web sites to access corporate information is probably a waste of paper. Counting the number of 'hits' on certain pages is more likely to yield useful information (Sinickas, 1998).

There are two basic options: choose a pre-existing instrument or develop one. There are benefits and liabilities to each approach. Pre-existing instruments generally have been scientifically tested and developed by professionals. Therefore auditors can be fairly sure that the survey is valid – it measures what they think it measures. And they can be reasonably certain that the instrument is reliable – the results are stable over time. Typically discussions of reliability and validity can be found in the research literature about the instrument. Moreover, normative data are often available that will allow some comparisons between organisations.

There are several potential disadvantages in using a pre-existing instrument. The authors may need to grant permission to use the survey. Some of the questions on the survey may not be applicable to the organisation. A few of the most frequently used questionnaires are too long to administer via modern communication technology, like e-mail.

Developing a custom designed questionnaire poses some unique challenges. Almost anybody can put together a list of seemingly insightful questions. But it is foolhardy to assume that this is what constitutes a useful instrument. There is an art to constructing a useful questionnaire. There are the scientific issues of validity and reliability to consider. For example, the wording of a question can have a significant impact on how it is answered. Consider the following survey item:

'Do you approve or disapprove of publishing the employee newsletter in order to improve organisational communication?'

This particular question introduces a number of problems. First, it is bipolar and offers respondents only two choices. What if employees have an attitude somewhere on the continuum between approve or disapprove? Second, the question makes the dubious assumption that a newsletter will actually improve 'organisational communication' (whatever that means). In fact, employees' attitudes about the newsletter and 'organisational communication' may be two separate issues. Finally, what could be done with the results gleaned from this question? In the unlikely event that significant numbers of employees 'disapproved', then what actions are implied? Should the newsletter actually be discontinued? Or are respondents asking for changes in the format of the newsletter? Or are employees upset about the content of the newsletter? These cautions are not meant to discourage but only to warn that framing appropriate questions is not as simple as it seems.

If auditors choose to develop a survey, it is important to consult the literature about how to do so (e.g. Edward *et al.*, 1997; Fink, 1995). This can be useful for a number of reasons. Well-developed custom-designed surveys are often better suited to employees of a particular organisation. They tend to use terms familiar to employees. Custom-designed surveys typically target more specific issues than their more generic cousins. For instance, none of the major instruments reviewed below asks about how effectively management communicates the need to control costs. Yet in one company I found this to be the most critical communication issue.

The choice of instruments is critical to the success of the audit process. As a rule of thumb, for those first learning about the process, it is best to use a pre-existing tool and then make adaptations to the instrument.

Step 4: Choose the instrument

Organisational communication scholars have used hundreds of instruments. The vast majority have only been used once. The ones routinely used can be classified into two types: process and comprehensive instruments (Downs *et al.*, 1994). The process instruments examine communication at a more micro level and investigate issues such as conflict management, team building, or communication competence. The comprehensive instruments examine communication practices on a more macro level. Both kinds of instruments have their place, but this section briefly reviews some of the most widely used instruments that are of a comprehensive nature. More extensive reviews of the instrument can be found in the existing literature. In most cases, complete versions of the surveys can be obtained from these sources (e.g. Downs, 1988; Greenbaum *et al.*, 1988; Rubin *et al.*, 1994). These instruments have generally proved to be reliable, valid and useful in a vast range of organisations.

Communication Satisfaction Questionnaire

When Downs and Hazen (1977) developed this instrument, they were investigating the relationship between communication and job satisfaction. They were successful. Generally, the more satisfied employees were with communication, the more satisfied they were with their jobs. However, certain types of communications, like those with the supervisor, tended to be more important than others. After extensive testing Downs and Hazen (1977) isolated eight key communication factors: communication climate, relationship to superiors, organisational integration, media quality, horizontal communication, organisational perspective, relationship with subordinates, and personal feedback. Other scholars have generally confirmed the reliability and validity of the instrument (Hecht, 1978; Crino and White, 1981; Clampitt and Girard, 1993, 1987; Pincus, 1986). The survey consists of forty core questions with five items devoted to each of the eight factors. In addition, there are six questions about job satisfaction and productivity. A databank exists that can be consulted for comparative purposes (Clampitt, 1991). It is relatively easy to administer and can be completed in less than 15 minutes. While the CSQ may not provide all the details necessary for specific action plans, it does provide a wonderful overview of potential problem areas that can be further investigated. The case studies in Chapters 12 and 13 both illustrate the utility of this instrument.

ICA Audit Survey

Gerald Goldhaber led a team of scholars from the International Communication Association in the development of a package of instruments designed to assess organisational communication practices (Goldhaber, 1976; Goldhaber and Krivonos, 1977; Goldhaber and Rogers, 1979; Downs, 1988). After over eight years of development, one of the principal diagnostic tools that emerged from this collaboration was the ICA Audit Survey or the Communication Audit Survey. The questionnaire consists of 122 questions divided into eight major sections:

- Amount of information received about various topics versus amount desired
- Amount of information sent about various topics versus amount desired
- Amount of follow-up versus amount desired
- Amount of information received from various sources versus amount desired
- Amount of information received from various channels versus amount desired
- Timeliness of information

- Organisational relationships
- Satisfaction with organisational outcomes

The first five sections use a similar scaling format. Employees are asked to rate on a 1 (very little) to 5 (very great) scale the amount of information they '*now receive*' on a given topic such as 'organisational policies'. In a parallel scale, respondents are asked about the amount of information they '*need to receive*' on 'organisational policies' or some other topic. Then a difference score can be generated that compares employees' information needs with the amount actually received. Some questions about the validity of the instrument and the utility of the difference scores have been raised (Downs *et al.*, 1981; DeWine *et al.*, 1985). Subsequent revisions of the instrument have tried to address these concerns (DeWine *et al.*, 1985; DeWine and James, 1988). In general, this instrument is one of the boldest and most comprehensive attempts to measure all aspects of an organisation's communication system. The case study in Chapter 10 illustrates how this instrument can be used as a benchmark in an initial audit against which to compare performance in follow up audits, and an adaptation of the ICA Questionnaire is included in the Appendix.

Organisational Communication Development audit questionnaire

Osmo Wiio and his Finnish colleagues developed the Organisational Communication Development (OCD) audit questionnaire as part of an assessment package built around the Delphi technique. Their purpose was straightforward, namely to: 'determine how well the communication system helps the organisation to translate its goals into desired end-results' (Greenbaum *et al.*, 1988, p. 259). The OCD is actually a refined version of an earlier survey (LTT) developed by Wiio and administered to some 6000 employees in 23 Finnish organisations. One version contains 76 items that are grouped into 12 dimensions:

1 Overall communication satisfaction
2 Amount of information received from different sources – now
3 Amount of information received from different sources – ideal
4 Amount of information received about specific job items – now
5 Amount of information received about specific job items – ideal
6 Areas of communication that need improvement
7 Job satisfaction
8 Availability of computer information system
9 Allocation of time in a working day
10 Respondent's general communication behaviour
11 Organisation-specific questions
12 Information-seeking patterns

More recently refined versions have fewer dimensions and items (Wiio, 1975, 1977). Because of confidentiality concerns, the instrument has not been subjected to some psychometric tests used to assess other surveys (Greenbaum *et al.*, 1988). Yet, the OCD addresses several issues that are not covered by the other instruments.

Organisational Communication Scale

Roberts and O'Reilly (1973) originally developed the Organisational Communication Scale (OCS) while working on research for the US Office of Naval Research. The scale was developed to compare communication practices across organisations. The OCS comprises 35 questions that can be broken down into 16 dimensions. Employees use seven-point Likert scales to respond to items about the following dimensions:

- Trust for Supervisor
- Influence of Supervisor
- Importance of Upward Mobility
- Desire for Interaction
- Accuracy
- Summarisation
- Gatekeeping
- Overload

Additional questions ask employees about the percentage of time they spend in the following communication activities: Upward Communication (factor 9), Downward Communication (10), and Lateral or Horizontal Communication (11). Another series of items ask about the percentage of time using various modes of communication (12–15). A final question (factor 16) asks about employees' general level of communication satisfaction. This instrument is by far the shortest one reviewed in this section. It has a couple of unique content areas like 'summarisation' and 'influence of supervisor' that other instruments do not contain. Other scholars have found that variables like this may have an important impact on organisational communication practices. Yet the brevity of the instrument may inhibit developing a more comprehensive view of other important communication issues like interdepartmental communication.

The obvious question is: Which instrument is best? That depends on the purpose of the audit and the constraints on the audit process. If, for example, time was limited, it would be difficult to use the ICA audit survey. The best advice is to carefully review all the alternatives. There are several works that can aid in that process (e.g. Greenbaum *et al.*, 1988; Rubin *et al.*, 1994). As a starting point, Table 3.1 provides points of comparison between the surveys reviewed above.

Table 3.1 Comparison of instruments

	CSQ	ICA	OCD2	OCS
Developer	Downs and Hazen (1977)	Goldhaber and Krivonos (1977)	Wiio (1975)	Roberts and O'Reilly (1973)
Number of items	46	122	76	35
Dimensions	10	8	12	16
Scaling device	Satisfaction level	Likert-type	Satisfaction level	Likert-type others
Open-ended questions	Yes	Yes	Yes	No
Databank available	Yes	Yes	No	No
Average completion time	10–15 minutes	45–60 minutes	30–40 minutes	5–10 minutes

Step 5: Make appropriate adaptations to the survey

Two types of modifications need to be considered. First, what demographic data are needed? Sometimes the demographic data can be helpful in isolating problem areas. For instance, in one audit I found that there were dramatic differences between the way females and males viewed the effectiveness of the communication system. Second, what departmental or unit breakdowns are needed? This is always a tricky issue. The breakdowns need to be specific enough to isolate areas of concern but not so specific that respondents feel their anonymity is compromised. A good rule of thumb: the smallest group size should be limited to seven people. Demographic and unit breakdown items should be included at the end of the survey. Thus, if the employees feel uneasy about providing that information, they will at least answer the substantive questions.

ADMINISTERING THE SURVEY

Sound administrative procedures are essential for an effective audit. This section provides a number of guidelines to improve the integrity of the administrative process.

1 Determine the sample size necessary to fulfil the objectives

Auditors have two basic choices: (a) survey everyone who wants to participate and (b) survey a sample of the population. As a rule of thumb, the first option is best for most organisations. There are two reasons for this recommendation. First, surveys are often used as a tool to set new organisational agendas, such as changing the performance appraisal system. If a sample is used, then those who did not participate can resist the change by arguing that they 'did not get a chance to provide any input'. In several cases we have encountered employees who said: 'Management picked the employees for the survey. They got just the answers they wanted.' Logical arguments about the statistical reliability of a sample hold little sway with folk who feel emotionally isolated because they were not included. Second, surveying the entire population allows auditors to provide specific actionable results for all groups in the company. Results often reveal remarkable differences between various working groups. First-level supervisors may have entirely different issues to address with their groups than the organisation as a whole needs to address. Few first-line supervisors would want only one person from their department to represent the views of the entire department.

Yet some uninformed managers misuse the data to draw exactly these kinds of conclusions about a work unit. Technically this problem is known as a lack of generalisability. They should not do it, but they do. Surveying the entire population can preclude this problem. That said, there is a place for sampling. Samples are an efficient way to make useful generalisations about the entire population. Samples provide a way to avoid the often large efforts needed to survey the entire population. There are different kinds of samples that can be used to make sure that the results are reasonably unbiased (Fink, 1995). The critical issue is randomisation. That is, everyone has an equal chance of being surveyed. However, some executives are tempted to be a little 'fast and loose' with this principle. So watch out.

2 Develop an administrative protocol

Failure to address administrative issues adequately is one of the more subtle ways to undermine a communication audit. The quality of the data may directly turn on how employees are motivated to participate, and how the survey is distributed. These issues are related to one another and the discussion below focuses on how to make the appropriate tradeoffs.

How can employees be motivated to participate?

Most organisations do not make completing a survey a mandatory job requirement. Therefore, auditors are faced with the task of motivating employees. This is becoming increasingly difficult because surveys are almost as common as junk mail. And many employees treat surveys just like another piece of junk mail. There are really two aspects to this quandary. First, how can employees' fears be disabused? Second, how can employees be persuaded that participation is important?

Employees often fear that somehow the results of their survey will come back to haunt them. For instance, an employee who candidly criticises his or her boss might be passed over for a promotion. Generally, this means that employees need to be guaranteed anonymity. Without that guarantee they are less likely to provide frank responses. Who should administer the survey? Usually, the supervisor is the worst choice and an outside consultant is usually the best choice. Even if employees *suspect* that their survey can fall into the hands of supervisors, there can be a problem. That is why interoffice mail is not the preferred method for collecting survey data (although the survey could be distributed via interoffice mail). In fact, we usually destroy individual surveys after the data are coded into the computer. When we use survey sessions to administer surveys we often make a theatrical production of placing completed surveys in a locked box.

How the data will be used is another motivational issue. One company used survey results to assign bonuses for supervisors. When the supervisors found out, they actively lobbied their workers for 'votes' on the survey. This is one of the worst uses of a communication audit imaginable. In another situation we discovered that, despite our best efforts, the data were tainted. After interviewing members of one unit it was clear that the results regarding training were useless. Many of the employees admitted that they artificially inflated the ratings on the training questions because they were sick of going to mandatory training classes. This example is less troubling. Over-reacting to audit data does not happen in very many organisations. This is a risk worth taking. But both of these situations highlight the motivational impact of the decisions regarding how the data will be used.

Assuming that employee fears can be minimised, there are a variety of ways to inspire participation. Frankly, some organisations 'bribe' employees with raffles, gifts and door prizes. Others publicise less direct or tangible rewards such as improvements in working conditions or the 'opportunity to express your opinion'. Either way, the WIIFM issue (What's In It For Me) is being addressed. There are more altruistic appeals that work in some companies, such as suggesting there is a kind of civic obligation to complete the questionnaire. One paper mill appealed to workers' sense of duty by comparing the survey process to maintenance procedures on machines. Mill workers may not like to do it, but it is necessary to keep the organisation running efficiently. These appeals could be characterised as WIIFO issues (What's In It For the Organisation). Typically, the WIIFM issues prove more effective than the WIIFO issues.

How will the data be collected?

There are several administrative options. One commonly used method is to administer the survey in a group setting. For instance, employees may be scheduled to complete the survey in the corporate training room. This method allows the auditor to brief participants before they take the survey. The briefing generally involves the following elements:

- describing the purpose of the audit;
- discussing how the data will be used;
- providing assurances about confidentiality;
- discussing the feedback process;
- explaining how to complete the survey;
- answering any questions.

Using this approach often increases employee trust in the process by decreasing their anxiety. Participants are also more likely to be motivated to complete the survey. Scheduling work groups often boosts participation rates.

One potential disadvantage of survey groups is that they can raise employee expectations too high. A synergy may be created in which employees may expect management to respond to concerns more quickly than is possible. Another potential disadvantage involves logistics. Can the audit team secure enough rooms to administer the survey? Does the team have enough time to set up the schedule and keep everyone informed? Do the rooms provide sufficient anonymity for participants? These are the kinds of questions that need to be considered when opting for this choice.

Sending the survey through the post or interoffice mail is probably the most common administrative procedure. Typically this is a cost-effective way to maximise coverage. You can conveniently reach employees who are geographically dispersed, work on different shifts or in different time zones. However, there are some tradeoffs. Confidentiality concerns may be raised if the completed surveys are returned via interoffice mail. It is also more difficult to motivate employees to participate in the process. Consequently, rates of return for mailed surveys are often relatively low when compared to other methods. For instance, one company distributed a survey in the mail to one division and scheduled survey sessions for a sister division. The participation rates were 25 per cent and 55 per cent respectively.

More recently, computer-based administrative procedures have been used. These work fairly well if the survey is short (one page or less) and to the point. Since most users will not fill out a lengthy survey in this medium, the auditor is restricted to a few relevant questions. This means the auditor is forced to make some tough decisions about which issues are relevant. The results are less comprehensive than those attained through other procedures. The confidentiality of the data is another issue. There are not many elegant ways to address this concern. However, the main advantage is the speed and the ease with which results can be tabulated. Computer-based surveys are an effective way to check the pulse of the communication system on a routine basis. Auditors can determine the concerns of employees and use the data to quickly address those issues. This is similar to how skilled politicians use opinion polls. They track public opinion on a few key issues and then fine-tune their messages accordingly.

One manufacturing plant with 1000 employees creates a 'pulse report' every week by e-mailing a survey to approximately fifty randomly selected employees

Box 3.2 Pulse report

Directions: Place an X in the appropriate space below.

Questions	Strongly Agree	Agree	Undecided	Disagree	Strongly Disagree
1. I understand where the plant is headed in the next quarter.					
2. I understand why the plant is heading in the direction it is.					
3. I believe we need to reduce costs in the plant.					
4. I have the tools to do my job effectively.					
5. I am actively trying to control costs in the plant.					

Directions: Place a number between 0–100 in the appropriate space.

Questions	Number 0–100
1. On your last shift, how many people made positive comments about the plant?	
2. On your last shift, how many people made negative comments about the plant?	
3. On your last shift, how many incidents did you witness where someone took an unnecessary safety risk?	

Directions: Please fill in a written response in the appropriate space.

Questions	Please write your response below
1. What is your most important job-related concern?	
2. If you could ask the plant manager one question, what would it be? Why?	

each week (see Box 3.2). Employees are asked eight closed-ended questions and two open-ended questions. They generally complete the survey in less than five minutes and are 'rewarded' with a raffle ticket. The company then posts the results and management responses to employee concerns on an electronic-bulletin board. The plant uses the data to continually track employee concerns and thus determines the effectiveness of the managerial communication strategy. This has proved to be particularly helpful in providing direction for meetings, suggesting articles for the newsletter, and planning for corporate changes.

The future possibilities for Internet/Intranet delivered surveys are fascinating. Consider a series of survey items arranged on several levels. A top layer of seven questions could address broad communication areas. Then several follow-up questions could be triggered depending on the employee's answers to the top-level questions. Therefore, the total survey would consist of ten questions, seven of which all participants would answer and three that would uniquely probe potential problem areas. This kind of survey could potentially provide the kind of depth and breadth necessary for a finely tuned communication strategy.

3 Decide how feedback will be provided

There are several crucial questions that need to be answered: What format will be used to present the results? How will the results be communicated? Will the auditor assist in the interpretation of the results? This section will address each of these issues.

What format will be used to present the results?

Quantitative data can be reported in any number of different ways and with varying levels of statistical sophistication. Some organisations want graphics. Others prefer simple numeric reporting, typically including the mean, standard deviation, and frequency. I worked with one organisation that only wanted the mean reported. In another, they ignored the mean and focused only on the frequency counts. While all these decisions do not need to be made before the survey is administered, they need to be discussed.

There are also options in reporting qualitative data. Some companies only want a listing of employee answers to open-ended questions. This is fairly easy to do but it often creates some difficulties. For instance, managers often play the 'who said that?' game when encountering a particularly touching or distressing statement. The focus of the discussion tends to be driven by the poignant or enraging statement. Thus a sense of balance and proportion is often lost. Others prefer that the data be content analysed. This approach tends to promote more thoughtful and balanced interpretations of the data. However, it does take a great deal of time and effort to content-analyse data properly.

How will the results be communicated?

Typically, the results are presented in both an oral and a written format (see Chapter 9). Senior management generally receives the report first. Then the results are rolled out to other levels in the organisation. Usually a written summary is prepared for all participants. Sometimes employees are offered the option of attending open briefing sessions.

Communicating the audit results is fairly straightforward. A more difficult issue involves answering a simple question: Now what? This phase is often called the 'action step' in which the following concerns are addressed:

1 What are the major issues?
2 When should they be addressed?
3 How should they be addressed?
4 Who should address them?

Clearly senior management needs to take some time to process the diagnostic phase of the audit before moving to the 'next step'. But the 'next step' varies from one organisation to another. There are three basic possibilities:

- In a few cases, senior management never releases the results to anyone. Long term, this is counterproductive because participation in future surveys is less likely.
- Sometimes senior management wants to have all the action plans in place before releasing the diagnostic data to employees. In that case, employees simultaneously receive a diagnostic report from the auditors and a set of responses in the form of an action plan from senior management.
- Other organisations value employee input and make a clearer distinction between the diagnosis and the prescription. Thus, they present the audit results and then merely outline the procedures that will be used to respond to the diagnosis.

In either case, it is important to draw a clear line between the diagnosis and the prescription. Auditors should avoid being tied to a particular programme. If the programme or action plan fails, then they can always find another way to address the underlying issues diagnosed in the audit. This is extremely important because the auditors' ability to generate useful data in the future should not be undermined by the failure of a particular action plan. Then the opportunity to learn in the future is severely limited.

Will the auditor assist in the interpretation of the results?

Some senior executives feel they need little assistance interpreting data. In fact, they may only hire an auditor to administer the survey and 'crunch the numbers'. This can present an ethical quandary because some executives believe they are qualified to interpret the data when in reality they are not. For instance, one of these 'qualified' executives drew the dubious conclusion that department A was much more effectively managed than department B. The basis for his opinion was a single survey question yielding the following results:

Department A = 6.2 mean (scale: 0–10, low–high)
Department B = 6.0 mean

This was not statistically significant, but the executive insisted that this result provided conclusive evidence. Because of similar instances, the auditor refused to work with the company on future projects. Clearly not all executives are like this. But most organisations need at least some help interpreting the results. Therefore, it is important to negotiate up front about these issues.

One way to address these issues strategically with the client is to provide sample output, reports and feedback protocols during the initial negotiations. Then auditors can be sure that the issues are discussed and the client can make any adjustments necessary.

4 Test the administrative procedures and questionnaire

This is a particularly helpful step when using a new instrument. You can determine what questions are difficult to understand and those that do not yield important information. Even with pre-existing questionnaires, it is important to test the instrument and administrative procedures. For example, one company selected a survey that made extensive use of the word 'team'. One unit in the company had just been through some poorly conceived and executed training about 'team-based' management. Whenever these employees heard the word 'team', they cringed. Consequently, this particular group systematically rated the survey questions containing the 'T-word' low. In short, the negative connotations trumped the intended denotations of the auditors. Therefore, they decided to replace the 'T-word' with 'work group'.

Testing the survey is typically done in a focus group format. A random selection of employees is asked to complete the survey. A facilitator then interviews the group asking questions such as:

- What did you like most about the survey?
- What did you like least?
- Were the instructions understandable?
- What questions were difficult to answer? Why?
- Were there any words that you did not understand?

Typically a funnel questioning sequence works best, starting with the general questions and then moving to the more specific ones. Using this approach allows auditors to discover issues they may not have thought of, like readability problems associated with the physical layout of the survey.

ANALYSING THE DATA

How quantitative and qualitative data are displayed has a profound impact on the ultimate interpretations of the information. Information displays influence our reasoning, inform our intuitions, and imply corrective action. Ineffective displays make it difficult to draw proper conclusions and can lead us into discussions of the trivial. Edward Tufte made this compelling argument:

Modern data graphics can do much more than simply substitute for small statistical tables. At their best, graphics are instruments for reasoning about quantitative information. Often the most effective way to describe, explore, and summarize a set of numbers – even a very large set – is to look at pictures of those numbers. Furthermore, of all methods for analyzing and communicating statistical information, well-designed data graphics are usually the simplest and at the same time the most powerful.

(Tufte, 1983, p. 9)

Therefore, auditors need to think carefully about the choices made in displaying the data. With that in mind, consider the following analytical options.

QUANTITATIVE DATA

A variety of techniques ranging from simple to complex can be used to present and analyse the numeric data. Some basic options are reviewed below.

Rank-order method

This method is relatively straightforward. Using the means from each question, simply rank related items from high to low. For instance, if auditors were using the ICA survey, then items about the timeliness of information could be ranked in one table. Another table would contain items regarding organisational relationships, and so forth. For the Communication Satisfaction Survey, we usually rank all 40 items in one table. Statistical tests can be used to group the items on the tables into high, medium and low 'zones'. These procedures can aid the auditor in identifying underlying themes or patterns in the data. Items will often appear in some natural conceptual clumps, like a group of items related to 'information dissemination' versus others related to 'supervisory relationships'. The major drawback of the rank-order method is that strengths and weakness are a necessary by-product of the technique. What if all the means are above (or below) the conceptual midpoint? How do auditors make sense of a situation like that? The next technique addresses that very issue.

Databank comparisons

Most of the commonly used surveys have databanks available. For instance, the Communication Satisfaction Questionnaire databank, composed of the results of 26 audits, has been published (Clampitt, 1991). This allows other auditors the option to compare their organisation's results with those in the databank. Many businesses are particularly keen on this approach because it is a form of 'best practice' comparison. Statistical tests can be used to assess significant differences between the norm and the targeted organisation.

The excitement generated by a databank comparison should be tempered by the inevitable problems those comparisons create. First, organisations often differ from one another in significant ways and it may be inappropriate to use the databank as a comparison point. For example, in a business organised around the team concept, a 'good' score compared to the databank may not be good enough. Other organisations that are less dependent on teams could find the same result gratifying. Second, sometimes the databank comparisons reveal seemingly contradictory findings to other analytical techniques. In one organisation, the highest ranked items on the survey revolved around supervisor communication, yet even these scores were well below the databank norms. Is supervisory communication a strength or weakness? That, of course, depends on whether auditors take an internal or external focus of analysis. This particular organisation was in a similar position to a football team with a 'star' player who was merely average when compared to others in the league.

Factor scores

Most of the standard audit surveys have been tested and reveal various key factors. These are groupings of questions that seem to measure similar underlying issues. Some are easy to spot, like all the questions relating to supervisory communication, while others are more difficult. These require more sophisticated statistical techniques like factor analysis, principal component analysis and regression analysis. These can often be helpful in determining key relationships between variables. Some auditors use the predetermined factors as the basis for their analysis. Statistically savvy researchers use a variety of techniques to draw their conclusions.

All these techniques are viable options for the preliminary analysis of your data. Often they are used in various combinations. The fundamental point is to recognise both the strengths and drawbacks of each technique.

QUALITATIVE DATA

Since many questionnaires contain at least a few open-ended questions, it is important to consider briefly how to scientifically analyse these data. The process is straightforward yet, at times, intellectually taxing:

1 One auditor should read over all the responses to a given question and look for underlying themes. Even though the respondents will use different terms to describe their concerns, usually a stable set of issues will emerge from the responses. Typical categories include 'upward communication', 'quality of information' and 'co-worker communication'. There is no way to determine the ideal number of the categories. However, generally, anywhere from five to

ten categories works best. If there are too few categories, it is difficult to make useful recommendations. If there are too many, the reliability becomes questionable. Content analysis is a blunt instrument; one can't put too fine a point on the categories. And there are always some responses that are so idiosyncratic that they defy classification. Best to put those in a category called 'other'.

2 Another auditor should repeat step 1 while being shielded from the classification system developed by the other auditor. This again is a way to help improve reliability and validity.

3 The firewall comes down and the two auditors should meet and share their respective category systems. After some discussion, they should agree on a category system.

4 The firewall goes back up. The auditors should separately go back to the original set of responses and tally up the number of responses in each category. Often a respondent will make a comment that falls into two categories. Both should be noted, but auditors should record the number of 'multiple coded items'. Sometimes the data sets are so large that it is impossible to review all the responses or devote the time of two researchers to the analysis of one question. In these cases sampling techniques are the best option.

5 The firewall comes back down (for the final time). The researchers compare their coding decisions and check the number of agreements. They reconcile any differences. This is the reliability test and should be 90 per cent or better. If not, the category system is flawed and needs to be revised.

6 Based on the data, the auditors should construct a chart summarising their data. There is an example of this in Table 12.2, Chapter 12.

Well-executed content analysis should provide a sense of organisation and proportion to the data. A particularly eloquent statement, venomous remark or catchy comment can skew the interpretation. Content analysis helps us to process these responses more rationally. Nevertheless, some clients will insist on seeing the entire list of employee comments. That is OK. In fact, in these situations, the content analysis can help defuse the inevitable emotional reactions of some clients.

INTERPRETING THE RESULTS

Properly interpreting the results of an audit requires discipline, insight and perspective. Auditors need to be disciplined enough not to jump quickly to conclusions. Insight is required to look beyond the surface and search for deeper patterns. Perspective allows auditors to distinguish the trivial from the important. The dedicated auditor will acquire these attributes with years of experience. However, heeding the following suggestions can hasten the learning process:

1 *Erect a temporary firewall between the qualitative and quantitative data*
The firewall provides discipline in the interpretative process. Numbers and words may paint different pictures. It is important to see both images before attempting to synthesise them. For instance, in a manufacturing plant the numeric data pointed to a problem with the general communication climate. Yet the chief complaint emerging from written questions involved 'trash' and the 'dirty working environment'. If the auditors relied solely on the numeric data, they would have ignored the trash problem. Even if they viewed the qualitative data through the lens of the quantitative data, they would have minimised this important concern. Instead, the firewall allowed them to see that the 'trash' problem was a legitimate concern that the numeric section was simply not sensitive enough to pick up.

    If there is a team of auditors, setting up a firewall is easy. Assign one group to examine the quantitative data and arrive at tentative conclusions. The other group does the same for the qualitative data. If this is not possible, then analyse one set of data and put aside the tentative conclusions. Then move to the other set of data. As a rule of thumb, it is best to start with the qualitative data. Why? Interpreting quantitative data is usually more straightforward and interpretations are less likely to be biased.

2 *Discern the difference between more and less important items*
Experienced auditors guided by research findings soon learn that some survey items are more important than others. For instance, the Communication Satisfaction Questionnaire contains the following item: 'extent to which my supervisor trusts me' (Downs, 1988). Previous studies have demonstrated a high correlation between this question and the general communication climate (Clampitt and Downs, 1993). As a rule of thumb, if this item is low, then all the other items have a similar tendency. It is a bell-wether question. Moreover, questions about supervisors tend to be the most important communication items because employees have a high preference for information from their supervisors. On the other hand, items about the corporate newsletter are usually less salient. That is, they usually have less impact on the entire communication climate than other issues. Of course, it is far easier to make specific recommendations to improve a newsletter than it is to restore the trust between employees and their supervisors.

3 *Distinguish between macro and micro level concerns*
When the stock market takes a tumble it does not mean that every stock or even every sector of the market is on the decline. Likewise, global results about the organisation's communication system may not be applicable to all departments and levels. For instance, the general results might indicate a problem with the timeliness of certain kinds of information, yet there may be one or more departments in which this is not the primary concern. Identifying these pockets is important for two reasons. First, a pocket may be a place to look for a 'best practice' lesson. If one department has mastered the 'timeliness' issue, it might

provide insights into how other departments could do the same. Second, action plans constructed for the entire organisation might not be applicable to every part of the organisation. In other words, by identifying the pockets you can avoid the 'one size fits all' mentality.

Identifying the pockets can provide specific focal points for each unit or department. Too often, global organisation-wide problems are quickly dismissed as everyone's problems. Often, if it is everybody's problem, then it really is nobody's. This means auditors need to be very careful when discussing macro level problems. Ideally the audit should identify major problems requiring specific actions that can be assigned to particular individuals or departments to solve. But the ideal is usually not the reality. 'Improving trust between management and employees' may be a worthy goal, but who really 'owns' that problem? Thus, it is particularly important when talking with senior management about macro concerns to temper the remarks with discussions of 'pocket' differences.

4 *Anticipate various interpretations of the questions*
Professional survey designers scrupulously try to avoid highly ambiguous questions. Despite their best efforts almost all surveys contain unclear items. Not only can words be interpreted in various ways; there is also the issue of the contextual parameters of the question. One commonly used survey asks employees about their satisfaction with communication regarding 'organisational changes'. In several audits, this item turned out to be a problem area. The question then became, 'what changes are the employees talking about?' The questions simply couldn't be answered with the existing data. Downs (1988) insightfully commented on the dilemma: 'The problem with questions such as these is not that the analysts cannot generate possible interpretations, but rather that these interpretations may not be faithful to the meanings intended by respondents' (p. 110).

There are two ways to address these dilemmas. First, auditors could make a best guess based on other available evidence. Self-deception is always a possibility in this case. Positive thinking can lead us to accept the more benign of the possible interpretations. Second, further research could be conducted using other methods such as interviews or focus groups. Time permitting, this is the preferred alternative. Then auditors can have enough specificity to clearly address the issue.

5 *Synthesise the results of the qualitative and quantitative analyses*
There are essentially two possibilities:

• *Similar themes*. These are conclusions that all the data sources point to. They tend to be highly salient issues, although they may be stated in somewhat different ways. For instance, employees may make written comments such as, 'I wish I knew how I was doing.' A survey question revealing dissatisfaction with the 'appraisal system' could indicate a similar concern.

- *Dissimilar themes*. Inevitably some themes emerge from one data source that do not emerge from another. This does not mean those issues are unimportant. All data gathering methods have biases and one of the methods may not be sensitive to certain concerns.

Determining which issues to highlight in the report is a challenging task requiring a thorough knowledge of the organisation and insight gleaned from the organisational communication literature. The quality of this synthesis often determines the value of an audit to the organisation.

6 Contemplate actions that might be taken
Audit results do not necessarily imply specific and direct actions. The ICA survey has one section asking employees to compare the amount of information they receive on various topics with the amount of information they desire. In several audits, the amount desired exceeded the amount actually received in every topic area. So what? What can be done with these results? We ultimately concluded that the answers to these questions actually constituted a 'curiosity index' (Downs *et al.*, 1981). If more information were provided on all the issues, then employees would be overwhelmed. Therefore, we had to use our judgement to discern which were the really significant information gaps. This meant we had to rely on our knowledge of the particular organisations as well as our general notions about organisational communication practices. For instance, we deemed information about job-related duties as more important than information about 'benefits', even though the benefits issue would have been easier to address.

As auditors enter the rather murky world of action plans, it is best to be tentative. Suggest several courses of actions that might address the issues. Then the client can choose those that are most compatible with the organisational culture. Clearly separate the diagnostic results from the prescriptions. This protects the auditor's credibility and allows the client to participate in the decision-making process. The result: a greater likelihood that the decisions will actually be implemented.

CONCLUSION

Scholars have devoted years of their lives to perfecting questionnaires and survey techniques. They have provided us with numerous valuable lessons and tools. A brief chapter cannot possibly summarise all the scholarship in this field. However, hopefully the foundation has been laid for a proper understanding of effective surveying procedures. In an age where surveys are as commonplace as weather forecasts, few people appreciate the art and science of the process. And like a weather forecast, few folks recognise all the effort required to produce a fairly accurate picture of an extraordinarily complex phenomenon – organisational communication.

Chapter 4

The interview approach

Rob Millar and Mary Gallagher

INTRODUCTION

The interview is considered to be one of the central tools within internal and external communication audits. Its utility is perhaps best illustrated by Downs's (1988) assertion that, if confined to using just one method, he would choose the interview. Given the nature of many organisations, in terms of numerous employees at different levels across departments and perhaps on different sites, and with a wide range of clients or customers, the survey questionnaire is often the first method which comes to mind. It is initially difficult to conceptualise how a method which involves 'talking to people' could possibly provide an accurate and reliable picture of communication in a complex environment. However, just like any other methodology, the secret of its success depends on giving thorough consideration to planning, development, implementation, analysis and interpretation (Payne, 1999). The purpose of this chapter is to identify and discuss those issues crucial to employing the interview as an effective audit method.

INITIAL CONSIDERATIONS

Why is the interview useful?

The interview has been defined by Millar *et al.* (1992) as:

> A face-to-face dyadic interaction in which one individual plays the role of interviewer and the other takes on the role of interviewee, and both of these roles carry clear expectations concerning behavioural and attitudinal approach. The interview is requested by one of the participants for a specific purpose and both participants are willing contributors.
>
> (Millar *et al.*, 1992, p. 3)

This definition emphasises the social nature of interviews, which is the main distinguishing feature of this method when compared to others. It is primarily a process of interpersonal interaction set within a particular context and with specific purposes (Hargie, 1997; Hargie and Tourish, 1999a). It will have primary goals, secondary goals, and a structure. The two-way flow of communication which characterises the interview method offers three main advantages over alternative information gathering strategies:

1 It is more likely to elicit unanticipated information and to enable a greater depth and meaning of communication experiences to be explored and recorded (King, 1994). Studies which limit themselves to questionnaire methods alone may miss crucial and meaningful information regarding communication. For instance, Ghoshal *et al.* (1994) acknowledged that the survey methods used in their study of communication in multinational organisations enabled frequency of communications to be analysed, but revealed little about the content or quality of such communication, information which is crucial for auditors.
2 Meetings with individuals may also enable auditors to get a better sense of the way in which organisational practices and issues are perceived and interpreted by staff, employees and, where relevant, service users.
3 The interview can also serve the need, both for auditors and respondents, for the audit to have a human and social aspect to discovery of information. The importance of fulfilling this need for both sides is perhaps best illustrated by comparing the audit interview with the selection interview. Despite having questionable validity and reliability in providing accurate and reliable information, the interview remains the most frequently used recruitment tool (Millar and Gallagher, 1997). Potential employers and employees are obviously reluctant to accept that a suitable decision could be reached without human interaction. For this reason, the interview has been retained, with recruiters focused on developing procedures which will minimise its shortcomings. In a similar vein, carrying out an audit without engaging in *any* face to face interaction would not be acceptable.

Thus specific procedures have been developed for audit interviews which enhance the accuracy and reliability of information obtained, whilst meeting the human and social expectations of participants.

When is the interview useful?

The interview can be used at a number of points during a communication audit:

1 Initial uses include interviewing key personnel to clarify the nature and type of audit which will best meet their needs. These interviews can also help auditors gain a background to the organisation and its general communication practices.
2 Interviews may be used as the first step in developing an audit questionnaire to be administered to a large number of respondents. Information obtained

from interviewing will enable salient, relevant and important areas to be included in the written instrument.

3 Interviews may be used alongside collection of quantitative data, in order to obtain in-depth and meaningful information from a sub-sample of respondents. Using interviews to complement other methods in the audit process helps to provide a more comprehensive and insightful formulation of the communicative climate (Zack and McKenney, 1995).

4 Even when auditors use wholly quantitative methods, following data analysis interviews with a selected sample can be a valuable way of helping them to understand, explain and interpret results.

5 Interviews can be used at differing times during the process in order to serve a variety of purposes. Initial exploratory interviews can help auditors to construct a guide to be used in more focused second round interviews. These can be scheduled to take place before and after interventions, allowing the impact and efficacy of communication initiatives to be evaluated.

PLANNING

The precise nature and depth of information required will strongly influence interview planning. With respect to communication audits, Downs (1988) detailed a number of purposes for interviews ranging from initial exploratory functions to the identification and probing of specific issues. None the less, most interviews take one of two forms; that is, *exploratory* where the purpose is to generate issues, or *focused* where the purpose is to obtain specific information on pre-selected subject areas. For example, the aim of surveying the formal communication structures within an organisation would be best achieved by conducting highly standardised focused interviews in which each communication structure and channel is covered in a systematic way (Stewart and Cash, 1988).

Conversely, if the auditor's aim is to gain a picture in some depth of the experiences of communication from the perspective of employees or service users, the exploratory interview is more useful. Whatever information is desired it is incumbent on the auditor to maximise the likelihood of it being relevant, reliable, valid (Brenner, 1981; Gorden, 1987) and authentic (Seidman, 1991). To this end, there are a number of very important planning decisions and procedures which need to be considered if the efficacy of the interview method is to be assured. The following questions need to be given careful consideration and attention.

Who will conduct the interviews?

Given the central role of communication skills to conducting effective interviews, it is essential that all interviewers involved in audits have highly developed skills. In order to ensure that this is indeed the case, and to maximise consistency across interviewers and interviews, specific training on the way in which the interview is to be conducted should be provided (van Tilberg, 1998). It is widely acknowledged that training enhances the validity and reliability of information gained through this method (Campion *et al.*, 1997; Pollner, 1998; Sias and Cahill, 1998). Collins (1997) identified two functions that training serves. First, interviewers need to be convinced that a standardised approach is essential. Second, training must 'develop a uniform level of skill in probing and obtaining information in depth' (p. 81). This training should directly address how to use the interview guide and focus on developing skills in opening, questioning, listening and closing the interview. Research evidence suggests that the most appropriate and effective medium in this respect is that of communication skills training programmes (Hargie and Tourish, 1994). The procedures and components of such programmes are well established and documented (Dickson *et al.*, 1997).

However, interpersonal skill is only one characteristic of the interviewer, and there are additional personal factors which can significantly impact on interview effectiveness and even on the credibility afforded the audit by the workforce. The influence of interviewer race, culture, gender and age must be given serious consideration (Hargie and Tourish, 1999a). For example:

- Is it likely that communication incidents perceived as sexual or racial harassment will be disclosed to the same degree to any interviewer?
- Will a young inexperienced interviewer obtain a wealth of information from a highly experienced senior manager?
- Should young white male interviewers carry out interviews of customers in an outlet where the clientele is exclusively female and predominantly Muslim?

As the research evidence indicates that these factors will indeed impact on the quality of interviews conducted (Collins, 1997; O'Muircheartaigh and Campanelli, 1998; Padfield and Procter, 1996; Sarangi, 1994), there should where necessary be a pool of interviewers with varying characteristics and backgrounds. Ideally, interviewees should be given the opportunity to express preferences, but in the absence of this the auditor must take such factors into account.

Who will be interviewed?

The gathering together of a pool of participants from which the required information will be collected is of paramount importance for any audit. In working with participants who are members of formal organisations this will necessitate gaining access through 'gatekeepers' who have responsibility for the operation of the site. Those high up the hierarchy should also provide a public endorsement of the audit, which in turn encourages those lower down to participate fully. Participants need to be representative of the range of different roles and also reflect all levels of the hierarchy. Likewise, in external audits, the entire client base should be covered. Furthermore, the final composition of samples should be by random selection across categories.

The need for close attention to sampling is illustrated by the findings of an investigation into communication within the North Yorkshire Constabulary. Interviews identified several common strands but also revealed the differing views of particular groupings which included the executive, middle managers, junior ranks and civilian support staff (Green, 1992). It is important to remember that at least two participants from each subgroup are required in order to protect anonymity of respondents in feedback, and it is normally recommended that all key personnel be included.

There are few concrete criteria to inform decisions about how many participants is enough. However, in following the above sampling criteria, a figure which represents the minimum number of individuals required can be formulated. The number of people in each subgroup should be sufficient such that reserves are in place if individuals decide not to participate, or for some other reason are prevented from taking part. In terms of the 'What's in it for me?' perspective, the willingness of interviewees to participate – especially in external audits – can be encouraged if incentives are on offer (see Chapter 5). Once the sample has been identified, the decision about whether to increase sample size depends on at least two factors:

1 *The type of communication audit.* If the audit is concerned with the provision only of a general overview of communication, then a minimum sample should be sufficient. However, if the audit is a basis for making specific and major changes, its findings and acceptability require a significant sample from each subgroup.
2 *The time and resources available.* Auditors must realistically estimate whether increasing the sample size is feasible within the audit timescale and the human and financial resources allocated. It is important to remember that interviewing is a very time consuming, labour intensive and expensive form of data gathering. Interviewers will have to schedule appointments, travel to and from interviews, and carry out the interviews. The processes of transcribing or writing up the content, and analysing the data, are also very time consuming. Furthermore, in internal audits the cost increases with sample size, as interviews are typically carried out in working hours.

The decision as to the number of participants is usually the result of balancing a number of competing demands for resources against the need to produce findings of sufficient reliability, validity and authenticity, and therefore entails a degree of compromise. The doable usually wins over the desirable.

How long should each interview last?

In practical terms, interviewers must decide on the length of time to be made available for interviewing each participant. To some extent the length of any particular interview will be closely related to the purpose for which the interviews have been arranged. The length of time scheduled is also dependent on the person being interviewed. Downs (1988) offered some advice on this issue when he suggested that managers may require a greater length of time (e.g. up to two hours) than non-managers (e.g. up to one hour). To take but two examples from actual studies, variations in time can be noted. Thus, Sias and Cahill's (1998) interviews, which focused on peer relationships at work, lasted an average of 20–30 minutes, whereas Gabriel's (1998) organisational storytelling interviews had a duration of between 45 and 75 minutes.

Once a time-frame has been decided it is important to inform all potential participants of such a time commitment prior to their agreement to be interviewed. They can then make an informed decision about participation, and schedule this accordingly. Furthermore, the agreed time limit must be adhered to. The temptation to just carry on for a little while longer is not only an unacceptable infringement of interviewees' time but in general reduces trust in the interviewer (Seidman, 1991), and inhibits purposeful communication (Gorden, 1987). Just as it is recognised that developing organisational trust improves organisational communication (See Chapter 1), so the development of trust within the interview is crucial to the quality of interpersonal communication achieved (Phelps and duFrene, 1989).

Developing the interview guide

Interviewers must have some form of interview guide or plan in order to ensure that the purpose of the interview will be achieved. The format and nature of this will differ significantly, depending on whether exploratory or focused interviews are being planned. Let us examine each of these.

Exploratory interviews

In the initial phase of the communication audit there is often uncertainty about what types of information might be available, what range of responses participants are likely to make and whether all areas high in salience have been anticipated. Under such circumstances, it is conceivable that an interview guide would not be used in order to allow respondents to express their perceptions of important processes spontaneously in the interview. The outcomes of such interviews can usefully contribute to the interview guide for the next phase, or the development of a questionnaire (Hofstede, 1998).

Nevertheless, even in exploratory interviews, it is useful to have some form of broad guide to the major topics to be covered. If participants raise and deal with the types of issues anticipated by the interviewer then such a guide may remain redundant. However, there is a possibility that interviewees might not raise some issues that interviewers hoped to explore. In these circumstances, reference to the guide reminds interviewers to suggest topics that hitherto had not been discussed. It also guards against the interviewer being drawn into detailed accounts of irrelevant issues or the interview turning into a chat.

The main body of the interview guide for exploratory interviews should consist of a list of broad opening questions which can then be followed up depending upon the responses of participants. There is no suggestion that all questions need to be predetermined nor asked in any particular set sequence. Indeed, herein lies the flexibility of the interview method. It is only important that all relevant questions be asked at some point during the process. This type of exploratory approach is also useful in the later stages of the audit where explanations for particular findings are being sought.

There are many examples of the successful use of exploratory interview guides in studies which have investigated communication processes across a range of contexts:

- In the medical context, King *et al.* (1994) employed a semi-structured interview guide which covered specific topics such as information gathering by doctors, their perceptions of uncertainty and risk, details of referral decisions, and doctors' relationships with patients.
- In his study of sexual harassment within an organisation, Clair (1994) developed an interview schedule comprised of 21 main questions.
- In a detailed exploratory interview guide in the organisational sphere, Goldhaber (1993) constructed a list of 11 main questions all of the open type and prefixed by 'What' or 'How' and requests to 'Describe' particular phenomena (see Box 4.1). This latter question type, referred to as a narrative/directive question (Dillon, 1997), can be very useful in that participants are asked to provide concrete details, actual behaviours and specific circumstances.
- In their study of communication in the clergy, Lount and Hargie (1997) asked individual clergy to reconstruct specific situations where communication between themselves and parishioners went well and where it did not (see Chapter 13).

Although, in each context, questions are used to focus participants on specific aspects of communication (e.g. formal and informal channels, decision-making processes, conflict, successful versus unsuccessful scenarios, and interpersonal communication experiences) participants are free to choose what disclosures to make in their personal responses. What characterises all these forms of interview as exploratory is that there is a general notion of subject areas to be covered, but ample opportunity for the interviewee freely to discuss these areas and to raise any additional issues. As illustrated by the above examples, the exact form of the interview guide to be developed will be largely influenced by the context in which the audit is taking place.

Focused interviews

In circumstances where interviewers are concerned with more factual type information, are time-constrained, or where meaningful quantification and comparability

---

Box 4.1 Exploratory interview questions in an internal audit

1 Describe your job (duties, function). What decisions do you usually make in your job? What information do you *need* to make those decisions and from where should you get it? What information do you *actually* get to make those decisions and from whom? Are there formal (written) or informal policies in your organization which determine how you get this information? Should any policies be added, changed or abandoned?
2 What are the major communication *strengths* of this organization? Be specific.
3 What are the major communication *weaknesses* of this organization?
4 Describe the *formal* channels through which you typically receive information about this organization. What kinds of information do you tend to receive? How often?
5 Describe the *informal* channels through which you typically receive information about this organization. What kinds of information do you tend to receive? How often?
6 How often, if ever, do you receive information about this organization which is of low value or use to you? If and when you do, what kinds of information do you receive? Be specific. From whom do you receive this?
7 What would you like to see done to improve information flow in this information? Why hasn't it been done yet?
8 Describe the way decisions are typically made in this organization.
9 When conflict occurs in this organization, what is the major cause? How is conflict typically resolved?
10 Describe the communication relationship you have with your immediate supervisor. Your co-workers. Middle management. Top management. Your subordinates (if appropriate).
11 How do you know when this organization has done a good or bad job toward accomplishing its goals? What measures of effectiveness are used in this organization?

Source: G. Goldhaber, *Organizational Communication*, 6th edition (Madison, Wisconsin: WCB Brown and Benchmark, 1993, p. 362). Reprinted with permission.

---

is sought, they need to adopt a much more highly structured or standardised approach to their interviews (Collins, 1997; Fowler and Mangione, 1990; King, 1994; Sias and Cahill, 1998). In the focused interview, most aspects of the interview are rigidly predetermined, from topics, to question types, sequence, and response alternatives (Downs, 1988).

It is important to remember, however, that the content of such questions will ideally have been generated from exploratory interviews. Focused interviews are characterised by the use of mainly closed questions relating to very specific areas of enquiry. They are typically less time consuming and can be very useful in checking out generalisability of information obtained in the initial phase of an audit. Moreover, responses can be more easily coded and analysed than those derived from exploratory interviews.

There is the danger, however, of exerting considerable direction and control over participants. Seidman (1991) cautioned interviewers against manipulating or restricting the responses of participants. Whereas some participants are happy to be directed through the use of short closed questions where alternative responses are provided, others may be considerably less satisfied with this approach. Where participants are over-communicative, interviewers may need to impose a higher degree of control and direction on the interview by frequently re-focusing participants through the use of more closed type questions. The key is that interviewers must be sensitive to the interview as experienced by participants.

As has been indicated, the type of interview will exert a powerful influence on the nature of interviewer behaviour. For example, the types of questions which are in keeping within the exploratory interview are quite different from those that are more useful in the focused interview. The next section will examine considerations which must be borne in mind in when interviewers actually carry out interviews.

CONDUCTING THE INTERVIEW

Both types of interviews require some form of structure in order to guide the interviewer from beginning to end. Training of interviewers should include practical experience of following the guide and conducting the interview in a standardised and skilful way. All interviews should be planned in terms of three basic stages; namely, (a) the opening, (b) the body and (c) the closing. Each stage requires that interviewers attend to the achievement of specific functions pertinent at each phase whether this be establishing a working relationship, providing orientation, developing trust, agreeing a mode of working ethically, gathering relevant information through effective use of questions, or closing the interview sensitively. Whilst the body of the interview will differ significantly in exploratory and focused interviews, conducting the opening and closing will share similar characteristics.

The opening

In any encounter between two individuals it is well documented that first impressions count (Hargie et al., 1994). Any interview should be held in comfortable surroundings which ensure privacy for the interaction. The interviewer should seem like someone who will conduct the interaction in a professional manner. The interviewee should be greeted by name and the name and associated role of the interviewer stated. An explanation should be given as to how the respondent was selected. The task of establishing rapport and a trusting relationship is crucial, particularly if collection of sensitive and truthful information is required

(Oakley, 1981). It is at this point that issues relating to the welfare of participants should be comprehensively covered. The interview guide should provide interviewers with specific statements which must be included in the opening. These should cover confidentiality, anonymity, rights of withdrawal, tape-recording and note-taking. This may simply be a process of reminding participants of assurances given previously, during the recruitment stages.

In addition to the relationship building aspects of the opening phase there is a more cognitively focused element which Stewart and Cash (1988) refer to as 'orientation'. Here the interviewer must indicate what the objectives are, propose ideas about how the interview will proceed, and give an indication of the structure, content and duration of the interview.

The body

Following the opening stage, interviewers begin by asking interviewees one or more questions. Given that respondents are unlikely to have developed any significant relationship so early in the process, it is normally best for the interviewer to begin by asking for factual or descriptive information. Examples from internal and external audits are:

- 'When did you join the company?'
- 'Could you tell me exactly what your job entails?'
- 'How many times a week would you come here?'
- 'For how long has Goodfolks been your main supplier?'

This gives the interviewee time to settle into the interview, without feeling threatened or interrogated. The implementation of the body of the interview will differ according to whether it is exploratory or focused.

Exploratory interviews

If the objectives of employing the exploratory interview are related to generating an understanding of phenomena which are not well known or where understanding the experience of others is of paramount importance, open questions are recommended. These offer considerable freedom, place responsibility on participants to choose what issues to raise, and allow interviewees to talk in some depth. Seidman (1991) gave the following illustrations of broad invitations to talk: 'Take me through a day in your work life', or 'Reconstruct your day for me from the time you wake up to the time you go to bed.' It is also useful to ask participants to recount more specific and limited experiences, such as a critical incident, a turning point, or a significant event. Examples of open questions are:

- 'Tell me about your job.'
- 'What are the communication strengths of your organisation?'

- 'Could you describe a situation where a lack of information affected your job performance?'
- 'Think about a positive (or negative) event which affected the quality of communication in the workplace and tell me about it.'

In general, the crucial advantage of open as opposed to closed questions is the low level of influence imposed on participants – where they can present their opinions, attitudes, thoughts, feelings and understandings unrestricted by the interviewer.

In exploratory interviews, the sequence of questioning is an important characteristic of effective interactions. The less structured interviews are, the more important it becomes to base questions on preceding material offered by participants. Interviewers often have to think on their feet and make on the spot decisions in the absence of tight structure. Not only does this 'verbal following' contribute to the flow of the interview but it sends a strong signal to respondents that interviewers are listening to what they are saying.

Of course, the utility of open questions can be lost if interviewers fail to listen actively to the messages contained in participants' responses. The situation can be further exacerbated where interviewers insist on posing very open questions and then persist in interrupting participants when they are responding. Appropriate use of silence allows interviewees time both to think about responses and to articulate them fully. Where respondents are enabled to disclose material to interviewers who in turn engage in effective listening, it is more likely that opportunities for using probing questions will arise.

It can be very difficult to follow what some interviewees are trying to say, what they mean by the words they use, or even to make any sense out of their replies at all. In such circumstances it is imperative that interviewers acknowledge these difficulties and develop a greater understanding by exploring responses in depth. Such exploration is progressed by extensive use of probing, or follow-up, questions. Failure to probe can result in the collection of superficial, ambiguous, vague and relatively meaningless information (Fowler and Mangione, 1990). This leads to the strong possibility that interpretation of the information will require many assumptions to be made by the interviewer, thereby distorting the data obtained.

There are a number of different types of probing questions, each of which can be effective in its own way. They should be introduced in a non-threatening manner such as 'You mentioned feeling as if you were kept in the dark about management decisions. I was wondering . . .'. Among the more relevant probes are those which:

- seek further *clarification* – 'Could you tell me exactly what you mean by that?'
- ask for *exemplification* – 'Could you give me an example of when you have felt like this?'

- check *accuracy* – 'You have *never* received this information?'
- question *relevance* – 'How do you think this affects communication?'
- request *further information* – 'Could you tell me a bit more about that?'

By employing such follow up probes, interviewers invite participants to disclose additional information which serves to reduce ambiguity, vagueness, and contradictions, to extend the story, and to sharpen detail, meaning and understanding.

The use of effective probing techniques can be problematic for interviewers to acquire, hence the importance of training. According to Collins (1997), where interviewers fail to establish satisfactory relationships with participants they may either fail to engage in sufficient probing or may give up very easily. Moreover, the ways in which interviewers probe can have a significant impact on the nature of information elicited. For instance, Houtkoop-Steenstra (1996) analysed interviewer behaviour in semi-open research interviews in order to discover the types of probes used. When faced with inadequate responses, interviewers employed a number of probing devices which included presenting several answer options, suggesting a response, or reformulating the response. It was concluded that the use of such leading probes compromised the validity of the information obtained. Therefore, the use of probes may not necessarily represent acceptable interviewer behaviour – the types of probes used and the way they are used is crucial if participants' responses are to be relied upon.

A further issue is worthy of note where the use of probes is being considered. By intent, these seek to delve deeper into the personal world of participants, to obtain more details from them, or to pin them down. The hope is that the use of probes will invite interviewees, albeit in a rather challenging way, to tell a little more about themselves and whatever context is pertinent. However, there is a possibility that their use may be perceived quite differently by participants. Indeed, they may be seen as means by which interviewers are invading their privacy, threatening their safety, increasing their vulnerability and increasing the need to defend themselves (Fletcher, 1992). So, there is a delicate balance to be sought between the needs of interviewers and participants.

If interviewers are to meet their objectives it is also imperative that they listen carefully to responses. The type of listening required in the interviewing process generally exceeds that which is witnessed in everyday encounters. For this reason, care must be taken to include breaks between interviews or have other tasks interspersed in the interviewers' schedules. Such listening requires interviewers to give their full and undivided attention to verbal and nonverbal responses (Hargie *et al.*, 1994). Listening is not simply a process of hearing or recording what is communicated but entails the more complex processes of understanding and evaluating the message (Bostrom, 1997). The importance of active listening assumes a pivotal role in the successful elicitation of relevant, reliable and sufficiently detailed information. One very influential way to demonstrate listening is to ensure that the types and sequence of questions posed during interviews display strong relationships to interviewee responses.

Focused interviews

Many of the general guidelines included in the previous section will apply in some way here. The major difference between the two is in the dominant question type included in the interview guide. In focused interviews, where the purpose is to collect specific information, question types need to be extremely precise and are typically closed. These might include simple recall questions such as, 'Who is your immediate boss?', 'Do you use e-mail?', or 'How often do you use e-mail?' In the case of the latter question options can convert the question into a multiple choice format. Respondents are required to use the alternatives provided by the interviewer in giving an answer to the question. For example, 'Do you think communication is (i) worse, (ii) better, or (iii) the same, as it was six months ago?' Where the required information tends to be factual, where rapid coding and quantitative analysis are necessary and where interview time is very limited, such closed type questions are appropriate.

However, the use of closed questions can present a major danger due to the impositional potential of this approach. As Dillon (1997) cautioned:

> The significance is that the questioner who asks closed questions may be specifying categories of thought that are unrepresentative of what respondents think, with the result that respondents confirm our own frame of reference without our even realising it.
>
> (Dillon, 1997, p. 120)

This threat will be minimised if the content of the interview guide has been informed by the findings of the exploratory interview phase, and the phrasing of questions adheres to the same criteria as are relevant to the construction of questionnaires (see Chapter 3).

In summary, if auditors engage in active listening, attend to participants, ask appropriate initial and follow-up questions, and use silence skilfully, they will collect relevant, appropriately detailed and trustworthy information in the interviews. This being the case it remains to close the interview.

The closing

In both interview contexts it is important to plan and allocate time for ending the interview as both a business transaction and a social encounter. To achieve an effective closure the ending should be viewed as a stage rather than an event and be built into the interview guide. The beginning of this closing phase should be marked with an indicator such as 'I'm aware that we only have a few minutes left so could we begin to draw our meeting to a close?' (Saunders, 1986). There should also be no doubt when the interview has finally concluded. Examples of concluding remarks would be 'Thanks again for your participation. I hope that things continue to go well for you' or 'Your input has been very helpful and is very much appreciated.'

Where a highly focused interview has been conducted there may be little to do but thank participants for their assistance; that is, a *social closure* (Hargie *et al.*, 1994). The inclusion of a social element in closure is not only courteous but also complies with one of the recommendations of Smith and Robertson (1993) for treating all interviewees in a fair and civilised manner. Respondents should leave their interview feeling appreciated. At the end of exploratory interviews, it is important that the interviewer also draws the encounter to a close by creating some coherent sense of the interview. This idea of offering some kind of summary constitutes one aspect of *cognitive closure*. It is a means of seeking agreement that the main themes of the communication have been accurately received and understood. In offering such a summary, respondents are afforded an opportunity to dispute or amend the interviewer's perception of what was communicated.

Similarly, where personal experiences are explored it is important that participants should not be allowed to leave interviews in any way damaged by the experience. For instance, in the case of an internal audit, suppose that when discussing communications with a supervisor the interviewee discloses an experience of sexual harassment and becomes visibly upset in recounting the incident. What does the interviewer do? Allowing the interviewee to leave the interview in a distressed state would certainly constitute unethical practice (Smith and Robertson, 1993). This type of situation poses clear ethical dilemmas for the interviewer, such as:

- Do you record the incident without comment and if you do, does this imply condonement?
- Do you encourage the employee to report the matter and if you do, is that your role?
- If it is a particularly serious incident, does your assurance of confidentiality preclude you from doing anything about it?
- Will your scheduled interview with that particular supervisor be coloured by this knowledge?

These possibilities illustrate the importance of formulating a very specific ethics and confidentiality policy and including it in the opening of the interview guide.

Some mention should also be made concerning the subsequent use of any information disclosed. During interviews, participants are required to respond to a variety of questions, some relatively factual whilst others will require deeper levels of self-disclosure. It is possible, as illustrated above, that such disclosure may leave the participant more vulnerable or exposed and quite likely feeling somewhat threatened having made the disclosure. Under such circumstances the source of the findings of an audit should not be traceable. Invoking Smith and Robertson's (1993) ethical principles whereby participants should not be damaged in any way by the experience, and that all information disclosed during an interview should not be misused or used to the detriment of the interviewee, interviewers need to deal with relevant concerns explicitly prior to the ending of an interview. Given that such matters are an essential part of opening interviews, additional reference to them during closure will reinforce the interviewer's desire to assure participants that they will be treated justly and with respect, and that what was agreed will be delivered.

A final aspect of effective closure relates to situations where subsequent follow up interviews have been scheduled as part of the audit process. It is important to discuss these future links so that participants are clear regarding any forthcoming commitments. This may relate to both time and to expectations of the purpose of further interviews and what might be covered with respect to content.

Conducting the interviews, in terms of the opening, body and closing, is therefore not straightforward and certainly involves much more than 'talking to people'. The preceding section has demonstrated the importance of having appropriate interview guides and skilled interviewers who can implement them effectively. We now move on to examine issues relating to the recording of interviewee responses.

RECORDING INFORMATION FROM INTERVIEWS

The importance of accurately recording participants' responses cannot be over-emphasised. Indeed, King (1994) recommended that *all* interviews of a qualitative nature should be routinely tape recorded. Tape recording clearly removes the need to take notes during interviews, a procedure which can be very disruptive to the flow of the interaction. However, if tape recording is adopted then the researcher must take cognisance of the following factors:

1 There must be clear reasons for using a tape recorder. This usually relates to being interested in the actual way participants articulate their experiences, rather than simply being interested in whether they mention a topic or not.
2 Participants must be informed of the reasons for using a tape recorder, and given a full explanation of why this is being requested, how their communications are to be used, to whom they will be available, and to what extent their responses will be identifiable. Issues of confidentiality and anonymity are of considerable importance to interviewees and should be dealt with at the beginning of the process. They are then in a position to give informed consent or not.
3 Active listening must continue throughout the interview and interviewers should not relax their attention because they know they will have the interview on tape. Audio recordings are not complete accounts of interactions, so interviewers must at all times be vigilant and observant of the wealth of nonverbal messages being communicated.
4 Participants must be offered the opportunity of opting out of a procedure that requires recording or be able to request that the tape recorder be turned off at any point.

5 There should be a contingency Plan B if the tape recorder fails to operate or where a participant requests that the machine not be used during the interview.
6 Interviewers should be fully familiar with the tape recorder. Technophobes should avoid this medium!

Where tape recording is not possible, the auditor must have developed a technique for taking down key words or phrases primarily as memory joggers. Indeed, the practice of routinely taking shorthand notes is useful, as there can be no absolute guarantee that the tape recording will be audible. Technology often fails us. Note-taking should be completed in a manner which will not create a tense and distant relationship between participants. It is then imperative that interviewers take time immediately following completion of the interview to reconstruct as much as possible of the content of responses. In this situation there will be implications for the scheduling of interviews in that adequate space must be built into the procedures to allow each interview to be reconstructed prior to any further interviews being conducted. Blind faith in our powers of recall is hazardous. Numerous errors are likely to occur when we rely on memory to reconstruct multiple events.

Downs (1988) suggested that an assistant, whose role is purely to take notes as the interview proceeds, could also participate in the interview. The auditor is free to listen and attend to the interviewee and what they have to say. This, of course, has disadvantages. The presence of a second party reduces the likelihood of depth interviewee disclosures, adds to costs, and requires additional permission from participants.

ANALYSING INTERVIEW DATA

By employing interview guides, the interview text is generally structured around a number of key questions. Initially it is the responses to these questions that are of most interest to the auditor. As indicated above, the outcome of the interview process will be a large amount of either audiotapes, or written text reconstructed immediately after each interview from notes. If interviews were tape recorded then the initial task is to transcribe the complete interaction – a very time consuming activity. Ultimately the basic data derived from the interview method is written text. There are several possible approaches to analysing qualitative interview data (see King, 1994; Mason, 1996; Seidman, 1991). These all involve three sequential steps.

Step 1: Become familiar with the interview data
Whatever approach is adopted the first stage is for the auditor to become very familiar with the interview data collected. This involves listening to the interview recordings and re-reading the interview transcripts several times. If more than one auditor is involved, group discussions are helpful where ideas, perceptions and themes can be shared and where new constructions can emerge.

Step 2: Search for categories in the interview data

Although it may be possible to consider textual data as amenable to quantitative analysis this is not always necessary in communication audits. However, there are occasions where the introduction of what King (1994) termed 'quasi-statistical approaches' may be helpful. Here, the content of responses to each question can be categorised into themes and the frequency with which each of them is expressed recorded as a percentage (see Chapter 15). This frequency data can then be tested statistically to establish differences between groups or levels, and indeed estimates of inter-auditor agreement can be computed. In areas where it may be important to provide supportive statistical evidence for findings, the inclusion of some quantitative analysis can provide a more persuasive argument.

Where a purely qualitative approach is adopted, familiarity with the interview data can be used to generate response categories or to construct a template or 'codebook' (King, 1994). This consists of a number of pertinent categories or themes which should be revised periodically as more interview data become available, possibly after each round of audit interviews. In this way, the categories emerge from the data and are regularly revised to ensure that they are reflective of the developing bank of textual data (for a detailed review of this area see O'Connell and Kowal, 1995). Auditors should carry out the following tasks:

1 Read and mark transcripts or written records according to identifiable categories.
2 Label all excerpts in such a way that their original locations within an interview transcript can be found swiftly.
3 Organise excerpts from the written text into the categories; once a round of interviews has been processed re-read the excerpts in an attempt to label the dominant theme(s) within a category. This will be a tentative process at this stage and auditors should not become set too soon, but should be prepared to change these tentative attempts as new data become available.
4 Ensure that categories presented as important are supported by excerpts extracted from as large a range of interviewees as possible. The auditor needs to guard against the accusation that a particular category of response is simply one idiosyncratic respondent rather than a definite theme.
5 Develop a suitable number of main categories. It is difficult to be precise about what this number should be, but more than ten begins to raise doubts about the reliability and comprehensibility of the system, and too few (say 2/3) is simply too crude to facilitate improved understanding and insight.

Step 3: Make thematic connections within and between categories

This involves a search for patterns or themes within categories and their revision if required. An open mind is essential if an adequate system of categories and linked themes is to evolve. This is essentially asking oneself what connects the experiences of those interviewed as part of the audit. It requires the auditor to look across responses to all questions included in the communication audit and not to be confined to responses to single questions.

REPORTING THE FINDINGS

The final task confronting the auditor is to present the findings in a concise but comprehensive form (see Chapter 9 for a full discussion of this issue). There are various methods available for reporting findings based on textual data, ranging from paraphrasing respondents' expressions to reporting considerable amounts of text verbatim. In general, the report of findings should include the following:

- A summary of the main and significant themes in the text.
- Inclusion of extracts from the interviews in the form of illustrative quotes which support the summary of themes. Indeed, King (1998) regards the inclusion of such quotations from participants as essential in reported findings, whatever approach is adopted.
- The report should read as a clear and coherent 'story', easily followed by the reader and well evidenced at all points. It may be useful to include larger extracts from selected interviews in addition to smaller chunks alluded to above. The inclusion of such extracts guards against accusations of prejudice and bias, which are more likely when reports are presented solely as paraphrased auditor summaries.

Finally, it is important to address concerns experienced by interviewees relating to identification and potential vulnerability. Where their exact words are presented as findings there is the possibility of them being traced as the source of the report. If assurances were provided at the commencement of the process then it is incumbent on the auditor to act accordingly; that is, ethically. In order to ensure anonymity the auditor may be required to:

- omit certain details which could be used to trace the identity of an interviewee (name, designation, location, etc.);
- disguise the details to prevent identification (locate the site in a different geographical location, change gender, etc.).

A well structured, clearly presented account which both summarises and provides evidence to support the main themes is more likely to be read and acted upon.

CONCLUSION

This chapter has presented the key stages in the audit interview process. Evidence has been drawn from a range of sources which document a widening variety of qualitative research techniques, including an increasing diversity of interviewing approaches. The status of the interview as a method for conducting communication audits has been supported through the transfer of knowledge and skills from organisational and other related contexts. The interview approach recognises the richness and authenticity of stories and narratives as a major source of information about organisations. Auditors must have the ability to listen to, understand, analyse, and report accurately what they are told by interviewees.

Chapter 5

The focus group approach

David Dickson

INTRODUCTION

The substance of communication audits can be non-numeric, captured in the actual words and forms of expression of those whose views and opinions have been sought. The value of such qualitative material as part of the auditing process has been highlighted (Tourish and Hargie, 1996c). Interviews are an investigatory technique associated with producing information in this form (see Chapter 4). The focus group can be thought of as a type of group interview (Fontana and Frey, 1998), in which a small number of participants who share certain characteristics of relevance to the research meet with a moderator to discuss in some depth a topic, or narrow range of topics, of interest to both parties. Such meetings have a number of main characteristics (Millward, 1995). They are:

- held at the behest of the moderator or research team to which s/he belongs;
- the topic is initiated by this person whose role it is to facilitate discussion focused upon the issues which it throws up;
- the discussion is typically recorded in some form to provide a permanent record for subsequent analysis;
- the purpose is to illuminate the experiences, understandings and perspectives of participants; and
- the findings are documented in some type of report.

The sort of information created by focus groups is a prime consideration in their use. It affords the researcher profound insights into the meanings and ways of understanding which members of the group bring to their experiences of the issues, events or circumstances of relevance to the research (Lunt and Livingstone, 1996). As such, focus groups are capable of providing a richness of knowledge that cannot be matched by, for instance, surveys. They serve a different function. Those who have failed to appreciate this fundamental fact have ended up misusing focus groups as a quicker and easier way of collecting surface information about habits and practices, generalisable to larger populations. This misrepresentation through malpractice is one reason why focus group research has acquired a dubious reputation in some quarters and borne the brunt of some barbed criticism (Gaber, 1996).

FOCUS GROUPS: WHAT THEY ARE AND WHAT THEY ARE NOT

Focus groups have been defined by Beck *et al.* (1986, p. 73) as 'an informal discussion among selected individuals about specific topics relevant to the situation at hand'. Similarly, Krueger (1986, p. 1) regarded them as 'organized group discussions which are focused around a single theme'. For D. Morgan (1998), the essence of what focus groups are can be captured in three pivotal criteria:

1 *They are a way of doing research to collect qualitative data.* Although the focus group is primarily a qualitative research technique, findings can also be expressed quantitatively. In any case the key purpose of the exercise is to produce information primarily to satisfy the needs of the researcher. This sets it apart from other types of group involvement established to satisfy the needs of the participants.
2 *The focus group offers a lens for directing attention onto a narrow topic or issue.* As such, an important starting point is in the framing of a well-defined and clearly delineated purpose. It is one of the responsibilities of the group moderator to ensure that the discussion does not overspill the topic boundaries so specified. This can be done by imposing varying degrees of structure on the interviewing process. At one extreme the moderator may have a set of precise and pre-specified questions to be posed. On the other hand, if the investigation is chiefly exploratory, it may be more productive to simply present the area of interest and leave it largely to the group to unpack the content that for them it contains. In either case, focus groups impose significantly fewer restrictions on the information gathering process than, for example, do questionnaires. More generally, focus groups are also focused in the sense that a considerable amount of information can be gathered in a relatively short, condensed period of time. D. Morgan (1998) contrasts the technique with participant observation in this respect.
3 *Information is created through group discussion.* Unlike the individual interview, the emphasis is not primarily upon interaction between the interviewer and the respondent, but rather on the interchanges amongst the participants as they compare, challenge or support, but ultimately extend the personal meanings and experiences that each contributes as they explore the topic. Compared to the one-to-one interview, however, the focus group seldom unearths the depth of understanding surrounding the experiences, attitudes or opinions of any one individual.

In addition to the content of talk, focus groups offer data of a different kind, of communication as process, that may be of interest to the researcher. As noted by Lunt and Livingstone (1996) the focus group is a social occasion in its own right that may sufficiently approximate the social setting of research interest as to warrant the drawing of distinct parallels. They explain how we can think of what happens during the discussion as 'a simulation of these routine but relatively inaccessible communication contexts that can help us discover the processes by which meaning is socially constructed through everyday talk' (p. 85). This dimension, of course, may well be of particular interest when seeking insights into how communication functions in organisations as part of the auditing task.

Several additional characteristics of focus groups are mentioned by Vaughn *et al.* (1996). They describe the group as a small informal assembly of relatively homogeneous members who share a perspective of interest to the researcher, brought together and guided by a trained moderator for the purpose of eliciting perceptions, attitudes and ideas on a selected issue. They make the further important point that it should not be part of the overall aim to obtain data with the intention of making firm generalisations to broader populations. This issue will be returned to shortly in the discussion of the focus group as qualitative research.

Other information-gathering procedures which, while involving groups, have been contrasted with focus groups include the nominal group technique, the Delphi technique (see Chapter 7), leaderless discussion groups, brainstorming and synectics (Stewart and Shamdasani, 1990). Points of demarcation hinge upon a lack of emphasis on the primacy of free discussion amongst participants, the absence of a person recognisably in the role of moderator, and the nature of the information created. Advances in information technology, including the internet, have opened up interesting opportunities for sharing ideas and exchanging views without ever coming into direct contact with other contributors. The virtual group is one such where members never physically come together, but are moderated over the internet, with everything that each types appearing on the screens of all others (Jones, 1998). The mechanics of operating an on-line focus group, together with issues raised by the computer-mediated environment, are also addressed by Gaiser (1997). Similarly, a telephone-mediated variant of the traditional focus group has been described by Greenbaum (1998) and used by White and Thomson (1995), to explore aspects of family physicians' contacts with their external publics. In the latter study, the anonymity afforded by telephone contact created a safe environment in which participants were able to discuss issues freely and was an aspect of the methodology that seemed to enhance the quality of the data generated.

THE POPULARITY OF FOCUS GROUPS

Focus group research has evolved through three distinct phases (D. Morgan, 1998), from origins in the social sciences in the 1920s, through growth and development in market research settings following the Second World War when the method first achieved a certain prominence, to its present resurgence in the social sciences and broader popularity across a range of areas of application (Merton, 1987). Focus groups have enjoyed a phenomenal growth in popularity, particularly over the past decade. They have been put to use in a range of diverse contexts including academic research, market research, advertising, healthcare and family planning, political campaigns, training evaluation and programme assessment, and communication auditing (Lount, 1997; Quible, 1998). While their contribution to improving corporate communication is less well documented, focus groups can be utilised in various ways, and at different stages of the auditing process. These include:

- to make an initial assessment and diagnosis of difficulty;
- as a preparatory stage to the formulation of a survey;
- to help interpret findings from surveys or other quantitative sources;
- to establish participants' anticipatory reactions to proposed change;
- as a means of evaluating new programmes and procedures once they are put in place.

Focus groups were used in an investigation by Wells (1996) of the attitudes held by external publics towards a health authority in England. They also formed a key component of the Management Development Group's initiative in assessing communication effectiveness in Scotland in the early 1990s (Management Development Group, 1992). As a mark of the heightened interest in the technique, it was estimated that, even by the late 1980s, some 700 specialised facilities for conducting focus groups were available (Goldman and McDonald, 1987). While the vast majority of these are in the USA, Fletcher (1995) also observed the speed with which numbers in the UK were growing. Furthermore, in addition to some $1 billion's worth of focus group research purchased by business annually, Morgan (1997) reckoned that over one hundred articles a year featuring this methodology are found in academic journals alone. The publication of key texts (e.g. D. Morgan, 1998; Krueger, 1998a; Greenbaum, 1987) and special issues of journals such as the *Journal of Qualitative Health Research* (Carey, 1995) represent further significant benchmarks in the establishment of the approach.

Reasons for this burgeoning interest in the focus group are multifarious. Referring particularly to the social sciences setting, Morgan (1997) pointed to, first, its well-established pedigree in market research circles, and second, a flexibility that makes it readily adaptable to academic tasks. More broadly speaking, the increasing acceptance of qualitative research perspectives in tracts of the social sciences such as psychology that have traditionally favoured positivist, quantitative alternatives (Banister *et al.*, 1994), has also created a receptive context for their use. For O'Donnell (1988), the fact that focus groups generate data that differ in nature from that of one-to-one interviews, coupled with the recognition that, for certain topics, no acceptable quantitative research alternative may be available, has led to their growing prevalence.

Others make reference to more pragmatic factors which, while promoting popularity, have not necessarily enhanced the reputation of the focus group as a bona fide investigatory instrument. Greenbaum (1991) pointed out that, since focus groups are cheaper and quicker than other methods such as surveys, this technique can seem compellingly attractive. Whether in fact focus groups are necessarily either cheap or quick is a moot point. In any case, such criteria should not be the prime considerations in making decisions about methodological appropriateness. Nevertheless, beliefs such as these have led to cases of focus groups being used injudiciously to furnish answers that they were never intended to address, attracting the vituperative comment of being 'cheap and nasty'.

Despite this recent upsurge of interest, it should be recognised that much of our knowledge about focus groups, and the bases for many of the recommendations about how they should be conducted, are still intuitive, experiential and rational rather than empirical (Morgan and Krueger, 1993).

FOCUS GROUPS AND QUALITATIVE RESEARCH

Focus groups are comfortably sited within the qualitative research tradition (Lee, 1999). Any attempt at a comprehensive account of the philosophical undergirdings of, and practical approaches to, this way of thinking about and doing research lies well outside the remit of this chapter. Nevertheless, a proper appreciation of the focus group, its uses and abuses, requires some level of acknowledgement of this background. Qualitative research defies a simple, universally accepted definition. For our purposes, though, it can be regarded, along the lines suggested by Banister *et al.* (1994, p. 3), as centring around '(a) an attempt to capture the sense that lies within, and that structures what we say about what we do; (b) an exploration, elaboration and systematization of the significance of an identified phenomenon; (c) the illuminative representation of the meaning of a delimited issue or problem'. In this sense it is juxtapositioned with, and can best be recognised against the relief of, quantitative research.

At the risk of confounding qualitative–quantitative and positivist–interpretive/constructivist polemics, quantitative research derives its inspiration from the natural sciences. Emphasis is placed upon the accurate measurement of objective phenomena in an independent, value-free way thereby enabling firm cause–effect relationships to be established and generalised beyond the immediate confines of the enquiry in the form of steadfast, universal laws. By contrast, qualitative enquiry concerns itself with the quest, through interpretation, to unravel the meanings and understandings which participants bestow upon their experiences. As put by Walker (1985, p. 3) it is designed more to establish 'what things "exist" than to determine how many such things there are'. Data collected relate to a phenomenal world, subjectively created, rather than to an objective, detached reality. This places the researcher in an altogether different and more egalitarian relationship with the participant whose role is elevated from that of passive 'subject' and whose perspective becomes the object of enquiry. As a corollary, the 'gathering of non-numeric data is deemed to be desirable within this paradigm because it frees researchers to explore and be sensitive to, the multiple interpretations and meanings which may be placed upon thoughts and behaviour when viewed in context' (Henwood and Pidgeon, 1995, pp. 115–116). This is not to say that qualitative researchers eschew all attempts at quantification. Some present their findings using numbers, but they tend to be less seduced by inferential statistics, avoiding the typically complex, multivariate analytical procedures that have become the hallmark of their quantitative counterparts (Denzin and Lincoln, 1998).

Qualitative research tends to be idiographic rather than nomothetic in orientation, although there is no logical requirement that it must be so (Smith *et al.*, 1995). Idiographic investigation is directed at an intensive understanding of the individual and the particular, considered in their own terms. Nomothetic research, by contrast, operates at the level of the collective, with individual data sacrificed to the group statistic in deriving universal laws. Ironically, such laws may afford little depth of understanding of any specific individual or case. Furthermore, qualitative research and focus group applications tend to produce data that is emic rather than etic, drawing upon the distinction made by Kippendorf (1980). Emic data emerge in 'natural' form in the sorts of uncontrived situations where they are normally found. Etic information, on the other hand, is shaped by the impositions of the researcher and his/her views of the situation. While both are 'pure types', data in the form of respondents expressing their views and preferences in their own language are more emic than, for example, that collected by ticking boxes on a researcher's questionnaire.

Tourish and Hargie (1996c) make a cogent appeal for a greater use of qualitative research methodology in conducting communication audits. While this should be in a complementary role to quantification, they argue that there is a need to permit staff within organisations to express freely and directly, in their own terms, their views and opinions on the communicative aspects of their work, 'rather than invariably [seeking] to reduce them to quantitative categories' (p. 40). According to Burnett (1991):

> By turning persons into research subjects with non-speaking parts in the script of social science, much investigation of interpersonal interaction can be seen like an elaborate prologue to a play in which the characters are denied their lines. Unless we let actors say what they mean, then the content of that play is reduced; however elaborate an outsider's commentary on the central action, it is no substitute for the story as told by insiders.
>
> (Burnett, 1991, p. 121)

To what extent can qualitative and quantitative research co-exist? The response depends upon whether an epistemological or merely technical question is being posed. As expounded by Bryman (1988a) the epistemological version of the qualitative/quantitative debate leads inextricably to profound issues of the fundamental nature of social science, the ontology of its subject matter, how inquiry should be pursued and what counts as valid knowledge. At this level, the two positions represent paradigms that are not only distinctive but in diametric opposition. Those who address the qualitative/quantitative bifurcation in more technical terms, on the other hand, are prepared to make choices between qualitative and quantitative techniques on largely pragmatic rather than epistemological grounds. As such, investigatory procedures selected, once stripped of possible doctrinal baggage, are those felt best suited to the particular research issue at hand. If need be, this may result in the utilisation of a judicious combination of qualitative and quantitative procedures, with little undue concern over the fundamental assumptions underpinning both. Many researchers use focus groups in this complementary way and argue in favour of doing so (Manfredi *et al.*, 1997). As we shall see in a further sub-section of the chapter dealing with the uses of focus groups, when employed in combination with surveys, for instance, the technique can make a significant contribution to the auditing of organisational communication.

USES OF FOCUS GROUPS IN AUDITING COMMUNICATION

Broadly speaking, focus groups can feature in three contrasting configurations of information gathering, described by Morgan (1997). They can be:

* utilised in a complementary arrangement with several other techniques;
* serve in a subsidiary role to the main information gathering instrument; or
* used as the sole approach to exploration.

1 *They can be included as one of a number of investigatory techniques in a multi-method strategy in which each contributes to the overall richness of the data gathered.* It has been argued that this approach, traditionally favoured by ethnographers, maximises the potential of the focus group and furnishes a fuller understanding of the topic than could be gleaned from the technique on its own (Agar and McDonald, 1995). Triangulation, as a research strategy, is based upon bringing several methods to bear on the issue (Cohen and Manion, 1980). By illuminating the subject from more than one vantage point, its textured richness and complexity can be captured in greater detail. In so doing, each technique can be used as a form of validation of the other two. In the investigation conducted by Egan *et al.* (1995), for example, focus groups were included together with mail survey and Delphi procedures to explore management knowledge, intentions and objectives. Likewise, in the commissioning of an audit on external communication, there may be a distinct advantage in cross-referencing, for instance,

- what sales staff say they do when dealing with customers, as represented by self-report data;
- the more insightful meanings that sales staff attach to their experiences as elicited by focus groups; and
- the actual behaviour of sales staff, together with levels of displayed interpersonal skill, revealed by observational techniques such as videotape analysis or mystery shopper (see Chapter 6).

2 *Focus groups can be included in a subsidiary role to another information-gathering technique which carries the bulk of the data generation.* Employed in this way, they can feature during the exploratory stage of a project in a relatively uncharted area as a source of initial ideas and hypotheses, to be subsequently investigated by other means (Stewart and Shamdasani, 1990). Indeed, this was the primary purpose that Merton envisaged for them back in the early days: 'for us, qualitative focused group-interviews were taken as a source of new ideas and hypotheses, not as demonstrated findings with regard to the extent and distribution of the provisionally identified qualitative patterns of response' (Merton, 1987, p. 558). Additionally, included during the initial phases of a study, they can be employed to obtain background information, identify issues, and perhaps locate problems or matters of concern, to be followed up with a more extensive survey of a larger sample of respondents. In the field of mental health, Coyne and Calarco (1995) drew upon the statements elicited in two focus groups, comprising recent and former depressed psychiatric patients, to construct a valid self-assessment survey instrument to measure depression. Commencing a communication audit in this way can help to establish how and why channels and modes of communication within the organisation, and between it and its external publics, are perceived and utilised as they are by different sections of the workforce or groups of service users and customers. Tourish (1996) stressed the importance of ensuring that the parameters of an audit are not shaped exclusively by management's perceptions and agenda, if it is to furnish an accurate picture of how communication is functioning across the organisation. A subsequent survey designed to quantify the extent of experiences revealed is more likely to address core issues and concerns, if premised in broader terms. Additional advantages of the preliminary use of focus groups are not only that topics of relevance can be more precisely targeted, but that specific forms of expression peculiar to those groups, let's say, can be reflected in the framing of questions in the questionnaire (Vaughn *et al.*, 1996).

An alternative follow-up arrangement involving the focus group in a secondary role switches attention to the other end of the investigator process. Here findings emerging from the major observation-based or, perhaps, survey-based part of the audit are examined in greater detail. The researcher may be keen to find out why particular patterns of communication observed on videotape are perpetuated, or why discrepancies have emerged between the evaluations of certain modes of communication by different groups of staff. According to

D. Morgan (1998) there is always room for a focus group perspective when an understanding of diversity is sought. Focus groups are a useful way of tapping the actual meanings that the participants attach to the behavioural observations or questionnaire responses recorded. Referring to market research, Greenbaum (1991) noted an increasing trend of focus group deployment in this way, following up quantitative studies to unearth reasons for the results obtained.

3 *The researcher may rely upon focus groups alone as the technique of choice.* In this stand-alone mode, care must be taken to ensure that the methodology is congruent with the goals of the investigation (see Chapter 16). As mentioned earlier, the strength of focus groups lies in their ability to uncover the meanings and experiences of participants relating to the process or event at issue. Estimating how often staff in the organisation use e-mail, or the proportion who would benefit from an assertiveness training intervention, is essentially the forte of quantitative procedures. To insist that the latter is in some way superior to qualitative alternatives, including the focus group, is to miss the point. In a spirit of new-found confidence and optimism surrounding focus group research, investigators are reacting strongly against a way of thinking that reduces the status of the technique to that of poor substitute for surveys or a cheaper and faster alternative to one-to-one interviews. Lunt and Livingstone (1996) argue in favour of focus groups being acknowledged as a legitimate research instrument in their own right. Their unique contribution is in the group-based nature of the discussion, offering 'a simulation of these routine but relatively inaccessible communicative contexts that can help us discover the processes by which meaning is socially constructed through everyday talk' (p. 85).

CONDUCTING FOCUS GROUPS

An increasing number of recent publications now exist offering detailed guidance on the 'how-to' of organising and operating focus group research (e.g. Krueger, 1994, 1998b; Hennink and Diamond, 1999). It should be noted at the outset, however, that while systematic inquiry into the technique and its efficacy is increasing (e.g. de Ruyter, 1996), a large proportion of the received wisdom on how best to run focus groups is epistemologically sourced from the practical experiences of those who have employed it extensively (e.g. Greenbaum, 1993). Advice is often buttressed by theory and research imported from cognate areas, including small group dynamics and interpersonal communication.

The process of making use of focus groups can be broken down into a series of broadly recognised stages or phases which indeed share much in common with those of other research methodologies. They are:

- planning and preparation;
- identifying and recruiting participants;

* moderating and recording the group interview;
* analysing the data and reporting the outcomes (D. Morgan, 1998).

Planning and preparation

The old adage 'well begun is half done' applies equally to focus group work as to other types of research. It is important that a vision of the project in its entirety be framed at an early stage (Morgan and Scannell, 1998). Unless the researcher has a sound working knowledge of the focus group approach, un-anticipated difficulties will constantly be confronted for the first time as the investigation unfolds. A lack of forethought inevitably means that prior decisions subsequently reduce preferred options for dealing with unexpected problems 'on the hoof', compromising the quality of the research. A range of points to consider at the outset are included in Box 5.1.

Box 5.1 Initial considerations

* What are the questions that the audit seeks to answer?
* Are focus groups the most suited approach?
* Who should be included as participants?
* How can they be recruited?
* How many will be required?
* How best to conduct the group interviews?
* Where will discussions be held?
* How should they be recorded?
* What is to be done with the recordings once they are made?
* How detailed does the final report have to be?
* How long will the audit take?

The objectives of the research

The starting point should be in establishing precisely what the project needs to find out. What are the questions that it addresses? The essential purpose of focus group research has already been explained but deserves repeating. It is basically to illuminate the meanings and interpretations that others place upon their experiences: to appreciate how they make sense of the communication systems and processes of the organisation, together with their function and utilisation. For example, why perhaps does a particular group of junior managers find weekly meetings of little benefit, according to the questionnaires that they have completed, when most other staff generally appreciate this channel of communication? Focus group research offers a path to get 'inside' the shared experiences of others and to begin to appreciate events from their perspective.

If the intention, on the other hand, is to make convenient use of the focus group as an easier or quicker way of gathering information, the strategy needs serious reconsideration. The chances are that the details garnered will not really enable the sorts of questions posed to be conclusively answered. That apart, while the information gathering stage of focus group research can be completed relatively quickly, subsequent transcription and analysis, if thorough, can be much more time-consuming than other techniques, such as small-scale surveys (D. Morgan, 1998). But cost should not be the primary concern. Ensuring that the methodology is suited to the purpose is much more important.

Who should be involved in the audit

The four main stakeholders in the typical focus group audit are the commissioning organisation, the research team, the moderator (who may or may not be an integral part of the team), and the participants. Deciding whether the research should be conducted 'in-house', by employees of the organisation such as the personnel department, or bought in from outside, is one of the first steps to be taken. Apart from issues of expertise, having the audit carried out by a section of the company can introduce the perception (if not the reality) of a 'political dimension' that may seriously compromise the enquiry and the extent to which employees are prepared to contribute fully and openly (Greenbaum, 1994). Employees may be reluctant to speak their minds on company policy, practice or personnel if they know that what they say in the focus group discussion can be ascribed to them personally and brought to the attention of management (Ettorre, 1997).

Selecting a suitable moderator is one of the most crucial decisions to be taken during planning. The depth of group discussion and richness of the information yielded ultimately depend upon the skill of this pivotal individual. Various qualities and requirements have been specified by Szybillo and Berger (1979). In addition to the more specialised skills of guiding group discussion, the moderator must:

- be acceptable to the participants;
- be familiar with the auditing process;
- have a firm grasp of the issues to be explored;
- be cognisant of the organisational background to the particular investigation;
- contribute to the preparation of the interview guide for the focus group;
- ideally play a central part in the subsequent analysis of the data.

Depending upon the expertise and skill mix of the commissioned research team, it may be sensible to buy in the services of a moderator with acknowledged expertise who can be briefed on the background to the particular audit.

Matters to do with identifying participants are also part of planning, but for convenience these will be discussed together with those of recruitment as the next stage of conducting focus group research.

Where to conduct the sessions

There is now a growing number of focus group facilities, mainly in the US but increasingly in the UK, specially designed for focus group work. These can be hired and are used mainly by market research organisations. They typically offer a comfortably sized room with good acoustics, furnished with a table and suitable chairs, together with an adjoining observation room beyond a one-way mirror. Resources for providing refreshments are an additional factor. Given that sessions may last up to two hours, a high premium is placed upon comfort and attractiveness of surroundings (Millward, 1995). It is crucial that room layout, furnishings and decor create an appropriate ambience, conducive to free and open interaction.

The observation room can be used by other members of the research team and, if necessary, messages passed to the moderator to pursue issues raised during the discussion. In doing so, it is important that this is not done intrusively, or the impression created that the moderator is merely someone else's mouthpiece.

Recording equipment is also required. Whilst audiorecording is the most common, video facilities enable nonverbal detail to also be included and has been strongly endorsed by Lydecker (1986). Identifying comments with individuals, during analysis, can also be much easier from videotape. CCTV equipment is an acceptable substitute for the lack of a one-way mirror, permitting the interaction to be monitored from outside the conference room. Prior permission of participants is of course required.

Whilst customised facilities have distinct advantages, they are far from essential. Most focus groups are carried out in lesser surroundings. Indeed a case has been made for taking small videocameras to where participants are normally found, whether it be in the workplace, their own homes or the shopping mall (Fletcher, 1995). One advantage of the latter strategy is convenience of location for those taking part, a significant factor when it comes to getting recruits to actually attend as and when required. Finding the videocamera off-putting at the beginning, for some participants, may be a potential disadvantage of this medium.

How to organise the focus group

Drawing up the moderator guide is a further planning task. This contributes a basic template for the session, specifying topics introduced, framing possible questions, and affording some degree of commonality across groups. The degree of structure thought necessary to impose on the discussion will shape the guide and in turn reflect the basic purpose of the focus group input in the overall auditing process. In situations where focus groups are used in an exploratory fashion to gain initial insights into workers' or customers' perceptions of forms of organisational communication, the guide may do little more than clarify and formalise the topic or topics to be addressed. On the other hand, as a follow-up to a survey or in evaluating a programme of change, the research team may decide upon a much more structured approach. Here specific points to be raised in the form of particular questions tend to be listed. (Further advice on topic-versus question-based guides can be found in Krueger, 1998a.) An alternative to either more or less structured approaches is the 'Funnel' option, whereby 'each group begins with a less structured approach that emphasises free discussion and then moves toward a more structured discussion of specific questions' (Morgan, 1997, p. 41).

For the most part, though, the moderator guide should not be thought of as a tightly prescribed set of specific primary and secondary questions that must be posed verbatim and adhered to religiously. It is less like a questionnaire in this sense, and more a reasonably relaxed framework for containing the discussion (Stewart and Shamdasani, 1990). In addition to specifying topics and/or questions for the session, the guide should earmark introductory procedures, cater for ways of getting the group relaxed in the situation and with each other, as well as including steps for smoothly bringing the discussion to an end (Vaughn et al., 1996; Greenbaum, 1998).

Anticipating analysis

The output of focus groups is talk (together possibly with nonverbal communication, if this has been collected). A final part of planning covers what to do with this material. During most discussions, the moderator, or an assistant, will keep notes on what takes place. If the purpose of the focus group is simply to tune into the typical terms and forms of expression used by a particular group when talking about a topic in their everyday language (in preparation for carrying out a survey, for instance), it may be possible to get by on recall of the discussion, bolstered by these field notes. Anything more than this most basic of processing requires recording of the discussion on audio or videotape for subsequent transcription and more rigorous analysis.

Identifying and recruiting participants

Identifying participants includes the tasks of deciding who best to include and how many to select. As far as the first is concerned, the aim is to involve those who have the most pertinent information to offer up and are prepared to do so. It is important to adopt a systematic strategy for segmenting the overall population into categories that are internally cohesive in respect of some variable which is conceptually of significance to the audit (Millward, 1995). Categories should be distinct from each other on a similar basis. For example, in the case of an internal audit, it may make sense initially to stratify the workforce from junior shop-floor staff through to senior management. Morgan and Scannell (1998) cautioned that it is almost always unwise to combine workers and supervisory staff in a single focus group, a view endorsed by Greenbaum (1994). It may also be desirable, depending on the purpose and background to the investigation, to group those staff who work together on some distinct task, form a section, or perhaps share a geographical location. The rule of thumb is to divide up the population in such a way that homogeneity within, but heterogeneity between, groupings is created (Morgan, 1997). Segmentation of the population of external publics could be based upon type of public, how often they have used the organisation, gender, age, income, education, or any of a number of demographic factors. Initial screening of recruits may be necessary to ensure that they satisfy these criteria.

Sampling for focus group work is typically nonprobability (Vaughn *et al.*, 1996). It is not the intention, unlike in quantitative research, to derive firm estimations of the extent of some practice or event in a population. Participants are therefore commonly selected using purposive sampling where the underlying concern is with the disclosure of sufficient quality information to maximise understanding of the event or happening, rather than with issues of empirical generalisability. That said, there may be occasions where it might make sense to randomly sample from amongst a number of possible participants, all of whom could theoretically make an equally useful contribution (Calder, 1980).

Focus groups are conducted in groups of 6–10 members (Lunt and Livingstone, 1996), although Greenbaum (1998) refers to minigroups of 4–6 participants as a possibility. Discussions usually last 1–2 hours. Most audits require 3–4 focus groups, the principle being that group sessions are continued until information saturation is reached with no new material forthcoming from additional interviews. Segmentation means that 3–4 groups may therefore be needed per segment of the population.

Once identified, potential members have to be recruited. With internal publics, this task is reasonably straightforward. Employees are easily identifiable. They are often motivated to make a contribution when the potential benefits to both them and the company are explained, when they are assured of anonymity, and when it can be done within normal working hours. Providing some food and refreshments over lunchtime is often an option, with the provisions serving as an acceptable recompense for forfeited time.

Recruiting from within external publics is usually more difficult. For a start there may be no obvious way of locating members of the population, although customer lists can help massively in this respect. Making cold telephone calls to screen for suitable participants is a worst-case scenario. Once contacted, these people may be less prepared to participate, making it necessary to introduce incentives in the form of direct payment, a meal, gift, or perhaps a paid trip to take part with free overnight accommodation. On the other hand, Lanigan (1997) pointed to the biasing effects of 'groupies' or 'professional respondents' who keep turning up at focus groups, often lying about personal detail in order to be recruited.

As a way of maximising the chances of having the desired number attend as and when required, it is common practice to 'over recruit' by arranging for one or two more than is actually needed to come along. Even so, a system of telephone reminders is also prudent, particularly with external publics.

Moderating and recording the group interview

The part played by the moderator in facilitating the focus group is a pivotal factor in the overall success of the investigation. The personal skills and attributes of this key member have a considerable bearing upon the nature and quality of the data collected (Sim, 1998). According to Krueger (1998b, p. 4) the role should be 'to guide the discussion and listen to what's said but not to participate, share views, engage in discussion, or shape the outcome of the group interview'. Being constantly on the alert to ways of inadvertently influencing the group is one way to avoid biasing the outcome.

While the specific moderating style adopted is tailored by the purpose of the focus group, together with the degree of structure envisaged, it should be one that conveys genuine interest in and respect for members and what they have to offer. It is they and their views that should take centre stage, with the moderator staying largely in the conversational background and becoming more actively involved only to keep the discussion going, guide it back on track or gently encourage the reticent to take a fuller part. Karger (1987) suggests that this is best served when the moderator:

> has unobtrusive chameleon-like qualities; gently drawing consumers into the process; deftly encouraging them to interact with one another for optimum synergy; lets the intercourse flow naturally with a minimum of intervention; listens openly and deeply; uses silence well; plays back consumer statements in a distilling way which brings out more refined thoughts or explanations; and remains completely nonauthoritarian and nonjudgemental.
>
> (Karger, 1987, p. 54)

Despite the fact that they are examples of group interviews, focus groups operate most effectively when the moderator concentrates on keeping participants discussing amongst themselves, rather than engaging in a question-and-answer session with each in turn. The advantages of the technique stem from the discursive element of the group encounter.

In addition to general style and sets of skills around information exchange, there are particular sub-tasks that have to be taken on board, as documented in the moderator guide (Vaughn *et al.*, 1996; Greenbaum, 1998). These include effecting introductions and 'setting the scene', easing the members into free and easy interchange and, once the discussion has run its course, negotiating closure.

Good quality discussion that is not captured in a good quality recording is often so much lost opportunity. For any other than the most rudimentary of analyses, a permanent record of what was said is indispensable. As already pointed out, this is usually done on audio or videotape. Video enables nonverbal contextualisations of what was said to be more fully taken into account, as well as making it easier to decide who said what in cases of overtalk. More important, though, are clear and distinct sound qualities. This means using a room with suitable acoustics and high-performance equipment. The microphone has been described as the most important tool of all (Krueger, 1998c), and having more than one strategically placed may be a requirement – especially with larger groups. Indeed operating several recording machines, in crucial cases, is a hedge against gremlins spoiling the whole enterprise.

Analysing the data and reporting outcomes

Analysing focus group output can be the most difficult and time-consuming part of the auditing exercise. As with moderating the discussion, there is considerable scope at this stage for subjective bias to be introduced thereby distorting conclusions reached. There is no one best way to carry out the task (Stewart and Shamdasani, 1990). Some approaches are much more rigorous and involved than others. That opted for will depend upon the goals of the research and the thoroughness of the report required. Krueger (1998c) mentioned three broad strategies for analysis:

- memory based;
- tape based; and
- transcript based.

Memory based

Using the first and least rigorous, the moderator relies upon recall, perhaps supplemented by field notes, to capture the substance of the discussion. Shortcomings include all the vagaries and distortions of memory that even the most experienced researcher can be prone to. However, when the interview has been watched by other members of the research team, some of these can be countered to a certain extent. If the focus group was held to simply get a feel for the words and types of expression used by groups of workers, as a preparatory step to a more detailed enquiry, perhaps this option would suffice. Nevertheless, it precludes anything other than the most cursory of analysis.

Tape based

With the second possibility, the researcher relies upon careful listening to the tape-recording, perhaps alongside an abridged transcript, to extract and interpret the essential findings. The permanency of the record facilitates a more involved examination of disclosures.

Transcript based

However, transcript-based analysis is the most common and affords the greatest depth of scrutiny. It is virtually obligatory, particularly when the focus group has been used as the sole methodology. Here recordings are accurately transcribed in their entirety for subsequent analysis, together with field notes. Transcribing is a time-consuming business. A group discussion lasting just one hour can take more than four hours to transcribe and yield some 20–25 pages of text. It may take a further 12 hours for even an experienced researcher to complete the analysis and document the findings (D. Morgan, 1998). Given that each group interview may last up to twice this length of time and that, with segmentation, each grouping of the population may require three or four focus groups, the total time commitment can be readily factored up. Under such circumstances the need to sample from the total content of group discussion becomes imperative. This should be done in a planned way to ensure the elements selected are representative of the whole.

Designs such as those above, with several focus groups conducted for each segment of the population, sometimes have the objective of making comparisons. When coupled with a structured interview guide, it may be possible to analyse the resulting data using a 'grid' technique described by Knodel (1993). A cell of this grid summarises the responses of a particular group to a certain question. When completed for each of the group's reactions to each of the questions posed, the matrix presents a useful panoramic view of the findings.

Transcriptions are typically processed by means of content analysis, defined by Kippendorf (1980, p. 21) as 'a research technique for making replicable and valid inferences from data to their context'. Three main forms of content analysis have been noted by Millward (1995): qualitative, quantitative and structural. Although all three have much in common, qualitative content analysis is concerned with codifying the data to reveal robust themes or patterns of meaning that can be illustrated and documented in well-chosen quotations from the text. The quantitative variant involves the analyst in carefully allocating units derived from the text to categories. Results are reported numerically indicating how often staff from different sections revealed a lack of trust over messages received from senior management. Morgan (1997) expressed the view that such 'Descriptive counting is especially useful in research projects that compare distinctively different groups to determine how often various topics are mentioned' (p. 61). Finally, structural content analysis extends the previous two by examining the 'rules governing the relationships between response categories' (Millward, 1995, p. 290). This may be a useful thing to do in analysing 'complex systems of which naturally occurring focus groups are an excellent example' (ibid.).

Content analysis comprises both mechanical and interpretative components, the two being closely linked (Kippendorf, 1980). The former has to do with the physical task of subdividing the text of the transcript into units to be systematically organised into categories: the latter with creating an internally coherent system of categories that is meaningful within the context of the enquiry. Analysis unfolds through cycles of coding and recording units as categories are extended or refined.

Vaughn et al. (1996) recommended that the process of analysis should begin directly after the interview, through reflection upon the 'big ideas' in what was said that seem to stand out as significant. These will probably be modified as the analysis proceeds but it is important that they don't get lost in the fine-grained work of breaking down the text into units. These units may be as small as a word or take in a paragraph. They may be referential (i.e. specify a particular person, event or thing such as the MD, e-mail, etc.), propositional (i.e. denote a certain property or attribute such as confusing, utility, etc.), or thematic (i.e. occasioning sets of broad recurring explanatory or interpretive statements) (Stewart and Shamdasani, 1990).

Categories can be largely pre-established on the basis of theory, prior knowledge, or the particular requirements of the research. Alternatively, they may be derived from the data themselves. It is here that the process most resembles what Krueger (1988) called 'detective work': 'One looks for clues, but in this case the clues are trends and patterns that reappear among various focus groups' (p. 109). It is important that the researcher be thorough, working systematically by defining categories and establishing rules for coding units. As analysis progresses, certain groupings may no longer be sustainable, resulting in sub-division or perhaps amalgamation. In any case a more refined and internally coherent system that can accommodate all units in discrete categories is the objective.

While the task of analysing content can still be done physically by 'cut and paste', a variety of computer software packages are available to ease data management. A range of these are reviewed by Vaughn et al. (1996).

Given the potential for personal bias and idiosyncratic interpretation to creep in, it is crucial to establish that the outcome of the analysis is not merely a figment of the creative imagination of the analyst. Procedures for establishing the degree of agreement, in the form of a numeric index, between the codings of two analysts include Cohen's Kappa (Cohen, 1960) which represents consistency as a coefficient value, taking chance agreements into account. Research carried out by Weinberger et al. (1998) raised concerns about the reproducibility of a single analyst's evaluations of focus group transcripts, making the need for such checks all the more telling. Vaughn et al. (1996) specify a stage of category negotiation in the steps that they recommend for handling the data. Here two members of the team, working independently along the lines already described, finally come together to compare their coded output and reconcile differences that may emerge.

CONCLUSION

Focus groups are a way of doing qualitative research, based upon group interviews. They are concerned not so much with establishing how extensive something is or how often it happens. That is essentially the domain of quantitative enquiry, which places a premium upon the generalisability of findings from a sample to the population from which it was drawn, utilising inferential statistics. While the results of focus groups can be represented in numbers, their function is rather with uncovering the meanings and interpretations that individuals, in their own terms, place upon their experiences.

Focus groups are enjoying a substantial growth in popularity, particularly in market research, health and social sciences research. They have much to contribute to the communication auditing process as either a 'stand alone' method of investigating or in combination with other techniques in the context of a broader project. As such, they can be used in the initial stages when investigating an issue or situation about which little is known, as a way of generating preliminary ideas and hypotheses. Alternatively, they can identify areas of concern to be explored more systematically by means of quantitative procedures. As a follow up to a survey, on the other hand, focus groups are an effective approach to illuminating in detail the significance of particular responses recorded. The quality of the output, however, depends upon guarding against individual bias and distortion creeping in, particularly at the stages of data collection and analysis.

Chapter 6

Data collection log-sheet methods

Owen Hargie and Dennis Tourish

INTRODUCTION

This chapter focuses upon two audit methods, both of which use a system of data collection log-sheet (DCL) to collect information. The DCL is a structured form on which specific items of detail have to be completed. The information content being sought, and the method of entry (tick box, Yes/No, Likert scale, open comment, etc.) are carefully determined, and the DCL is thoroughly field-tested prior to the audit exercise. This method differs from the questionnaire approach in that here the respondent measures and evaluates *actual* communication experiences immediately after they have occurred. With questionnaires, the respondent is asked to reflect back on, and evaluate, past general communication trends and patterns, rather than focus on the specific here-and-now.

In audits, DCLs can either be completed by the member of staff, or by an outside observer. Indeed, the two main approaches presented in this chapter differ on this dimension. In the first, diaries and logs, the respondent is responsible for the completion of DCLs. In the second, undercover auditing, an independent evaluator fills these in after an interaction with the person being observed.

DIARIES AND LOGS

As defined by Breakwell and Wood (1995, p. 293), the diary audit technique encompasses: 'Any data collection strategy which entails getting respondents to provide information linked to a temporal framework.' Analysis over time is therefore a key determinant in deciding to use this approach. If a 'snapshot' is required then other methods, such as questionnaires, are simpler and easier to apply. However, if the objective is to study communications across a set period, then the use of a systematic 'diary' or 'log' is appropriate.

Although the title of this section suggests that what we all know as traditional diaries should be scrutinised and audited, this in fact is not the case. While the well known and much loved 'Dear Diary' can be a fascinating storehouse of information and opinion about communication with others, it is at best a subjective and erratic source of data. For example, King George V, who died in 1936, had spent 25 years on the throne through some very turbulent and violent periods. It was hoped that his diaries would offer an opportunity to study carefully the deepest insights of a key player. However, in fact the King only kept a diary for the first few days of each year, during which time he merely recorded less than enthralling impressions of the weather, in terms such as 'Rainy' and 'Cold'. Likewise, at the time of the Russian revolution, when seismic changes were sweeping the country, the diary of Tsar Nicholas II was not exactly analytical or insightful. In those tumultuous times, when most people in his circle were panic stricken, typical diary entries read: 'Got dressed and rode a bicycle to the bathing beach and bathed enjoyably in the sea' and 'Walked long and killed two crows. Drank tea by daylight'. More insight into the nature of the period could be gleaned from reading tea-leaves than from the Tsar's entries. One reason for the disparity between experiences and diary entries may be that, as explained by the Scottish writer J.M. Barrie, 'The life of every man is a diary in which he means to write one story, and writes another.'

On the other hand, there are detailed diaries that have informed and inspired generations, a prime example being the poignant record kept by Anne Frank in her terrifying and brief life under Nazi occupation in Amsterdam. Although certain diarists are assiduous in maintaining a daily record of events, and indeed some do so with a view to publication (e.g. Benn, 1992), their entries vary greatly in structure, length, focus and depth of analysis. Thus, although personal diaries are an interesting form of historical record and social artefact, and can be studied as forms of social science data in their own right, they are not really useful as audit tools within organisations. While they can provide an overview of who staff have interacted with, how often, about what topics and for what duration, the problem is that in the organisational context it is usually only formal meetings and contacts which are entered into diaries, and so other information will not be included.

The audit diary method described in this chapter involves obtaining written responses from participants on a carefully prepared proforma or data collection log-sheet (DCL), on which they itemise and evaluate communicative activities over a set period. The International Communication Association Diary (Goldhaber and Rogers, 1979) provides a useful DCL template that can be adapted to meet particular requirements. (An example of this is given in Chapter 11.)

Diaries and network analysis

While audit texts (e.g. Goldhaber and Rogers, 1979; Downs, 1988) make a distinction between 'diaries' and 'network analysis', in essence these both use variations of the DCL method. The main difference is that the former, also known as 'the duty study' (Goldhaber, 1993), involves detailing one's *own* communications, while the latter entails an estimate of how the respondent interacts with *others*.

Network analysis is now widely used in social science to investigate how individuals perceive the nature of causal links between events. For example, in studying the phenomenon of loneliness, the researcher using network analysis attempts to ascertain how people perceive the connections between possible causes of loneliness, such as shyness, physical unattractiveness, lack of trying, fear of rejection, pessimism, lack of opportunity for contact, and so on (Muncer and Gillen, 1997). This allows central causes to be distinguished from more peripheral ones, and also illustrates the network of relationships between each of the sub-areas (e.g. is shyness closely linked to pessimism?).

Sociometry

Network analysis is a variant of sociometry – a term derived from the Latin *socius* (companion) and the Greek *metron* (measure). Sociometry was developed by Moreno (1953) as a method for analysing the pattern of relationships in peer groups. In its original format, it requested all members of a group to nominate those members they would and would not like to associate with in a particular activity (Bukowski and Cillessen, 1998). For example, pupils in a school class may be asked who they would choose and not choose to sit beside in class, play with in the playground, or invite home for tea. In the organisational context, staff could be asked who they would most like, or would definitely not want, to share an office with, work on a special project with, or socialise with after work. The lists of choices are then analysed and converted into a 'sociogram', or 'com-municogram' (Weinshall, 1979), which diagrammatically portrays the network of choices.

Let us take a hypothetical group of 13 people who have been asked to accept or reject one another on a given issue. The results are then as follows:

A chooses K and rejects no one
B chooses C, D and E and rejects H
C chooses B and D and rejects no one
D chooses B and L and rejects H
E chooses D and rejects H
F chooses G and L and rejects no one
G chooses F and L and rejects no one
H chooses I and rejects no one
I chooses D and rejects H
J chooses D and I and rejects no one
K chooses A and rejects no one
L chooses D, F and G and rejects no one
M chooses no one and rejects no one

This information is difficult to interpret as presented, but when converted into sociogram format it becomes much easier to evaluate (Figure 6.1). On the basis of choices made, it is possible to identify 'stars' at one end of the continuum

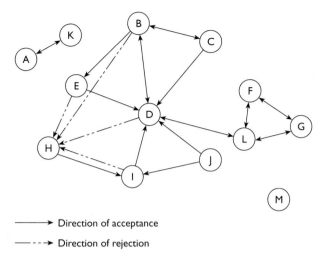

→ Direction of acceptance

-- -→ Direction of rejection

Figure 6.1 Sociogram

(very popular individuals who are nominated by numerous others in their group as their choice) – and 'isolates' at the other (people who neither make nor receive any nominations). In Figure 6.1 person D is the star, and M an isolate. Other identified categories are neglectees (people who make choices but receive none) and rejectees (those not just unchosen but actively rejected). In Figure 6.1, J is a neglectee while H is a rejectee. On the basis of reciprocal choices, mutual pairs (A and K) and triangles or cliques (F, L and G) can also be determined. While sociometric choices do not always reflect actual friendship patterns in practice, reciprocal choices have been shown to be a highly accurate indicator of strong interpersonal relationships (Ashley, 1992).

This is a straightforward, yet robust, method for gaining insight into how individuals in groups regard one another. It has been shown to be a useful method for analysing the work of teams within organisations (Lucius and Kuhnert, 1997). A refinement of, and evolution from, sociometry is *social network analysis* (SNA). As stated by Oliver and Ebers (1998, p. 551), the purpose of network analysis, at both the intra- and inter-organisational levels, is to identify 'sets of recurring ties (e.g. resource, friendship, informational ties) among a set of actors (e.g. individuals, groups, organisations)' and identify 'why actors forge which specific linkages under different circumstances, and what consequences entail'. The eventual aim is 'to produce representations of social structures and positions inherent in dyads or groups' (Koehly and Shivy, 1998, p. 3). The SNA methodology embraces a range of techniques to collect data, which are then analysed using a set of sophisticated and complex mathematical and statistical tools, together with specially designed computer packages (Wasserman and Faust, 1994). Indeed, some of the specialist SNA analytical and representational techniques used to evaluate and present data require considerable time and training to acquire (Scott, 1991).

However, a range of useful survey instruments, such as the Social Support Questionnaire and the Social Network List, have been developed for use in SNA (see Bass and Stein, 1997 for a review). In addition, more open format questionnaires have been employed to chart the social networks of individuals within organisations (e.g. Stackman and Pinder, 1999). In general, SNA uses the range of audit methods covered in this text (questionnaires, interviews, etc.) to investigate linkages between people in terms of:

- their evaluations of one another (liking, trust, friendship, etc.);
- task relationships (the structures through which people interrelate to get the job done);
- information exchange (the direction, speed, accuracy, etc. of information flow);
- associations and affiliations (e.g. race, gender, age, membership of same clubs);
- physical linkages (e.g. sharing an office, located on different sites);
- formal roles (colleagues, supervisors, senior managers, etc.);
- behavioural interactions (how often, through which channels, and about which topics, people communicate).

When used to audit communication, network analysis is usually concerned with how often or how well particular individuals communicate with other members of staff in the organisation (or with relevant personnel in other organisations). For example Goldhaber and Rogers (1979) used a DCL on which respondents identified, from a given list of named personnel, each person they communicated with in a typical work day. For each selection, the individual had, first, to estimate how many times a day communication occurred, and second to evaluate on a five-point scale how important these contacts were. Both parts were completed twice, once for formal channels (meetings, memos, etc.) and once for informal or grapevine contacts. This information then provides a sociometric database which is used to chart the volume and perceived importance of communications between specific members of staff within the organisation. By combining individuals in the same unit, it is also possible to examine inter-departmental communications as a whole. An example of such analysis is presented later in the chapter.

ECCO

Another example of a DCL method is what has been termed 'Episodic Communication Channels in Organisation (ECCO) Analysis', initially developed by Davis (1953). This is a DCL which is specially designed 'to analyze and map communication networks and measure rates of flow, distortion of messages, and redundancy' (Goldhaber, 1993, p. 374). The ECCO is used to monitor the progress of a specific piece of information through the organisation. The information to be tracked should be (1) true, (2) expected to be widely known by most if not all staff, (3) basic and straightforward, (4) recent, and (5) released through a specific channel.

Respondents are asked to list on a DCL:

1   whether or not they know all or part of the information;
2   if they know about it to cite the parts they know;
3   if they do know about it, when they first learned of it;
4   where they were when they first became aware of it;
5   by which channel (memo, phone call, newsletter, etc.) the message was delivered;
6   what was the source (manager, colleague) of it.

An analysis of completed ECCO DCLs provides a picture of whether or not communication is flowing well, how long it takes information to reach certain destinations, which media seem to be most effective in disseminating messages, and where there appear to be problems. The ECCO questionnaire is brief and can be easily completed in a few minutes. This means that it can be administered to a large sample of staff. Among its disadvantages are that some staff may be reluctant to identify sources, while others are loath to admit that they are in ignorance of what will then be perceived to be an important piece of information.

An example of an ECCO DCL based upon one we used in an actual audit is presented in Box 6.1. The information had in this case been communicated through the company Newsletter. The results enabled us to conduct various analyses. Interestingly, we found that some 6 per cent of respondents did not know that Sue Bloggs had been head of customer services, let alone that she was

---

Box 6.1 Example of an ECCO DCL

Gender: ❒ Female   ❒ Male
Age: ❒ Under 20 years   ❒ 21–30   ❒ 31–40   ❒ 41–50   ❒ Over 50 yrs
Post: ❒ Full-time   ❒ Part-time   ❒ Temporary full-time
            ❒ Temporary part-time
How long employed: ❒ Under 1 year   ❒ 1–5 yrs   ❒ 6–10 yrs
                        ❒ 11–15 yrs   ❒ Over 15 yrs
Present position: ❒ I don't supervise anyone   ❒ First-line manager
                       ❒ Middle manager   ❒ Senior manager
Other (please specify) _____
What is your job? _____

Please tick the box beside each of the statements below if you knew this information before you completed this Questionnaire. If you did not know it, please leave the box blank. If you leave all boxes blank do not complete any more of the Questionnaire.

❒ Sue Bloggs is leaving
❒ Sue Bloggs is going to Head Office
❒ Sue Bloggs was Head of Customer Services
❒ The post of Head of Customer Services will not be re-advertised

Box 6.1 (cont'd)

❒ The new Head of Communications is Davinder Patel
❒ Davinder Patel will now be responsible for customer services

From what *source* did you first hear or read about this information (please tick only one box)

Written medium
❒ Company newsletter
❒ Notice on staff board
❒ Formal memo
❒ E-mail
Other (please specify)_____

Talking medium
❒ Colleague
❒ Line manager
❒ Senior manager
❒ Overheard someone

Through which *channel* did you learn about this information?

❒ Staff meeting
❒ Company video
❒ Written communication
Other (please specify)_____

❒ Informal conversation
❒ Telephone call

When did you first learn about this information (please circle only one)?

Days ago   Today 1   2   3   4   5   6
Weeks ago   1   2   3   4

Where were you when you first learned about this information?

❒ Staff canteen
❒ While visiting another department
❒ Outside of the company
Other (please specify)_____

❒ At my normal working location
❒ At a formal staff meeting

leaving or that a new structure was in place (see Box 6.1)! However, over 60 per cent of staff claimed to have heard all parts of the information and most had received it from the Newsletter, with the next most common channel being a colleague. The one part of the message that had failed to penetrate was the final one relating to the fact that the head of communications was now in charge of customer services – less that 30 per cent of the workforce claimed knowledge of this. As a result, the next edition of the Newsletter carried a main feature on Davinder Patel and his role in the company.

Advantages and disadvantages of diaries and logs

There are both pros and cons in using self-report DCLs (Breakwell and Wood, 1995). The advantages are as follows:

1 *Diaries are ubiquitous*! The diary is a familiar, user-friendly artefact for most people and so the task of keeping one is viewed as fairly unproblematic. Respondents understand and accept the notion, and the validity, of keeping a personal record. While precise instructions, and in some cases training, about exactly what is required are important, half the battle is won through familiarity with the diary concept.

2 *Where repeat information is required from respondents over a period of time, it is a cost-effective approach.* Once respondents are fully informed and understand exactly the nature of the assignment, they can be left to get on with it. The auditor does not have to be on site to collect the logs. This is done at the end of the observational period (or at interim periods if the timescale is long). However, if the logs are to be completed over a prolonged period, at least one motivational reminder letter from the auditor is useful.

3 *Diaries provide information about the temporal sequence of events.* They also give the auditor specific detail about the source, recipient, nature and perceived effectiveness of each individual communication. The range, depth and variety of the information which can be obtained is potentially enormous. Such data would be very difficult to obtain through other means.

4 *Classification is made by the person doing the job.* An observer may not have access to, or fully comprehend, the full range of interactions engaged in by members of staff. Their perspective is also that of 'outsider' while the diary is completed from an 'insider' view (Weinshall, 1979).

The disadvantages are:

1 *It relies upon staff to conscientiously complete the DCLs – the auditor has no real control over how well this is done.* As expressed by Breakwell and Wood (1995, p. 296) 'getting people to remember to make entries at the right time about the right things can be difficult, even when they have goodwill towards the research and every intention of complying with your instructions'. Obviously, the likelihood of regular completion diminishes in direct proportion to the extent to which respondents have doubts or are unconvinced about the value of the exercise. Goldhaber and Rogers (1979) described how they faced resistance to the diary method from individuals in organisations, owing to its time-consuming nature, or to a lack of conviction about its validity. They cited the case of how in one instance they received initial commitment from a hospital to use this approach. However, at the training session for staff one surgeon baulked at the task. As they explain: 'One doctor told us, "when I come out of an operation with blood on my hands, just how do you expect me to get serious about this diary"' (p. 30).

Some years ago, one of our former university colleagues decided to carry out a study into temporal variations in sexual intimacy. As part of this project, he issued diaries to staff in the Faculty and requested that they enter a tick in the relevant day each time they had sexual intercourse. Anonymity was guaranteed and diaries were to be returned through the Internal mail. Not surprisingly the results were erratic. The return rate was very low, and some individuals who did return their diaries seemed to have an impossibly prodigious rate of sexual activity! The study was abandoned. Interestingly, as a substitute method, he carried out a daily count of the number of condoms that appeared in the sedimentation tanks of the Belfast city sewage plant. After monitoring activity for a period of 333 days he produced his results, which showed a weekly rhythm as well as a seasonal fluctuation in mating frequency (Tittmar, 1978).

2　This latter study reveals a second problem, namely *the veracity of what is reported*. It is difficult to know whether respondents are reporting truthfully, or whether they have embroidered or reconstructed the actuality. For this reason, diaries are best used in conjunction with other audit methods, the data from which serve as a source of evidence for reliability checks.

3　*Another drawback is that what is termed 'sample maintenance' is low.* In other words, there is likely to be a high drop-out rate and hence a low level of returns. This increases in line with the complexity and duration of the observation period.

4　*The auditor needs to be aware of the possibility of 'reactance', which refers to the process whereby a research intervention can affect the subject.* Reactance is not peculiar to this method, but the ongoing nature of the diary approach means it is more likely to occur. Thus, the very task of having to complete a diary and analyse communications may in itself influence the respondent's thoughts, perceptions, feelings and behaviour. Breakwell and Wood (1995) gave as one example Freud's study of his dreams. When he started recording these, he found that he began to wake at points in the sleep cycle where he was able to remember the dream. In this way, the act of logging his dreams changed his sleep patterns.

When respondents begin to complete a diary, it can become a significant part of their daily activities. They may, for example, begin to initiate communications with others in order to be able to make more entries in their log. It can also make them very aware on a moment-by-moment basis of who is communicating with them, and to what effect. The act of recording and rating past communications may, in turn, affect the nature, purpose and content of future interactions. As Duck (1991, p. 153) put it: 'subjects' recall of communication influences their approach to those interactions by providing opportunities to recapitulate, ponder, or plan for the future'. The extent and impact of reactance are almost impossible to determine, but the auditor should take steps to minimise its effects. Respondents should be made aware of this phenomenon and encouraged to respond as naturally as possible. In audits of a prolonged duration, a reminder of the possibility of reactance should be included in mid-audit 'motivational' communications from the auditor to all respondents.

Optimising diaries and logs

In order to gain the maximum benefits from this method, the following points should be borne in mind:

- As with all audit methods, *planning is very important*. The auditor has to decide *who* is to be included in the analysis, *what* issues are to be investigated, and *how* data are to be recorded.
- Where numbers dictate that it is impossible to collect diaries from all staff, *a consistent sampling frame must be devised*. Some audit researchers argue that randomisation in this type of exercise in necessary to ensure a valid data set, and that 50 per cent of respondents in each work group should be audited (Porter, 1988). However, an alternative view was proposed by Goldhaber and Rogers (1979), who argued that purposive (or judgemental) sampling is a viable alternative to randomisation. There is no hard and fast rule here. In essence, the sampling method used will be determined by the objectives of the audit.
- *The content of the DCL should clearly reflect, and directly measure, the goals of the audit.* These can range across various issues, such as how often certain sections of the organisation communicate, what channels tend to be most and least used, the duration of communications, and so on.
- *Choose the most appropriate recording system for the target group.* More complex systems may be suitable for senior managers, but for shop-floor workers the method for recording data should be kept as simple as possible. In all cases, the layout of the DCL should look professional, and provide enough space for the data which has to be entered in each row/column. Another important factor is that the DCL must not appear daunting or off-putting to respondents. An initial 'gulp' response to first viewing of the sheets can set respondents to believe that the exercise is unrealistic and very difficult. The DCLs should therefore be thoroughly pilot-tested and modified to meet specific requirements before being shown to respondents.
- *Staff should be given as much preparation and training as possible in how to complete the logs.* The ideal is to have a training session with all respondents, during which one or more dummy runs are carried out. In fact, most sources regard training as an essential prerequisite to using this method. As expressed by Goldhaber and Rogers (1979, p. 30) 'The major lesson we have learned is to only use the diary when there are very good reasons, when specialized training is provided, and when adequate controls are possible.'
- *Accompanying instructions should be carefully designed and pilot tested.* These should be readily comprehensible and at a level appropriate for the target

audience. It is important to provide a contact telephone number (help-line) which respondents can use to clear up any queries they have.

- *It has been said that one picture is worth one thousand words and one example is worth one thousand pictures.* For this reason, it is useful to give respondents an example of a completed DCL, to illustrate what exactly is required. However, care should be taken to emphasise that this is not an exact template and that variations are acceptable.
- *Entries should be made as soon as possible after each communicative episode.* Delays in completing the logs tend to result in inaccuracies, since respondents then rely upon memory (a notoriously faulty faculty!). They also result in a higher number of incompletions, and an increased drop-out rate.
- *Regular contact with respondents is useful.* It helps to improve sample maintenance, and allows the auditor to answer any queries about the exercise.
- *Incentives, in the form of payments or inclusion in a prize lottery, also facilitate sample retention.*
- *If the objective is to obtain very detailed information on logs, it has been shown that it is best to use what is known as a foot-in-the-door approach* (Hargie *et al.*, 1999). This involves asking initially for brief details and then increasing the amount required once respondents have been involved for a period. So, the tactic is to begin with a relatively brief diary and then up the ante. When presented with what seems a very difficult task at the outset, the respondent drop-out rate is high. However, once they are committed to the audit exercise a request for some more detail does not seem so unreasonable.
- *Given the demands of this method, DCL audits should be time-limited.* In our experience, if respondents are asked to complete detailed forms for any more than one week, the drop-out rate becomes unacceptable.
- Finally, given the nature of this method, *DCLs are more appropriate for use with the upper echelons of an organisation.* Managers are used to form-filling and record-keeping and for them filling in DCL sheets becomes just another administrative task. However, shop-floor workers are less familiar with such bureaucratic niceties. If DCLs are to be used with the latter group their level of complexity should be kept to a minimum.

The data obtained from diary analysis can be most insightful, since they provide patterns of typical communicative encounters engaged in by relevant sections of the organisation (see Chapter 11). The results from this audit system are probably as close as it is possible to get to obtaining an overall picture of the pattern of communication within any organisation. How the results are analysed depends upon the exact purpose of the audit, and the precise nature of the information that has been gathered. Usually, both quantitative and qualitative analyses are possible. Furthermore, temporal, sequential and reciprocal matrices can be developed to provide communication network analyses from the results. For auditors who require intensive numerical investigation, detailed and specialised statistical analyses are available for analysing and interpreting diary-type data (see Norton, 1980; Porter, 1988; von Eye, 1990).

Box 6.2 Communication analysis sheets

Instructions for completion

On the sheets attached please record all communications received by you during the week **24–28 April**, inclusive, from other staff within the Organisation. Please list each communication in a separate numbered row. Give details under each heading as follows:

Source   – State whether the communication was from a middle manager, a senior manager or another member of staff. If the communication was not from management please specify the occupational group concerned.

Topic   – State the purpose of the communication

Channel   – State the communication channel (**face to face; telephone; fax; letter; memorandum; etc.**)

Length/   – State either the length of the communication (e.g. **2 page**
Duration   memorandum) or the duration (e.g. **5 minute** telephone call).

Feedback   – State whether the communication was **one way** and you were simply a recipient, or **two way** in that you were expected to respond with your views or give information.

Evaluation – Please rate how effective you feel each communication episode was from your perspective, using the following ratings:

        7 = Totally effective
        6 = Very effective
        5 = Quite effective
        4 = Neither effective nor ineffective
        3 = Quite ineffective
        2 = Very ineffective
        1 = Totally ineffective

Example of a diary audit

One audit that we conducted was concerned with the quality of communication across senior levels of the National Health Service (NHS) in one region of the UK (Hargie and Tourish, 1996a). Specifically, the audit examined communication at senior management levels between staff in the Region (R), District (D) and the Trusts (T) within that district. As part of this audit, DCLs were sent to all managers in order to chart communication patterns. These requested respondents to provide details of all communications received during a one-week period from the other two relevant sources (see Box 6.2 and Figure 6.2). Thus:

- T staff completed DCLs regarding their communications with R and D;
- R staff completed DCLs regarding their communications with D and T;
- D staff completed DCLs regarding their communications with T and R.

NAME ....   LOCATION ....

SOURCE	TOPIC	CHANNEL	LENGTH/ DURATION	FEEDBACK	EVALUATION
1					
2					
3					
4					
5					
6					
7					
8					
9					

Figure 6.2 Communication analysis sheet

Respondents were asked to list the source of the communication, the topic, the channel, the length or duration, whether it was one- or two-way, and finally to rate the effectiveness of the communication. A total of 40 per cent completed DCLs was received from D staff, 64 per cent from T staff; and 76 per cent from R staff. These figures were fairly representative of levels of communication between these three areas, with a high proportion of D staff indicating that they had no communication whatsoever with T or R during the week of the audit. The satisfactory level of returns in this investigation was facilitated by two strongly supportive letters sent to all staff from the Chief Executive Officer. One was delivered before the data collection period, and the second on the first day of the audit week.

An example of the type of results from this part of the audit is shown in Table 6.1. Communications recorded by T staff revealed an overall total of 195, of which 151 (77 per cent) were in writing, 31 (16 per cent) by telephone and 13 (7 per cent) face-to-face. While T staff rated communications as between 'quite'

Table 6.1 Results of DCLs completed by T staff

		R	D
Total communications		162	33
Average evaluation		5.2*	5.6*
Total two-way communications		83	
Total one-way communications		112	
Number/duration	Telephone n = 31	Average duration = 4.9 minutes	
of communications	Face-to-face n = 13	Average duration = 112 minutes	
	Written n = 151	Average length = 4.3 pages	

Scoring Key: 1 = Totally ineffective; 2 = Very ineffective; 3 = Quite ineffective; 4 = Neither effective nor ineffective; 5 = Quite effective; 6 = Very effective; 7 = Totally effective

and 'very' effective, those with D received a higher score than those from R. The results showed that a much larger proportion of the T communications was in writing and the average length of document dealt with was also lengthier at 4.3 pages (compared to 2.8 for R and 2.3 for D). Furthermore the T staff indicated that the bulk of these communications were one-way with no feedback required (whereas both R and D recorded a higher proportion of two-way communications). In fact, the lowest level of face-to-face contact was indicated by T staff, with only 13 (7 per cent) of their total communicative episodes via this channel (as opposed to 39 per cent for D and 27 per cent for R).

The interpretation of the results from the DCLs was further informed by the anticipated levels of contact, given the organisational structure, together with the responses to an accompanying detailed questionnaire. One picture to emerge from the results of this audit was that of T staff constantly communicating at length in the written medium, with a minority of their communications involving no response from others. We recommended that this finding be further investigated, given the potential for isolation raised by such a *modus operandi*. An overall analysis of the total of 364 communications recorded by all staff revealed that 197 (54 per cent) of these were written, 105 (29 per cent) were by telephone, and 62 (17 per cent) were face to face. Another of our recommendations therefore was that attention be paid to methods whereby the latter channel of communication could be more widely employed.

Thus, this diary method unearthed some very interesting findings and provided a rich seam of data. The results allowed senior managers to appraise their existing patterns of communication, and indicated areas of serious concern as well as existing strengths to be built upon. In addition to the diary, the results from the questionnaire administered in this study (Hargie and Tourish, 1996a) confirmed the trends identified in the DCLs.

UNDERCOVER AUDITING

One audit approach that has developed rapidly in recent years is that of 'mystery-customer research' (MCR). This technique, also known as 'mystery shopping' or 'service shopping', has been defined as 'the process wherein trained marketing research personnel go to establishments and evaluate their service standards and identify problem areas' (Burnside, 1994, p. 32). It involves observers (or 'shoppers') visiting (or telephoning) a location and 'acting' as consumers, while carefully noting the behaviour of the service provider. As the title of this section indicates, it is a form of 'undercover audit' wherein the assessor poses as a consumer and actually experiences the service. MCR is therefore a type of covert participant observation. This approach has been termed 'the "moment of truth" when the customer meets the salespeople' (Holbert and Speece, 1993, p. 93). MCR now operates in a wide range of both private and public sectors, including finance, automotive, food, hotel, leisure and tourism, retail, telecommunications, the utilities, and local government (Miller, 1998). It is a major industry, with an estimated £30 million being spent on this service per year in the UK alone (Wilson, 1998).

Historically, MCR has its roots in the field of cultural anthropology, where anthropologists lived as part of a tribe in order to gain an in-depth insight into their patterns of living (Wilson and Gutmann, 1998). The key aspect here was that the researcher actually *experienced* what was happening. Similarly, the important dimension of MCR is that the person acts just like a 'real' consumer and plays out the entire scenario in this role. Only afterwards are detailed notes taken. Usually some form of data collection log-sheet (DCL) is used to structure the audit. This is not displayed in the location, but is completed immediately following the visit. The DCL may also be a hand-held computer into which the results are entered, since this can facilitate later analysis. The exact nature of observation depends upon the context. In a sales context it would include questions such as:

- How long was it before a salesperson approached you?
- Did the salesperson offer a greeting or other welcoming remarks?
- Did the salesperson engage in eye contact throughout the interaction?
- Did the salesperson close the encounter with a friendly comment?

In the banking sector (Leeds, 1995) the investigator scrutinises actions such as whether the member of staff:

✓ shakes hands
✓ smiles
✓ offers a seat
✓ presents a business card
✓ asks relevant questions
✓ recommends the best product to meet the presented needs
✓ asks for the business

✓ helps in completing the application form
✓ offers a follow-up service

In other locations the mystery shopper will observe situation-specific aspects such as whether:

✓ shelves in a supermarket are well stocked
✓ ashtrays in a pub are frequently emptied
✓ a sales assistant in a fashion store offers help within two minutes
✓ background music is being played in a restaurant
✓ prices are clearly displayed in a car showroom
✓ all ticket machines in a train station are in working order
✓ a telephone call to a company is answered within six rings

Part of the inspection may involve a request being made (e.g. seeking assistance, asking a specific question about a product), followed by careful monitoring as to how it is dealt with. Alternatively, the assessor may be sent to an outlet to audit an entire procedure, such as going to a bank and opening an account, visiting a local tourist attraction, or actually purchasing a specific item from a shop. In the latter case, this will apply only if the cost is not prohibitive. For example, if the investigation were into the standard of service in a luxury car showroom, then obviously a purchase would not be feasible! In such instances, the evaluator backs off just before the point of commitment.

Box 6.3 The main purposes of MCR

To:
1 identify the extent to which consumer needs are being met
2 chart precise strengths and weaknesses in current practice
3 assess whether new initiatives have been implemented on the ground
4 check for consistency of standards across outlets
5 inform performance incentive schemes and guide the payment of bonuses
6 evaluate the effectiveness of staff training programmes
7 enable managers and staff to improve overall performance

Cobb (1997) identified a number of key objectives served by MCR (Box 6.3), while Cramp (1994) enumerated four operational fundamentals of the process (Box 6.4). In fact, the following key steps are essential to promote an effective mystery shopping process (Biere, 1998; Leeds, 1995):

1 *Define clearly the specific goals of the process at the outset.* Also, determine in advance how problems will be resolved if and when they are identified. To fail to prepare at this stage is to prepare to fail.

Box 6.4 Four main fundamentals of MCR

- *Realism.* It should mirror reality. Thus, if 80 per cent of consumers are couples, then two evaluators should visit the location together.
- *Unobtrusive.* The shopper should not create a scene or pose unusual difficulties for the person being assessed.
- *Objectivity.* The main purpose of the evaluation should be to check measurable aspects of the service. While some subjectivity may be permissible, this should be kept to a minimum.
- *Consistency.* Shoppers should receive rigorous training to ensure consistency of evaluation across outlets. Everyone should be measuring the same things in the same way.

---

2 *Design the programme specifically to meet the set goals.* The standards against which personnel are to be judged need to be clearly delineated. These should then be explained fully to staff so that they know exactly what is expected of them. They should also be as specific and objective as possible. For example 'Was your meal served within twenty minutes of being seated?' is high in objectivity, whereas 'Were the staff friendly?' entails an element of subjectivity. Questions such as the latter need more detailed specification ('Did the waiter smile?', 'Were you asked if your meal was OK?', etc.). Assessment drives effort. But if staff do not know what benchmarks are being employed they cannot endeavour to shape their behaviour in this direction. These standards must be agreed and supported by staff – this is absolutely essential. Ideally, staff should be involved in their identification.

3 *A DCL measurement system that is simple, yet robust, should be developed, and fully pre-tested to ensure it is both reliable and valid.* For example, Burnside (1994) describes how Victoria Wine actively involved both customers and staff in the eventual identification of 34 key service aspects for measurement across all outlets, in its 'Working Together for Customers' quality programme. Following initial testing, a weighting process was applied to ensure that different types of outlet were judged fairly in relation to one another. Results from visits were quickly fed back to staff who then demonstrated a commitment to improving service through a range of identified actions.

4 *Select the appropriate type of auditor for the location being assessed.* Some organisations recruit evaluators from their own client base rather than using professional contract ones. This has a number of advantages. It means that feedback comes from a 'real' user's perspective, that staff are less likely to identify auditors (since these are actual clients), and it is usually more cost-effective than employing outside consultants. In selecting auditors, Cobb (1997) recommended that they should:

- represent the same geodemographic spread as actual consumers – thus, if consumers are both male and female, auditors of both gender should be employed.
- possess qualities such as good retentive memory and high levels of visual and aural observation skills. While there is evidence that females are more accurate in this type of evaluation, it is also the case that males and females are often dealt with differently, and so males need to be used as evaluators and may require more extensive training (Morrison *et al.*, 1997).
- not be over-aggressive personalities – professional complainers are not appropriate!
- behave appropriately. The objective is to allow staff to perform to their optimum level, not to put them under stress. It is certainly not the role of the auditor to be an *agent provocateur*, deliberately creating difficulties for the service provider.

5 *Tell staff that they will be shopped (but not exactly when or by whom).* Staff may initially display negative reactions and these have to be handled sensitively. The exact purposes of the programme should be explained, and the actual DCL to be used should be given to all staff. The positive aspects (e.g. incentives and rewards) should be highlighted. Reassurance needs to be given that, when analysing and interpreting the audit findings, the emphasis will be placed on overall trends, and that the results will not be used as an employability criterion.

6 *Thoroughly train the auditors.* Inform them fully about the exact goals of the exercise (e.g. compliance with set procedures, part of a bonus payment initiative). If it is to be reliable, then evaluators need to receive extensive training in observation and recording methods. There are well documented cognitive processes, including attentional focus, attitudinal biases, conformity pressures, knowledge base, and expectancy effects, which influence the extent to which the observer will be objective and therefore effective (Morrison *et al.*, 1997). Training can help to overcome these contaminating factors. It is especially important where a team is employed to simultaneously investigate different sites within the same organisation. All assessors should receive the same standardised training, and preliminary reliability checks should be made to ensure that their reports are comparable and compatible.

7 *Implement an ongoing programme of evaluations.* There is research to show that performance gains are significantly greater where regular consumer auditing, rather than sporadic or one-off appraisals, takes place (Biere, 1998). The aim should be that of a continuous improvement cycle. An infrequent system of evaluation provides only a limited insight, and perhaps even an inaccurate or unrepresentative snapshot, of performance (all staff have off-days!).

8 *Link the results of mystery shopping directly to incentive schemes to motivate and reward staff.* It should be clear that exceptional performance will be rewarded, so that carrots rather than sticks are very much in evidence. What gets measured and rewarded generally gets done, hence the effectiveness of

this method. Some organisations actually link their surveys to employee contests complete with accompanying rewards for 'winners'. These rewards range from letters from senior management, through 'congratulations' notices (e.g. employee of the month) prominently displayed, to actual monetary rewards. Care needs to be taken here, however, since the introduction of such performance-related rewards may result in jealousy or resentment, and so be counter-productive to the fostering of a good team spirit. Indeed, the available evidence suggests that performance-related pay demotivates staff, does not help organisations keep their best people or get rid of their worst performers, and generally creates a feeling of injustice (Hargie *et al.*, 1999).

9 *Provide detailed results in a concise, comprehensible and actionable format, highlighting both strengths and weaknesses.* The objective is not just to collect data, but rather to allow the information gathered to be converted into action plans, which will then effect improvements in performance.

10 *As part of the MCR process, it is important that supervisors as well as first line staff receive briefings and training* (Leeds, 1992). This should include training in how to interpret findings and what their implications are.

The mystery shopper method provides a more direct, detailed, scientific and structured approach than simply asking consumers to recall their experiences (Hague and Jackson, 1995). As summarised by Chisnall (1997, p. 46), 'when undertaken with sufficiently large samples and systematically organized MCR can provide valuable insights'. In addition, there are bottom line benefits. Biere (1998) describes how financial institutions that implemented MCR raised their performance levels by some 20 per cent inside 15 months. In noting such developments, Miller (1998, p. 27) argues that 'Mystery shopping is finally shedding its cloak-and-dagger image and has become a mainstream market-research technique that companies cannot afford to ignore.'

MCR as espionage

A variation on this theme is that of 'competitor mystery shopping', where an assessor from one company visits rival outlets to note how well they handle consumers, and to learn from them if possible. In other words, this method is employed as a form of industrial 'espionage'. It has been employed in this way for years by consumer magazines such as *Which* and *Money Magazine* to report to subscribers on the performance of different companies. The technique has witnessed an ever-increasing usage.

For example, Holbert and Speece (1993) illustrated how before the hotel chain Marriott launched its subsidiary, the Fairfield Inn chain, they sent a team on a six-month intelligence mission to gather information on existing hotels with which they would be competing in the same price band. Strengths and weaknesses of all aspects of the competitors, from check-in, to sound-proofing in bedrooms, toiletries in the bathroom, and through to check-out, were carefully itemised. As a result, the design and service standards of the Fairfield Inn chain were based on solid research evidence. The success of this chain proved that the investment was worth while.

Another variant here is 'matched pair' auditing. In this procedure, two auditors, similar in most respects but with at least one vital difference, both visit the same location. In the USA, the Equal Credit Opportunity Act (ECOA) prohibits discrimination in lending. To monitor the implementation of the ECOA, a matched pair of assessors (e.g. one African-American and one non-minority) will separately visit a bank to enquire about a loan (Leeds, 1995). The results from their experiences are checked and compared for differences, and if any occur further evaluations are then carried out to check for a possible pattern of differential treatment. A similar matched pairs procedure can be followed to determine bias in the treatment of those of different gender, age, and so on.

Finally, in the medical sphere there is what is known as the 'pseudo patient' method. This was used in an early study by Rosenhan (1973). He and seven of his students had themselves admitted to different mental hospitals. They each said they had heard voices and were diagnosed as schizophrenic. The average length of stay was 19 days. None of the staff spotted the fact that they were being deceived, although about a third of the patients did. The psychiatrists did not change their initial diagnoses, but marked the case notes of the 'patients' as 'schizophrenia in remission'. Among their interesting findings was that when a patient and psychiatrist met casually the latter only made eye contact on 29 per cent of the occasions. When casual meetings between strangers were surveyed, eye contact always occurred. In the sphere of general hospitals, mystery shopping also occurs (Meyer, 1997). Here, a pseudo patient checks into hospital, and, posing as a patient with a specific complaint, undergoes everything from X-rays to blood tests. Over a typical two-day stay a detailed check is made of the behaviour of staff in admissions, the emergency department, nursing, human resources, security and maintenance, as well as other facilities such as car parking, food services and housekeeping.

Ethical issues

There are several ethical dilemmas surrounding the MCR audit method (Cramp, 1994). First, staff time and effort is wasted in dealing with a 'false' client. Thus, in the hospital example cited above, the valuable skills of health professionals are spent dealing with a 'phoney' patient, when they could have been devoted to genuinely sick individuals. Furthermore, where a worker's pay is linked to bonuses (e.g. in the automotive trade) this wasted effort is especially unfair, and some would argue morally untenable, since it literally costs the person part of their wages.

Second, there is a strong odour of dishonesty about the entire process. Since it entails 'undercover testing' (Leeds, 1995), it is a form of secretive inspection regime which smacks of sneaking, snooping and subterfuge. Is it really justifiable for management to send incognito assessors on the sly to check up on their personnel? Companies respond to this criticism by arguing that they always inform staff that MCR will be taking place, and that the evaluations then occur with their informed consent. Indeed, some organisations regularly use mystery shoppers, and so staff know that at some stage the person in front of them will in fact be a 'spy'. In other cases, the company tells staff that within a set time-frame (e.g. three months) they will be audited by a trained evaluator posing as a real client. However, this 'informed consent' is not consent at all. Staff cannot really refuse to be investigated. In some instances the process of MCR actually forms part of the contract of employment. If you want the job you accept the assessment – it is not negotiable. An interesting point of speculation here is how managers would feel if trade unions adopted mystery shopping methods to monitor management performance!

Third, there are reservations about the effects of the procedure upon the evaluators. Rawlins (1998, p. 376) notes the dangers of a system where: 'Cloaking oneself while scrutinizing others, the detached observer achieves a sense of vicarious social connection, without assuming any obligations to other persons or for mutually beneficial comportment.' Indeed, it can be argued that the mystery shopper is a relative of the paid informer. Where undercover operations are for the wider good of society they are morally acceptable. However, when they are designed primarily to improve the profit margins of a corporation they are at the very least ethically questionable. The assessors are at the cutting edge of the entire process and are likely at some stage to have qualms of conscience about their activities.

Fourth, the ramifications of MCR for those being assessed have to be considered. The knowledge that someone will eventually appear and pose as a consumer is bound to affect staff behaviour. There is an inevitable (if not always conscious) grain of ingratiation, coupled with a sprinkling of suspicion as consumers are dealt with. This was humorously depicted in the classic sitcom *Fawlty Towers* by the behaviour of the hotel owner Basil Fawlty, as he reacted towards guests he viewed as possible inspectors. MCR is regularly used to monitor the performance of service staff who are already under severe pressure because of what has been termed 'emotional labour' (Briner, 1998). This term is used to describe the form of employment in which the employee is expected to constantly display a certain type of affect (e.g. the friendly, smiling hotel receptionist). The long-term pressure of this emotional labour, coupled with the effects of being spied upon intermittently, is a matter for conjecture, but few of us would relish the prospect. As expressed some years ago by Selltiz *et al.* (1976):

> the investigator who proposes to enter a situation without revealing his research purpose has an obligation to ask himself whether there is any possibility that his disguised activities will harm any of the people in the situation and if so, whether the potential results of his research are valuable enough to justify their acquisition under these circumstances.
>
> (Selltiz *et al.*, 1976, p. 218)

Finally, there is a growing and worrying trend towards maximum surveillance of people at work – what has been termed the 'Big Brother syndrome' in organisations (Milne, 1999). Employers are increasingly checking on all aspects of the work of staff, by logging telephone calls, checking e-mails, and monitoring behaviour on hidden spy cameras. This, in turn, can lead to an erosion of the workforce's individual and collective autonomy (Ford, 1999). The use of MCR is another example of this surveillance mindset. What managers need to remember is that employees who perceive themselves to be not trusted will be less loyal. They are also likely to rise to the perceived challenge of devising ways of beating the surveillance system (Webb and Palmer, 1998).

In competitive mystery shopping several suggestions have been made (Dawson and Hillier, 1995) to help reduce the associated ethical problems. Indeed, in the UK, the Market Research Society (1997) has produced a booklet specifically designed to encourage ethical usage and best practice in MCR. Among the key recommendations are:

✓ Staff must be informed that MCR will be occurring, and what it involves, if reporting is at an outlet or individual level.
✓ If staff are to be identified individually this should be part of their contracts.
✓ Clearance should also be sought from unions or other relevant staff associations.
✓ The results should not be used to discipline staff.
✓ Staff should not attempt to 'evaluator spot', to avoid any interference with genuine customers.
✓ Evaluators should be thoroughly trained.
✓ The assessor should spend no longer than a normal consumer in any outlet or on any telephone call.
✓ Visits or telephone calls should not be tape recorded.
✓ An item should be purchased where possible.
✓ No follow-up action should be requested.
✓ Visits should not be made at busy periods.
✓ No more that one visit per quarter should be made.

While these ethical guidelines, if fully implemented, help to offset the concerns about MCR, they have their limitations. In practice, they are often ignored. For example, in her analysis of the area Miller (1998) cited the positive views expressed by industry personnel from various fields. One of these sources states that: 'One of mystery shopping's benefits is that you often get recordings of people doing wonderful jobs which you can use as an example to others.' So much for the ethical principle above, about no use of tape recordings! Also, one wonders what usage is made of the tapes when a member of staff is not perceived to be doing a good job. Similarly, Leeds (1992, p. 25), in discussing the need to optimise MCR outcomes, argues that supervisors need to be trained 'to interpret the mystery shopper's findings, how to correct mistakes, and how to discipline'. Again, such advice flies in the face of the above ethical guideline that MCR should *not* be used as part of the discipline process. We personally know of organisations that check on how their staff respond to telephone enquiries, by audio-recording calls from mystery shoppers. These recordings are then used as part of the ongoing feedback and discipline cycle with staff.

Clearly, there are strengths and weaknesses associated with MCR. A major drawback is the lack of hard evidence as to the effectiveness of this approach. As noted by Morrison *et al.* (1997, p. 351) 'Published data on the accuracy (reliability and validity) of mystery customer research appear to be non-existent.' However, it is widely used, popular across a wide range of sectors, and when rigorously implemented does seem to produce performance improvements. It is therefore not likely to disappear. Detailed research is needed into all aspects of the process including the design of DCLs, and the effects of age, gender, race, and other geodemographic variables on the assessment procedure.

There is also a need for a strict ethical code to determine its use. In analysing some of the issues involved, Miles (1993) quoted one person involved in the business of MCR as saying 'We are trying to find a compromise between high moral tone and pragmatism.' The worry, of course, is that in the world of business, pragmatism usually wins. It may be for these reasons that some European countries are less enthusiastic about MCR than their UK and US counterparts. Thus, trade unions in Germany and France regard mystery shopping as a threat, and in the former country objections have been raised on data protection grounds.

Anyone using this audit approach treads a fine line between the desire for hard data about how clients are actually being dealt with, and an awareness that such information arrives in questionable ethical baggage. MCR is more acceptable when the audit is at outlet level, and the results do not 'finger' specific individuals. Problems can then be dealt with by local management in a low-key rather than high-profile manner. In general, it is our view that auditors should only use MCR if there are no viable alternatives, and when they do so they should ensure that proper ethical safeguards are put in place – and adhered to.

CONCLUSION

In this chapter we have reviewed two separate types of audit method, both of which have been employed extensively in many differing contexts. They are similar in that the core methodology involves the completion of carefully designed log-sheets. A major difference is that in one case the process is one of self-report by the individual involved, while the other involves an evaluation of a member of staff by a trained observer. The first, diaries and logs, requires that staff analyse their own communications on a pre-set sheet as soon as possible after they occur. In the second, undercover auditing, an observer pretending to be a consumer engages in an interaction with a member of staff and immediately afterwards fills in an assessment form.

Although the DCL methods described in this chapter do not analyse behaviour *in vivo*, in the absence of video or audio recordings they are as close as it is possible to get to charting the topography of organisational communications. Both methods have strengths and weaknesses. Self-reports are prone to inaccuracy. We all reconstruct to some extent when asked to recount our experiences – and we usually do so to show ourselves in a better light! Bias in diaries is therefore to be expected and anticipated. With proper pilot-testing of the DCLs, coupled with preparation and training of respondents, such effects can be minimised. In the case of MCR, there are problems of intra- and inter-observer reliability, but again these can be lessened by rigorous field-testing and training of auditors. A more serious issue here is the dubious nature of the ethics of using subterfuge to collect data, unbeknown to the person being investigated.

Chapter 7

Auditing professional practice

Owen Hargie and Dennis Tourish

> Audit is the latest example of a drive in social policy over the last decade towards evaluation, particularly in the area of assessment of performance.
>
> (R. Malby, 1995, p. 9)

INTRODUCTION

The audit principle is now very familiar in all professions. Financial audit, medical audit, clinical audit, organisational audit, and so on, are all commonplace terms (Baker *et al.*, 1999). Likewise, the concept of communication audit is well recognised and accepted by most professional bodies. Indeed, the audit approach has developed rapidly in relation to the analysis of the interpersonal performance of a wide range of professionals. Much of this development was initiated in the 1980s, a time when changes were sweeping through the professions. Prior to this, as Marinker (1986) pointed out:

> professional standards were very much a matter for the professions themselves. They were jealously guarded not only by professional institutions but by individual conscience. The move from private to public accountability is . . . best understood in relation to the growth of information in society, and a new sophistication among members of the public.
>
> (Marinker, 1986, p. 15)

As the public demanded better service from professionals, methods had to be found to satisfy this demand. The reason for this is simply that 'The evaluation of professional practice is central to every aspect of the organisation, delivery and quality of services' (Reid, 1988, p. 230).

Audits of professional practice occur at all levels. An example of a small-scale audit is that conducted by Markar and Mahadeshwar (1998) into written communications between two professional groups – GPs and psychiatrists – in relation to the outpatient assessment of patients with learning disabilities. In a more comprehensive audit study, Skipper and Hargie interviewed all health professionals associated with a particular clinic in a large hospital (see Chapter 11). At a general level, government-backed audits have been implemented. Thus, in the UK the Audit Commission regularly investigates various parts of the public services and produces detailed reports on their findings. In 1994 they published two major reports. The first found a wide disparity with respect to how effectively local council authorities answered telephones and letters from members of the public, and made recommendations regarding acceptable standards in this area (Audit Commission, 1994a). The second highlighted poor communication as a key factor in the under-performance of National Health Service Trusts (Audit Commission, 1994b). In the same year a major survey of the communication objectives and practices of chief executives in the NHS was conducted by the Office for Public Management (1994), which pinpointed strengths and weaknesses in both internal and external communications.

Likewise, in 1993 the Audit Commission carried out a detailed audit of acute general hospitals in England and Wales. This set standards as to what patients were entitled to expect in hospital, and measured these against the actuality. This audit examined, *inter alia*:

- patient information leaflets;
- hospital notice boards and signposts;
- telephone communications with patients;
- written communications from hospitals to patients;
- the discharge process;
- the main problems experienced by patients – both practical in terms of being in hospital and clinical in relation to their consultations with health professionals;
- patient complaints and how hospitals deal with them;
- how the specific problems faced by non-English-speaking patients are handled.

Some of the above are quite basic, yet very important, elements of communication. For example, signposts should be clearly marked, large enough to read easily, consistent (all the signs for a location should point in the same direction – this is not always the case!), and simple. There is no point in having a map with a red circle declaring 'You are here' if the person cannot figure out how to get from 'here' to their destination. Likewise notice boards are an often forgotten communication medium. In their review of a number of audits, Hargie *et al.* (1994) found that these were usually ignored by staff. Common complaints about boards were that they were over-posted, disorganised, or plastered with out-of-date or useless notices. Furthermore, they were often felt to be in the wrong location. To avoid such chaos, a designated member of staff must be given responsibility for the management of each board, keeping it tidy, removing irrelevant or out-of-date notices, and having a categorisation system for information displayed. Like all animals, humans are territorial and do not like to move too far away from habitual paths and lairs. Boards should therefore be positioned in a central part of the 'patch' of staff for whom they are intended.

The utility of the Audit Commission's approach can be illustrated by examining only one small part of the 1993 hospital audit. This investigated the treatment received by female outpatients with breast lumps who were referred to hospital for clinical examination. Eight key treatment standards were formulated and 12 consultant surgeons were then audited on these. As shown below, the results revealed few surgeons using each standard, as indicated by the numbers in parentheses:

1 Written information used (n = 1)
2 Discussion of radiotherapy before a decision taken on surgery (n = 2)
3 Patient dressed on meeting the surgeon (n = 2)
4 Nurse included in the discussion of treatment (n = 3)
5 Patient dressed for discussion of the prognosis (n = 4)
6 Patient invited to bring a companion (n = 6)
7 More than one chance to discuss the treatment (n = 6)
8 Consultant working with a breast nurse (n = 7)

One surgeon did not score on *any* of the standards, three scored on only one, and the best score was one surgeon who used seven out of the eight. Furthermore, the Audit Commission found that the clinical protocol usually involved the patients arriving at hospital, being asked by a nurse to strip naked, medical staff arriving and not introducing themselves by name, conducting the entire procedure – including medical history, reasons for referral, clinical examination, and treatment options – all with the patient undressed and usually lying on the treatment couch with only a sheet to cover her. The conclusion was that such a 'way of conducting the consultation strips patients of their dignity as well as their clothes, and because it increases their feelings of vulnerability, makes it even more difficult for them to focus on what is being said and questions to ask' (p. 26). Not surprisingly, when interviewed, patients expressed considerable dissatisfaction with their treatment.

A system for auditing GP surgeries was devised by the Royal College of General Practitioners, which involved two assessors visiting the surgery for one day (Schofield and Pendleton, 1986). This procedure involves six main steps:

1 a general analysis of the overall profile of the practice;
2 direct observation of the facilities, equipment, and functioning of the practice;
3 discussions with ancillary staff and all of the practice healthcare team;
4 inspections of all written records, indexes and registers;
5 a review of video recordings of some of the doctor's recent consultations with patients, together with relevant records and the doctor's summary;
6 an in-depth and comprehensive interview with the doctor.

Various audit methodologies have therefore been employed in studies designed to monitor, evaluate and improve the communication performance of professionals across a broad spectrum. Indeed, all of the methods covered in the previous chapters are relevant. Questionnaire surveys, in-depth interviews, focus groups, diary logs, and undercover methods have all been utilised to gauge information about professional practice. For example, in the pharmacy profession alone, questionnaire and interview surveys have been conducted to determine consumer views (e.g. Hargie *et al.*, 1992); pharmacist self-report measures of performance have also been employed (e.g. Povey *et al.*, 1990); and the undercover approach has been utilised to test pharmacist responses to patients presenting with specific problems (e.g. Consumers' Association, 1991).

This chapter examines two further methods for examining professional practice; namely, the critical incident technique and constitutive ethnography. It also briefly describes a third approach, the Delphi technique.

CRITICAL INCIDENT TECHNIQUE

This is a specific methodology which is used to educe concrete instances of effective and ineffective behaviour in any context. It is based upon the view that internal feelings of satisfaction or dissatisfaction with a person, profession or organisation are the result of actual experiences. In particular, the way in which events that are 'out of the ordinary' are experienced are central to judgement formation, and lead to the eventual attribution of positive or negative attitudes towards the source. These attitudes then influence how future encounters are 'seen', categorised, and responded to. This perspective was neatly summarised by the former British Prime Minister, Benjamin Disraeli: 'Experience is the child of Thought, and Thought is the child of Action.'

When asked for a 'critical' example, it is argued, the experience which is chosen reflects a wider general view about how the person feels – the incident is retrieved from the relevant memory 'file'. An exploration of what individuals see as important experiences, or incidents, therefore provides pertinent information about their attitudes to a particular group of people, or to an organisation in general. It also offers practical insight into key areas of both good and dysfunctional performance. As a simple example, we expect things to progress normally when we go for a meal to a restaurant. But what happens when the waiter spills a bottle of red wine over your new suit? How such a 'critical' incident is handled by the manager and staff will have a key impact upon your attitude to the restaurant.

The critical incident (CI) method was pioneered by Flanagan (1948, 1954), who first used it to investigate the specific competencies of air pilots in the Second World War. He asked experienced pilots to reflect back on the last time they saw a trainee pilot do something that was effective or ineffective (i.e. the 'critical incident') and then to answer three main questions:

- What led up to this situation?
- What exactly did the man do?
- Why was it effective/ineffective?

Based upon their responses it was possible to identify actual instances of positive and negative behaviours, which in turn led to a compilation of key pilot competencies. Following the early pioneering work of Flanagan, thousands of investigations have been carried out using this approach. The CI procedure itself involves three main phases (Caves, 1988):

1 *Defining the target population.* The main issue here is how precise to be in setting the parameters for inclusion. There is a tradeoff between exclusivity of focus and generalisability of findings – the 'bandwidth-fidelity problem' as it is often referred to. For example, in a study of the key skills of lawyers the researcher would have to consider the types of specialism and range of functions of different members of the profession. Decisions would then have to be taken about whether to include *all* qualified lawyers in a single study, or to have separate studies for those specialising in specific areas (corporation, litigation, etc.). Other decisions would have to be made, for instance about whether prosecuting counsel and public defenders should be studied separately.

   The next issue is who to employ as the 'subject matter experts' (SMEs) (Anderson and Wilson, 1997) who will identify and analyse the incidents. In most studies this is usually restricted to experienced practitioners and in-structors. However, consumers and other professional groups can also provide informed insight. For instance, in one study of the role of the cancer nurse, the expertise of patients, carers, nurses and doctors was all gleaned and combined to identify key competencies (Cox *et al.*, 1993).

2 *Obtaining the description of incidents.* Two factors need to be considered here. First, how many incidents in total should be collected? Second, what method should be used for collecting them? There is no correct answer to either question. In relation to overall number, Caves (1988, p. 206) noted how in most studies 'the usual practice has been to seek refuge in large numbers of incidents'. However, the larger the sample size, the fewer the incidents required from each person. In general, between two and four incidents seems to be the upper and lower limits of studies which have used CI (Dunn and Hamilton, 1986; Lount and Hargie, 1997). In relation to the method for collecting data, there are two main alternatives, questionnaires and interviews (see Chapters 3 and 4 for a full review of each method).

   Where the latter approach is adopted, SMEs need to be notified well in advance about what is expected of them. They should have identified and thought carefully about the incidents *prior to the interview or questionnaire completion.* Interviews should be recorded for later transcription and analysis, with the role of interviewer being that of guide, facilitator and listener. Anderson and Wilson (1997) recommend using workshops to collect CIs. They advise that each workshop should last for three hours, the first 30 minutes of which is devoted to training; there should be 10–20 SMEs per session, with each individual attending only one workshop. The advantage of this group approach is that

Box 7.1 Identification of critical incidents in practice

Think of one or more occasions recently where you witnessed good or poor communication practice. Under each of the following headings, describe *exactly* what happened.

Where did the event take place?

Who were the people involved?

What features of the individuals were important in the interaction?

What actually occurred in the interaction?

What was the outcome?

Why was the interaction considered to be effective/ineffective?

What were the implications of this incident for interpersonal communication performance?

it saves time – one explanation of the CI methodology suffices for up to 20 SMEs.

Regardless of which approach is adopted, the guidelines identified by Dickson *et al.* (1997) (Box 7.1) provide a useful data collection template. When asked to select a critical incident, SMEs should be told to select an example that (a) deviates significantly in either a positive or negative fashion from the norm and (b) can be described in detail (Bejou *et al.*, 1996).

3 *Identifying the competencies.* This is a very important stage of the process. It involves careful content analysis to convert the data obtained into discrete and clearly distinguishable competencies. In practice, this task is almost always completed by the researchers, both because of its time-consuming nature and the data analysis skills required. However, Caves (1988) strongly advises that the SMEs should also be involved at some stage, ideally to help to validate the content validity of the final list of competencies. In other words, the 'insider' knowledge of professionals is useful to complement the more 'objective' perspective of the researcher.

A case study will help to illuminate the discussion at this point. In their study of the priesthood, Lount and Hargie (1997) used the CI technique to identify key interpersonal skills of Catholic priests. Having negotiated access with the bishop of one diocese in Ireland, they randomly selected 33 priests, representing 25 per cent of the total number of priests in the diocese. These SMEs were contacted by telephone and, having agreed to participate, were asked to think in advance about personal experiences of what for them were important communication incidents in their work. This procedure was employed to give the priests time to reflect on key experiences and so reduce the likelihood of trivial incidents being selected. The priests were then interviewed by the researchers in the former's environment and were assured of absolute confidentiality. The standard format for this type of interview was followed (see Box 7.1).

A total of 184 critical incidents was obtained from the interviews. Analysis of these showed that they included 84 different types of people (from an architect to an undertaker), and 15 main categories of problem. The most frequently reported problem dealt with was that of marital disharmony, followed by bereavement. In dealing with such problems, priests used a total of 89 different interpersonal skills. A list of the 25 most reported skills was then compiled and sent to all 135 priests in the diocese, who were asked to rate each skill on a five-point scale, and then to identify and rank order what they considered to be the five most important skills. The analysis of these data then allowed the researchers to compile a final schedule of the key skills as perceived by priests themselves. Of these, the top five were listening, understanding, honesty, confidentiality, and showing care/concern. These data formed part of an overall audit of professional practice in the priesthood (see Chapter 13).

The simple, yet robust, nature of the CI method has led to its widespread usage across a wide variety of contexts, including, *inter alia*, dentistry, nursing, teaching, university lecturing, speech therapy, medicine, surgery, pharmacy, the priesthood and management (Lount, 1997). The exact purposes of research studies employing this methodology vary far and wide. For example, in the professional sphere it has been used to:

- investigate the perceptions of nurses, other health professionals, residents of old people's dwellings and their families, as to the most important dimensions of the nurse's contribution to the care of the aged (Cheek *et al.*, 1997);
- survey training directors of APA-accredited programmes in the USA and Canada about the exact nature and implications of ethical transgressions made by psychology graduate students (Fly *et al.*, 1997);
- chart the factors taken into consideration by professionals working in family courts when they make their final decision about where a child should reside (Banach, 1998).

The method can also be used to audit external publics. For example the CI method has been used to:

- ascertain patient satisfaction or dissatisfaction levels with various aspects of their care (Pryce-Jones, 1993)
- identify the precise factors that provoked customers of service firms to switch their patronage from one outlet to another (Keaveney, 1995)
- determine the effects of service failures on customer attitudes to airlines (Bejou *et al.*, 1996)
- distinguish situations in which the emotional needs of patients attending a cancer unit were not met by staff (Kent *et al.*, 1996)
- detail the impact which the presence of other customers had upon individuals in a shared service environment (Grove and Fisk, 1997)
- chart the specific business-to-business context of problems experienced by buyers in retail wine outlets (off-licences, pubs, hotels, restaurants, etc.) in their dealings with wine suppliers (Lockshin and McDougall, 1998).

Using the critical incidents technique within organisations

In the specific communication audit context, the CI method has been widely employed. As noted by Downs (1988, p. 133) 'The technique is well respected and it can be a valuable audit tool.' However, interestingly, he changed the Communication Satisfaction Questionnaire section title from 'Critical Communication Experience' to 'Communication Experience'. This was after receiving negative feedback from senior management who baulked at the connotations associated with the term 'critical', perceiving it to be an appeal to respondents to record only negative experiences. We have found a similar response from senior staff with whom we have worked on audits, coupled with confusion from respondents about the exact meaning of 'critical' (particularly when conducting audits in the health sector!). As a result, and while the method remains exactly the same, we recommend that auditors use the term 'Communication Experience' to gather data about critical incidents (see the main questionnaire in the Appendix).

The data gleaned from this part of the questionnaire reveal some very important information (Tourish and Hargie, 1996c). First, a comparison can be made of how many reported instances are effective and how many are ineffective instances of communication. This then provides a rough measure of the overall communication climate. If the vast proportion of reported examples are overwhelmingly negative, then there are clearly problems with communications. In organisations where communications are functioning reasonably well, one would expect an effective/ineffective ratio of at least 50/50 to prevail. Higher or lower ratios provide a useful barometer of communication pressures. Second, the sources of effective or ineffective communication can be delineated. A detailed examination of responses will reveal exactly where these high and low pressure points are located. For example, in one audit we found that the overwhelming source of dissatisfaction was not with working colleagues or managers, but with a service department within the company. We were therefore able to identify the exact department and the precise reasons for dissatisfaction. In essence, what the service department viewed as priorities did not concur with the views of staff in the recipient departments. Consequently, new standards of service were agreed and monitored to overcome the problem.

While, in general, this method is used to give respondents complete freedom to select whatever example they wish, in some audits the focus is narrowed to specific areas. For instance, SMEs may be asked to focus specifically upon a staff group (such as communication with managers or with staff from other sites), or a communication medium (such as telephone or e-mail), and restrict their example entirely to that category. In fact, the original ICA Audit Questionnaire had a 'critical incident' sheet attached to *every* section, so that respondents had to provide a separate incident relating to channels of information, sources of information, and so on. However, in our experience this amounts to overkill, and the time and duplication required to complete all of these incident sections meets with resistance from managers and staff alike. On the other hand, the inclusion of a single incident allows respondents the freedom to select from all of their experiences what they consider to be most typical of communication in their organisation. As a consequence, this one section often acts as a form of thermometer, identifying hot and cold areas of organisational communication temperature.

Points for consideration

In evaluating the CI technique, the following points should be borne in mind.

Face validity

The notion of providing a personal example of communication makes sense to most people, who will readily concur with the following sentiments of the Scottish philosopher Thomas Carlyle:

> What is all knowledge too but recorded experience, and a product of history; of which, therefore, reasoning and belief, no less than action and passion, are essential materials?

We all spend a fair proportion of our lives telling family, friends and colleagues about things that have happened to us in our dealings with others, what we said or did, and how we felt. Indeed, many respondents relish the opportunity to complete this section of a questionnaire, or interview, detailing their key experiences.

Respondent-centred nature

Since the method brings to centre stage the frame of reference of respondents, it is free from the 'designer bias' which can contaminate the quantitative sections of questionnaires. The incidents, and how they are reported, are created by respondents – this section of the questionnaire is left open for them to select and describe freely what they wish. Of course, if interviews are used to collect the incidents these can result in bias if these are not conducted properly (see Chapter 4).

Methodological reservations

The qualitative nature of this method has produced some criticisms about the reliability and validity of the results – mainly along the lines that it does not allow for statistical analyses. However, when implemented in a systematic and consistent fashion, the CI approach has been shown to be a sophisticated data collection methodology (Ronan and Latham, 1974), and one in which the advantages far outweigh any disadvantages (Johnston, 1995). It provides an in-depth analysis of what respondents perceive to be the main issues, and allows them to describe these in detail. In an organisational context, this can serve to put flesh on the bare bones of quantitative data gathered in the main body of a questionnaire. As expressed by Pryce-Jones (1993, p. 95): 'Quantitative methods are designed to produce numerical statements of effects (numbers of opinions held) without identifying primary causes. Critical incident technique pinpoints individual causes of dissatisfaction.' In other words, the main body of the questionnaire may reveal that staff are very unhappy with senior managers. However, it does not reveal *why* this is the case – the CI approach will provide this detail. In essence, number crunching methods produce a clear picture of the event under scrutiny, but it is often a monochrome image – the addition of qualitative methods can help to convert this into full technicolour.

Illumination of minority views

If recurring causes of deep dissatisfaction are found across even a small minority of respondents, then this can be very significant. In quantitative sections of the questionnaire such insight may be lost, since the majority of respondents will not have rated this as a problem – and so its overall rating will be at least in the 'satisfactory' band. For instance, most people may be happy with the company Intranet, yet a few people in one part of the organisation may be having terrible problems with it. The CI section will bring this to light, and detail the specific reasons why this is the case.

Inclusion of rating scores

While the CI method is primarily qualitative, it also allows for a certain degree of quantification. For example, counts can be made of the number of times specific incidents recur, or particular people are mentioned. An additional approach is to have respondents rate various aspects of the incidents. These ratings can then be used to measure different dimensions of the issue under investigation. Thus, in their study of wine retailers' experiences with wholesale suppliers, Lockshin and McDougall (1998) asked respondents to rate the following on a scale of 1–10:

- how serious the identified incident was;
- the way in which the problem was dealt with;
- how frequently this particular problem occurred;
- how important this supplier was to the respondent's business;
- their overall level of satisfaction in their dealings with this supplier.

These ratings provided additional insight into the views of retailers. They revealed that respondents were less satisfied with the way in which routine as opposed to non-routine incidents were handled. This suggests that clients expect normal procedures to be followed as a matter of course and can get annoyed if this is not the case, but where a problem that is more unusual occurs they will be more tolerant in their expectations of the time needed to resolve it. In terms of recovery strategy, or how the problem was dealt with, if it was solved after one telephone call as opposed to two or more calls, ratings of satisfaction with the way it was handled and with the supplier *per se* were higher, the problem was rated as more minor, and the product line was viewed as more important to the business.

Time and labour

As with most qualitative techniques, the CI method can be very demanding. If interviews are used, these in themselves are time consuming. The content analysis of results is then a laborious and slow process, involving detailed scrutiny of either written or tape-recorded responses. This means that this is by no means an inexpensive audit methodology.

Positive models

Because the CI method asks for effective as well as ineffective instances of communication, it identifies and illuminates existing best practice. Many managers (and indeed staff) may initially see the audit as a form of Spanish Inquisition. However, audits produce many good news stories, and these can serve as useful role models for the promotion of best practice. The CI approach allows the auditor to provide detailed insight into exactly where, why, and with whom satisfaction with communication is high. When these are highlighted in the audit report (see Chapter 9), it becomes clear to all that, far from an inquisition, the audit can be an excuse for a celebration!

CONSTITUTIVE ETHNOGRAPHY

The nature, implementation and identification of the central components of expert performance is a complex field of study (for a full review of this area see Ericsson and Smith, 1991). Indeed, a salutary warning was sounded by the former British Prime Minister, Lord Salisbury, when he advised as long ago as

1887: 'No lesson seems to be so deeply inculcated by the experience of life as that you should never trust experts'! Different perspectives are held on the best way of accessing the behavioural components of expertise. For example, one view is that social scientists have the necessary skills to identify and analyse interpersonal performance. The corollary perspective is that this is not the case, but that rather only those who practise within a given situation or profession are capable of charting the core components, since only they can fully understand both the central context and the subtle nuances involved. The latter view largely guides the technique known as constitutive ethnography (CE), although this methodology also recognises the role of social scientists in navigating the procedure.

The term 'constitutive ethnography' was first coined by Meehan (1979), who developed this research approach as part of his investigations into teacher–pupil interactions in school classrooms. As he summarised it: 'A description of the interactional work of participants that assembles the structure of these events is the goal of this style of research' (p. 8). Meehan was particularly concerned with an examination of the social organisation of interpersonal encounters – in his case classroom lessons. In describing this methodology, he noted: 'constitutive ethnography requires that three criteria be met: first, the organization described by the researcher must, in fact, be the organization employed by the participants; second, the analysis must be retrievable from the materials; and third, the analysis must be comprehensive' (p. 35).

This approach was later further developed and refined by Saunders and Caves (1986) and Hargie *et al.* (1993), who tailored it to meet the specific requirements of skill identification in professional contexts. The important part of these refinements was that the professionals themselves were moved to centre stage in the overall research methodology. The main function of this later form of CE is that of 'analysing and identifying aspects of interpersonal behaviour which occur in social interactions in order to chart those skills and strategies that go to producing skilled performance' (Dickson *et al.*, 1997, p. 197). It uses an 'expert-systems approach' within what has been termed the 'consultative' research paradigm (Caves, 1988). In other words, consultation is central to the whole ethos, with professionals playing a key role as 'experts' in investigating their own practice.

CE involves obtaining video recordings of actual interactions between professionals and clients, and then subjecting these to detailed peer analysis. As Meehan (1979, p. 19) pointed out: 'Constitutive studies employ videotape and film . . . because they preserve data in close to their original form. Videotape serves as an external memory that allows researchers to examine materials extensively and repeatedly.' It is therefore useful at this stage to examine briefly some of the issues relating to this medium.

Video recording

Cameras are now ubiquitous. They are to be found, *inter alia*, at sports grounds, in stores, in pubs and hotels, in city centre streets, on main arterial routes (to catch speedsters), in university computer rooms, and in hospital corridors. It has been estimated that the average New Yorker appears on camera some 20 times per day (Gumpert and Drucker, 1998). In the UK, which is the country with the greatest number of cameras per head of population, in many urban areas people can be filmed by up to 300 cameras per day (Gadher, 1999). In an era of spy satellites and television exposé programmes featuring hidden cameras, we no longer find it unusual to think that someone might be watching us. Since 1975 cameras have been used in stores to study the buying behaviour of customers (Chisnall, 1997). For example, how long are customers in the store before they make a purchase? Do they read the information on labels before they buy a product? Are they more or less likely to purchase following an approach by a member of staff?

In the UK, the Market Research Society's code of ethics states that consumers should not be filmed unless they are in a location where they could reasonably expect to be seen or heard. This rules out, for example, the use of cameras in changing rooms. However, as Gumpert and Drucker (1998, p. 414) point out: 'The act of entering a bank, office building or housing complex implies consent to photograph, videotape, or both in order to prevent crime.' The notion of surveillance, and its acceptance by the general public, is now widespread. Despite this, and especially in research studies, Dowrick (1991) highlighted the importance of consent in the use of video. He argued that subjects should sign a consent form which:

1 communicates the purpose of the project and whether or not it is for research or other purposes;
2 gives the reason/need for recording the participant;
3 presents the steps which will be taken to ensure confidentiality;
4 states the absolute right of the subject to withdraw at any time and for any reason;
5 describes what will happen to the tapes and when they will be erased.

However, it is not always possible to secure the informed consent of every participant on an individual basis. For example, the Hargie *et al.* (1993) study described below involved an overall total of 105 hours of video recording actual pharmacist–patient consultations. The pharmacists in this study (who owned their stores) did not want their customers to be approached by a researcher, either before or just after entering the shop, to be informed about the nature of the research project. It was felt that such 'interference' by the researchers might lose them potential business. As a result, the method of individual informed consent could not be employed.

To enable the study to continue, an alternative method was adopted, which used the generic approach of having large posters displayed prominently on windows, doors and around all areas of the shop for one full week leading up each video-recording session. These described the nature and purpose of the project, assured individuals that all recordings would only be seen by the research team, and that tapes would be erased at the end of the study. Posters were 'updated' on the days of recording, stating clearly that videotaping was taking place that day. The camera was placed on a tripod at the side of the counter so that patients would be aware visually of its presence. This method has been used in other similar studies (Wilson *et al.*, 1989; Smith *et al.*, 1990).

Constitutive ethnography in practice

Once recordings have been obtained, professionals then analyse these in depth, both individually and in groups, in order to identify and describe the *constituents* of effective and ineffective performance. It is behaviour analysis by those involved in the actual interactions and so is *ethnographic* in design. The pattern of analysis involves building from individual opinion and analysis through to group sharing and pooling of knowledge. This results in the eventual itemisation of the verbal and nonverbal behaviours deemed essential for effective professional communication.

This method can best be explained by reference to an actual study. A major investigation of community pharmacy practice using this methodology was carried out by Hargie *et al.* (1993). In this investigation, 15 pharmacists agreed to have their consultations with patients video recorded for later analysis. A total of 20 consultations was recorded for each pharmacist. These were then analysed in four stages.

Stage I: individual analysis

Here, pharmacists were given an analysis form on which they had to judge whether each consultation (episode) was effective or ineffective, and give reasons for their choice (Box 7.2). They then had to view their tapes and select their five most effective and five most ineffective consultations, and complete a more detailed written assessment of their performance on these ten episodes, including comments on the specific professional situation depicted, and the frequency with which it typically occurred (Box 7.3). They also recorded any background detail which, while perhaps not obvious from the video, was in their opinion relevant to the assessment of communication. This information then facilitates discussion at Stage 2. Finally, they made suggestions about how the communication could have been improved. Since at this stage participants in CE are watching recordings of their own interactions for the first time, issues relating to self-viewing need to be borne in mind. The project team must be sensitive to participants as they assimilate their own self-image, and allow time for this process to bed down, only after which can meaningful behaviour analysis occur (see Dickson *et al.*, 1997 for a review of this area).

Box 7.2 Classification of recorded episodes

Instructions to pharmacists

During this individual viewing session we would like you to view each of your recorded episodes and broadly classify whether, in your opinion, your communication with patients was **effective** or **ineffective**, stating briefly the reason for your choice.

Format of individual viewing session record sheet:

Episode no.	Effective	Ineffective	Reason
1			
2			
3			
4			
5			
6			
7			
8			
9			
10			

Stage 2: triad sessions

At this part of the analysis, pharmacists met in groups of three to share their expertise and evaluations and also to scrutinise the consultations of each other. They were asked to review their own ten consultation episodes and the ten identified by each of the other two in the group, their task being to consensually select the most effective and least effective consultation for each individual (see

Box 7.3 Schedule used for selection of effective/ineffective episodes

Instructions to pharmacists

During this individual viewing session you are requested to select the 10 episodes of your own communication with patients for further analysis by the study group. We would like you to select 5 episodes that in your opinion are examples of **effective** communication and 5 that you think are **ineffective**. Please complete the following details as fully as possible.

Name   Episode No. [ ]

What is the situation?

This is an example of **effective/ineffective** communication because

In my view, the communication in this situation is **effective/ineffective** because

I would consider this situation to be a rare occurrence: Yes[ ]   No[ ]

I would deal with this situation: once a day[ ] once a week[ ] once a month[ ] once a year[ ]

Points to be borne in mind from the tape (not immediately obvious) when assessing the communication in this episode are:

What I would do differently to improve communication in this situation would be:

Box 7.4). The triad then completed a schedule for each of these six episodes (Box 7.5). This required them to clearly identify seven behaviours of the pharmacist which were instances of good pharmacist–patient communication. In addition, they were instructed to identify any behaviours that the pharmacist could have taken to improve the consultation.

Box 7.4 Instructions for triad selection of core episodes

Now that everyone has completed Stage I of the project we are interested in generating some discussion about what constitutes effective and ineffective communication within community pharmacy practice. During this triad session we would like you to view your selected episodes again along with the 10 episodes from the other members of your group, and for the triad to select one effective and one ineffective episode per pharmacist. These will be included in the 'pool' of episodes that will be seen by the entire study group. We would like you as a triad to complete the 'selected' episode sheet provided so that at this session we have a completed viewing sheet for each of the 3 effective and 3 ineffective episodes selected by the triad. For the purpose of the exercise you should appoint a co-ordinator and secretary for each pharmacist.

For your 6 selected episodes please try to identify 7 different actions of the pharmacist which are, in your opinion, instances of effective pharmacist–patient communication. If this task seems rather abstract, make it more concrete by imagining that you have a pre-registration pharmacist beside you. Use the tape to point out to the inexperienced pharmacist instances of communication that they would do well to attend to. We would like you to describe what is going on in such a way that what you put on paper would be meaningful to someone who has not seen the videotape.

In column I we would like you to write down what the pharmacist did (actions) that, in your opinion, made the interaction either effective or ineffective. In column II we would like you to describe the message(s) that the action(s) listed conveyed (meaning). Finally, in column III we would like you to indicate whether the action was an example of ineffective or effective communication for both the pharmacist and the patient. e.g. As a triad you might analyse the action described in the following way.

I. Action	II. Meaning	III. Effective(E)/Ineffective(I)	
		For the pharmacist	For the patient
1. Pharmacist interrupts their conversation with patient, to ask assistant to lock up	Pharmacist wants to get away (after all it's 5.30 pm)	E (as they wished, brought interaction to a close)	I (obviously had more to say but pharmacist closure meant no opportunity to express feelings)

We appreciate that you may want to include more than one definition of the pharmacist's action and, correspondingly, more than one meaning. However, having reached consensus within your triad we would like you to provide **only one** definition of every action and meaning in each episode. Please provide a minimum of 7 listed actions.

Box 7.5 Triad viewing sheet

Name _____   Episode No. _____

This episode was chosen as example of   Effective communication (E) [ ]
                                         Ineffective communication (I) [ ]

The 7 actions which, in our opinion, are instances of **good** pharmacist–patient
communication in this episode are as follows:

I. Action	II. Meaning	III. Effective(E) / Ineffective(I)	
		For the pharmacist	For the patient
1.			
2.			
3.			
4.			
5.			
6.			
7.			

Stage 3: categorisation of behaviours

After the triad sessions the next task was that of classifying all of the identified
behaviours into categories and labelling these. Given the very time-consuming
nature of this part of the project, the social scientists on the research team carried
out this initial categorisation task. While ideally this would be carried out by the
professionals themselves, in practice this is unrealistic. However, to emphasise
the consultative nature of the study, the initial categorisations were presented as
a tentative first step, to be subjected to rigorous analysis by the pharmacists.
Following further discussion, an eventual list of effective communication categories and related sub-categories was agreed. All 30 recorded consultations
were then viewed by the project team, who were asked to evaluate each using
this category list. This process led to further discussion and refinements, resulting in a final agreed classification.

Stage 4: individual ratings of essential behaviours

In this final phase, pharmacists individually viewed the 30 consultations again and rated on a six-point Likert scale the extent to which each of the identified communication skills was essential for effective pharmacist–patient communication in that context. In addition, pharmacists were asked to indicate on a separate scale the extent to which they felt that each of the skills was essential for effective pharmacist–patient communication *as a general rule*. This allowed an estimate to be made of the perceived contribution of specific skills to effective pharmacist–patient interaction generally. These ratings were then used to weight the relative importance of the identified skills and sub-skills.

Following all of these stages, it was possible to compile a detailed list of 45 key communication behaviours, which were in turn categorised into 11 main skill areas. The two most important skill areas identified were those of rapport-building with, and explanation to, patients, Similar projects using the constitutive ethnographic framework have been carried out in the fields of speech therapy (Saunders and Caves, 1986), physiotherapy (Adams *et al.*, 1994) and university lecturing (Saunders and Saunders, 1993a).

Points for consideration

In evaluating the CE approach, the following points should be borne in mind.

Logistics

Since professionals themselves are at the heart of CE, it necessitates considerable commitment from them. Methods have to be found for recruiting sufficient numbers to make the investigation viable (allowing for a potential drop-out). A range of material and other resources are also needed, including time, finance and technology. In the study described above, research funding was obtained to pay for locum cover to release the community pharmacists from their work and to purchase specialised audio-recording equipment. Inevitably, however, the pharmacists had to devote more time than the locum cover paid for. Their goodwill and personal commitment were therefore necessary to ensure the successful completion of the study. The arrangements for video recording and timetabling of viewing sessions are also time-consuming, sometimes quite complicated, and inevitably demanding. This all takes place before any data analysis can occur, so this method is not one for the faint-hearted auditor! In practice, therefore, CE is a method usually employed in well-funded research investigations.

Face validity

The results obtained from CE have very high face validity within any profession. This is primarily because identification of skills comes directly from members of the profession – they are neither imposed nor invented by others. It is possible for social scientists to follow much of the CE protocol described above, but then to carry out the analysis and interpretation of data themselves (see for example Rackham and Carlisle, 1978). However, this is open to the criticism that the analysis has been conducted by 'outsiders' and so lacks an 'insider' view of what is happening, and the interpretations are therefore less relevant.

Generalisability

One criticism is that CE only represents the views of a small number of people, who may or may not be representative. In reality, and given the commitment expected of them, the professionals who take part will be volunteers. It is not possible to select them randomly. In discussing this issue in relation to the recruitment of community pharmacists in their study, Hargie *et al.* (1993) commented:

> Since participation would necessitate allowing the research team to video record all of their interactions over a set period and would then require a substantial time commitment to the ensuing analyses of these recordings – often in the evenings – it was clear that it would not be possible to randomly select a set number of pharmacists and request that they participate!
>
> (Hargie *et al.*, 1993, p. 18)

Rather, to recruit pharmacists, what they did was to publicise the study widely, both with direct mail shots and media publicity, and ask for volunteers. What must also be remembered here, of course, is that CE is a qualitative research methodology, and so issues of statistical relevance are not centre-stage (see Chapter 5 for a discussion of this issue).

Expertise

Where possible, attempts should be made to identify 'expert' professionals, and also to consider specialised areas of sub-expertise, in recruiting the sample. Thus, in their study, Adams *et al.* (1994) asked senior physiotherapists to nominate 'expert' therapists within the specialist fields of neurology, obstetrics, outpatients and paediatrics, whom they thought should be included. Likewise, Saunders and Saunders (1993b), in recruiting 37 lecturing staff to take part in their investigation into effective university teaching skills, asked the deans of the seven faculties at the selected university to nominate appropriate lecturers across the main discipline areas within their faculties. What makes an expert will, of course, vary across contexts. For instance, in their investigation into the skills of effective negotiators, Rackham and Carlisle (1978) used three criteria to select expert negotiators; namely, that they:

- had a track record of significant success over time;
- were rated as effective by *both* sides;
- had a high incidence of implementation success in reaching agreements that proved to be viable.

Analytical ability

Another criticism is that professionals may not have the requisite skills to carry out meaningful evaluations of the behaviour of themselves and their colleagues. This is where the role of the social scientist is essential. Training and guidance may be needed at various stages, and the progress of each participant must be monitored on an ongoing basis.

Professional-centred nature

The client's perspective is not really taken into account in CE. While professionals may be asked to consider this perspective, this is very different from accessing it first hand. This means that in order to gain a complete picture of professional–client communications, other audit approaches (client interviews, focus groups, questionnaire surveys, etc.) need to be used to supplement CE in terms of gauging the client's perspective.

DELPHI TECHNIQUE

This method was developed in the USA in the early 1950s by Olaf Helmer and his colleagues (Helmer and Rescher, 1959). Their work at the Rand Corporation, on 'Project Delphi', concerned an analysis of the probable targets and outcomes of a possible Russian bombing campaign (Dalkey and Helmer, 1963). As noted by Reid (1988), it may therefore be viewed as one of the positive spin-offs from the cold war! The technique is named after Apollo's Delphic Oracle, an ancient Greek myth which purported that a 'chosen one' living on the island of Delphi could predict the future with infallibility. The approach is similar to CE in that it elicits the views of a panel of experts in a procedure that involves building from individual perspectives to reach an eventual overall group consensus (Linstone and Turoff, 1975). The main difference is that under the rubric of the Delphi technique (DT) the participants never actually meet. In fact the DT has five defining features:

1 *A panel of 'experts' is recruited to conduct the analysis.* As discussed earlier, the notion of 'expert' is in itself a moot topic, and in reality panel members are usually selected on the basis of what has been vaguely referred to as their 'reputations' (Dickson *et al.*, 1997). The size of panels has also varied widely, ranging in number from 10 to 1685; in essence, the larger the panel the higher

the drop-out rate, with panels of 20 and under tending to retain all their members (Reid, 1988). However, Clayton (1997, pp. 377–378) argued, 'Because Delphi is a tool to aid understanding or decision-making, it will only be an effective process if those decision-makers who will ultimately act upon the results of the Delphi are actively involved throughout the process.'

2 *These experts never meet face to face.* All information is sent to them individually in writing and they return their written responses directly to the central source. Participants are guaranteed complete anonymity. The reason for this is to encourage openness and honesty – people are more likely to express their real opinions in private than in public. It also removes those psychological influences, such as dominant personalities and status differentials, which influence committee-style discussions. While in theory it also gives respondents the time to give considered views, a down side of anonymity is that it can also lead to hasty, ill-judged opinions and a lack of accountability. Because of this, what has been termed 'quasi-anonymity' has been recommended, where respondents know who else is involved in the overall exercise but all individual contributions remain strictly anonymous (Rauch, 1979). An alternative approach is that of the 'nominal group technique' (NGT), which in essence is face-to-face Delphi. Using the NGT, the group members are actually all in the same room but they make their contributions in writing individually and independently of the others present. As with the DT these individual contributions are then collated and presented (on a flipchart or board) for further individual scrutiny – no discussions occur.

3 *The exercise is conducted in writing, with the project leader co-ordinating the whole process.* The advent of e-mail has facilitated this part of the DT procedure. Within an organisation, the process can easily be completed using the Intranet. The fact that respondents do not have to be brought together for discussions also reduces many of the logistical and resource problems associated with CE. One drawback of the DT is that, given the ongoing demands of involvement, the response rate can drop off significantly after the first round. McKenna (1994) found that using face-to-face interviews in this first stage significantly increased later returns; this is not surprising since the development of a personal relationship has been shown to increase commitment to a task (Hargie *et al.*, 1999).

4 *Two or more 'rounds' take place, in between which the project leader sends a summary of the results of the previous round to panel members.* The full range of opinions is fed back, together with an indication of the extent of consensus on each, and a request for further evaluation and comment on each item. A five- or seven-point Likert scale with a zero (neutral) mid-point is often employed, with respondents being asked to rate each item. This allows a numerical analysis of consensus to be computed.

5 *An eventual identification of final areas of concordance and discordance is compiled at the end of the process.* As expressed by Jeffery *et al.* (1995, p. 48), 'After three to four rounds of discussion, opinions and revision, a much better defined opinion, one with high consensus, is the result.'

The DT can be used to examine what key 'players' agree to be the most important communication issues in any profession or organisation. It continues to be used in a range of studies in different professions including, for example, distance education (Thach and Murphy, 1995), family therapy (Jenkins, 1996), teaching (Houtz and Weinerman, 1997), and nursing (Davidson et al., 1997). It has also been used widely in organisational contexts. Indeed, Varney (1990) carried out an interesting study using DT in which a random selection of organisation development (O.D.) professionals on the O.D. Network Roster were asked to identify and then evaluate the significance of key books and articles in the O.D. field. This led to the production of a list of what were viewed to be the key publications central to this area. Also in the O.D. domain, Reid et al. (1990) identified the potential applications of DT as including an examination of:

- how staff view the future of the organisation;
- role definition and clarification regarding exact responsibilities and duties;
- goal setting and the determination of key organisational priorities;
- the resolution of conflicts and differences between staff;
- the identification of current information and communication concerns.

As summarised by Reid et al. (1990):

> The Delphi Technique has been widely used by organizations as an aid to decision-making. Its features and several of the applications which have been reported in the management and planning literature . . . suggest . . . many potential uses in activities which are essential to the work of organization development.
>
> (Reid et al., 1990, p. 40)

CONCLUSION

To improve practice it is necessary to audit existing levels of performance, identify areas of strength and weakness, and devise action plans to remedy identified deficits. In the professional sphere, as noted by Reid (1988, p. 232): 'The challenge is to find some means of evaluating professional practice that is both acceptable and credible with the professions, and which has some scientific standing and will produce hard data.' In fact, the techniques employed to audit professional communications will be dependent upon a range of factors, including the expertise of the auditors, the time and resources available, and the motivation of the professionals themselves. For example, in relation to the latter point, Goldhaber and Rogers (1979) found that their attempt to use a diary method with hospital staff was thwarted by the resistance of surgeons to what they saw as a time-consuming and seemingly pointless methodology (see Chapter 6). Thus, the method chosen needs to be one which has high face validity with those who will be required to implement it.

In this chapter we have examined in detail two such methods, the critical incident technique and constitutive ethnography, and briefly reviewed a third, the Delphi technique. While all three methods have different procedures and formats, what they have in common is that they can all be employed to carry out an in-depth investigation of professional communication. They are also all flexible enough to allow for some modifications to meet the demands of particular areas or specific resource limitations. The templates as covered in this chapter can therefore be adjusted depending upon objectives and circumstances. This issue is discussed in more depth in Chapter 16.

Chapter 8

Auditing the communications revolution

Dennis Tourish and Owen Hargie

INTRODUCTION

The revolution in information technology is transforming how organisations communicate internally, and with their customers, clients, and suppliers. A larger volume of information can be exchanged more rapidly between greater numbers of people than ever before. The bleep of mobile phones, once the staple ingredient of every stand-up comic's nightly routine, no longer evokes a second glance. We no longer ask people: 'Do you have e-mail?' Instead, we say: 'What is your e-mail address?' These developments pose new challenges for the business world, and for communication auditors.

In this chapter, we look at four key issues. First, we explore the implications of the intranet. This can be defined as electronic systems for in-company communication, which includes e-mail but is not restricted to it. Second, given that e-mail is the form of electronic communication with which people are still most familiar, we devote particular attention to its growing role. Third, we look at the internet, increasingly mined for information on every conceivable topic, and used as a means of transacting business. Fourth, we examine issues raised in the auditing of telephone usage.

It is easy to feel overwhelmed by the new and ever-expanding range of technological innovations being dangled in front of us. Our purpose is to indicate both the strengths and the weaknesses of these options, in order to assist organisations make more appropriate choices in line with their business needs. Audits can help organisations decide if rational and productive choices are being made, or whether people have purchased the latest gear for no better reason than that it was there. The intention is to summarise emerging trends in the research, enabling readers to learn from the experiences of those who have been there before them. It isn't always necessary to touch a stove to find out whether it burns. How hot or cold is the information revolution likely to be for organisations in the twenty-first century?

Box 8.1 Intranet applications

- E-mail
- Videos of managers providing briefings
- Facilities for people to sign up for distance learning courses, without leaving their desks
- Giving staff access to their payroll records
- Tutorial materials readily available, with opportunities to interact with tutors
- Organisation charts, best practice benchmarks and procurement issues available on-line
- Internal phone directories, and policy and procedure manuals, available
- Electronic newsletters
- Bulletin boards
- Stock prices posted daily

ENTER THE INTRANET?

The growth of the intranet has been explosive. Over 90 per cent of US companies who responded to one survey either already had an intranet system in place or were planning to adopt one (Taaffe, 1996). Various estimates put spending on internal communications software at more than double the levels of investment in internet sites (Welch, 1996).

Many people still assume that intranet is a fancy expression for e-mail. Most intranet systems incorporate e-mail, but seek to do much more. Box 8.1 lists a number of intranet applications, widely reported in the general literature and also derived from our own consulting experience.

There are a number of advantages and, inevitably, some emerging disadvantages to the intranet. Advantages include the following (Gray, 1997; Greengard, 1998):

1 *The elimination of unnecessary hierarchy.* In principle, employees can begin to organise themselves around clusters of information and common practices, rather than in traditional departmental tribes. Thus, a human resources person can access finance knowledge more quickly to solve a particular problem, and vice versa. It therefore seems likely that the intranet will lead to new organisational configurations. For example, it is generally anticipated that communication chains will become shorter, have fewer intermediaries and encourage more openness between people (Hougaard and Duus, 1999). Such developments will have enormous implications for styles of management. Research is needed into their impact on performance, profitability, communication and satisfaction with the working environment. Auditors can also help explore the

obstacles that will inevitably present themselves. Many people, fearful of losing their place in the gatekeeping hierarchy, already resist the unimpeded flow of ideas. They are busy felling logs and building dams. What is likely to be the impact of such resistance, and what might be the most appropriate response?

2 *Employee self-service*. In some companies, employees log-on and input the necessary information when they secure promotion, move departments or leave the organisation.

3 *Access*. People can get information when they need it, rather than having to wait for a response from someone else. Thus, information exchange is speeded up.

4 *Time*. Delivery times can be reduced, as well as the costs of paper, postage and delivery. For example, the Ford Motor Company used its intranet to connect 120,000 computers and reduce the time required to introduce new models from 36 months to 24 (Cronin, 1998). The savings have been enormous.

The disadvantages are less well documented at the moment. Three of the most obvious include:

1 *Costs*. Direct costs include hardware and software installation. IT companies are investing a great deal of money in designing new intranet systems. It can be predicted with confidence that they will then attempt to scare the life out of their clients, and convince them that only a huge investment in the latest systems is capable of averting bankruptcy. Who asks questions when clinging to a precipice? We know of some companies, infected by the fear virus, who have already spent millions of dollars on the intranet. Others have succeeded with a much more modest spend. *The correct level of investment depends on each organisation's unique business needs*. On the other hand, most organisations already have a great deal of expensive hardware (computers) in place, and need only a minimal investment in additional software applications. The cost of people's time in developing the system also needs to be borne in mind. Intranets require widespread participation if they are to work. The best advice available counsels against leaving the issue entirely in the hands of IT specialists, who often become mesmerised by 'the toy factor' rather than the profit motive. Linked to this, the development of Intranets raises new training needs.

2 *Impact on other forms of communication*. Face-to-face interaction remains best – a theme we elaborate below in our discussion of e-mail use. Intranets are not for every organisation. Even when they are, the objective should not be to produce a new generation of nerds, glued to computer screens. If people's vocal chords deteriorate through lack of use, it is a clear sign that you have a problem.

3 *Impact on innovation*. This is still an under-researched area. However, it has been pointed out that one of the main uses of the intranet is the storage and dissemination of existing best practices inside and outside the organisation. This form of benchmarking can stimulate improved performance, and greater creativity. But whether such gains are achieved depends on how the system is

managed. If top executives respond to each new idea by enquiring whether it has been compared to Performance Standard Y on File X (*'Don't you know it's on the Intranet?'*) the stream of new ideas will quickly dry up (Schrage, 1999). Despite its potential to have a levelling effect, the intranet in the wrong hands can become a new means of stifling dissent, and of enforcing conformity and compliance. The underlying philosophy of management, and the values and principles it lives by, is crucial.

Some guidelines on effective intranet use have begun to emerge (Abernathy, 1998; Chamine, 1998). We discuss these here, and suggest that they should inform an audit process homing in on the intranet. Many of the audit tools discussed in this book (e.g. questionnaires, interviews and focus groups) can be readily adapted to monitor these issues in-depth:

1 *Measure the intranet's return on investment*
A basic premise of any communication strategy is that it should strengthen business performance. Without this, the side effects (i.e. costs) outweigh any gains obtained from the treatment. They might even become toxic. Thus, intranet applications should improve sales, productivity and competitiveness. En route, their effectiveness can be judged by whether they deliver improvements in such areas as

- order management;
- inter-departmental collaboration;
- customer service;
- database access; and
- inventory management.

Each organisation should select its own performance indicators, and measure intranet effectiveness by these yardsticks.

2 *Make the site user friendly*
Its purpose is to serve employee needs in language they themselves use and understand. Thus, organisations should involve wide numbers of staff in intranet design, rather than leave the task to IT specialists. Users can also assist in ongoing audits of its effectiveness.

3 *Make it unique, but keep it calm*
The site should have special features of its own, rather than merely reproduce written documents with which people have been familiar in the past. We make a bigger impression when we dress up for special occasions. Novel features on an intranet site can increase utilisation rates, and hence effectiveness. On the other hand, they should not make people feel they have wandered into an alternative psychedelic universe. Purple swirls and dancing bears distract rather than inform.

4 *Lower the barriers to entry*
We know of some organisations which encourage all employees to post information on the company intranet. Surprisingly, early indications are that this does not lead to information overload. On the contrary. It suggests empowerment, and keeps the sites user-friendly, accessible and relevant.

5 *Make it useful*
What needs will it serve? How will it transform people's work? What services can it provide on-line? Information provision for its own sake leads to congested sites and low utilisation rates.

6 *Keep it current*
Regular updates are essential. Some intranets have systems which tell individual employees what has changed since they last logged on. Again, this simplifies access and encourages regular use. Antique sites abound, and although they make for fascinating archaeology they also suggest organisations mired in the past rather than facing the future.

7 *Get feedback*
This is a fundamental principle of audit. It is entirely possible for a system which looks unbeatable at the design stage to miss people's real needs by a mile. Even bad ideas attract enthusiastic champions. In particular, many people believe that reality is morally obliged to conform to the fine detail of their strategic plans. The audit tools discussed in this book will help tell companies if their intranet spends are genuinely capable of meeting their needs. Frequently, the exotic beast glimpsed in the distance, and thought to be a computer solution, turns out to be another white elephant.

8 *Be creative*
As with most other forms of communication, snap, crackle and pop improves the impact of the information. Sites perceived as boring and irrelevant lose friends, influence no one and accumulate enemies.

The challenges of auditing the intranet are enormous, given the diverse applications reviewed here. In principle, most of the tools discussed in this book can be adapted to encompass the variety of intranet forms currently in use. For example, the methods which Charles Patti and his colleagues describe in Chapter 14, utilised in an external audit of written communications between a superannuation fund and its clients, could be readily adapted to audit electronic newsletters, posted on the intranet. They could also inform a detailed analysis of bulletin boards. On the other hand, if a wide range of intranet tools are in use and a broad picture of their effectiveness is required, it is more likely that focus groups, interviews and some form of questionnaire could yield sufficient data for most purposes. As we discuss in Chapter 16, there is no one obviously correct and universally applicable approach to auditing communication which can be dusted down and applied under all conditions. What works depends on a careful examination of each organisation's own unique situation, and the needs which flow from this. However, based on this review of the existing literature, we would propose that an intranet audit should be concerned with exploring the following issues. The available techniques should be assessed by would-be auditors in the light of whether they are capable of addressing the questions we raise here:

- *Access*. Do people feel that the system can be accessed by them with minimum trouble, and quickly? In consequence, how frequently do most people use its facilities? If sites slumber, despite earthquakes in the outside marketplace, they are unlikely to achieve their primary objective – the rapid dissemination of useful information.
- *Utility*. Do people feel that the intranet meets their needs, and that the investment is therefore justified? Does it add real value to the enterprise? Or is it seen as an expensive stunt, the equivalent of a Concorde flight from Kennedy Airport to Manhattan?
- *Timeliness*. Is the system updated frequently (ideally, on a daily basis), and therefore judged to be a channel through which people derive up to date information? Potentially, the intranet is one of the most effective methods yet devised for short-circuiting the grapevine and enabling top managers to interact directly with all levels of their organisation.
- *Feedback potential*. Are there systems for people to interact with the Intranet, and use it as a further means of feeding their ideas into the organisation? As in a marriage, one-way communication is usually a recipe for boredom and breakdown. Many organisations deliberately set extremely low barriers to entry, in order to encourage frequent and informal communication, with its concomitant impact on status differentials. A key test for any intranet audit, therefore, is to measure the range of people who input to the system. If it is seen as the plaything of a few geeks, sheltering from reality behind computer consoles, it will fail to deliver on its potential.

A number of these issues can be routinely audited, using existing software. For example, most intranet systems will automatically record the number of 'hits' on individual sites. This is a crude form of measurement, but valuable to a point. The additional tools discussed in this book should be considered, and adapted, for some of the more fine-grained analysis suggested above.

THE GROWTH OF E-MAIL

E-mail has been the fastest growing aspect of the intranet, and the area with which people are most familiar. The USA had 20 million e-mail addresses in the mid-1990s. More than half of these had gone on-line during a single calendar year: a phenomenal rate of expansion (Baig, 1994). Some countries, such as Sweden, gave every citizen an e-mail address. This has multiplied the exchange of information between people, much of which would not exist without e-mail. When the e-mail communications of one Fortune 500 company were scrutinised, in an early investigation of the area, it was discovered that 60 per cent of the messages exchanged by this means would not have been sent via other channels (Kiesler, 1986).

This relatively new channel of communication has reached into the furthest recesses of even those organisations most resistant to change. The British Foreign Office, hardly renowned for pioneering global revolutions, traditionally communicated with its overseas offices through a telegraph network system which dated back to the nineteenth century. This has now been replaced with a £69 million investment in e-mail software (Hibbs, 1999): 4400 personal computers were installed in over 250 British overseas posts, linking them to 1200 domestic users. The effect has been to streamline hierarchy. Previously, submissions were passed upwards through a rigid chain of command. During transmission, critical opinion frequently transmuted into its opposite, or drowned under a deluge of red ink. E-mail has enabled young and inexperienced officials to interface with people at the top much more frequently than in the past, thereby improving diagonal communication, and the circulation of innovative ideas.

There is some evidence that staff view superiors as less intimidating in e-mail settings (possibly because many of the non-verbal signals that we normally rely upon to decode status are absent). Hence, one study found that detailed and frank discussions were more likely to take place using e-mail than with more conventional forms of communication (Kiesler, 1986). Top managers have also used e-mail to drive around traditional communication roadblocks. Jacques Nasser, Ford's CEO, instituted what he termed a 'Let's Chat About the Business Routine', which involved him sending e-mails to about 100,000 employees every Friday afternoon. As he put it: 'They're just another way to share as much information – unfiltered – as broadly as possible throughout the company and to encourage dialogue at all levels' (Wetlaufer, 1999, p. 87).

E-mail has enormous advantages as a means of communication. The most apparent are:

- *The rapid exchange of information.* It is hard to imagine any other system which would enable a CEO to communicate so quickly with 100,000 employees each week.
- *The elimination of hierarchical barriers.* People at the top and bottom can interact without having to seek permission from innumerable gatekeepers.
- *Status differentials can be enormously reduced.* Such differentials tend to act as a block on effective functioning.
- *Inter-departmental communication can be facilitated.* This has the potential, as Ford has already shown, to speed up decision-making, and hence reduce the time required to get new products into the marketplace.

• *External communication, with customers, is also enormously facilitated.* It is now common practice for organisations to publicise their e-mail address alongside their postal address and telephone and fax numbers.

However, all opportunities also bring dangers. For example, a survey of 293 communications professionals in the UK found that, in their organisations, e-mail had become the most frequently used media for internal communication, replacing one to one meetings with supervisors (Stewart, 1999). Forty-six per cent of respondents to another survey also said that e-mail had reduced face-to-face communication in their workplace, and that this had led to less co-operation, greater internal conflict among colleagues, bullying and a more unpleasant working atmosphere (Utley, 1997). Organisations can be media rich, but interpersonally famished. In such conditions e-mail has the potential to supplant rather than supplement face-to-face communication. Yet it is the latter which remains most popular as a means of people hearing about important issues facing their organisation, and which is also vital to cement strong relationships in the workplace. Such contact has been termed the 'human moment', defined as 'an authentic psychological encounter that can happen only when two people share the same physical space' (Hallowell, 1999, p. 59). When human moments become infrequent, the communication process is marked by lack of sensitivity, self-doubt and abrasive curtness. This, in turn, damages relationships, communication and, eventually, organisational effectiveness.

Quirke (1996) reported precisely such a difficulty with Apple Computers, which developed a culture of each employee having a computer on their desks. Everyone loved the technology. In fact, they came to rely on it so much that face-to-face communication was neglected. Apple responded by holding a series of conferences for different levels of management, specifically to promote more direct communication. This led to systems for face-to-face briefings, the development of national publications and the convening of cross functional communication meetings. High tech needs high touch if it is to build the relationships that ultimately underlie performance and business success. The lesson is that the role and impact of e-mail should be carefully monitored, to ensure that it does not displace the old 'technology' of people talking to people.

A related difficulty is the prevalence of abusive e-mails, now widely known as 'flame mails'. More than half of the 1000 users who responded to one major survey had received flame mails, which they said had irreparably damaged working relationships (Utley, 1997). Fifty-four per cent of antisocial e-mails reported in this study were from managers to their staff and one in six of all respondents reported being officially disciplined via e-mail. In a survey carried out by Novell, a software design company, 23 per cent of respondents reported that they received flame mails several times a week; 48 per cent received them several times a month. Over 5 per cent of respondents said that they had left a job as a result of these problems (Hilpern, 1999). E-mail lacks the facial and tonal cues associated with non-verbal communication. As a result, it appears that less consideration is given to its consequences than when we compose letters and faxes, which we assume are more likely to form part of a permanent written record. E-mail also provides for instant communication, at a time when tempers are running high and both parties may require a cooling off period, rather than further interaction. There are times when words become a highly combustible fuel.

A key aspect of this is defamation. E-mail is less confidential than many people think. Even when it is deleted, records are kept in the employer's back-up tapes and can be accessed for use during legal proceedings (Coles, 1999). This cost Norwich Union, an insurance company in the UK, £450,000 in damages after defamatory messages about a health insurer were circulated in its e-mail system. Some US companies have also been forced to pay employees million dollar levels of compensation, when courts have judged that sexist e-mails con- stituted unacceptable harassment. Auditors need to assess awareness levels on this issue, and the extent to which people bear it in mind when transmitting messages.

In such a volatile context, managers are often suspicious of how their staff use e-mail. A survey of the UK's top 1000 companies, by Integralis, found that 85 per cent of companies thought it was adding to office rumours (Integralis, 1999). E-mail has so augmented the grapevine's legendary potential for disseminating gossip that in many quarters the technology is now referred to as 'the e-vine'. Twenty-two per cent of companies in the Integralis survey reported that they had already disciplined some staff for e-mail misuse. Furthermore, most re- spondents thought that staff wasted something like two hours a day on sending e-mails and surfing the internet. An earlier study of 1000 users seemed to confirm at least some of these anxieties, finding that over 90 per cent of respondents spent up to an hour a day reading, responding to and deleting irrelevant messages (Lewis, 1997).

The problem is that the ease and ubiquity of the technology has the potential to replace information *underload*, a frequent problem in the past, with informa- tion *overload* today. Thus, Gladstone (1998) cited one middle ranking sales person as reporting that he received an average of 125 e-mails per day. Worse still, the chief financial officer of a large Silicon Valley firm returned to work after a week's vacation to find 2000 e-mails waiting (Cairncross, 1998). What would you do? In despair, this man deleted them all, unread, and moved on to next business.

Given the relative newness of the technology, research into its role and impact on organisational communication is at an early stage. However, it is possible to identify several themes in the literature, which should be considered during audits of such communications. These are:

1 *The volume of e-mails sent and received.* These data can inform further in- vestigations of many questions, including what proportion of messages:

   • relate to business issues;
   • deal with purely personal matters;

- cover internal/ external issues;
- absorb too much time, in an average working day;
- are timely, relevant and lead to focused action plans;
- strengthen or damage relationships;
- improve horizontal, vertical and diagonal communication.

2 *How e-mail complements or substitutes for other channels of communication.* It is vital that it does not entirely replace face-to-face interaction between colleagues, or between managers and their staff. As a rule of thumb, if the audit shows that e-mail has become the predominant channel of communication for dealing with important issues it is likely that too many 'human moments' are missing. This will weaken the prevailing organisational culture. It may therefore be time to revisit first principles. As part of this process, it might also be helpful to create special opportunities for face-to-face communication. Hallowell (1999), for example, cited a CEO who required all employees working from home to come into the office once a month for some unstructured face time. More research is needed into the effects of such initiatives.

3 *The extent to which e-mails contain information which would not be sent by other means.* As we have noted, many messages would never be transmitted without e-mail. To a point, this is positive. Frequent informal interaction between people builds relationships and improves team spirit. All other things being equal, people who enjoy coming into work for the fun factor will be more productive than those smitten by gloom. It is hard to innovate if you believe that the four horsemen of the Apocalypse are about to gallop across the nearest horizon. In addition, the greater the amount of information people exchange on work issues the stronger the possibility of spontaneous insights emerging, capable of adding value to the business. On the other hand, if e-mail is used primarily for whizzing jokes around the office, companies will have achieved little other than to invest in an expensive in-house entertainment system. Comic books on every desk would be cheaper.

4 *The quality of communication between managers and staff.* Given the absence of non-verbal cues, it is possible that the arrival of e-mail may drive out supportive communication, and install a punitive regime in its place. Managers need continually to ask people for their ideas, deliver praise and encouragement, and seek corrective feedback on decisions made. If people perceive that e-mail is being used mainly to apply more pressure and stifle discussion it will have become more of a roadblock than a freeway.

5 *Whether e-mails frequently become flame mails.* It may be necessary to train people to reflect on the messages they write before they send them, and consider whether other communication channels are more appropriate for dealing with particular problems. Protocols for the effective and civilised use of e-mails are increasingly being developed (e.g. Hargie *et al.*, 1999) and should be circulated to staff.

6 *Whether targets for responsiveness have been set, and achieved.* E-mail is fundamentally another dimension of written communication, and its content can be conceptualised as a cross between a letter (given its format) and a phone call (given its mode of transmission, and instantaneous impact). Its efficiency is thus improved if e-mails exchanged inside the organisation are viewed as communications between internal customers. Likewise, external e-mails are essentially interactions with paying customers. In the UK, the Audit Commission (1994a) proposed that targets should be set for written replies to letters. There is no reason why this approach could not be applied to e-mail, and audits employed to find out if the targets have been achieved. Thus, organisations should:

- set a corporate target for the whole organisation;
- set departmental targets, as well as a corporate target;
- set targets which stretch each department, and so help improve performance;
- inform staff and the public what the targets are;
- review progress regularly to make sure that performance continues to improve.

More research is required into each of these areas. For example, investigation is needed into the tradeoff between rapid response times (presumed desirable) and communications which genuinely inform people. Organisations surveyed in the Audit Commission Report had widely divergent targets for responses to letters, ranging from three days for a full reply to six weeks. These normally included a distinction between *acknowledgement* replies and *actual* replies. We have worked with one organisation where ambitious targets were set for instant acknowledgements to all incoming mail. Staff indeed met these targets – but did so by sending out form letters which could not yet actually answer the information needs of their customers. Meanwhile, having acknowledged the original mail, there was correspondingly less urgency in responding to its content within a reasonable time-frame. Our audit found that some people were becoming quite irate at this. It was necessary to set slightly more relaxed targets, and empower people to take more initiatives when answering customer queries.

Taking account of the emerging research, a number of issues stand out, which audits of e-mail communication should be designed to assess. We identify a number of these in Box 8.2. This is not intended to be an exhaustive inventory of questions, but are suggestive of what seems to be most important at this stage.

A number of audit options are available, in exploring these and other questions. First, the *questionnaire* which we reproduce in the Appendix lists e-mail as one of the main channels of communication, and asks respondents to identify how much information they receive and send through it, and how timely it is. This enables auditors to assess the impact of e-mail relative to the other main channels being utilised.

Second, a *diary analysis* could be kept of e-mail usage. We offer, in Chapter 6, an example of a diary format used by us in an audit of a public sector organisation. In this instance, e-mail had not yet been introduced, and so was not

---

Box 8.2 Assessing e-mail communication

- The number of e-mails people receive in an average day.
- The extent to which such e-mails:

  - relate mostly to business issues
  - improve relationships
  - harm relationships
  - raise issues which people would not hear about by other means
  - are mostly social and friendly in nature

- The extent to which e-mail complements or replaces other channels of communication, particularly face to face.
- The nature of e-mails received from more senior people in a given organisation, and the extent to which they:

  - give instructions
  - ask for the recipient's ideas
  - give praise
  - criticise performance
  - provide useful information
  - ask for information
  - demand immediate action

- The prevalence or otherwise of 'flame mails'.
- Respondents' perceptions of e-mail's strengths and weaknesses, and their suggestions for improving its use.

---

listed with the other channels investigated – telephone, written, etc. However, it could easily be incorporated into this or a variety of other diary formats.

Third, we discuss *mystery shopping* in Chapter 7. Again, this technique could be adapted to the e-mail context. A 'mystery e-mailer' could send a number of messages to an organisation. Responses could then be measured along such dimensions as informativeness, timeliness, relevance, and friendliness.

Interviews and *critical incident analysis*, both discussed in detail in this book, can also be employed in this context. The precise approach, as so often, depends on the needs of the organisation, the time allowed for the audit, and the resources available, including budgets.

THE INTERNET

The term 'internet' refers to the system which inter-connects computers, databases, and software applications on a global scale. It therefore encompasses multi media (pictures, music, colour, moving images, data and text). It is capable of handling any data which can be reduced to a digital format, and thus seems likely to deliver wholly new applications in the decade ahead. In essence, it is the cornerstone of the intranet and e-mail systems we have already looked at in this chapter.

The growth of the internet continues to be explosive. During the decade up to the mid-1990s the number of people using it doubled every 12 months. Though this exponential growth has since slowed, it still continues at extremely high levels (Cairncross, 1998). The number of users is generally expected to exceed 300 million early in the new millennium, and catch up with the number of telephones in the world not long after that. Yet it was only in the mid-1990s that the World Wide Web enabled it to utilise on-line graphics, sound and moving pictures, enhancing the interest value of the whole enterprise (Anderson, 1995). Here, we look very briefly at some of its principal applications, and outline the main challenges posed for auditors.

E-mail   It has been estimated that two-thirds of people who use the internet do so only for sending e-mails (Cairncross, 1998). For many, this is the point of entry into the whole system. As internet retailing and other applications become more readily available, it is unlikely that so many people will continue to use it only for the limited purpose of e-mail.

Finding information   More and more information is posted on internet sites, and it is now widely expected that all organisations will have an internet address. The upside of this is greater communication opportunity. The downside is the growing problem of information overload (Cortese, 1997). Search engines throw up hundreds of sites dealing with any and every issue under the sun. This ease of access has been described as creating an 'information democracy' (Thompson, 1996, p. 9). However, sifting through the junk in search of pearls can take an inordinate amount of time.

Provision of on-line services   Internet shopping is now a reality, creating virtual companies in some sectors which only do business by this means. The terms 'e-commerce' and 'e-business' are widely used to describe such transactions. Many companies, such as the Amazon book retail outlet, have seen the value of their shares soar, despite never turning in a profit. The market's valuation has been based as much on the potential of the technology as on immediate economic performance. Nevertheless, in many sectors traditional retail shopping is being seriously challenged by 'e-tail' shopping on the internet.

Speeding information flow, and hence product development   Communication between companies via the web, and between companies and regulative bodies, can slash product development cycles. Perhaps the most publicised drug of the 1990s was Viagra, the anti-impotence treatment. In the USA, approval time for such drugs, after clinical trials, normally takes a year. In this case it was granted after six months. It might be suspected that regulators had a personal interest in the issue, and were responding to pressure from home. However, the manufacturer credits the fast result to the internet. Rather than having to physically transport thousands of documents to various agencies everything was digitalised, with consequently more rapid outcomes (Hamm and Stephanek, 1999). It is therefore not surprising that the term *the digital economy* is gaining greater currency (Hougaard and Duus, 1999).

There are also problems. The principal one is that the internet requires access to both computer hardware and telephone lines so that signals can be downloaded. Even with the price of such equipment in freefall, it still represents a significant barrier to entry for many people.

The second problem is security. One survey found that over 30 per cent of internet sites had no programme to prevent intrusion (Kehoe, 1996). The consequences can be severe. Citibank in the USA lost $10 million when Russian computer hackers transferred the money from its cash management network. (Most of the money was subsequently recovered.) Clearly, this creates customer suspicion when cash transactions or sensitive personal information is at stake.

Third, and linked to the security issue, the internet has become an excellent medium for transmitting computer viruses. Many software programmes are free, and can be downloaded directly through the internet. They frequently bring infections with them. In one year alone, virus infections in US companies grew tenfold (Kehoe, 1996). Evidently, the concept of 'safe socialising' has yet to catch on with sufficient numbers of internet users!

Fourth, congestion is a huge problem. We discuss, below, consumer impatience with having to wait as long as a minute for someone to answer a telephone. However, it is not unusual for several minutes to pass without a response from an internet site. This occurs when companies do not have sufficient connections to handle the demand from customers. Surprisingly, this is a major problem even for some companies who do most of their business on-line. It would, unfortunately, be libellous to specify which of them are most at fault.

Given that the growth of the internet is such a recent development, research into it from a communication perspective is at an extremely early stage. Many sites are left untended for long periods, and hence look like derelict shop windows, exhibiting the fashion sensations from an earlier decade. Others are cluttered, hard to read, have poor links between sections and sometimes prioritise appearance above content. They have a mission to confuse. There is, as yet, a dearth of well established standards to guide those developing and maintaining internet sites. It is likely that audits will shed much light on such issues, and inform the development of best practice standards in the years ahead. Most of the issues which we identify above in connection to the intranet and e-mail clearly apply here as well, and should be a central focus of audit investigations. Accordingly, we would suggest that the following are among the key issues for auditors focusing on the internet:

- *The quality of information on a site*   In particular, is it well structured, does it facilitate movement between sections through the use of transitions and signposts, and is the information clearly presented? The proformas proposed in Chapter 14 for analysing written communication would be of use here.

- *The extent of information underload or overload*   In the final analysis, the needs of the site's users determine whether it is blighted by either of these afflictions. Extensive work by auditors, taking account of communication theory, is the logical means of bringing such needs to the fore and influencing site design. As with wider communication issues, this should be an ongoing process. Few audiences maintain the same information needs over an indefinite timespan: just because they have been audited once does not mean that they can be ignored thereafter. Focus groups, depth interviews or questionnaires could all be employed in addressing these issues.
- *Is there evidence of effective security precautions?*   In particular, the ease with which people's personal information may be accessed is a vital question, and can be evaluated using versions of the mystery shopping technique. Auditors could set the system access challenges to discover whether it locks them out or beckons them in.
- *Utilisation levels*   The number of hits can be monitored with existing software, and gives some indication of a site's likely impact on customers. Bearing in mind the number of transactions made by other means, organisations can set their own targets for the volume of contact expected via the internet. These would serve as rough measures of the site's attractiveness, relevance and ability to win business.
- *The timeliness of information provided*   If customers believe that a site is changed too frequently or infrequently it is clear that their needs are not being met. Questionnaires can address this issue. It could also be a key topic explored during focus group or interview investigations.

TELEPHONE COMMUNICATIONS

The advertising slogan for Audi motors for many years was '*Vorsprung durch Technik*' ('Progress through technology'). But technology itself does not equal progress. Rather it is how it is managed and used that brings results. Of all the advances in technology, without a doubt the telephone has been one of the most important and significant. Since its development in 1876 it has been at the cutting edge of the communications revolution. It is both important as a communication medium in its own right, and has also been the key to numerous other developments (fax, e-mail, the internet, paging, video-phones, etc.). In essence, the wiring of the world began with the development of the telephone (Cairncross, 1998).

The telephone in business

The telephone is a core constituent of the DNA of the business organism. As a whole, telecommunications is a huge industry, with an annual spend of some $1000 million (Hargie *et al.*, 1999). One UK study showed that while 15 per cent of members of the public contacted organisations by letter, four times that number (60 per cent) did so by telephone (Audit Commission, 1994a). In some sectors the figure is even higher. For instance, 80 per cent of all financial transactions are carried out by telephone. Effective firms make optimum use of the telephone, both internally for intra-company communications and externally in their dealings with clients.

The telephone is an indispensable part of everyday life. There are now over one billion telephones in the world. In western society, most cities have more telephones than people. To illustrate the growth of this phenomenon, let us present but three facts in evidence (OPCS, 1992; Irwin, 1998; Hargie *et al.*, 1999) from the UK alone:

- In 1972 the percentage of households with a telephone was 42 per cent, but by 1992 this figure had more than doubled to 92 per cent.
- In 1985 the market for mobile phones was minimal, with only 25 thousand users. By 1999 this number had risen to 13 million and the growth rate has shown no evidence of a slow-down.
- In 1997 a total of 40 million calls to mobile phones were made from land lines, with a total talk-time of five billion minutes, a growth of 40 per cent from the previous year.

In relation to the latter point, the advantages offered by mobile phones has contributed considerably to the increases in telephone usage (Jagoda and de Villepin, 1993). The introduction of satellite as well as terrestrial transmitters means that calls can be made from almost anywhere. Also, the caller can do something else at the same time as dialling and waiting for the call to be answered. The temptation to surrender to that warm little phone in the pocket or handbag is ever-present. In the early stage of development these phones were like house bricks – heavy to carry, hard to hold and only to be used by those with special expertise. However, their increasing miniaturisation quickly enhanced their popularity. They are now not much bulkier than a credit card, and will soon be reduced to the size of a button. It is not surprising that this has been the fastest growing part of the entire telecommunications industry (Irwin, 1998). In the near future one in two phones will be a mobile.

Techno stress

A downside here is that these developments in telecommunications have meant that there is no real escape from the umbilical organisational cord. As telephones have shrunk in size, their impact upon organisational communication has grown in an exponential fashion. Mobile phones, pagers, faxes, and e-mail have colonised the world and increased the pressure upon people to communicate. There are few hiding places left. This has resulted in a condition that has been alternatively termed 'information fatigue syndrome', 'multiphrenia', 'techno stress', and 'future shock'. To put it simply, we become overwhelmed by the barrage of electronic communications and find it either very difficult or impossible to cope.

We seek sanctuary by turning off our mobiles, using voice-mail as a matter of course, and removing our numbers from the telephone directory. Indeed, there has been a rapid increase in ex-directory numbers, with some 56 per cent of subscribers in the city of London requesting exclusion from the directory in 1998 (Kennedy, 1998).

This stress has been heightened by the increased expectations of the public for excellent service. It is also the case that organisations who subject their personnel to techno stress will not survive. Services to clients suffer, efficiency drops, and the daily agenda becomes dominated by sick leave reports. Sick people mean sick companies. Thus, there must be a clear strategy for handling tele-communications, in which the pressures on staff are recognised and catered for. It needs to be recognised that staff whose work involves continuous 'emotional labour' (see Chapter 6), such as being pleasant all of the time on the telephone, will suffer from burn-out unless provided with support.

While some large companies have their own specialised departments to deal with calls from the public, many others hand over responsibility for such tele-phone contacts to independent call centres. By the end of 1997 there were 5000 such centres in England, employing 250,000 people. Recent research into the effects of working in such an environment has identified a condition known as RBI or 'repetitive brain injury' (Irwin, 1999). This occurs after about six months into the job, when people reach the stage where they feel unable to deal with yet another query or handle even one more complaint. The stress is exacerbated by the fact that their work is heavily monitored, a large amount of data are compiled about each individual's performance (e.g. average duration of call), and their calls are often recorded or listened into by supervisors. Staff turnover is therefore high. If organisations are sub-contracting work to call centres they should investigate how workers are treated in these centres. This, we believe, is yet another challenge emerging for those interested in auditing communications. The clients on the receiving end of someone suffering from RBI will believe they are being spoken to by the organisation itself, and not by someone hired at a distance to work by proxy. Any damage caused is not to the call centre, but to the hiring organisation.

Freephone services

One reason for the increase in public contact with companies has been the introduction of freephone, or toll-free, services. This innovation was introduced in the USA by the telecommunications company AT&T in 1967, resulting in what then seemed to be a huge total of 7 million free calls. However, 30 years later, AT&T alone registered 20 billion. Customers are readily seduced by the idea of free calls, and regard this service as an indicator that the organisation wants to communicate. As but one example, when a toll-free number is included in an advert, customer enquiries increase by about 140 per cent.

Of course, this means that steps must be taken to deal with the deluge. There is little point in allowing members of the public to ring you free of charge so that you can then treat them in an offhand manner or insult them! Paying for bad publicity in this way could be the theme for a *Monty Python* sketch. Rather, staff need to be both tooled and psyched up to maximise the opportunity proffered by freephone availability. The benefits can be enormous. For example, the insurance company Direct Line launched its telephone business service in 1985. Using automatic call distribution systems, it was able simultaneously to answer 3000 calls within a second. The public liked it. By 1997 it had become the UK's largest insurer with well over two million customers and 4000 staff.

It is clear that those who handle a large volume of telephone calls need training. Interestingly, it is usually staff lower down the hierarchy (receptionists, tele-sales staff, secretaries, and complaints personnel) who are trained in telephone techniques. On the other hand, managerial staff seldom receive such tuition. This is a wasted opportunity. A knowledge of how to use the telephone to best effect can pay handsome dividends at all levels. For example, within any particular organisation when and in what circumstances is it best to use face-to-face, telephone, written or e-mail communication? In one study, managers rated the most powerful influencing medium as being the telephone, yet it was actually used most often in horizontal interactions between those at the same level (Barry and Bateman, 1992). For vertical communication, face-to-face or written communications were preferred. However, such findings will vary from one context to another, and so managers need to be aware of, and measure, whether internal telecommunications are achieving the best results.

Features of telephone communications

The following features of telephone interactions should be borne in mind when evaluating an organisation's usage of this medium.

Interactions are briefer

While the word itself is a combination of the Greek words for far (*tele*) and voice (*phone*), the effect of the telephone is to literally bring distant voices up close. However, there is a degree of unreality about a disembodied voice beaming into our ear – what you have is interaction without the 'social' dimension. There is no process of meeting, greeting and seating. This is the main reason why when calls are compared to parallel face-to-face encounters, there is a huge chasm in time differentials (Hargie *et al.*, 1999). Telephone interactions last for only a fraction of the time of comparable face-to-face contacts. Most of the discussion is task centred, with little social chit chat and less humour. Much of the interaction is taken up with questions and answers. This means that people expect businesses to deal with these mediated interactions in a rapid, yet efficient, fashion.

Relationship development is more difficult

The above time differentials have been explained by what is known as 'the coffee and biscuits problem' (Short *et al.*, 1976). When people meet they do not rush madly into the business to be transacted. Rather, there is a period of small talk and social niceties, during which the host provides refreshments (tea, coffee, biscuits etc.). Such 'social hokum' takes time, but has evolved for a good reason. It is part of a human bonding ritual that allows relationships to develop. It also enables both 'sides' to size one another up and make judgements about acceptable responses (e.g. is humour appropriate?). This in turn oils the interactional wheels so that when the conversation moves on to business it will flow smoothly. In telephone encounters there is no coffee and biscuits interlude. Furthermore, the social problems are compounded by the lack of visual and body language cues that are often vital in judging the true feelings, attitudes and beliefs of others. The lack of such cues can be summarised simply as an absence of presence. On the telephone, a degree of relational compensation can be effected through using first names, engaging in some small talk, discussing family and friends, and employing humour. All other things being equal, people will prefer to do repeat business with people they like rather than those they do not like.

Incidents of aggression and rudeness increase

There is an estimated 65 per cent and 9 per cent chance of rudeness, respectively, for telephone and face-to-face interactions (MacErlean, 1997). As with e-mail, the fact that the other person is not physically present makes it easier to be aggressive and assertive. For example, refusal rates to survey requests are higher on the telephone than face to face (Frey, 1989). In interpersonal encounters, being rude or aggressive carries the possible danger of physical violence. This is removed on the telephone and the concomitant lack of fear may contribute to aggression. Aggression can also be provoked in the caller by the recipient using one of a number of behaviours (Tracy and Tracy, 1998), including:

- interruptions – not allowing the person to finish speaking before interjecting;
- increased voice volume;
- controlled enunciation – pausing briefly and deliberately between each emphasised word (What. Exactly. Are. You. Looking. For?);
- metacommunicative directives – commands or enquiries that question the caller's ability ('Do you understand what I am trying to tell you?');
- assertion/counterassertion (Caller: 'I don't like your attitude.' Recipient: 'Well, I don't care much for yours either');
- confrontation/denial (Caller: 'You should have told me that earlier.' Recipient: 'I did');
- stance indicators – negative attitude towards the caller expressed implicitly through choice of words and phrases ('If that really did happen . . .').

These should be avoided wherever possible when dealing with the public, and when auditing telephone complaints these should form the basis of behavioural checks. For organisations, the key is to ensure that staff do not react negatively or provocatively. We have worked with a major broadcasting company in Northern Ireland over many of the years of inter-community conflict. At tense times when tempers are running dangerously high, people phone in at full steam to complain bitterly about a programme. By reacting with courtesy, showing an appreciation of their *feelings* (not their sentiments), speaking softly (as recommended in the Bible 'A soft answer turns away wrath'), allowing them to rant without interruption, and reassuring them that their complaint will be noted, their behaviour is almost always transformed. They generally end up thanking the member of staff for listening and offering some sort of apology and explanation for their emotional state.

Public dislikes

Surveys of top telephone hates reveal that the top two most disliked practices are, first, the call not being answered for a long time, and second, being met by a recorded message. Let us look at each of these.

Delays in answering

The advice of the sixteenth-century poet Robert Southwell should be heeded in formulating a telephone answering strategy: 'Shun delays, they breed remorse.' Two UK surveys carried out in 1997 identified problems with pick-up times. In the first, the *Financial Mail* found that a quarter of all calls were still unanswered after one minute, with a wide disparity of performance between the best company answering in one second and the worst in 7 minutes 30 seconds. In the second, carried out by British Telecom, almost one-third of all calls to small businesses were still unanswered after 15 rings. This can be rectified. To paraphrase Bob Dylan, the answer to a ringing telephone is not to leave it blowin' in the wind. For instance, Citibank in London set a target frame for calls to be answered in between 10 and 30 seconds and discovered that over 500 calls per day were not meeting this benchmark. To overcome this deficit they invested £120,000 in new equipment, after which some 95 per cent of the 5000 daily calls to the bank were responded to in less than 10 seconds.

Voice-mail

The Swiss novelist Max Frisch defined technology as 'the knack of so arranging the world that we need not experience it'. It seems that many people use voice-mail in this way – as a screening device to decide whether and when to deal with people. For live telephone interaction to occur, the other person must be available when you call. Before the introduction of voice-mail, what was referred to as 'telephone tag' occurred in large firms, with callers phoning round and trying to get hold of the other person. This was very time-consuming and wasteful. As a result, in many organisations voice-mail has become an accepted internal communication norm. But it has been consistently shown to be disliked by external customers. The most hated system is 'voicemail jail' where callers are met by what is regarded as a sadistic recorded voice advising: 'If you want to do X, press 1, if you want to do Y press 2 . . .' Two-thirds of people respond to voice-mail jail with the 'slam-down' reflex (i.e. they hang up!). Not good business.

Auditing telephone communications

The ubiquitous nature of telephones means that this is a communication medium in which organisational personnel must show high levels of skill. Staff should be trained in the key skills of receiving and sending calls. A British Telecom survey of customers in 1997 found that 90 per cent of those who experienced unanswered or poorly handled calls stopped dealing with that organisation. On the other hand, when calls are dealt with in a caring, professional way, an impression of efficiency and competence is conveyed and customer loyalty bonds strengthened. For the ringing of telephones to be converted into the jingling of cash in the company's coffers, external callers must experience an excellent service.

Organisations need to set targets for answers to telephone calls. We discussed above, in connection to e-mail, how targets could be set for organisations as a whole, for individual departments, and on issues such as responsiveness. A similar approach can be readily applied to telephones. For example, targets can be for responses within a specified number of rings, or time in seconds. In practice, the latter criterion is most widely used, and targets can vary far and wide. Thus, the Audit Commission (1994a) found that local authorities in England and Wales had targets for answering ranging between less than four seconds at the best end of the continuum to under one minute at the worst (few people will wait that long!). It is important for targets to be set at such a level that they can be met at even the busiest time of the week or year. If the standard is too high staff will become demoralised, and if too low it becomes inconsequential. The secret is to set achievable targets that challenge staff to improve their performance.

There are various ways and levels at which an audit can be carried out into telephone usage. For example, organisations should have a proforma for taking messages that lists the name/address/phone number of the caller, date/time of call, main points of the message, and when the person is available for call back (see Box 8.3). The auditor can conduct a content analysis of these proformas over a set period (e.g. one week), to ascertain the extent to which all information has been logged, and where improvements are required.

At another level, electronic call logging systems give accurate information about how many calls are made to and from each extension number, how long before incoming calls are answered, the duration of each interaction, what the cost to the company is of each external call and to whom it was made. This information is important in informing task analysis (e.g. what percentage of a

---

Box 8.3 Telephone messages proforma

Message for _____ Date/Time _____

Caller's name _____ Designation _____

Caller's Tel. No. _____ Fax. _____ E-mail _____

Times when caller will be available to take a return call:

_____

Main reason for the call _____

_____

Message:

_____
_____
_____
_____
_____
_____
_____

      Message taken by _____

---

worker's time is spent on the telephone), and in attributing costs to relevant departments. However, while it produces an accurate measure of the dimensions of the artefact, such analysis gives no information about its quality. It can also be inaccurate.

The Audit Commission (1994a) cited the example of an organisation where performance in call answering had deteriorated. The Chief Executive exhorted all staff to address this matter, but the next read-out from the call logger showed a further drop in performance. Frustrated, he examined the full details and found one extension where performance was dreadful. This turned out to be an extension number in the office next door to his, which was occupied by the external auditor! When this number was removed, performance levels improved dramatically.

Many of the methods described in previous chapters can be employed to audit telephone answering. Thus, questionnaires can assess internal staff perspectives (see Appendix). We conducted an audit of a health authority in which, on the quantitative section, we noticed marked dissatisfaction with telephone communications in one particular section of the organisation. Analysis of the open questions then revealed that the problem was that there were only two extensions for 15 staff. This situation had been raised through formal channels but forgotten about until the audit. It was quickly rectified.

Customer surveys and interviews can be employed in external audits. However, the most common method used to assess this field is that of mystery shopping (see Chapter 6). Here, a 'pretend' client makes the call and checks how it is dealt with against a range of criteria such as:

- Was the call answered within three rings (or four seconds)?
- Did the person sound genuinely pleased to be taking the call?
- Did the person begin with a greeting, followed by location, name, and position (i.e. 'Good afternoon, Booking Office, Jane Hodges, Client Executive speaking')?
- Was an offer of help made? (e.g. 'How may I help?')
- Was your name ascertained at the outset?
- How often in total was your name used?
- Were your needs and requirements established at the outset?
- Were these checked for fulfilment at the end?
- If relevant, was the call transferred swiftly to the right department (within ten seconds)?
- If you were left hanging on, was an explanation given as to why?
- Was your permission obtained for this (e.g. 'Could you excuse me for a few seconds, while I get that file?')?
- If the person could not deal with the enquiry immediately, was a reason given?
- Did the person explain precisely what would happen next?
- Were you told when someone would return the call?
- Were key points fed back to you during the call to show concerted listening, and to check that these were your main concerns?
- Were regular signals of active listening used (e.g. 'Ah ha', 'Right', 'Yeah', 'OK')?
- Was action-reassurance given about the time-frame within which relevant issues raised would be dealt with?
- If making a complaint, were you given time to ventilate without interruption? Did the person speak gently? Did they acknowledge your emotions (e.g. 'I can understand that you feel very strongly about this')?
- Were the main points summarised at the end of the call?
- Were you rewarded for calling (e.g. 'Thank you for calling', 'I'm glad you let us know')?

Some organisations have an in-house checking facility. For example, North Yorkshire County Council has an internal team of five clerks who carry out four mystery shopper surveys per year (Audit Commission, 1994a). Each survey checks 500 calls in a particular week against predetermined criteria. Calls are routed so that they appear to be from an external source. Staff know they will be monitored but do not know when. Other companies use external consultants to carry out this function.

An analysis of the purpose of telephone calls can be very insightful. For example, one local authority in the UK discovered that many callers were seeking similar basic information (e.g. public holidays, opening hours), and so switchboard operators were trained to ascertain what service the caller wanted and to provide this information if required, rather than transferring the call to a service department (Audit Commission, 1994a). This simple measure reduced the response time considerably, improved customer care and removed a very routine, repetitive task from the staff in service departments. It also brought some more variety into the jobs of the switchboard operators.

CONCLUSION

All the technologies reviewed in this chapter offer the prospect of further enormous changes in the immediate future, despite the frantic speed of developments already witnessed. This means that organisations themselves will be transformed. The manner in which information is now exchanged tends to up-end power relationships, and frequently demolishes the most imposing of organisational structures. Virtual companies are becoming commonplace. Even mainstream companies find that they have a reduced need for gatekeepers. Traditional departmental structures are becoming more translucent, as information flows through boundaries that once seemed opaque. There is no room left for technophobia. A few years ago, it was possible to boast that one did not know the difference between a megabyte and an insect bite. Today, such an attitude is career suicide, and would set any organisation which tolerated it firmly on the road to ruin.

Communication audits will assist researchers and practitioners to monitor these issues more closely. There is, for example, a need for clearer protocols in all these areas (e.g. in Intranet/Internet design, e-mail manners and telephone answering targets), which take account of best practice. Yet what is best practice? There is still insufficient clarity on this important issue. As we have argued here, audits can help to resolve this problem.

Most of the tools discussed in this book can be adapted to audit the communications revolution. As elsewhere, it has not been our intention to recommend a stock inventory of techniques for all situations. A variety of tools can be utilised to explore different aspects of the technologies discussed in this chapter. However, the general process of audit and the strategic framework for its implementation which we proposed in Chapter 2 will be vital to the development of a deeper understanding of these issues. The communications revolution offers a rising tide of technological innovations. With the aid of audits, organisations can seize the new opportunities which abound, rather than perish under the flood.

Chapter 9

Crafting the audit report

Dennis Tourish and Owen Hargie

INTRODUCTION

Once the audit has been implemented, and the data collected and analysed, there is then the key task of presenting the results in the form of a report. This is a defining point in the whole exercise. Considerable care may have been devoted to the implementation of the audit, but if this is not reflected in the final written presentation all the planning, script conferences and dress rehearsals will have stopped short of a convincing public performance.

For example, it is possible to:

- overemphasise the difficulties which lie ahead;
- baffle the organisation with an over-abundance of statistics;
- outline a sweeping change agenda, which inspires panic rather than action;
- deal summatively with the audit's main findings, generating lethargy rather than energy.

We have also encountered audit reports written by some consulting firms, in which the recommendations have been principally framed to avoid offending anyone and so lose the firm future business. The consequence is that they are of little use as a guide to action for the organisation concerned. (Incidentally, we have found that most organisations *prefer* a frank rather than a diplomatic appraisal of their communication climate.)

Our goal, in this chapter, is to enable readers to avoid these pitfalls. Accordingly, we propose an overall structure for a typical audit report and outline what each section is intended to achieve. Given that a report will present both positive and negative findings, and that the latter may be threatening for some people, we discuss how 'bad news' can best be broken. A good deskside manner is as vital for auditors as a bedside one is for medics. In particular, we pay close attention to developing the recommendations which should flow from the audit findings. Furthermore, we argue that, if such recommendations are to take root, wide constituencies of opinion must be persuaded of their benefits, so that they become motivated and committed to seeing them through. In consequence, we outline some of the key levers of persuasion suggested by the research literature, which seem particularly pertinent in this context, and explore how they can be employed in the course of constructing an audit report.

STRUCTURING AN AUDIT REPORT

Bowman and Branchaw (1983, p. 7) described reports as 'an organised presentation of information to a specific audience for the purpose of helping an organisation achieve an objective'. Effective reports can be defined as 'a guide to action'. All other issues (e.g. the amount of detail required, statistical sophistication, and literary style) are subordinate to this clear imperative. Additionally, people have a particular expectation that an audit report dealing with communication will be an exceptionally crafted demonstration of good communication practice. As Downs (1988, p. 204) argued, this means that 'the final report must be a superb form of communication about communication'.

The defining traits of effective reports are widely agreed (Padget, 1983; Hargie et al., 1999). Typically, excellent reports are assumed to be:

1 *Timely:* This refers to both the production of the report and its contents. Ideally, it should arrive before it is due (but certainly no later), and contain the most up-to-date information available on the problem at hand. An audit report should display an awareness of the most current and relevant techniques in the field, combined with an acute focus on the current business needs of the organisation involved. It should answer today's problems rather than yesterday's, while preparing everyone for the challenges of tomorrow.

2 *Well written:* The report should be clear, concise, and interesting; it should grab the reader's attention and hold it throughout; it should avoid errors in grammar, spelling, punctuation and factual content. One factual error damages the credibility of your whole case, much as a single lie shatters a manager's reputation for honesty. Above all, it should be driven by a bias towards action, which solves a problem, identifies the next steps the report's readers can and must take, and be directly related to the underlying business objectives of the organisation.

3 *Well organised:* A good report is designed to be read selectively, so that the reader can pay attention only to its most necessary parts. Most reports have multiple audiences, and will have few readers interested in its entire content. For this reason, an executive summary (listing main findings and recommendations) is obligatory. Surprisingly, compiling such a summary is often the most difficult part of the exercise, since it implies a careful identification of the most important themes and a judicious selection of the most relevant supporting details. Perhaps this process explains Mark Twain's fabled comment to a friend, on sending him a lengthy letter. Twain complained that he hadn't had time to write a short letter, so a long one would have to do.

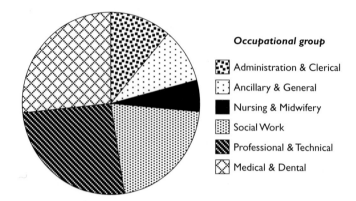

Figure 9.1 Breakdown of the sample (1)

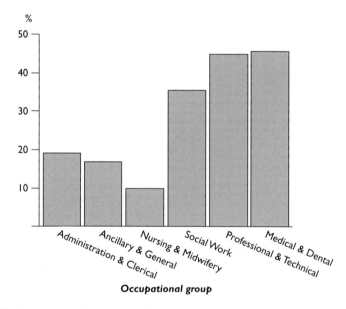

Figure 9.2 Breakdown of the sample (2)

4 *Attractive:* It should be clearly labelled, arrive in good condition, and be
   presented with an attractive typeface and layout. Graphics, bar charts, pictures
   and diagrams present data in accessible forms, simplify the job of the reader
   and also enhance the attractiveness and impact of a report (Blundel, 1998).
   Figure 9.1 provides an example of a pie chart from one of our audits, summarising a breakdown of the staff who were surveyed, to illustrate the point.
   Figure 9.2 reproduces the same data as a histogram. Either is preferable to
   simply listing the numbers of each. First impressions count. They shape ex-

pectations about the overall import of the report. Thus, a professional cover and good binding are also essential. A well presented report projects a favourable impression of the audit exercise, and creates an aura of attractiveness around its central recommendations.

5 *Cost effective:* The report's recommendations should be designed to solve real problems facing its readership, and should be clearly explained, possible to implement, and cost effective. Although there are no guidelines on the maximum number of recommendations it should contain, it is important to remember that an organisation with 40 priorities in reality has none. On the other hand, a small number of key proposals is known as an action plan. We return to this issue later in this chapter.

6 *A report begins before the beginning*, with the terms of reference set for its production. These identify the problem(s) it will be expected to solve, set explicit limits on the range of issues to be addressed, and identify specific outcomes towards which the report should aspire.

Standard formats exist for the structure of a report, and in general retain their validity in the case of communication audit reports. It has been suggested (Hargie *et al.*, 1999) that they should normally contain the following:

- Title page
- Contents
- Acknowledgements
- Executive Summary
- Introduction

- Methodology
- Findings/Conclusions
- Recommendations
- Appendices
- References

The *Acknowledgements* are an opportunity to identify important change agents within the organisation who have participated in the most important aspects of the communication audit exercise. This, of course, suggests that such people will have been involved in designing the audit process, or collecting data, and that key findings will have been shared with them as they emerge. It is certainly unhelpful to present senior people with a nasty surprise at the end of the audit, and then expect their enthusiastic support (Barrington, 1992). By involving them, and sharing the credit in the eventual report, auditors will gain a valuable reputation as team players, and establish that the entire exercise has been rooted in the business needs of the organisation.

The importance of involving vital players has been noted by, among others, Conger (1998, p. 89), who advocated that those attempting to persuade should 'make a concerted effort to meet one-on-one with all the key people you plan to persuade. This is not the time to outline your position but rather to get a range of perspectives on the issue at hand.' Such an approach also has the added advantage of spreading responsibility for awkward issues raised and difficult decisions proposed: it is harder for people to reject the audit conclusions outright, if the Chief Executive has been identified as a key figure in drawing up the team's terms of reference, gathering the data and devising the recommendations.

A reason for this, suggested in the research literature on persuasion, is that the credibility of a message source is a key factor in determining a message's persuasive impact (Perloff, 1993). One of the key dimensions of credibility is *power* (Morrow and Hargie, 1996). Top executives in an organisation are likely to possess *legitimate power* (i.e. their hierarchical position possesses innate authority and confers extra legitimacy on the office holder's perceptions and actions); *coercive power* (i.e. they are perceived as having the ability to enforce their will by having the capacity to apply sanctions); and *expert power* (i.e. their recognised expertise or in-depth knowledge can directly persuade another of the value of a particular course of action). Associating the report with powerful and hence credible figures, capable of exercising these and other forms of power, is an important means of enhancing its persuasive impact.

The *Summary* should outline both the main findings and recommendations. Typically, a report will have multiple audiences, with vastly differing information needs (Roberts-Gray, 1992). Therefore, most people will read only this section. One research investigation, into the efficacy of a particular approach to report writing, found that three-quarters of readers merely skimmed the report (Stallworth and Roberts-Gray, 1987), with only one-quarter reading it thoroughly. Likewise, most readers tend to read only the abstracts which appear at the beginning of articles in academic journals, much as those of us who write them would like to think otherwise. Given that the end purpose of the audit exercise is to promote action and change, this reinforces the need for a cogent, comprehensive summary.

However, the rest of the report lends authority to the summary. Readers who query a particular finding or recommendation can delve into the appropriate section in more depth, to reassure themselves that the audit has been rigorously conducted, data genuinely representative of communication transactions within the organisation collected, and that the report's recommendations are based on solid evidence. Otherwise, it may be assumed that they are either a wish fulfilment list drawn up by alienated malcontents, or a top manager's ideal image of what should be rather than what is. Such supporting testimony is excised from the summary, which needs to combine brevity with a comprehensive account of the most salient issues.

The *Introduction* should explain who commissioned the communication audit, who was responsible for the overall conduct of the exercise, and the purpose of the report. It should briefly outline the method of inquiry which was adopted and the terms of reference which were set. It should also explain how the data have been assembled and arranged, how the report is structured, and whatever general background factors are considered to be most crucial. In general, this means identifying the importance of communication to the organisation at this stage. The temptation here is to assume that, since the issue is by now over-familiar to the audit team, it will be equally familiar to everyone else.

The *Methodology* outlines, in detail, the steps taken to assemble the audit data. It is generally agreed (Downs, 1988) that the key issues which must be explained include the following:

Table 9.1 Breakdown of the sample

Occupational groups	Staff in post	Sample size	Percentage of occupational group
Admin. and Clerical	53	10	18.8
Ancillary and General	84	14	16.6
Nursing and Midwifery	332	33	9.9
Social Work	28	10	35.7
Professional and Technical	9	4	44.4
Medical and Dental	11	5	45.5
Total	517	76	14.7% of workforce

- What techniques were employed in the audit?
- Why were these techniques selected in preference to any others?
- How, and by whom, was the data collection carried out?
- How many staff, clients or customers were audited?
- How were they selected?
- If everyone was not included, what percentage sample was used?

It is also useful to provide a summary table which describes the total breakdown of the sample. We provide an example in Table 9.1, derived from an audit conducted by us in an NHS Trust. The data it contains were presented earlier in this chapter in the form of a histogram and a pie chart. Readers can compare these, and decide which they feel presents the data in the most striking and accessible form. For many data sets histograms, bar charts and pie charts are a more striking and hence preferable mode of presentation, and with the advent of desktop publishing are now widely used.

The *Findings/Conclusions* section details precisely what you have discovered. It should also analyse the importance of your findings. If 80 per cent of the organisation's employees are satisfied with information received from top management, what precisely does this mean for the organisation's communication strategy? What are the implications for trust, loyalty and commitment? How well does it compare to previous surveys, or contemporaneous surveys in other organisations within this business area? Does it mean that plain sailing lies ahead, or are there storms on the immediate horizon?

The *Recommendations* is the section of the report where you most clearly link data to action. Research into the effect of feedback in the context of clinical audit has distinguished between passive feedback (i.e. information on performance *without* suggestions for improvement) and active feedback (i.e. information about performance *with* suggestions for improvement). In general, such research has found that active feedback is more likely to promote improvements in performance (Mugford *et al.*, 1991; Baker, 1999). As Roberts-Gray (1992, p. 177) put it: 'data presented without recommendations can frustrate and immobilise rather than facilitate decision making'. Recommendations should emerge clearly from the findings, rather than appear unheralded in the middle of the conclusions. The benefits which key change agents in the organisation will obtain, if they implement the recommendations, should be fully explained. The principal finding (judged by its importance to the organisation, and as identified in the terms of reference) should attract the most emphasis in the recommendations.

To capture attention, an audit report should expend most of its energy in outlining the particular difficulties which communication problems are creating for the organisation at present, rather than potential difficulties to which current practices might give rise in the hypothetical future. As the eminent economist John Maynard Keynes once famously remarked, 'In the long run, we are all dead.' Managers are therefore biased in favour of addressing immediate problems rather than distant tornadoes, which they hope might pass them by. As two early researchers in this area stressed, they use communication as a corrective rather than a preventative process (Greenbaum and White, 1976). Consequently, recommendations are more likely to attract attention, and support, when they focus overwhelmingly on real and present dangers.

An important question is how many recommendations the report should contain. We have scrutinised audit reports where the number of discernible recommendations has varied from 3 to 43! There are no absolutely clear-cut rules or research findings in this area. However, research into change management suggests that an excessive number of action points produces paralysis rather than action, by preventing a consistent focus on the clear vision which is a precondition for success (Kanter, 1983). People in general value habit in their work lives – i.e. they prefer to do a job the way in which it has been learned, performed and reinforced through practice (Moorhead and Griffin, 1989). The disruption of habit on an excessive scale sparks increased uncertainty, in spite of the fact that uncertainty reduction is both a driving force behind many interpersonal communication episodes (Berger, 1987), and a characteristic of an organisational context capable of sustaining successful innovation (Pearson, 1991). An atmosphere of heightened uncertainty is also likely to promote organisational politicking and hence disrupt that process of coalition building which is, again, a vital factor in successful innovation and change (Kanter, 1991).

In short, when faced with a call for action on every front, people find it difficult to discern clear priorities or to focus their energies on any one issue to the point where they can see it through to completion. An overwhelming agenda also makes it difficult for managers to track and hence benchmark the impact of particular initiatives. Given what is known about human memory, and the limited attention span of the average TV viewer, it was probably wise for God to give Moses ten commandments, rather than 110. In our experience, and we acknowledge the need for further research into this question, ten major recommendations is sufficient to stimulate both action and further reflection within any organisation.

Kramlinger (1998) has argued that, in constructing a message people can easily learn, it is vital to address employees' real concerns, and make a connection to whatever values are shared throughout the organisation. Clearly, recommendations which promote actual change must assume a simple form which people can memorise, become inspired by, act upon and convince others to respond to. The eminent psychologist B.F. Skinner (1954) concluded that the two most powerful reinforcers are *success* and *an awareness that progress has been made*. This suggests that an audit report should talk about the strengths of action plans as well as the weaknesses they are designed to address, thereby (in marketing parlance) promising the organisation a clear set of benefits.

It is vital that recommendations are relevant to the organisation which has been audited, and that managers will be able to implement them. Good generals know never to give an order which cannot be obeyed. The result is demoralisation and an erosion of their authority. Recommendations which may have worked in other organisations before might be impractical in a different context. Suggesting that they be implemented when this is likely to be a stretch too far does not facilitate action, nor improvements in communication.

It is useful if the recommendations seek to build upon positive behaviours which at least some sections of the organisation are already displaying, rather than if they represent an entirely new set of values, behaviours and relationships which everyone will have to learn from scratch. In these terms, and selecting from suggestions made by Kramlinger (1998), it is vital to frame recommendations so that they tell people:

- Why were we doing the wrong thing before?
- How does this change fit with previous changes?
- What will remain constant?
- How is this change grounded in our values and commitments?
- What will the organisation look like in six months? In a year?
- What will we gain or lose personally?
- What support will we get to make the change?
- What will executives do to make sure the change works?

(Kramlinger, 1998, p. 46)

The cardinal question to be addressed is: what can the organisation do differently to that which it already does, and how will this make a difference to the main problems which it currently faces? Goldhaber (1993, p. 369) listed a number of recommendations which were implemented by a variety of ICA clients. Some of these are identified here, combined with commentaries from our own auditing experience:

- The use of new formal communication channels, such as newsletters, bulletin boards, new meeting structures. Increasingly, our research would add e-mail, the Internet and the Intranet to this list.

- Development of communication goals, objectives and policies, and the disclosure of these to relevant publics.
- Open disclosure policies on certain issues. Frequently, we have found that
people imagine managers to be more secretive on a range of issues than they
are. We have therefore recommended that a 'A Freedom of Information Act'
be announced, which explicitly declares that managers can be approached on a
number of identified issues and will be prepared to provide any information
available on them.
- Better upward input solicited by top management to improve the planning
process. Frequently, this has involved intensive follow-up effort, to transform
team briefings into a system for promoting two-way communication and hence
involvement.

This is by no means a definitive inventory of likely recommendations, which always
relate to the unique findings of the audit which has been conducted. The case study
chapters contained in Part III of this book discuss particular organisational interventions to which various audits gave rise, and which should enable readers to
begin a debate into the most relevant changes which seem pertinent to their needs.

The *Appendices* contain supporting material that is important to the overall
case, but which does not belong logically in the main body of the report. These
include examples of data collection instruments (e.g. questionnaires, survey instruments, observation schedules), tables which are of interest to some readers
but are marginal to the main issues being explored, or more lengthy extracts
from interviews with people who have been surveyed. Few readers will explore
this section in-depth, just as few patients will ever inspect a doctor's credentials.
However, the knowledge that they are there reassures people that the report's
diagnosis is based on a rigorous methodology, solid evidence and hard work.

The *References* is a list of main sources cited in the text – books, reports,
newspaper articles, journal articles or official statements. Again, this reassures
readers that the methods, findings and recommendations contained in the report
rest on a tangible body of research and experience, rather than the sort of
inspiration born of missed or impending deadlines. There is no need for a huge
number of references – a report is a guide to action, rather than an academic
masterpiece. A small number of references (probably in the region of about ten)
should be sufficient to enable anyone who wishes to explore a particular issue in
more detail to do so. Such follow up is also likely to strengthen their interest and
hence commitment to the issues raised in the report. This reinforces the report's
credibility. Credibility is central to successful persuasion, and hence to change.

A number of other key issues in writing an audit report are now considered.

THE SIGNIFICANCE OF STATISTICS

Roberts-Gray (1992) counsels that reports should present statistical information
simply. Stephen Hawking, in the acknowledgements to his best selling *A Brief*

History of Time, wrote: 'Someone told me that each equation I included in the book would halve the sales' (p. vi). He therefore includes only one equation in his book – that for relativity ($E = mc^2$). A similar approach to statistics in reports is vital. Investigations of teachers and administrators in schools explored precisely this question (Brown and Newman, 1983). They found that teachers and administrators were

- much more receptive and supportive of recommendations emerging from short reports which contained no statistics;
- slightly more supportive if frequency data and percentages were included;
- tended to reject the same set of recommendations if the report contained notations for type of statistical analysis and significance levels.

In part, as has been well documented, this is because most people have a poor grasp of statistics and the laws of probability (Sutherland, 1992). This explains the popularity of national lotteries, once defined as 'a tax on stupidity'. However irrational it may be, we tend to place more trust in stories and individual experiences which we can recall vividly than we do in statistical averages (Dawes, 1994). For this reason, smokers find the fact that they know someone who has survived the habit a convincing reason to continue with it, while pooh-poohing the epidemiological evidence that it damages health. Additionally, many of us distrust those who wield figures in argument, recalling Mark Twain's famous comment that 'there are lies, damned lies and statistics'.

It is clear that statistics require careful interpretation (Edwards *et al.*, 1997). First, statistics are useful to provide evidence – i.e. as an indicator of what the main trends in communication are, and as a means of persuading people that certain changes are necessary. However, although statistics are important in this endeavour, it has been pointed out that the most effective persuaders

> supplement numerical data with examples, stories, metaphors, and analogies to make their positions come alive. That use of language paints a vivid word picture and, in doing so, lends a compelling and tangible quality to the persuader's point of view.
>
> (Conger, 1998, p. 90)

It is therefore necessary to integrate statistical findings with the real words of real people in the organisation, who can explain in the language of individual experience what the facts and figures really mean.

In addition, many readers of the report will approach any and all findings with trepidation, fearing that their reputation or that of their departments is in some way on the line. They may therefore be inclined to exaggerate or understate precisely the most important findings, in the service of internal political agendas. People may also attack the statistical tests used, metamorphising within seconds into mathematical geniuses, intent on recruiting adherents to the good old cause of the status quo. A communication audit report should minimise the scope for such misunderstandings and gamesmanship. This means that its authors should consider such issues as:

- If a score of 4.1 is achieved on a five-point scale (such as that utilised in the ICA instrument, and discussed in Chapter 3), what does it *mean*? Is the communication climate freezing cold? Or, on the contrary, has springtime arrived early?
- If 80 per cent of staff are moderately dissatisfied with communication, should this be a cause for panic? Or does it compare favourably with levels achieved by other competitors in this industry?
- What are the subgroup scores within the organisation? Do most groupings feel the same, or are there pockets either of great satisfaction or total alienation? Where, in other words, is the greatest need for rapid action, and where can we encourage people to immediately celebrate their achievements?
- What are the optimum scores which can be achieved with the particular research instrument employed in this investigation? It is rare, in our experience, for organisations to achieve scores above 4 when a five-point scale has been used. Central tendency would suggest that scores tend to settle on a mid-point range. This puts what might appear to be initially low scores in context.
- It is also helpful to compare present scores with those for the same or similar items on previous surveys, either within this organisation or in audits conducted in other organisations (Edwards *et al.*, 1997). For example, we worked with one organisation in which senior managers were initially depressed at an overall satisfaction score of 3.7, on a five-point scale. It was necessary to point out that in this particular sector of industry 3.7 was actually in the upper quadrant of organisations which we had surveyed, and close in any event to what experience suggested was the maximum that could be achieved.
- Consider carefully how to report issues of statistical significance. The problem is that managers often become obsessed by what is statistically rather than what is practically significant. The difficulty, and one possible solution, is neatly summarised as follows by Edwards *et al.* (1997, p. 130): 'because statistical significance tests are affected by sample sizes, surveys conducted with samples of several hundred or several thousand respondents may obtain significant results even with group differences as small as .1 or .2 on a 5-point scale. These differences, though statistically significant, may have little practical application in organizations . . . At times, we have used a 10 percentage point difference as a predetermined level of practical significance.' Thus, if a five-point scale is converted to percentages 10 per cent would represent a value of 0.5, which these guidelines suggest could be used as a measure of practical significance.

BREAKING BAD NEWS

A communication audit report should be an *honest* and *accurate* account of the communication climate found within the organisation concerned. However, this general imperative does not exhaust the vexed question of how to present what might be termed bad news to senior managers. We have already alluded, in this chapter, to the difficulty of interpreting data, particularly of a statistical kind. In addition, communication audit results are always subject to 'political' interpretation, creating the possibility of a 'shoot the messenger syndrome' which might well derail the whole process (Badaracco, 1988).

Thus, it is vital that the report draws attention to both the strengths and weaknesses of communication. When only the latter is highlighted people feel powerless to effect change, imagining that there are no instances of effective practice for them to build upon. Consistent negative feedback, and the absence of positive reinforcement, promotes the conviction that things can only get worse, whatever people do. This syndrome is known as 'learned helplessness' (Peterson *et al.*, 1993). Those who fall victim to it may reject the entire report, and disparage the audit exercise. Everyone then gets very busy, preparing for failure. In reality, communication sometimes works well in even the most dysfunctional of organisations. Likewise, all organisations have problems, and their existence may be more a reflection of the breakdowns and viruses that inevitably afflict human communication than, for example, the leadership ability of a particular chief executive (Quirke, 1996). Despite such qualifications, there is, as Downs (1988, p. 190) has pointed out, 'a common tendency . . . to focus almost exclusively on the negative; tackling problems seems to be more interesting and more challenging. Therefore, the negative must be kept in perspective, balanced with the positive.'

When this is not done, senior management teams often respond by rejecting the audit findings out of hand. As Quirke (1996) noted:

> It is remarkable how, in a presentation of the findings, senior managers suddenly become experts in research methodology, asking questions about statistical validity, phrasing of questions in the questionnaire, individuals selected for interview, five-point scales and false positives. Resistance to uncomfortable findings is expressed in questions about the way the research has been conducted. The findings are then talked out of court without any real discussion or acceptance of their validity, and hope of commitment to action disappears.
>
> (Quirke, 1996, p. 203)

Thus, staff can become viewed as whiners, malingerers or troublemakers – and the audit findings again rejected (Wilmot and McClelland, 1990).

We have conducted 'repair' work with one organisation where precisely this occurred in a particularly disastrous form. An internal audit team had carried out its work with great energy, determination and enthusiasm – but neglected to keep the senior management team informed of its progress. When they presented modestly critical findings, in an oral presentation to the top management team, their methodology was queried, the validity of the findings rejected and the group disbanded in disgrace. In consequence, a highly talented and important group of people became demoralised, while two years passed before the organisation dared to re-examine its communication practices again. It was necessary to start work with both the group and senior managers from the very beginning, while placing an enormous stress on the importance of ongoing communication between the two.

How can such disasters be averted? Fundamentally, we would argue that many of the principles which apply when breaking bad news to employees also hold in this context (Cook, 1991). A number of suggestions are offered here, based on what the research literature suggests to be most effective:

1 When positive and negative feedback has to be communicated about a person, object, process or organisation the message recipient is more likely to believe the message when it begins with the positive comment (Jacobs *et al.*, 1973). This may be because a variety of self-serving biases cause most of us routinely to exaggerate our proficiency as communicators (Sutherland, 1992). Drivers often appear to imagine that the roads would be safe, providing everyone else stayed at home: a recent survey of British drivers found that 95 per cent rated themselves as better than the average driver (Hargie *et al.*, 1999). Likewise, most people seem to believe that they could communicate perfectly, if only there was no one else around to get in the way. In consequence, a message which begins by confirming what we think we already know (i.e. *what I am doing well*) has a greater intuitive validity for most people, and leaves them more favourably disposed to accept what follows. A report should begin by accentuating the positive, in the form of stating whatever good news it honestly can.

2 Indicate how the findings compare with surveys of this kind in other organisations, or how much further improvement could be realistically expected at this juncture of its history (Morris and LoVerde, 1993). Context is vital to promote understanding and facilitate action.

3 The report should be written in non-inflammatory and neutral language, offering solutions rather than a grievance list (Badaracco, 1988). It should be sensitive to the internal politics, language and values of the organisation concerned. Rather than identify scapegoats, responsibility for problems should be shared as widely as is honestly possible, thereby encouraging a collective determination to do something about them. Naming and shaming leads to aggravation, conflagration and retaliation.

4 Reinforcing the previous point, it is vital that critical feedback be constructed as non-judgementally as possible (Murray, 1989). This means that it should avoid negatively labelling the people involved (e.g. 'human resources in this organisation is causing communication blockages for every other department, and therefore creating nothing but trouble'). Such an approach attacks people's face needs, and is thus likely to provoke their immediate opposition rather than attract their support (Donohue and Kolt, 1992). On the other hand, a constructive focus on detailed behaviours which can be changed is likely to

be perceived as helpful feedback, and spur further change (Whetten and Cameron, 1991). Thus, a report *could* usefully say: 'Employees require more information about the impact of the reorganisation plan on job security. We recommend that a short statement be prepared by human resources on this issue, in conjunction with communications staff.' Non-judgemental feedback is generally perceived as one of the foundation stones of supportive communication (Albrecht *et al.*, 1994).

5 Managers will also be faced with a difficult decision if the report has uncovered a great deal of bad news. Should they circulate it, or try to keep it quiet? Auditors may well be called upon to make recommendations on this point also. It is worth remembering that widespread feedback to all employees of the main audit findings is correlated with increased faith in the possibility of the audit leading to meaningful change. Edwards *et al.* (1997) cited findings in one organisation, where only 11 per cent of people who received feedback felt that survey results would not be used well. This figure rose to 84 per cent among those who were not in receipt of such feedback. A number of researchers (e.g. Scarpello and Vandenberg, 1991; Johnson, 1993) have recommended holding employee feedback sessions, which management may or may not attend, and which are designed to achieve the fullest possible dissemination of both critical and positive audit findings. In this context, it is worth noting the finding from other research to the effect that when managers openly accept critical feedback, rather than seek only positive strokes on their performance, their stature actually rises (Ashford and Tsui, 1991). A further study by Tsui *et al.* (1995), involving a survey of almost 3000 managers, peers, superiors and subordinates found that exerting extra effort and explaining decisions was positively associated with managers being viewed as effective. Thus, feedback sessions should openly acknowledge the difficulties faced by the organisation in terms of communication, as well as celebrate its strengths.

INFLUENCING AND PERSUADING TO EFFECT CHANGE

As mentioned several times in this chapter, the ultimate purpose of an audit report is to persuade the organisation concerned to implement the recommendations which the report will outline. Persuasion has been defined (Reardon, 1991, p. 2) as a process of 'guiding people towards the adoption of some behaviour, belief or attitude preferred by the persuader through reasoning or emotional appeals'. Wells and Spinks (1996) proposed that persuasive messages should therefore seek to:

(1) attract attention;
(2) arouse psychological needs;
(3) present persuasive information showing the receiver how to satisfy those psychological needs;

(4) present evidence to support claims;
(5) urge action.

(Wells and Spinks, 1996, p. 27)

We have, in several instances, pointed to particular levers of persuasion (e.g. the use of power as a means of enhancing credibility) which can serve to accomplish these goals. Other persuasion levers should also be considered at this stage. In particular, we would draw attention to the following:

Threat/fear

This tactic involves the use of fear-arousing messages and the threat of negative outcomes, in order to secure compliance with a desired course of action (Pratkanis and Aronson, 1992). The success of this strategy is dependent upon three critical elements (Hargie *et al.*, 1999). First, the magnitude and severity of the negative outcome; second, its probability of occurring if nothing is done to avoid it and, third, the effectiveness of the recommended response to remove the threat. For example: 'Successfully implementing these recommendations will transform the communication climate within this organisation. Failure to do so will see a further deterioration, and the prospect of industrial action during the forthcoming pay round. We believe that these proposals can avert such a danger.'

Logical argument

An appeal to reason and logic is the cornerstone of many persuasion efforts (Allen and Preiss, 1998). It is therefore useful to examine strategies which can maximise the impact of this approach.

Reason has been defined (Buchanan and Huczynski, 1997, p. 695) as 'a strategy of influencing which relies on the presentation of data and information as the basis for a logical argument that supports a request'. There are well established features of arguments, and of the way they are delivered, which increase their persuasive power:

1 The message should be fully *comprehensible* – the meaning must be clear and unambiguous. As argued earlier, adding clear interpretation to audit findings reduces ambiguity and accomplishes this goal.
2 The report should be *shared* with a few key people inside the organisation before it is finally printed. This enables them to identify obvious factual mistakes, or suggest areas which might require further analysis, if the logic of the recommendations is to be readily apparent to readers. Handled carefully, such a process of consultation adds force to the report's arguments and credibility to the efforts of the audit team. Care should be taken to ensure that it does not become a means of top executives enforcing a whitewash job, in which all sins become virtues and each disaster is described as 'a rapidly

accelerating, upwardly mobile learning curve'. A report which celebrates every Little Bighorn as the organisation's finest hour will have no credibility, and will spur cynicism rather than action.

3 The important aspects of the argument should be *emphasised* to underline them. Bearing in mind that the report will be read in its entirety by only a few people, this suggests that the main findings should be repeated at several points, particularly in the summary and conclusion.

4 The *advantages* of the recommended course of action, and the *disadvantages* of the alternatives, should be firmly stated and supporting evidence cited. This is referred to as *sidedness* in message delivery. Two-sided messages, while emphasising the positive aspects of the message, also recognise negatives, whereas one-sided ones are partisan and only accentuate the positive. In general, the former are more effective (Pratkanis and Aronson, 1992). Thus, an audit report can acknowledge the difficulties in implementing particular recommendations and perhaps concede that there may be parts of the organisation not yet ready for a particular approach.

5 Reports benefit from the use of *vivid examples*, which have been shown to be a powerful technique for effecting influence. For example, the communication audit questionnaire reproduced in the Appendix of this book contains a section asking respondents to identify an example of communication which most typifies the quality of communication inside their organisation. They are then asked to indicate whether this experience was positive or negative. A communication audit report can use these data in two ways. First, it can tabulate the ratio of positive to negative examples offered. The higher this is in favour of positive examples the healthier the communication climate is likely to be. (Examples of this are provided in Chapter 10, reporting an audit in an NHS Trust.) Second, the report can extract representative comments from the examples, to buttress the auditors' case. For example, a major finding that people feel under-informed about a key change issue could be supported by a representative sample of quotations. These strengthen the argument in favour of the audit team's recommendations.

6 Clear *conclusions* should be evident to the report's readers. In particular, the reader should have no doubt about the overall nature of the findings, and be fully aware of the main action points being proposed.

DELIVERING THE REPORT ORALLY

Finally, the audit report will normally be presented orally to the top management team. This is frequently the most challenging, and decisive, part of the whole exercise. Many managers will have only skimmed the report. In particular, they will have been looking for issues which relate directly to their part of the organisation's function. It is therefore essential that the presentation provides a summary of the audit's overall main findings. In addition, it is important to recognise that if critical comments have been made, some managers who feel most directly affected may well arrive in attack mode, and anxious to ridicule the entire project. Rather than wearing a crash helmet and flak jacket, the best defence is the shield of top class presentational skills. There are many texts which advise on this (e.g. Turk, 1985; Hargie *et al.*, 1999), and we do not intend to dwell on the point here.

In essence, how a message is delivered is often as crucial in determining its impact as the nature of the message itself. The medium is the message. Confidence, clarity and a focus on essentials are vital. The audit team should practise the presentation as much as possible. In particular, at least one member of the team should play the role of critical evaluator, anticipating as many objections to the report as possible. The objective is to ensure that no question will be asked whose answer has not been thoroughly prepared in advance. As with the whole nature of the audit report, the presentation should be presented in a professional manner. Audio-visual aids, such as Powerpoint, are increasingly regarded as standard, and their use is therefore expected. The presentation must show that the team appreciates the organisation's strengths, has accurately diagnosed its weaknesses and – above all – has a clear programme of action which will solve its problems.

CONCLUSION

This chapter has outlined a structure for compiling a communication audit report, a process for persuading key people of its merits, and suggestions for the widespread dissemination of the report's main findings and recommendations. Too many reports languish on shelves, or find themselves instantly consigned to the nearest waste-bin. Our main point has been that audit reports can avoid these fates if they are planned as an integral part of the audit process and if they are designed as a guide to action. It is vital that senior managers are on board throughout. This can be accomplished by, for example, getting them to respond to draft surveys, reports and recommendations, or otherwise commenting on the nature of the findings (Barrington, 1992).

Thus, attention must be paid to:

• producing accurate data;
• achieving a balance between negative and positive findings;
• devising recommendations which address real problems, and which are 'doable'; and
• persuading the organisation at large of the merits of the audit team's proposals.

Communication audits can make a major contribution to organisational success. But the audit itself does none of this. In the final analysis, the audit report is the most visible product of the audit team's efforts, and hence the most potent factor of all in determining the impact the exercise will have within the organisation concerned.

Part III

Audits in action

Chapter 10

Charting communication performance in a healthcare organisation

Owen Hargie and Dennis Tourish

INTRODUCTION

The National Health Service (NHS) is by far the largest employer in the UK and one of the largest in the world, with over one million employees. It was formed in 1948 to provide health services free of charge to all citizens. Not surprisingly, the demand for these services rose rapidly. The pressures produced by this resultant demand, coupled with the logistics of running such a huge, nation-wide organisation, soon led to an obsession with administrative structures and costs (Harrison *et al.*, 1990). Inevitably, given its scale of operation and budgetary demands, government is centrally involved in the affairs of the NHS. When the impact of political changes enforced by the diametrically opposing ideologies of Conservative and Labour governments about how healthcare should be delivered is sprinkled on, the NHS mix becomes highly unstable. Indeed, the management structure of the NHS is rather like flat pack furniture – difficult to put together, the instructions received by the person expected to manage the activity often appear to make little sense, the bits do not always fit neatly, and it never seems to be designed to last.

This has meant that staff working in this field have tended to live in very uncertain times with regard to how NHS facilities are organised and managed. Our own audit is testimony to this changing environment. In this chapter we describe two audits conducted within one major NHS facility (called a 'Trust') over a two year period. The first audit (which we will refer to as Audit1) was conducted when the government in power was Conservative, and had just introduced seismic changes within the NHS. However, at the time of the second audit (Audit2) they had been replaced by Labour, who came to power promising sweeping changes to the NHS, many of which were specifically intended to undo the reforms introduced by their predecessors! Meanwhile, managers and staff have to get on with the day-by-day task of delivering health services to the public.

Our involvement in this audit stemmed from our extensive work in the NHS (e.g. Hargie and Tourish, 1993, 1996a; Tourish and Hargie, 1996b, 1998). The audit publications that we produced attracted considerable attention and led to numerous invitations to assist in communication programmes. In this case, when we were first approached by the Trust about the possibility of running an audit of communications, our initial step was to arrange a meeting with the Chief Executive and the Head of the Corporate Communications Department, to gain some insight into the organisation itself and their objectives for the exercise. It soon became obvious that we were dealing with two disciples wishing to spread the gospel of the importance of effective organisational communication. What they wanted to achieve in the first instance was an objective and accurate picture of existing strengths and weaknesses, to enable them to build upon areas of identified best practice while implementing changes to rectify deficits. What they needed, but did not have in place, was a coherent communications strategy, and the audits led directly to the construction of one. The problems they faced can best be appreciated by examining the nature of the facility they have to manage.

THE ORGANISATION

This particular NHS Trust is a large organisation. It provides health and social services across eight main programme areas:

- Child Health
- Family and Child Care
- Elderly
- Mental Health
- Learning Disability
- Physical and Sensory Disability
- Health Promotion and Disease Prevention
- Primary Care and Adult Community

The scale of operation is reflected by the fact that the Trust:

- has an annual budget of over £100 million;
- employs 4000 staff;
- spans a geographical area of 1149 square miles, covering a diverse mix of urban and rural areas;
- provides health and social care services for a population of some 320,000 people;
- runs 90 different health and social care facilities, such as residential childcare units, centres for adults with learning disabilities, residential care homes for the elderly, and a major psychiatric hospital;
- arranges care for 8000 people in their homes each day;

- engages in a total of 700,000 contacts per year with patients and clients;
- employs the complete spectrum of health and social care professionals (consultants, doctors, nurses, occupational therapists, speech therapists, social workers, etc.), together with the related swathe of administrative, estates, clerical, secretarial, technical and ancillary staff.

The total of 4000 staff in the Trust includes some 800 home helps. These are workers who are employed, mainly on an hourly basis, to provide help (cleaning, cooking, shopping, etc.) to the elderly and infirm in their homes. The questionnaire employed in the main phase of this audit (see Appendix) was inappropriate for this target group, since it addressed a wide range of issues which were largely irrelevant to the communication issues faced by them. Accordingly, home helps were audited by an open-ended questionnaire, in which they were asked to list three main strengths and three main weaknesses in the way people communicated with them, and to suggest any changes which would improve current communication practices. In this chapter we do not have space to present the findings from the home help audit, but rather will concentrate on the main body of the workforce who completed the full audit questionnaire.

OBJECTIVES

Following the initial discussion with the Chief Executive and Head of Communications, detailed planning meetings were held with the Communications team to work out how, and in what ways, an audit could best be carried out. Given the geographical spread and the wide range of staff groups involved, it was eventually decided that a depth questionnaire would offer the most detailed picture of the Trust-wide operation. A Communications Workshop was then run by the authors, at which time the proposal for an audit was presented to the Senior Management Team (SMT). The rationale for the exercise, the proposed questionnaire methodology, and the broad aims of the audit were explained. As a result of concerted deliberations and debate, the key issues about which the Trust should be communicating were formulated and agreed for inclusion in the questionnaire. The exact objectives for the audit were also delineated.

This Workshop served to ensure that all members of the SMT were fully apprised of the audit and had the opportunity to help form its final shape. This involvement served to increase their commitment to the exercise. Since they would also be involved in organising the release of some of their staff to complete audit materials, it was vital that they fully understood its importance and were able to cascade this down the hierarchy. Given that participation is a proven tool for effecting influence in organisations (Hargie et al., 1999), we would commend to auditors that they involve as many key players as possible in the initial stages of the audit exercise.

An important output from the detailed planning sessions with staff from the Corporate Communications team, and the consequent feedback from the SMT, was that six objectives were agreed for Audit1 and carried forward to Audit2:

1 To examine in-depth the attitudes of staff in the Trust towards internal communications.
2 To use a depth validated questionnaire to gauge the views of a 5 per cent sample of the total staff population, stratified across staff groups and geographical locations.
3 To identify key issues current within the Trust for specific inclusion in this questionnaire.
4 To produce qualitative and quantitative findings which would guide related action plans and act as a benchmark for future audits.
5 To investigate separately the view of home helps, using an open format postal questionnaire and to produce a set of recommendations relating to the findings.
6 To produce a report on all of the main findings from the audit, to also contain a set of recommendations for action.

For Audit2, and again following the same planning and consultation cycle, an additional seventh objective was formulated:

7 To compare and contrast the findings from the present audit with those obtained from the audit conducted two years previously. (Audit1 therefore provided benchmarking standards against which progress was measured two years later.)

THE AUDIT INSTRUMENT

Once the planning cycle had been completed, it was clear that what the Trust both wanted and needed was an organisation-wide analysis of communication. No previous such systematic evaluation had occurred, and so no information was available regarding the state of communications generally or in specific locations in particular. As explained above, it was therefore agreed that a comprehensive questionnaire should be employed as the main instrument.

The questionnaire utilised in this audit was an adaptation of the ICA Questionnaire. This instrument has a sound conceptual framework and has been shown to have validity, reliability and utility in auditing organisational communication (see Chapter 3). It produces a great deal of quantitative data and thus provides benchmarks against which to measure future performance. It also includes open questions that allow respondents freely to express their views about aspects of communication. The original ICA Questionnaire was modified by us, following audits we conducted in a range of NHS sectors (Tourish and Hargie, 1998). Four main changes were made (see the Appendix for a full discussion of the questionnaire):

1 The language was modified to reflect the norms of this sector. As a simple example, the term 'middle management' was used rather than 'immediate supervisor'.

2 We added an open-format first question, asking respondents to list three main strengths and three main weaknesses in the way other staff communicate with them. This allows respondents to reflect generally on their own views about what is good or bad about current practices, before being 'set' in any way by the standard questions that follow.

3 The original ICA instrument had a 'critical incident' sheet alongside every page (see Chapter 7). We found that staff viewed the completion of these sheets as a very time-consuming and tedious task. As a result we reduced this, while retaining the concept, by requesting respondents to give *one* critical incident of their choice, which was most typical of communication within the organisation. We made this the penultimate question.

4 A final question was added asking respondents to recommend three changes that would improve communication. We have found that the responses to this question produce a wealth of useful suggestions, and sweeps in valuable information which would otherwise be lost.

In addition, the questionnaire has a section devoted to what are considered to be the main issues facing the organisation at the particular time of audit. In this audit some of these issues remained the same from Audit1 to Audit2 ('Relocation of services'; 'Development of new services'), while others changed (e.g. Audit1 'Transition to Trust status': Audit2 'New Government plans for changing the services'). Our revised version of the questionnaire is presented in full in the Appendix.

THE AUDITS

An identical procedure was followed in both audits. All staff were informed by a letter from the Chief Executive that an audit would be taking place in the near future. The main objectives of the audit were explained and it was pointed out that some staff would be chosen at random to participate. The next step was to select the survey sample.

This type of audit necessitates selecting a sample population genuinely representative of key subgroups as the basis for data collection. In theory, an organisation comprising 600 staff could be audited by surveying 10 per cent of the staff ($n = 60$) selected at random. However, in practice most organisations have a range of discrete occupational groups and managerial levels, all performing different roles, and with possibly very different perspectives on communication effectiveness. Furthermore, some of these groups may be small in number, yet of key importance. Since a 10 per cent sample of ten staff would mean that only one person would be audited, a simple crude percentage approach will result in

Box 10.1 Categories and numbers of staff audited

	Audit1	Audit2
Administrative and Clerical	34	42
Works and Maintenance	4	2
Ancillary and General	14	16
Nursing and Midwifery	37	44
Social Work	20	16
Professional and Technical	14	12
Medical and Dental	14	8
Other	23	16
Totals	160	156

such influential groups being under-represented. This means that a weighted stratified sampling technique is needed. Where numbers are over 100, a sample of 5 per cent is usually sufficient. When less than 100, we have used the following weightings as a basis for sampling within a number of audits (Hargie and Tourish, 1993):

No. in sample	90+	60–89	40–59	30–39	20–29	15–19	10–14	1–9
% surveyed	10	15	25	30	45	60	80	90

Using this sampling frame, and bearing in mind other important considerations such as gender and managerial level, a randomly selected, stratified cross-section of staff was then chosen by us from the Trust's Personnel Information Management System (PIMS) print-out. Thus, the gender balance in both audits was 80%F:20%M, reflecting the staffing complement; likewise the proportions of staff at various levels of management, and on full-time or part-time contracts, were representative. Staffing categories used by the Trust, together with audit totals, are shown in Box 10.1, and again these figures were in proportion to overall staffing numbers.

As previously explained, the Trust has seven main sub-regions. Questionnaires were distributed in person by the authors in a suitable room at each of these seven main central locations. The selected staff were given one hour off work to engage in the exercise. This method of administration was adopted for several reasons. It allowed us to:

1 explain that we personally selected staff at random and that no one was chosen by the Trust to take part;
2 make it clear that we were university lecturers and so independent of the organisation;

3 give a personal assurance that all information would be treated in the strictest confidence, that completed questionnaires would only be seen by us, and that no names were to be put on the questionnaires;

4 emphasise the fact that since a fairly large number of staff had been given an hour off work to complete the audit, their views were clearly of importance to the Trust;

5 carefully describe the questionnaire and answer any queries regarding its completion;

6 raise the response rate well above that which would have been achieved by a postal administration.

An attendance list was taken for each administration so that we could track and follow-up any missing staff (this was explained to respondents). Once the first set of completed audit questionnaires had been obtained from the locational distribution, a postal drop was then carried out to reach those staff who had not been able to attend. As a result, a final total of 160 Audit1 and 156 Audit2 questionnaires were obtained, representing over 5 per cent of the total staff (excluding home helps) in both cases.

RESULTS

The questionnaire is divided into a number of sections, each dealing with a different aspect of communication (such as *information received*, *information sent*, and *action taken on information received*). The sections contain a number of very specific questions, and respondents are asked to rate each, using a five-point scale, along two dimensions which in essence measure 'how it is now' and 'how they would like it to be' (see Table 10.1). This allows for comparisons regarding staff views about current (real) and desired (ideal) communication practices (see Appendix). The totals for each section are then summed to give overall scores for that aspect of communication. Scores in the questionnaire can then be converted into percentage satisfaction scores. For example, as can be seen from Table 10.1, the total Audit2 score for information sent now was 2.5 as opposed to a desired score of 3.3. These scores are converted into percentage scores by multiplying by a factor of 20 (given the five-point scale used). Thus, the percentage satisfaction score of 2.5 for 'Information Being Sent' in Audit2 represents 50 per cent satisfaction as opposed to a desired score of 3.3, or 66 per cent. To put it another way, there was a 16 per cent shortfall between perceptions of amount of information actually sent as compared to what is perceived to be needed.

In addition, the differences between the scores for each of the items and the overall totals can be tested for significance using the Wilcoxon signed ranks test. Although the Wilcoxon test employs ranked scores, in our audit reports we present mean scores (as in Table 10.1), since we have found these to be the most

Table 10.1 Amount of information being sent (Audit2)

Topic area	Information received now	Information needed	Rank
Performance appraisal systems	2.0	3.2*	1
How decisions that affect my job are reached	2.6	3.6*	2
Promotion opportunities	2.2	3.2*	2
Staff development opportunities	2.5	3.5*	2
Important new service developments	2.1	3.1*	2
The goals of the organisation	2.2	3.2*	2
The development of the organisation as a single, coherent Trust	2.0	2.9*	7
Major management decisions	2.4	3.3*	7
Improvements in services, or how services are delivered	2.4	3.3*	7
How my job contributes to the organisation	2.8	3.6*	10
Specific problems faced by the organisation	2.3	3.1*	10
Pay, benefits and conditions	2.1	2.9*	10
Things that go wrong in my organisation	2.7	3.5*	10
My performance in my job	3.0	3.5	14
The total range of services offered	2.9	3.4	14
How problems which I report in my job are dealt with	3.4	3.8	16
What is expected from me in my job	3.0	3.4	17
Mean total	**2.5**	**3.3***	

Scoring key: 1 = very little; 2 = little; 3 = some; 4 = great; 5 = very great

Note: *p<0.01 (Wilcoxon). Rankings based on differences between means for information sent and needing to be sent.

readily understood and digestible measure of central tendency. The average individual understands the notion of average scores, whereas medians and modes can cause indigestion for many people.

Overall levels of 'satisfaction with communication' scores are calculated by summing each individual's raw scores for each item for communication as it 'is now' (in sections with two columns, this is the left-hand column scores) and dividing by the total number of items in the questionnaire. Cross-tabulations are carried out between these overall satisfaction scores and background information criteria, using chi-square tests. The objective here is to determine whether a correlation exists between levels of satisfaction with communication and factors such as gender, location and occupational grouping. Let us now turn to the main findings of the audit.

Box 10.2 Comparison of scores for main questionnaire areas

	Audit1	Audit2	Change
Information received	2.4	2.8	+0.4 (8%)
Information received on important issues facing the Trust	2.1	2.4	+0.3 (6%)
Information received from various sources	2.6	3.0	+0.4 (8%)
Information received through various channels	2.4	2.7	+0.3 (6%)
Timeliness of information received	3.2	3.5	+0.3 (6%)
Information sent	2.5	2.5	0
Action taken on information sent	2.9	3.1	+0.2 (4%)
Information sent on important issues facing the Trust	1.8	1.8	0
Working relationships	3.4	3.7	+0.3 (6%)
Overall satisfaction score	**2.6**	**2.9**	**+0.3 (6%)**

Audit1–Audit2 comparisons

Cross-tabulations

In Audit1 the only significant difference to emerge was between geographical locations, with three of the seven regions recording significantly lower satisfaction scores than the other four. As a result, we ran focus groups at these three locations to tease out why such differences existed. We asked three main questions:

- How do you feel in general about communications between staff and managers within the Trust?
- What are your main views about communications within the area where you work – what are the main strengths and weaknesses?
- What specific additional measures would you like managers to take to improve communication in your area?

We found that staff in these areas did not have specific grievances, but rather they felt more strongly about those issues which were generally perceived to be problematic by all respondents. In Audit2 no significant differences were found between satisfaction scores and background information criteria, indicating that any locational problems that may have existed had been overcome.

Overall satisfaction levels

As the figures in Box 10.2 illustrate, there was a definite overall improvement in the scores for Audit2 as compared to Audit1, with an overall mean improvement of 0.3 (6 per cent increased approval rating). On almost every section of the questionnaire, the Audit2 results were an improvement upon the findings from Audit1. Other important findings in relation to satisfaction were as follows.

Information received

The largest change scores were for information received. Following the finding from Audit1 that there was a problem with the amount of information being received by staff, two of our recommendations were that: 'More information should be disseminated about all aspects of the work of the Trust, and the key management concerns which are current' and 'There should be more face-to-face communication between senior managers and staff.' As a result, the Trust put in action a plan to improve its performance on this aspect of communication. Three main strategies were introduced:

1 A monthly letter was sent by the Chief Executive directly to all staff at their home addresses in which he presented up-to-date information on Trust matters and itemised the main decisions made by the Trust Board. A point of contact was also included for feedback from staff.
2 A Trust Newsletter was introduced and again sent to all staff at home. This Newsletter was used to inform staff about the results of both audits, and provide details about the communications strategy which would be introduced to meet identified deficits. It was also used to publicise the fact that Audit2 would be taking place.
3 The Chief Executive initiated a series of regular visits to all sub-regions at which he met with staff, listened to their views and explained current Trust policy.

These actions clearly produced positive results, as measured by the improvement scores of between 6 and 8 per cent for satisfaction with the amount of information received in general, information on important issues facing the Trust, and information from various sources and different channels (Box 10.2).

Information sent

Conversely, there was no change at all in the figures for amount of information sent, although there was a smaller improvement (4 per cent) regarding action taken on any information that had been sent (Box 10.2). This indicated that an important task for the Trust following Audit2 was to explore ways in which staff participation in its operation could be increased. In making our recommendations we pointed out that the desire of staff to send more information (see Table 10.1) indicated their willingness to become involved in the operation of the Trust, and strongly advised that this should be built upon. To facilitate this, one of our Audit2 recommendations was that the system of team briefings be reviewed to include a *requirement* that staff list items they wished to have referred up the line to more senior managers. Another was that plans should be

Box 10.3 Comparison of difference scores for main questionnaire areas

	Audit1	*Audit2*	*Change*
Information received	1.5	1.0	0.5 (10%)
Information received on important issues facing the Trust	2.0	1.4	0.6 (12%)
Information received from various sources	1.1	0.8	0.3 (6%)
Information received through various channels	1.2	0.7	0.5 (10%)
Information sent	0.9	0.8	0.1 (2%)
Action taken on information sent	0.9	0.7	0.2 (4%)
Information sent on important issues facing the Trust	0.9	0.7	0.2 (4%)
Overall mean difference scores	**1.2**	**0.8**	**0.4 (8%)**

drawn up to foster greater inter-departmental communication and involvement in the work of the organisation.

The results from Table 10.1 also highlight the importance of audits to be timely. At the time of Audit2 the Trust was introducing a new system of staff appraisal, and the questionnaire data showed this to be the area of greatest concern for respondents. Indeed the 1.2 (24 per cent) shortfall here between information received and that needed was one of the largest deficits in the entire audit. Our actual recommendation here was that 'The Trust should investigate why the issue of performance appraisal is causing concern, and should engage in more communications with staff about this aspect of their work.'

Working relationships

Following Audit1 it was evident that one of the solid building blocks on which to erect a firm communication edifice was the fact that working relationships among staff within the Trust were good. People on the ground expressed high levels of trust for colleagues and line managers, with somewhat lower levels for middle and senior managers. These bonds were further strengthened by Audit2, with an overall 6 per cent increase in relational satisfaction (Box 10.2), and this rate of increase was consistent for colleagues and managers. Thus, as communications improved, working relationships were perceived to be better. Following the rule that good news should always come first in audit reports (see Chapter 9), our first recommendation in Audit2 was that 'The Trust should ensure that this level of harmony is maintained and enhanced.'

Comparison of difference scores

As previously explained, on most sections of the questionnaire there are two columns. In the first column, respondents rate on a five-point scale their actual

Box 10.4 Actual and ideal satisfaction scores: Audit2

Source	Actual Satisfaction Score	Ideal Satisfaction Score	Shortfall
Colleagues	4.0 (80%)	4.3 (86%)	0.3 (6%)
Immediate managers	3.7 (74%)	4.2 (84%)	0.5 (10%)
Middle managers	3.3 (66%)	3.8 (76%)	0.5 (10%)
Senior managers	3.0 (60%)	3.7 (74%)	0.7 (14%)
Chief Executive	3.0 (60%)	3.5 (70%)	0.5 (10%)

level of satisfaction with communication at present. In the second column they rate their ideal satisfaction level. The difference between these two scores then represents a score for current level of satisfaction or dissatisfaction. Box 10.3 presents comparisons between the *difference* scores obtained in the two audits. The lower these change scores, the more satisfied staff are with communication – an ideal difference score would be '0'. As can be seen, there was again a definite overall improvement in Audit2 across all areas, with a total improvement score of 0.4 (8 per cent). The mean score for satisfaction across all respondents in Audit2 was 2.9, as opposed to 2.6 in Audit1 (Box 10.2). This indicated that respondents felt that while internal communications were on an upwards trend, there was still room for improvement. The target overall ideal satisfaction score, as set by respondents in both audits, was 3.5. This indicated that staff wished communications to be functioning at a moderately good level. In our experience, organisations rarely achieve scores of above 4.0. We recommended therefore that a realistic general communication target score for the Trust to set for the next audit was 3.2.

Satisfaction with managers

The questionnaire can be used to measure satisfaction with various levels of management. Thus, in Audit2 the scores in Box 10.4 for colleagues and managers were obtained by combining the ratings from various sections of the questionnaire for each source and then calculating the mean score for each. The interesting aspect of these audit results is that these converted scores are realistic in two senses. First, they are close to the actual targets set by many large corporations who audit on a regular basis. Second, staff recognised that middle and senior managers, and the Chief Executive, cannot be expected to achieve as high satisfaction scores as colleagues or immediate managers. It is worthy of note here that an important advantage of the questionnaire used in this audit is that it quantifies communication in terms of communication scores, so that targets can be set for managers at all levels to improve their current satisfaction

Box 10.5 Comparison of examples		
Year	*Positive examples*	*Negative examples*
Audit1	19	96
Audit2	63	61

scores. For example, an examination of Box 10.4 suggests that a realistic target for immediate managers to achieve in Audit3 would be 3.9 (78 per cent).

Communication examples

As part of the questionnaire, respondents are asked to select and describe one effective or ineffective experience that is for them most typical of communication within the organisation (see Appendix). Perhaps the most striking feature of comparison between the two audits was the ratio of positive to negative examples cited (Box 10.5). As discussed in Chapter 7, the 'critical incidents' that staff report as being typical of communication provide insight into whether staff feel positive or negative about the organisation as a whole. Where communication is functioning at a reasonable level we would expect a positive/negative ratio of at least 50/50 to be reached. However, the ratio in Audit1 was 5:1 in favour of negative examples. By Audit2 this had been transformed, with positive examples outnumbering negative ones. This was a considerable achievement, and another clear indicator that the communication strategies introduced after Audit1 had effected positive change during the intervening two years. A closer examination of these examples revealed that in both audits some two-thirds of all positive examples related to communication with line managers, illustrating the key role they play in ensuring organisational effectiveness.

Open questions

The questionnaire includes three other open questions, which ask respondents to give examples of: (1) three main communication strengths, (2) three main weaknesses, and (3) suggestions for improvement in communications. These questions produce a mass of information, which when content-analysed reveals recurring trends, together with some fascinating comments about organisational functioning. In both Audit1 and Audit2 the open-question results confirmed the direction of findings from the quantitative section of the questionnaire. For instance, in terms of specific cited strengths of communication, the two main changes from Audit1 to Audit2 were *the Chief Executive's direct communications* and *the Newsletter*. It will be recalled that these were both initiated following Audit1, and the comments from staff in the open sections were a clear indicator that these innovations had been well received.

The other strengths mentioned in both audits confirmed the good working relationships with colleagues and line managers. Furthermore, in Audit1 a commonly stated weakness was the lack of information from senior managers, but this was not a main theme in Audit2, again confirming the success of these initiatives. Reflecting the electronic era, the need for improvements to the e-mail/Intranet system, and for more information to be delivered in the medium of video, were highlighted in Audit2 and therefore these were included as part of our recommendations.

A final issue that emerged in both audits was that of the problems faced by the Trust's split-site operation. This included communication difficulties for staff working within the same occupational grouping but across different sites; concerns regarding the fact that some departments which provided important services were located some distance away; and general communication problems such as difficulties with internal mail, e-mail, and telephone. Staff also repeatedly expressed a wish to meet and share more with colleagues working on other Trust sites. Our recommendation here was that 'The Trust should therefore develop plans to foster greater inter-departmental communication.' Given its geographical spread, there were no easy solutions to this. However, as ways in which distal contacts could be facilitated, we recommended that:

- important Trust meetings (including the SMT) should be rotated around the different locations;
- effective technological communication channels be given priority;
- cross-site conferences and training days be organised on a regular basis;
- the criterion of cross-site location be a key consideration in the formation of task forces, working teams, and so on.

The fact that staff expressed such a strong desire for contact with colleagues in other parts of the Trust suggested a strong sense of corporate identity and we also recommended that this should be fostered.

CONCLUSIONS

Like people, all audits are different, although with some commonalities. The experienced auditor must to be able to tailor general audit measures to meet the specific needs of particular organisations. For the reasons stated, a depth questionnaire was the most appropriate measurement tool in the two audits reported in this chapter. It allowed the Trust-wide communications picture to be brought into sharper focus. Like an X-ray, it showed up areas where problems were located while also illustrating the healthy regions of the organisational body. The check-up after two years using identical measurement tools also enabled the progress of organisational health to be directly charted. The precise diagnostic nature of the questionnaire allowed an informed prescription to be made to treat areas of dysfunction. The fact that more than one method can be usefully employed was illustrated in Audit1, when focus groups were used to investigate a specific area of difference identified from the questionnaire.

In this audit we followed the recommended template as presented in Chapter 2, which can be summarised as follows:

- The support and enthusiasm of the Chief Executive was confirmed at the outset.
- The Senior Management Team were fully involved in the early planning decisions.
- Clear audit objectives were delineated.
- All staff were informed that the audit would be taking place and its purpose was fully explained.
- The same audit tool was employed to diagnose initial problems and measure progress – in other words like was compared with like.
- The auditors were external to, and independent of, the organisation.
- The results of the audit were disseminated to all staff.
- A set of achievable recommendations was drawn up, together with related action plans, and these were also explained to staff.
- Following Audit1 an overall Communications Strategy was formulated for the Trust and this was used to guide and direct policy and practice in this area.

The findings from this case study illustrate clearly the contribution that audits can make to improved performance. Once areas of weakness have been identified through auditing, an action plan can be put in place to rectify identified deficits. Follow-up audits then allow the success or otherwise of the intervention to be accurately tracked. The results from this audit also help to counter the view held by some managers that no matter what you do, staff will simply ask for more (Zimmerman *et al.*, 1996). We found that when staff realised that senior management was making a concerted effort to improve communications, there was a tangible increment in overall ratings throughout the questionnaire, coupled with realistic expectations of the levels at which managers could be expected to perform.

* We would like to thank Christie Colhoun and Marlene Kinghan for all their help, support and advice throughout both of the audits described in this chapter.

Chapter 11

A communication audit of a hospital clinic

Myra Skipper and Owen Hargie

BACKGROUND

The previous chapter described an internal audit of staff in a large facility (Trust) within the National Health Service (NHS). This chapter is also concerned with an audit of communications in the NHS, and again the audit has a 'research' impetus (see Chapter 16) in that it was intended that the results would be of interest to the wider health community. The focus of this audit is upon a Swallowing Clinic operated by a small team of designated staff, but sited within a large hospital in Belfast, Northern Ireland (N.I.). While the core team of Clinic staff was small, its operation necessitated ongoing communications with health professionals and patients from across N.I. The audit of the Clinic therefore had to encompass an analysis of both internal and external communications. It also used three main tools to evaluate communication:

- depth interviews;
- diary analysis;
- analysis of video recordings of interactions.

Staff in the NHS are employed in regional facilities with a clear line management structure, to which they are immediately answerable. However, most are also members of professional groups with which they have a strong allegiance (doctors, nurses, speech and language therapists, etc.), all with specific aims, roles and responsibilities. Furthermore, the way in which different groups perceive the exact nature of the roles and responsibilities of their own and other professions often varies, making communication and relationships somewhat problematic (Dickson *et al.*, 1997). The stated aim of the NHS – to ensure that the interests of patients are the driving force of the entire system (HMSO, 1996) – can at times be difficult to effect given such a context.

The Swallowing Clinic which was the centrepiece for this audit operated within this real world NHS setting. The Clinic had been in operation for a period of four years, and while the numbers attending were initially small, they had been gradually increasing as knowledge of the facility grew. It was a relatively new service using a technique called 'videofluoroscopy', which records moving X-ray images onto videotape. Here, the patient swallows a small amount of food together with barium and this enables images to be filmed and captured on tape at all stages in the swallowing cycle. The purpose of the Clinic was to assist in the treatment of the condition known as 'dysphagia' – disorders of swallowing at any point between the ingestion of food into the mouth and its arrival in the stomach. At its most serious dysphagia is life-threatening since it becomes impossible for food to be eaten by the patient without risk of aspiration (the passage of ingested material into the lungs with the consequent risk of choking and infection). The main benefit of videofluoroscopy is that it facilitates accurate diagnostic treatment decisions to be made with greater safety and speed.

The Clinic was located within a large teaching hospital with 600 beds, situated within the Belfast conurbation. The videofluoroscopy assessment method described above had not been previously available, and no similar facilities were offered anywhere else in N.I. Furthermore, the specialised technical equipment is not portable and so could not be moved from site to site. Thus, as well as serving the immediate urban catchment area of some 250,000 people, the Clinic served the entire country. Referrals were accepted from a range of different professionals in other hospitals and practices elsewhere, with the regional speech and language therapists acting in a gatekeeper role. This means that the accurate flow of information to and from the Clinic is a key aspect of its functioning.

All patients attending the Clinic were experiencing swallowing difficulties, the majority as a result of neurological damage following stroke. However, since the hospital was the main centre for surgical intervention in N.I. for patients with head and neck cancer, the Clinic also served this patient group. Others with progressive neurological disorders, such as Parkinson's disease and motor neurone disease, were also referred. At the time of audit, the Clinic was staffed by a team of three professionals all specialising in dysphagia: a speech and language therapist, a dietitian and a radiologist. Part-time secretarial/ administrative support was also provided.

The key challenge to Clinic staff was to make information easily understood and quickly accessible to all those involved. However, some communication problems had been identified by staff. As time passed, it became increasingly evident that communications did not appear to be as effective as they should have been, with the result that the work carried out was not offering maximum benefit to patients. The perceived problems included:

- expressed confusion by some professionals about the Clinic's services as compared to the services provided by the radiology department;
- an apparent lack of clarity about the role of different professions in the assessment procedure;
- the fact that advice given seemed to be sometimes ignored by other staff;

- the receipt of information by the Clinic was often inadequate, and staff were unsure about whether the messages they transmitted to patients and other professionals were effective.

In relation to the latter point, there is considerable evidence in the literature that patients often feel their concerns are not addressed (Hargie *et al.*, 1998) and that information between professionals is frequently misunderstood (Audit Commission, 1993). The extent to which these factors were prevalent in the operation of the Clinic was unclear. The health professionals within and without the Clinic were undoubtedly caring and competent individuals all working for the best interests of their patients. However, good intentions are but essential raw materials – they need to be shaped and co-ordinated to produce optimum outputs (in this case the highest quality of patient care). It was in this area of co-ordination and communication that there seemed to be room for improvement. At the same time, problems are often only in the eye of the beholder, and while difficulties had been identified by staff, it was not clear if these concurred with those perceived by those using the Clinic. Indeed, no formal attempt had been made to ascertain the views of clients, or to investigate the communicative functioning of this facility. Accordingly, a decision was taken to initiate a formal audit.

THE COMMUNICATION AUDIT

The idea of systematically examining communication issues was initiated by one member of the Clinic team (the first author), but was given complete support and backing by the other staff. Collaboration in the preparation and implementation of an audit was sought from the Department of Communication at the local university and as a result a member of staff from the university (the second author) became involved. Following discussion and collaboration with all staff, the following objectives were agreed for the audit; namely, to:

1 investigate the functioning of other similar clinics throughout the UK, so as to obtain a comparative frame for the audit and ascertain the extent to which the results would be widely applicable;
2 conduct a pilot study in one of these clinics, to test the methods to be employed in the audit;
3 examine the extent to which the appointment and referral system between the Clinic and its clients was effective;
4 gauge the views of all professional staff and patients who used the Clinic;
5 analyse the actual interaction patterns which occurred during the assessment procedure itself;
6 identify strengths and weaknesses in communication practices and make recommendations about how existing procedures could be improved.

Pre-audit survey

Since similar clinics were in operation elsewhere in the UK, the first step was to examine whether there were commonly recurring issues which could inform the main audit. This would also enable comparisons to be made with the site Clinic, thereby revealing whether the findings would be relevant to other such NHS facilities. All existing clinics were therefore surveyed using a postal questionnaire sent to the organiser of each clinic. Questions related not only to the methods used in the assessment procedure but also to the size of the catchment area, designated staff involved, patient profiles, the process of referral and feedback of assessment results, the perceived value of the clinic, and general difficulties experienced.

The results of this survey showed that the site Clinic was representative of what was happening elsewhere. The assessment methods used, range of patient groups, and referral patterns by health professionals were all similar. Thus, the findings from the in-depth site audit would definitely be of wider relevance. Likewise, those operating other clinics expressed difficulties in communicating effectively with all those involved. The exact role of Clinic staff was not always clear to outsiders. This confirmed the importance of investigating the issue of role ambiguity in the main audit.

It was also reported that the main method used to transmit Clinic results was via written reports, but that other media were also regularly employed (ward notes, face-to-face communication, telephone). No definite analyses had been carried out on this area. Since it is clear that the medium can directly affect the message (Hargie *et al.*, 1999), the audit objective of analysing exact patterns of information flow was confirmed as being important.

Another common issue to emerge was that a number of people as well as the patient were often present at the assessment (e.g. relatives, nursing staff, regional speech and language therapists), and the view was expressed that this may affect how the patient was dealt with. In order to investigate the relative influences of the range of personnel on the assessment process, it was therefore decided to video record the Clinic sessions, and conduct fine-grained behavioural analyses of the interaction patterns that occurred.

The final theme of note from the survey was that respondents highlighted the problem of advice given by the Clinic being rejected by those directly responsible for the patient's care. This underlined the need to investigate in the main audit the views of all staff regarding the value of the assessment, and actual impact upon patient care.

The pilot study

While the Clinic staff had ideas about what the direction of the interviews with staff and patients should be, it was decided that a more informed navigational system was required. A hospital clinic in England was identified from the survey as being directly comparable to the site Clinic, and arrangements were then made to conduct a pilot study of interviews with six patients and nine staff (from across the full range of professional groups). This enabled the format of the interview process and procedures to be field-tested and also allowed information to be gathered in order to inform the main audit interviews. Interestingly, while ethical approval for the entire audit had been obtained in N.I., since different staff and patients were involved in this pilot study, the hospital deemed that it was necessary to seek ethical approval from the local ethical committee in England. Although this was readily secured, it represents a good example of one of the hurdles that often have to be jumped by audit researchers!

The audio-recording system used to tape interviews was found to work very well and so no modifications were required. The interview format and schedule were also tested, and minor modifications made prior to the main audit. In terms of areas of focus, it became clear that the following themes were important for patients:

- prior expectations of the assessment and its outcomes;
- exact reasons for the assessment;
- advice given, by whom, and how comprehensible it was;
- relationships with health professionals;
- expectations and hopes for the future;
- anxieties and how they are handled;
- their overall role in the assessment procedure.

These themes therefore formed the core of the actual interviews. In addition, from interviews with patients at different stages of their condition, it appeared that their perspectives may well change with time. As a result, it was decided to interview patients on two occasions: immediately following the assessment, and then some four weeks later.

In relation to staff interviews, the core recurring themes to emerge were:

- the nature and purpose of the assessment itself;
- perceived advantages of the procedure;
- the pressures of time in relation to competing demands;
- relative knowledge and experience of different staff;
- emotional issues surrounding the swallowing domain – for both staff and patients;
- perceptions of the roles and responsibilities of different professional groups;
- organisational issues surrounding the operation of the Clinic.

Following the survey and pilot-testing stages, the main audit was implemented. Over a period of nine weeks, all communications with the Clinic were charted and analysed. The methods used, and total numbers involved in each, were as follows:

- *Data collection log-sheets* (n = 63) were kept so that all communications with the Clinic could be logged.

- Clinic assessments were *video recorded* (n = 22) *and analysed* to determine *interaction patterns*.
- *Interviews* were conducted with all *professionals* (n = 61) who had contact with the Clinic.
- Two *interviews* were conducted with *patients* (n = 35) – the first immediately following assessment and the second four weeks later.

AUDIT FINDINGS

The audit produced a large amount of data, and we will here summarise the main trends in each phase.

Data collection log-sheets

In order to chart the flow of communications to and from the Clinic, a diary method was employed (see Chapter 6). A data collection log-sheet was devised, based upon the ICA instrument (Goldhaber and Rogers, 1979). This required Clinic staff to detail all their contacts in terms of who initiated the communication, what channel was used and whether the reason for it was to do with organisational matters (e.g. dates of appointment) or substantive issues of information (e.g. feedback of assessment results). After pilot-testing, all staff were trained in the use of the log-sheet prior to the audit itself.

A separate log-sheet was completed for every patient by each member of the Clinic team (Figure 11.1). All communications with each patient, and with professionals associated with the patient, were logged daily from the time the patient was first referred until the final Clinic assessment was sent to the referring agent. Though simple in its format and conception, this method provided a comprehensive list of everyone involved with each patient, and gave important details about the exact nature of Clinic communications.

The log-sheet findings (Table 11.1) demonstrated that speech and language therapists were key players. They were in communication with the assessment team more than any other professional group, although their actual numbers were comparatively smaller (e.g. less than half that of medical staff). They also initiated contacts with the Clinic more frequently than any other group. Dietitians were identified as another important profession – for example proportionally they initiated contact with the Clinic (25 per cent) twice as frequently as nursing staff (12.5 per cent). The results also showed that the written channel was the main method for communications with the medical profession, unlike nursing where the primary medium was face to face. In the case of dietitians the telephone predominated. For speech and language therapists, the phone and face to face were both important channels, and they also at times received a video recording of the assessment in addition to the written report.

These results paint an interesting picture. There is growing evidence to show that most people prefer face-to-face communication, followed by telephone, and

Page _____   Name of patient: _____

Number _____   Completed by: _____   Position _____

Period covered: From .... to ....

	Consecutive communications										
Communication with	1	2	3	4	5	6	7	8	9	10	11
Initiated by Self											
Other											
Channel used Face to face											
Telephone											
Written											
Video											
Type of communication Organisation											
Information											

Figure 11.1 Data collection log-sheet

Table 11.1 Data collection log-sheet results for communications between staff

Communication with	Method				Total	Initiated by	
	Face to face	Phone	Written	Video		Clinic staff	Other
Speech therapist (n = 10)	24 (34%)	25 (35%)	15 (21%)	7 (10%)	71	49 (69%)	22 (31%)
Dietitian (n = 9)	4 (17%)	13 (54%)	7 (29%)	—	24	18 (75%)	6 (25%)
Doctor (n = 30)	9 (14%)	12 (19%)	43 (67%)	—	64	49 (76%)	15 (24%)
Nurse (n = 18)	36 (64%)	13 (23%)	7 (12.5%)	—	56	49 (87.5%)	7 (12.5%)
Occupational therapist (n = 2)	1 (33%)	1 (33%)	1 (33%)	—	3	3 (100%)	0
Physiotherapist (n = 5)	5 (45%)	5 (45%)	1 (10%)	—	11	9 (82%)	2 (18%)
Radiographer (n = 5)	10 (42%)	12 (50%)	2 (8%)	—	24	22 (92%)	2 (8%)
Secretary (n = 1)	12 (44%)	7 (26%)	8 (30%)	—	27	18 (67%)	9 (33%)
Total communication	101 (36%)	88 (31%)	84 (30%)	7 (3%)	280	217 (77.5%)	63 (22.5%)

that the written channel is least preferred (Hargie *et al.*, 1999). Levels of intimacy, warmth and commitment decrease across these three. Yet, face to face is the most time-consuming medium, followed by phone and then written methods.

The source of over three-quarters of all communications was the assessment team. Further analysis revealed the primacy of the role of the speech and language therapist, in that 77 per cent of these Clinic staff communications were actually initiated by her, and she also directly received 68 per cent of all outside contacts with the Clinic. A similar pattern emerged in relation to contacts with patients and their relatives, where again the speech and language therapist was the prime mover. The data further revealed that only a very small proportion of contacts (4 per cent) were initiated by patients and relatives, and that these were primarily face to face. This finding suggests that the patient played a passive role in the process.

In relation to substantive matters, communication with radiographers and the secretary largely concerned the organisation of the Clinic (80 per cent). By contrast, contacts with other health professionals related mainly to information dissemination (78 per cent). With relatives, again the main content was to do with the exchange of information, although organisational issues were also important.

Overall, the results revealed that a core 'gatekeeping' and information-giving role is played by the speech and language therapist. The primary method of communication was face to face except in the case of doctors, where over two-thirds of communications were written, and dietitians, who used the telephone for the majority of their communications. These log-sheet findings helped to map the topography of the Clinic. On the higher ground were doctors, who tended to send messages from a distance. Lower down the slope was the base camp where the communication patterns were face to face and where the other health professionals could be found talking directly with the Clinic team about patients (Table 11.1). Scaling across all of the terrain was the speech and language therapist, who had the full picture and was at the centre of the operation.

Video recordings of the Clinic

Prior to their arrival at the site Clinic, patients were informed by their speech and language therapist (who had been fully apprised about the nature of the audit) that the assessment would be video recorded if they gave permission. Each patient was given a consent form on which the details of the study were outlined, and which was signed if permission was given for recording. No patient refused consent for this part of the study.

Two fixed cameras were placed on the wall in such a way that they covered the entire room. No attempt was made to hide these, since everyone knew that the session would be filmed. However, as they were above head height it was usually a case of 'out of sight out of mind', and both staff and patients reported that once the 'action' started they forgot about the cameras. As the assessment procedure itself took place in different parts of the room, a mixer system was

Table 11.2 Percentage talk-times in the clinic

	Speech therapist (C)	Radiologist	Speech therapist (O)	Patient	Relative	Dietitian	Nurse (O)
Percentage of talk-time	25.6	17.4	13	12.4	12.2	11.7	7.7

S&LT (C) = Clinic speech and language therapist
S&LT (O) = Speech and language therapist from outside the Clinic who was accompanying the patient
Nurse (O) = Nurse from outside the Clinic who was accompanying the patient

installed to allow the recorded view to be switched from one camera to another. Pilot-testing revealed that this eliminated blind spots and was able to capture the entire procedure. Piloting also revealed that to overcome the noise from the X-ray equipment, two microphones were required. One was placed above the lead screen to record intra-staff interactions, and the other was suspended from the ceiling in the area where the patient was seated.

The video recordings were analysed in relation to talk-times, number and source of questions, and the information and instructions given. The results showed that patients' talk-time accounted for just over 12 per cent of the total (Table 11.2). It was also found that the amount of time taken by relatives increased when patients were unable to communicate verbally themselves. Thus, relatives of non-speaking patients had almost 19 per cent of the talk-time, as compared to 6 per cent for the other group of relatives. However, the largest proportion of talk-time was filled by the Clinic team members, with the speech and language therapist herself accounting for over one-quarter of the total.

In terms of the source of communication, when the total figures in Table 11.3 are converted into percentages, it transpired that the Clinic team was responsible for initiating 80 per cent of communications, accompanying professionals for a further 6 per cent, patients initiated 11 per cent of the interactions, and the remaining 3 per cent came from relatives. A total of 46 per cent of interactions were directed to the assessment team as compared to 42 per cent to the patients, 7 per cent to visiting professionals and 5 per cent to relatives. Again, the central figure was the speech and language therapist who was responsible for initiating 39 per cent of all communications.

In line with the emerging picture, once more the Clinic speech and language therapist was again centre stage. She was involved, as source or recipient, in sequences comprising a total of 434 questions, 801 information-giving inter-actions and 329 instructions. In fact, she asked the highest number of questions, and gave the highest amount of information and instructions (Table 11.3). As confirmation of the findings from other research in the health context (Hargie *et al.*, 1994), the patient played a subsidiary role, asking few questions but receiving many, and being given a high proportion of instructions and information.

Table 11.3 Source and recipient of questions, information and instructions

	Source of:				Recipient of:			
	Questions	Information	Instructions	Total	Questions	Information	Instructions	Total
Speech therapist (C)	259	477	312	1048	175	324	17	516
Radiologist	102	333	156	591	107	202	28	337
Dietitian	212	156	133	501	67	136	213	416
Patient	93	194	12	299	329	511	316	1156
Speech therapist (O)	21	83	7	111	21	59	11	91
Relative	19	67	9	95	20	77	34	131
Nurse (O)	29	30	10	69	16	31	20	67
Totals	735	1340	639	2714	735	1340	639	2714

S&LT (C) = Clinic speech and language therapist
S&LT (O) = Speech and language therapist from outside the Clinic who was accompanying the patient
Nurse (O) = Nurse from outside the Clinic who was accompanying the patient

Patient interviews

Two interviews were planned with each of 21 patients. The first took place immediately after the assessment and the second some four weeks later. Owing to the increased illness and incapacity, or death, of some patients, follow-up was not possible in seven cases. Thus, 35 interviews were audio recorded. Content analysis revealed a number of core themes.

Although the procedure had been explained by the speech and language therapists prior to attendance, patients reported *differing expectations of the assessment* and had varying levels of *understanding of its nature*. Thus, 18 per cent said they had 'no idea' what the exact purpose of the examination was, with the same percentage being confused about the videofluoroscopy. The two main reasons proffered by patients for their Clinic assessment were the general and vague ones that staff wanted to 'see what is happening' (41 per cent) and 'confirm all is well' (24 per cent). It was also clear that patients *with language problems* in addition to their swallowing difficulty had *greater difficulties in understanding*. They were less certain of what to expect, less clear as to who the various members of the Clinic were, and more unsure about the reason for the assessment. This finding underlined the need for specific and concerted attention to be devoted to explaining the purpose of the Clinic visit carefully to this group of patients both before and during the assessment.

In general, patients were *positive about their experience* in the Clinic. Although they generally felt that no unanswered questions remained, they still expressed *concerns about receiving conflicting advice*. Interestingly, these were not voiced at the time of assessment. This indicated that a step needed to be placed in the procedure where the patient would be encouraged to express such worries and have them answered. They also felt that *the assessment was required by staff* and it was *their place to comply*, or, as expressed by one respondent, 'do what you are told'. This confirms their 'subservient' expectations, as found in other parts of the audit, and highlighted that the matter of patient empowerment was in need of development. The importance of this can be illustrated by one respondent who said that he did not feel able to query the textures used in the Clinic, although the fact that he felt they were unrepresentative of what he had been attempting to eat on the ward made him severely doubt the validity of the result.

Overall, 61 per cent of patients indicated that the assessment had made a difference to the action taken by themselves and others, but 22 per cent indicated that the results had not done so. It is also interesting to note here that while the evidence from other parts of the audit consistently highlighted the major role of the speech and language therapist, patients were almost totally unaware of this. Some 11 per cent commented that her role was concerned with speech, 9 per cent said she played very little part in the assessment and the remaining 80 per cent had no comment to make about her role! The doctor and dietitian were seen as the main operators. This suggested that speech and language therapists needed

Table 11.4 Health professionals involved in interviews

Profession	Staff based at the Clinical Hospital Site	Staff based at other sites
Doctors		
Consultants	5	8
Registrar	2	—
SHO	1	—
JHO	2	2
GP	—	2
Total	10	12
Nurses		
Sisters	3	—
Staff nurses	6	3
SEN	—	1
Student	1	—
Total	10	4
Others		
Dietitians	5	5
Speech and language therapists	2	7
Physiotherapists	3	1
Occupational therapists	1	1
Total	11	14
Overall total	31	30

to convey to patients the core role they played in the entire procedure, and show that they were knowledgeable professionals in this field.

Staff interviews

From the 80 staff identified as having involvement with the Clinic, 61 were interviewed from across the full range of professions (Table 11.4). No one refused to take part and the sample atrophy was caused by staff moving jobs, being on leave, or unable to fix a time due to work schedules. The results revealed that the majority of respondents *were positive about the Clinic*. They felt *it had influenced their perceptions of the assessment and management of swallowing problems*, and *provided information not available by other means*. It was also found that *medical staff in the site hospital had a clearer understanding of the procedure than those from outside*, a difference that was less evident with therapists. Likewise, the degree to which swallowing was seen as a priority differed considerably among the staff groups, with the site respondents not surprisingly believing it to be more important than those from elsewhere.

Concerns relating to communication were felt most keenly *by speech and language therapy staff, who expressed the view that the procedure was not fully understood by other professional groups*. They also were worried that *the assessment results might not be accepted by other groups*. A common theme in the interviews was that staff overwhelmingly *recognised the importance of ensuring patient understanding of the process*. Yet, as we have seen, in reality this was not achieved, revealing a communication crevice in need of repair.

A final communication issue was *the different perspectives held by respondents of the roles and responsibilities of their own and other professionals, and of the problem itself*. In relation to the latter, one junior doctor with limited experience, expressed the view: 'Swallowing problems is not anything major or anything like diagnosis of cancer and I feel that even the junior staff can speak to the patients or a relative about a swallowing problem.' This was in sharp contrast to the views of a nurse with considerable experience of patients with swallowing disorders who commented: 'It's a big handicap and it can ruin your life . . . just about everything is affected by it . . . It's a big nursing problem and a big problem for the patient.'

This was reflected in the responses of various professionals to the roles of one another. One speech and language therapist in noting the discrepancies which existed said: 'You could have a lot of people working on the problem but not necessarily as a team, so they would be giving conflicting advice.' The need for co-ordination and consistency was also recognised by a doctor who in being aware that staff may not be cognisant of what others have told patients and relatives concluded: 'It is a question of communication, and this I think is perhaps the most difficult and most neglected area.' Thus, there was a clearly expressed need *for greater team-work and collaboration to be developed* and fostered among all those dealing with patients with dysphagia. This is reflected in the general literature where problems of interrole conflict have been well documented (Gaska and Frey, 1996).

CONCLUSIONS

This audit used a combination of three main methods – diary analysis using data collection log-sheets, interviews and video recordings – to obtain a complete picture of the operation of a Swallowing Clinic. This triangulation of methods provided a panorama from these different but equally important perspectives. The main findings were:

- the speech and language therapist played a central role in organising referrals to the Clinic and in the assessment procedure itself;
- although this role was accepted by most staff it was not recognised by patients;
- doctors differed from other professionals in that their communications about patients were mainly in writing;
- the patient's perceived role was that of being co-operative and compliant;
- there was a lack of patient understanding of the assessment procedure and this was particularly marked amongst patients with language difficulties;
- even when they did not understand, patients felt unable to express this openly;

- there were differing views amongst professional about roles and responsibilities, and a feeling that more teamwork was needed.

Following the audit, the findings were disseminated through a series of presentations to different professional groups in both formal and informal settings. This allowed the results to be shared, but also served as useful forums to publicise the need to rectify the above-listed findings, and especially the need for greater inter-professional collaboration. The results influenced the conduct of the Clinic in specific ways. For example, it became standard procedure in the acceptance of referrals to ask the referring agent how any change in management would be dealt with if the need for such changes was indicated by the results. This highlighted the issue of management options, allowing the Clinic to have a clearer understanding of the perspective of those involved. It also prevented patients from having to cope with the stress of the assessment if no benefit was going to accrue for them. A signed referral form was required so that it was clear to all those involved that agreement to proceed was made on this basis.

Report writing was also influenced by the finding that the import of the assessments was not always understood by all staff. Feedback was altered to underline to all involved that recommendations were based on a specific set of factors and that the patient could be put at risk if, for example, larger amounts of food or different consistencies were given. In light of their identified key role, it also became policy to insist on the involvement of a speech and language therapist, so that the necessary monitoring could continue after the assessment.

Since the completion of the study, other clinics were introduced in N.I., and staff who gained their experience through attendance at the site Clinic were centrally involved in their organisation. The audit undoubtedly played a part here in raising the profile of this assessment method. Given the increasing prominence of dysphagia for many professional groups, the study also provided valuable hard evidence about the assessment and management of this condition. Information on data from the audit was cited in a document on evidence-based practice produced by the Royal College of Speech and Language Therapists (van der Gaag and Reid, 1998).

An important aspect of this audit was not only that it sought to examine the functioning of one clinic through a multi-faceted approach, but also attempted to establish its representative nature so that the results could be applied in a wider setting. It was also a good example of a 'partnership' audit. The professional speech and language therapy experience of the first author proved to be of value in determining the need for the research, and the involvement of a communications specialist provided the additional navigational skills to help chart the direction of the audit. Together, it was possible to combine expertise in both the content of the area and the process of audit.

Chapter 12

A communication audit of a paper mill

Phillip G. Clampitt and Laurey Berk

INTRODUCTION

The intern readily admitted that her telephone call was a 'shot in the dark'. She was phoning all the local universities to see if 'anyone there knew how to create a world class communication system for a paper mill'. She was not having much luck until she stumbled into our voice mail system. When we finally contacted her, she was vague about what she wanted but eager to have us talk with the members of the plant's 'communications task force'. We agreed. Assembled around the table were the plant manager, the human resource manager, several supervisors, an hourly worker, and the intern. With some trepidation we began by asking about the issues they were hoping to address. The plant manager simply said, 'We want to develop a world class communication system. How do we do that?' He was disturbed by climate survey results that consistently indicated employee concerns with the communication system. This was the conversation that eventually led to a series of communication audits and other related projects.

In this case study, we want to discuss how audit results can be used to continuously improve the communication system. The process is simple and straightforward (see Box 12.1). The audit or assessment suggests areas of improvement. (The term 'assessment' connotes to many clients something less onerous than the word 'audit'.) Special projects are developed to target these areas of improvement. The loop continues by conducting another audit that assesses the effectiveness of the projects implemented.

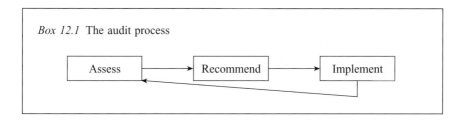

Box 12.1 The audit process

Box 12.2 100 facts about the mill (partial listing)

The numbers
- 650 employees
- 4 shifts
- 26 departments
- 73% male

Communication system
- E-mail
- Electronic bulletin boards
- Dozens of regular bulletin boards
- No regular mill-wide meetings
- Monthly newsletter

BACKGROUND

Like any good detective, we started by gathering relevant facts about the mill. We examined past survey data, employee publications, corporate reports, and bulletin boards. We interviewed key members of the staff. The result was a disjointed list of over a hundred factual statements about the mill (see Box 12.2).

At the time of the first audit, the mill employed over six hundred employees working around the clock in four rotating shifts. Most of the employees were middle-aged males with strong family values. The plant manager was held in high esteem by both union and non-union employees. In order to improve relations with the union, he set up a joint labour management (JLM) team that met every fortnight to discuss issues of mutual interest. The mill was one of several mills and plants that comprised a company, which was, in turn, owned by a multinational corporation. The company was regarded as the 'cash cow' of the corporation, which was having some difficulties with its European companies.

COMMUNICATION ENVIRONMENT

The mill made several attempts to improve the communication system. The Executive Team had developed a 'Communications Bill of Rights' (see Box 12.3), which was a document to stir conversations about communication effectiveness by the senior staff. The document was instructive on several accounts. First, it identified some of the issues the staff was trying to address. Second, it pointed to some of the underlying problems that the senior staff unwittingly spawned. The most obvious was that the Bill of Rights focused entirely on communication rights with no mention of responsibilities. The underlying assumption was that the senior staff bore almost total responsibility for the effectiveness of communication. Indeed, at the root of much of their frustration was that they put enormous resources into communicating 'properly' but had very little to show for their efforts. Fortunately, the Bill of Rights was never adopted and circulated to employees. It

---

Box 12.3 Communications Bill of Rights

We the people, recognising the advantages of a successful communications programme at the Mill, do hereby declare that all employees have the right:

- To clear, understandable, and unambiguous communication.
- To ongoing communication – not just in times of crisis or need.
- To information before, not after, important events.
- To give feedback on issues and have all two-way horizontal and vertical communications lines open and clear.
- To be told about issues affecting their company, their jobs, and their responsibilities.
- To be recognised for their accomplishments and achievements so they feel like 'somebodys' on their job every day.
- To know why the company adopts its policies and procedures and to know about changes in the business and social environment the company works in.
- To an explanation of the company's community relations activity and to share in the responsibility for civic and community projects.
- To a continual overview of successes and failure with products or services, and company growth and vision.

---

was, however, an exquisite example of senior management's thinking. To their credit, the team recognised that 'something was askew'.

So much for the mind-set of the management team. What were the key components of the communication system? In addition to the typical departmental meetings, the plant relied on the following communication channels:

- *Bulletin boards*. The boards were scattered throughout the plant. Some had designated functions like 'safety information' or 'job postings' but most were under departmental control. Even though the boards were considered one of the mill's most important communication channels, they were unevenly maintained and updated.
- *Newsletter*. The newsletter was distributed once a month and contained the following regular features: union news, birthdays and work anniversaries, safety updates, general plant information and personal interest stories. The general consensus was that the newsletter enjoyed a wide and thorough readership. Audit results would confirm this perception.
- *E-mail system*. The system was widely used by administrative employees to communicate with one another. They assumed that this was also an effective tool to communicate with hourly employees. All administrative employees had dedicated computer terminals at their desks; hourly employees had to share terminals.

- *JLM.* Union representatives and management discussed major issues in these meetings. The hope was that union representatives would share relevant information with their fellow union brothers and sisters.

Senior management often communicated key messages via all four channels.

However, data from an organisational climate survey conducted two years prior still indicated there were problems. In particular, the management team was worried about two survey items:

- Over 80 per cent of hourly employees felt that 'employees responded [negatively] to formal and informal communications from plant management personnel'.
- Over 80 per cent of hourly employees felt negatively about the 'extent [to which] plant management shares organisational information' with each other.

These results, coupled with the frustrations wrought by the management team's musings regarding a 'Bill of Rights', prompted a strategic change in approach. They decided to seek professional assistance in dealing with the communication issues. Thus, their strategic goal for the year was simple: 'Conduct a professional survey on communication. Determine what world class communication systems look like.'

THE FIRST COMMUNICATION AUDIT

After the Communications Committee agreed on the basic assessment process, we sought input from several key groups, including other members of the top management team, union officials, and a number of supervisors. Our aim was to have these opinion leaders shape the audit process and thus motivate others to fully participate. Accordingly, we asked how the process could be beneficial to them and sought their advice on various audit procedures. Although we used the Communication Satisfaction Questionnaire developed by Downs and Hazen (1977) as the centrepiece of the audit, we encouraged union officials, supervisors, and employees to add other appropriate questions. This proved particularly helpful in motivating these opinion leaders. We also ended up adding 13 questions to the survey to target certain specific concerns.

Other important issues arose during this initial consultation:

- Could the results be used to seek retribution against dissatisfied employees?
- Would the results be used to promote or demote supervisors?
- Would the administration of the survey place even more burdens on supervisors?

These were all legitimate concerns that we addressed in three ways. First, we were very clear about the purpose of the audit process. All our messages to employees about the process highlighted our central objective: to improve communication processes at the mill. We assured employees in face-to-face meetings that the focus was organisational processes and not personalities. Second, we guaranteed the anonymity of employee responses. Because we were an outside consulting firm, we, rather than the company, were able to control the data. In fact, we even mentioned to employees that after the data were coded into the computer, their individual surveys would be shredded. This also signalled to supervisors that we would be doing most of the work. Third, we assured employees that we would not report results of groups containing fewer than seven employees. These measures apparently alleviated most of the employee concerns.

Components

After the initial consultation with these groups, we developed an audit package that included the following:

- *Communication satisfaction survey.* The survey consisted of 46 standard questions and 13 items unique to the mill. The survey also contained four open-ended questions that allowed us insight into some of the 'big picture' issues. At the end of the survey, employees were asked to provide various demographic data and indicate a shift and departmental code.
- *Channel assessment.* Content analysis was performed on three of the most frequently used channels: bulletin boards, monthly newsletter and monthly report. Our purpose was to study empirically the *actual* messages sent through formal channels. Those data were compared to the *intended* messages of the senior staff.
- *Follow-up interviews.* After a preliminary assessment of the survey data, we randomly interviewed 43 employees. Our objective was both to confirm tentative conclusions drawn from the quantitative data and to probe for more details on certain issues of concern.

The Communications Committee then reviewed and approved the 'final' package. In addition, we presented a flow chart of all the activities involved in administering the package and providing feedback to the various groups. The last step before the administration was pre-testing the survey with a group of volunteers. Based on their feedback, we made a few minor wording changes to the instrument.

Promotion and administration

Since the Communications Committee determined that participation would be voluntary, we felt that motivating employees to participate was critical. Therefore, we publicised the process with bulletin board and payslip announcements (see Box 12.4) as well as personal communications to supervisors. This process was a bit paradoxical since we had to use the very communication system we were

Box 12.4 Sample publicity for the survey sessions
(this was inserted in employee payslips)

We need your help

As part of our commitment to continuous improvement, we will be evaluating
the strengths and areas for improvement in our communication system within the
mill. We will be looking at the effectiveness of various means of communication
such as memos, bulletin board announcements, the employee newsletter, and
verbal communication. To conduct the evaluation, *we need your help*. We need to
know your views on how well we communicate with one another. We have asked
MetaComm, a consulting firm specialising in internal organisational communication, to co-ordinate the evaluation.

Here's how we will proceed:

1. MetaComm will be administering a brief survey to all employees. **All
   responses will be completely confidential.**
2. The surveys will be taken in groups of approximately 30 employees.
3. MetaComm will conduct these sessions in the Assembly Room and will collect
   the surveys at the end of a 30-minute session.
4. Sign-up sheets will be posted on the entryway wall the week of July 20th.
5. All employees will receive a summary of the findings in November.

Special times have been designated for each shift. For those on vacation, a confidential mail-in survey will be provided.

Here's the schedule:

We are aiming for 100% participation. Your input is vital. In appreciation for your
participation, a door prize will be given out at each session. The door prize will be
on display at the mill entrance. If you have any questions about the survey process,
please feel free to call Paul M. at ex. 2348.

---

auditing to inform employees about the audit. Some incentives proved useful.
Hourly employees were paid overtime wages to participate. In addition, a raffle
for coolers and gift certificates was held for those who completed the survey.

Approximately twelve survey sessions were scheduled around the clock to
administer the questionnaire. We designated times for certain departments to
take the survey, but others were allowed to participate at their own convenience.
When employees arrived, we orally briefed them about the objectives, guidelines, and the feedback process (see Box 12.5). When they completed the survey
we again reminded them of the 'next steps', including random employee interviews and briefings over the results.

Box 12.5 Survey session introduction

1 Objectives of the survey
2 Responses are **confidential**
3 No right or wrong answers
4 Background on survey
   a *History*
   b *Approximate completion time*
5 Follow-up
   a *Interviews*
   b *Report findings*
6 Instructions
   a *Scale*
   b *Department codes*

RESULTS

Over 55 per cent of employees participated in survey sessions. Thirty-six per cent of the respondents were salaried and 64 per cent were hourly. The salaried were somewhat over-represented as respondents as they comprised 23 per cent of the mill employees. During follow-up interviews we found that many of those who chose not to participate reported that they were suffering from 'survey fatigue'. That is, they had filled out too many surveys that yielded too few benefits. This is a fairly common complaint in many organisations (Management Decisions Systems, 1993).

We prepared a table that rank-ordered all the quantitative results and also showed a comparison to our databank norms (see Table 12.1). The databank norms were drawn from assessments conducted in 26 companies, many conducted through our consulting company, MetaComm (Clampitt, 1991). Initially, we looked for trends based on the mill results alone. Then we used the databank norms to analyse the data from a broader perspective by examining how this mill compared to other companies. In addition, we prepared tables based on the content analyses of the open-ended questions, the channel assessment, and interview data (see Table 12.2). All of these tools were used to draw conclusions about the general communication issues faced by the mill. We also prepared more specific tables, breaking down the results by department and shift.

We made a clear separation between data analyses and conclusions. In fact, two separate booklets were prepared. One contained all the charts discussed above. The other was a report that synthesised the results, providing tentative conclusions and recommendations. Our strategy was to secure everyone's agreement on the basic analyses before suggesting any specific conclusions or recommendations. Indeed, we reviewed the data booklet with the staff first. Our strategic

Table 12.1 Rank order and norms of survey items

The numeric survey questions are ranked in descending order according to respondents' satisfaction with the following factors on a 0–10 scale ('0' represents no satisfaction, '5' represents average satisfaction, and '10' represents high satisfaction)

Rank	Question	Mill mean	MetaComm norm	Significance
1	Job satisfaction	6.69	6.79	
2	Supervisor trusts me	6.62	7.45	*
3	Right amount of supervision	6.53	7.14	*
4	Information on policies and goals	6.47	5.73	*
5	Activity of grapevine	6.41	6.39	
6	Subordinate responsive to directives	6.23	6.88	*
7	Compatible work group	6.11	7.07	*
8	Subordinate anticipates my information needs	6.10	6.53	
9	Effectiveness of employee newsletter	6.05	n/a	
10	Supervisor open to new ideas	6.01	6.69	*

Note: $^* p < 0.05$

Table 12.2 Sample content analysis of interview data

'What do you think are the greatest communication strengths of the mill?'

Rank	Category	%	No.	Sample comments
1	Climate: openness/keeps us informed	45	27	• 'Open atmosphere, sharing.' • 'More open – information given freely.' • 'Open about business conditions and how company is doing; open to customer feedback.'
2	Leadership of top management/downward communication	17	10	• 'Bob D. has good presentations; good general information – everyone knew about the No. 7 paper machine project.' • 'Leadership is good; no secrecy.' • 'Bob D. comes down on floor and talks with us – open climate.'
3	Channels/accessibility	17	10	• 'PA system throughout mill, notices on changes sent to everyone, have many information meetings.' • 'Accessibility to people – voice mail, pagers that maintenance and supervisors carry . . .'
4	Good intentions/attempts at improving	12	7	• 'Improving – used to be secrecy.' • 'They're trying – there's still not a precise way of getting communication around.'
5	Miscellaneous	9	5	• 'Communication with union is great – especially regarding injuries.' • 'Educational programmes have improved.'

Reliability = 97%
Responses   = 59
Respondents = 42

tentativeness paid off in a number of ways. First, it allowed the senior staff to shape the action plans. This, in turn, provided them with more motivation to implement the plans. Second, the senior staff made a number of perceptive observations about the raw data that we simply overlooked because we lacked intimate knowledge of the mill. Third, it boosted our credibility as auditors because it demonstrated that we were unlike many 'vendors' who used surveys to sell training programmes.

We used a cascade approach to provide feedback. The senior management team was orally briefed on the mill-wide results and given the booklets to peruse at their leisure. Then the various department heads were briefed on the mill-wide and their specific departmental results. Finally, we prepared a two-page summary of the major conclusions, which was distributed to all employees. The mill manager attached a written response to our summary that outlined the next steps. In addition, we held a couple of open meetings for employees who wished to review the results in more depth.

The basic conclusions of the audit were as follows:

- Satisfaction with *supervisory communication* was strong at the mill. The second most highly rated survey item was employee satisfaction with the extent to which 'my supervisor trusts me'. Employees also felt satisfied with the amount of supervision they were given and that their supervisors were open to new ideas.
- Employees were also highly satisfied with their *work groups*. They often mentioned a 'family theme' when describing their work groups. Employees like the friendship and camaraderie with their co-workers.
- Employees felt that a great strength was the *mill-wide communication climate* of 'openness' and accessibility to information. However, while information was accessible, people often mentioned that the information was not understandable and they did not know how to use it.
- There was a relatively high level of satisfaction with the *employee newsletter* and *bulletin boards*. However, our studies revealed that each could be used more effectively.
- Employees expressed dissatisfaction with *feedback* on how they were being judged, recognition of their efforts and information on their job progress. Feedback was often mentioned to be infrequent, inconsistent or non-existent.
- There was dissatisfaction with the flow of *routine information*. Employees felt the greatest weakness of the communication system was that they were not kept informed on daily operations and that they did not receive their job information on time.
- There was dissatisfaction with *interdepartmental communication*. Comments such as 'one hand doesn't know what the other is doing' were common.
- Many employees did not see how they fit into the '*big picture*'. They felt like a 'missing puzzle piece'. There was confusion about what important committees were doing and how their decisions were made.

- Employees felt that improving *problem-solving* with their supervisor could increase their satisfaction and productivity. There was a feeling that superiors did not understand job problems and that problems in 'my job' could be handled better.

Both quantitative and qualitative data were used as evidence for almost every issue. The senior staff basically agreed with these findings. Then we discussed the 'next step'.

NEXT STEP

When it came to action plans, we were venturing into unknown territory. Diagnosing problems is one thing, knowing what to do about them is another matter altogether. As we discovered, the analysis was the easy part. Nevertheless, we accepted the challenge and continued to work with the mill by attacking some of the root problems. Interestingly, one of the key issues was redefining the senior staff's view of communication effectiveness. Recall the 'Communication Bill of Rights'. After further discussions, the staff began to see the inherent problems of that approach. We reoriented the staff's thinking by suggesting that a World Class Communication System had five key attributes:

- The leadership team has a *strategic commitment* to effective communication.
- Employees at all levels have the appropriate *communication skills.*
- There is a proper *infrastructure of channels* to meet mill objectives.
- There are proper *communication policies and procedures* to meet mill objectives.
- *Information is managed* in a way to meet mill objectives.

This strategic view of communication, while not perfect, reoriented the discussion around a system of interlocking issues rather than exclusively focusing on the needs of employees (see Box 12.6). We were trying to challenge the notion that senior management was solely responsible for the effectiveness of the entire communication system. Hourly employees and newsletter editors also had responsibilities. Even the taken-for-granted ways of communicating needed to be challenged.

We used these core strategic issues to filter the results and weigh the significance of issues raised in the audit. In fact, we even rated the mill on each of the core issues using a 'meter' with 'low', 'medium', and 'high' ratings (see Table 12.3). This was an admittedly subjective process based on our experience with dozens of other audits. Even though we readily admitted the subjective nature of our analysis at this point, the leadership team agreed and actually found it a useful way to prioritise action plans. This may be instructive to other auditors. There is an intuitive element to auditing; expertise is not totally based on facts and figures. With this new strategic approach to communication, we attacked the core problems with the following specific projects:

Box 12.6 Attributes of a world class communication system

Strategic commitment
1 There is a strategic commitment from top management to promote and practise effective communication. This means:

- There is a clear vision of the objectives of the communication system.
- There is a compelling desire to continually improve the system.
- There is a commitment to provide the financial resources necessary to enact the vision.

2 There is a commitment by management and employees to uphold ethical stands for communication.

Communication skills
3 Top management has the ability, desire and means to inspire a vision in the employees.
4 Managerial employees have superior communication skills.
5 All employees have above-average communication skills.
6 Employees know how they are performing against recognised standards of performance.

Channel infrastructure
7 The organisation has an effective infrastructure of channels to meet three communication challenges:

- quickly handle emergencies;
- disseminate day-to-day information;
- present a realistic vision of the business environment.

8 Channels used by communicators are congruent with employee needs, management's objectives, and the message capacity of the channel.

Communication policies and procedures
9 Employees know how they fit into the 'big picture' and believe they are empowered to carry out the organisational mission.
10 Dynamic programmes are in place to make sure employee concerns are heard and acted on.
11 Departments interact with one another effectively.
12 The communication system is routinely evaluated.

Information management
13 Employees have relatively easy access to all information they deem necessary, with some minor exceptions.
14 Active measures are in place to make sure that employees receive relevant and timely information but not more than necessary.
15 There are safety valves built into the communication system to circumvent communication breakdowns.

Table 12.3 Core issue ratings

Core issue	Rating
Strategic commitment	High
Communication skills	Medium
Channel infrastructure	Medium
Communication policies and procedures	Medium-low
Information management	Medium-low

1 *Redesigning the employee newsletter.* We suggested a realignment of informa-tion priorities and the inclusion of regular standing columns based on the priorities. Employee recognition and personal interest issues would remain, given the organisational culture, but visionary commentary from top adminis-trators and stories that celebrate mill values would take on added importance.

2 *Introducing a new channel: quarterly 'State of the Mill' address.* This channel would enable top management to more effectively link individual employee's efforts and roles with the mill 'big picture'. This oral channel would allow for discussion of key industry trends and general corporate responses to the trends, along with evaluating the current state of the company in light of goals and values.

3 *Changing the format and content of the 'Monthly Report'.* This report, in-tended for mill-wide distribution, resembled a 'grab bag' due to the inclusion of so many different components (key indicators, future directions, key external events, on-going projects) often buried in one paragraph. We suggested clarifying the core audience for the monthly report (hourly workers) and organising the report around the mill values (productivity and cost, quality, service and safety), with key indicators measuring each value. To help authors in preparing and submitting information for inclusion in the monthly report, we also developed a more user-friendly 'feeder report'.

4 *Developing leadership skills.* The survey and interviews revealed that this was an area in need of further development. We developed training sessions on enhancing communication effectiveness in the areas of conflict management, problem-solving, listening, feedback, recognition, and channel selection. We planned to use role-playing to provide insight about each participant's com-munication style.

The senior staff also decided that after these projects were underway, we should conduct another audit in a couple of years to determine the effectiveness of the changes. Meanwhile, we assisted in the planning and implementation of many of these projects. This approach fitted nicely with the mill's basic commit-ment to 'continuous improvement'. If the projects did not address the problems, then we would try something else.

Table 12.4 Comparison of audits 1 and 2

Item	Audit 1	Audit 2
Information on finances	5.5	6.4
Information on major changes	5.6	6.0
Communication with top management	5.6	5.2
Effectiveness of employee newsletter	6.0	5.9
Clarity of written communication	5.7	5.8
How conflicts are handled	4.6	4.6
Interdepartmental communication	4.8	4.2

THE SECOND AUDIT

As often happens, larger events intervened in our plans. Most of the action plans discussed above were actually implemented. However, on the second go-around, the parent company decided to expand both the size and scope of the audit. They asked us to survey all the plants in the company and expand the content to include a vast array of other issues. Our intent, therefore, to determine the effectiveness of our communication projects at the mill, was compromised a bit. Nevertheless, we were able to compare the results on several items.

We used the same 0–10 satisfaction scale ('0' representing low satisfaction, '10' representing high satisfaction) for many of the items. The results were as shown in Table 12.4.

Many of the results were pleasing. One of first projects we implemented after the initial audit was the introduction of a new channel, the quarterly 'State of the Mill' address by the plant manager. Therefore, it was gratifying to see improved satisfaction levels with information on finances and major changes. The modest decline with the item on top management may appear puzzling. But interview data revealed that when most employees answered this question, they were referring to senior company management, not the on-site mill manager.

Several projects were completed a few weeks prior to the second audit. In fact, because change is often resisted, we would not have been surprised by a modest decrease in related items (Clampitt and Berk, 1996). For instance the format changes in the newsletter only appeared in two prior issues. So it was not terribly surprising, and in fact somewhat comforting, to discover that satisfaction with 'the effectiveness of the employee newsletter' remained stable. Likewise, satisfaction with the 'clarity of written communication' showed little change. The changes in the format and content of the monthly report were only recently introduced. These changes probably did not directly address this survey item. There were numerous other written channels of communication that needed improvement. After discussing this item in more depth, we decided that this item was partially a skill issue based on the writing abilities of managers. This discussion was particularly instructive because it reminded us once again of how difficult it is to correctly interpret some survey items and subsequently develop an appropriate response.

Although we had several projects in the works dealing with leadership development, these had not been rolled out in all areas of the plant. Thus, the results on certain items, while disappointing, were not terribly surprising. For instance, employee satisfaction with 'how conflicts are handled' was virtually unchanged while satisfaction with interdepartmental communication declined. Interdepartmental communication typically is a particularly vexing issue (Clampitt, 1991). In this case the issue was compounded by the fact that over fifty employees were added to the plant in the intervening years.

We included several special items in the second survey. On an agree/disagree scale ('1' representing strongly disagree and '7' representing strongly agree), a question directly focusing on the monthly report was asked: 'The new monthly report is better than the former.' The mean of 5.1 showed significant agreement with the statement.

In general, these were encouraging findings. Changes in the channel infrastructure were particularly well received. However, the results also indicated the difficulty in making significant changes in a well-entrenched communication system.

SO WHAT?

There are many lessons to be learned from this audit. First, it helps to illuminate some of the audit procedures discussed in this book (questionnaire survey, interviews, etc.). The procedures used in this case study can be adapted to virtually any company. Second, this audit illustrates how the classic notion of continuous improvement can be used to enhance a communication system. In particular, the leap between the diagnostic and prescription phases is one that is rarely discussed in the literature. This audit provided some insight into how to do that, although admittedly we were not as prepared as we should have been for this transition.

We have since developed more specific procedures for addressing common communication problems (Clampitt, 1991; Clampitt and Berk, 1996). Yet, we believe the key is to maintain a strategic tentativeness in regard to actual solutions. However, we should note that this sentiment is not one shared by all consultants. Many believe that their role is to 'solve' the problems. We take a more interactive view and believe that our role is to act as a catalyst for developing appropriate responses.

Finally, the case demonstrates the importance of having a firm understanding of organisational communication theory. Without that theoretical basis we never could have answered the 'world class communication system' question. Intuition, tempered in the organisational communication literature, allows auditors to go beyond the data provided by the inherently limited investigative tools and to suggest new approaches to novel issues. In short, we learned that effective auditing is both a science and an art.

Chapter 13

Auditing communication practices in the Church

A study of a Catholic diocese

Owen Hargie and Mark Lount

INTRODUCTION

This chapter describes an audit carried out within a Catholic diocese in Ireland. The investigation is novel, in that no previous audit of the priesthood has been undertaken. In the chapter we will discuss the rationale for the audit, describe the Catholic diocese where it was conducted, present the main findings, and highlight some of the benefits and difficulties of the approach adopted. The audit was conducted as part of a research investigation into the communicative 'world' of the Catholic priest. The need for research in this area was identified following a review of literature, which revealed the paucity of inquiry in this field.

The study detailed here was part of a wider project into the training and interpersonal practice of priests, which included three other investigations:

- a critical incidents analysis undertaken to identify key interpersonal skills used by priests in their communications with laypeople and colleagues (Lount and Hargie, 1997);
- an examination of seminarians' views on the interpersonal dimensions of the education and training they had received as a preparation for their future mission as priests (Lount and Hargie, 1998);
- a focus group study of the attitudes of Catholic laypeople towards their priests (Lount, 1997).

One of the reasons that few empirical investigations have been carried out into the communication practices of priests is the difficulty of gaining access. Much of the work of priests is, by definition, confidential, and this makes data collection problematic. At each stage of the present audit, therefore, full agreement was reached with the main 'gatekeeper', the auxiliary bishop in charge of the diocese. The methods, procedures and processes to be undertaken were all agreed with him in advance. The audit was seen as beneficial not only to the authors in terms of academic research but also to the bishop in the form of feedback on current communication practices. As part of the 'contract' negotiated prior to the audit, full confidentiality was guaranteed for individual priests. Also, a comprehensive report was to be presented to the diocese, detailing all of the main findings.

The main purpose of this investigation was to obtain a detailed account from priests of their experiences of the diocesan communication system, and examine its quantity and the quality, both vertically and horizontally. Like staff in any organisation, priests carry out their responsibilities within a specific environment, and an important part of this audit was to examine their perceptions of this work context. Churches are hierarchically organised, with full-time professionals, developed procedures, articulated belief systems, and well developed routines and procedures to deal with their activities. This tends to produce the line of authority, differentiation of functions and specification of tasks typical of all bureaucratic organisations. The present audit set out to examine the effects of this particular setting and situation upon communication patterns.

Despite the number of books written on the priesthood, it appears that there has been no systematic attempt to examine and typify the interpersonal context of priestly practice. Most studies on clergymen have focused on one of two areas: (a) personality and personal background studies of individual clergymen, or of *in situ* clergy contrasted with 'dropouts', or comparisons with other occupational groups; and (b) wider sociological attitude surveys (Lount, 1997). For example, the analysis by Rice (1990) of priests who leave the Church did not really address the issue of communication. Likewise, the investigation by Francis and Jones (1996) into psychological perspectives on Christian ministry included material selected to encompass as wide a range of topics and empirical methods as possible. Yet, none of this material specifically focused on Catholic clergy in relation to interpersonal communication.

THE ORGANISATIONAL ENVIRONMENT

In a fairly obvious sense, the Catholic Church is a huge multinational organisation. That is, it is an organisation that has 'branches' in almost every country throughout the world. The Church is both a religious system and a bureaucratic entity. As a bureaucracy, it portrays many of Weber's (1947) characteristics of the ideal type of bureaucratic administrative structure:

- a rational-legal basis of authority;
- clearly defined sphere of legal competence for each office;
- appointment (not selection) of members to offices;
- definition of the office as the sole (or at least primary) occupation of the incumbent;
- membership in the organisation seen as a career;
- office holder subject to strict and systematic control in the conduct of his office.

In secular terms, within the Roman ecclesiastical structure, line-management descends from the Roman Pontiff (the Pope), the bishop of the entire Roman Church, to the bishops of dioceses who take responsibility for the local church, to the priests, the immediate point of contact between clerical personnel and the laity. Between ordination and the advancement to parish priest (priest-in-charge), priests will spend many years as curates (assistants), responding to the way in which the different parish priests exercise their authority. There are no inter-mediate formal hierarchical steps between curate and parish priest. Beyond this there is the bishopric or the honorary title of monsignor.

The diocesan bishop has immense potential autonomy and authority. He owes allegiance only to the Pope. All of his offices and commissions, notably the chancery office (all administrative or bureaucratic functions) exist at his discretion and are merely advisory bodies. The absolute dependence of priests on the bishop in their ministry is the other side of the total responsibility for the diocese, which in both belief and practice is under the remit of the bishop. However, the relation of the bishops to priests and laypeople, the concept of 'office' itself, and the scope of Episcopal authority, have all been the subject of ongoing development and vicissitudes (Osbourne, 1988; Dunn, 1990). The Second Vatican Council sought to balance the chain of command by an awareness of 'collegiality' – a process of discernment, co-responsibility and joint decision-making in which the Church, clergy and laypeople, all participate.

The Catholic Church in Ireland is organised on an all-Ireland basis, unaffected by political structures. The key unit is the diocese, each with a clear geograph-ical boundary, in turn divided into parishes, again usually geographically de-fined. In larger parishes the parish priest is assisted by one or more curates. Many parishes have established pastoral councils. These are not meant to be executive committees on the model of secular business administration. Rather, they are a core group in the faith community of the parish, whose role is to work with priests and laypeople in deciding the direction in which the com-munity is going and in helping to facilitate the growth and activity of the local church.

The particular diocese in this audit was selected because the university campus was situated within its boundary and this facilitated both access and data collection. This diocese, which has 52 parishes, covers a substantial area with a present population of some 200,000. The ratio of priests to laypersons is approximately 1:1321. The priests who are the subjects of this research are described as diocesan priests – that is, they work and operate in the context and environment of a diocese in Ireland. The day-to-day task of leadership in the Catholic Christian community is in the hands of these priests, the vast major-ity of whom work unobtrusively in parishes and are devoted to the pastoral ministry. While the main roles are those of parish priest or curate, others may have 'special' assignments, such as full-time teaching, university or hospital chaplaincy, newspaper work, or liturgical commission activities.

AUDIT OBJECTIVES

This communication audit had the following objectives:

- to examine the quantity and quality of information flow between priests at all levels;
- to examine the quantity and quality of news and information about activities and events in the diocese and parish;
- to explore the priests' levels of satisfaction with communication;
- to investigate the extent to which current communication practices encouraged priests to identify with the diocese;
- to investigate what opportunities existed for priests to have access to a colleague in the event of experiencing difficulties;
- to examine the level of priests' satisfaction with decision-making processes.

THE AUDIT PROCESS

All priests in the diocese were included in the audit. As no previously validated instrument was available to specifically measure the attitudes of priests, the Downs and Hazen Communication Satisfaction Questionnaire (CSQ) was selected as the guiding framework for analysing the source, method and content of communication surrounding the work of the priests. The CSQ, which has been shown to have wide utility (see Chapter 3 for details), was slightly modified to meet specific contextual requirements. The terminology was adjusted in various ways – one example is that the term 'manager' was replaced with the context-relevant term 'priest-in-charge'. Also, some questions were not suitable, such as 'Information about relationship with unions', or 'Information about government action affecting my company'. Following consultations with the bishop and six randomly selected priests, these questions were replaced by parallel questions. The revised CSQ was again then reviewed by the same six priests. Following minor modifications it was further pilot-tested with the bishop and eight diocesan priests.

The final agreed CSQ comprised 16 pages with an overall total of 66 questions. Actual questions used are presented within the tables later in the chapter. The questionnaire contained seven sub-sections:

1 Section A elicited personal background information (e.g. age, number of years working in the diocese).
2 Section B was concerned with the nature of the priest's work and his level of job satisfaction.
3 Section C charted the *quantity* of information being received about a range of issues.
4 Section D focused upon the *quality* of information flow.
5 Section E examined information flow upwards, downwards and horizontally.

6 Section F contained questions about working relationships with fellow priests.
7 Section G was designed specifically for priests with a managerial/supervisory responsibility. This section also included three questions developed by Ransom *et al.* (1977). The first of these required priests to evaluate how much *influence* the various members of the diocese (from bishops through to laypeople) had in decision-making. The second described seven main *functions* of the priestly ministry and asked priests to rank-order these in terms of their priority. The third requested priests to *characterise the diocese* as being 'highly centralised', 'centralised', 'decentralised' or 'highly decentralised'. Finally two open questions were included:

(a) What do you believe parishioners expect of you as their priest?
(b) If the communication associated with your work could be changed in any way to facilitate you, please indicate how.

AUDIT RESULTS

The CSQ, and a pre-paid return envelope, was posted to all 137 priests in the diocese. The questionnaire was anonymous, and respondents were assured that answers would be treated in the strictest confidence. A reminder letter, with a questionnaire and pre-paid envelope, was posted one month later.

Seventy eight completed CSQs were received (57 per cent). There was a broad spread in terms both of age breakdown (Box 13.1) and years of experience (Box 13.2).

The 'role' of the sample, in terms of their actual work, was that the majority (53 per cent) were curates, followed by priests (27 per cent), and parish administration (8 per cent), while 12 per cent described themselves as carrying out 'other' duties (e.g. teaching, full-time chaplain). In fulfilling these roles, there was an even spread across the number of years the priests had worked in this diocese, so that 10 per cent had been there for less than four years while 12 per cent had been with the diocese for over forty years. Finally, respondents were asked to record the length of time they had held their present post, and here

---

Box 13.1 Age range of priests

Age	Number
under 30 years	6
30–39 years	22
40–49 years	15
50–59 years	17
60–69 years	16
70+ years	2

Box 13.2 Range of years ordained

Years ordained	Number
0–4 years	8
5–9 years	12
10–14 years	10
15–19 years	7
20–24 years	8
25–29 years	7
30–34 years	8
35–39 years	9
40+ years	9

47 per cent indicated less than four years, 36 per cent between five and nine years, and 11 per cent between ten and fourteen years. One individual had been in the same position for over forty years, while the remaining 5 per cent were in their current post for between twenty and twenty-four years.

The results indicated that there were many strengths in the diocesan network of communication. These included:

- the bishop's accessibility to priests;
- his perceived trust in them;
- his openness and honesty;
- the opportunities made available for priests to consult someone else in the diocese over difficulties (personal and/or work related);
- the feedback priests received horizontally from colleagues.

However, the modal values as shown in the frequency analysis tables (see Tables 13.1–13.6) indicated that for most questions the reported level of satisfaction was 'moderate' showing that for the majority of priests, and across many communication issues, there was room for improvement. At the same time, some aspects of interpersonal communication in the diocese produced a high modal score.

The main findings to emerge were as follows:

1 There was a high level of personal identity with the diocese. The majority of priests were satisfied with their work and felt highly involved (see Table 13.6). This measure reflects the extent of personal identification with and commitment to the organisation – in other words, the level of emotional attraction felt for the organisation (Allen and Meyer, 1990).
2 Although the priests felt a strong sense of identification with the diocese, this appears to be in contrast with the way the majority of them felt about the

Table 13.1 Ratings of *amount* of feedback being received by priests

Questions	1*	2*	3*	4*	5*	M
Information regarding the detail of what is required of me in the performance of my duties	14	45	28	5	8	2
Feedback given by the *bishop* about the way I carry out my duties	10	19	36	29	6	3
Feedback given by the *priest-in-charge* about the way I carry out my duties	6	21	29	12	32	5
Feedback given by *fellow priests* about the way I carry out my duties	9	38	31	16	6	2
Feedback given by *laypeople* about the way I carry out my duties	18	44	27	9	2	2
Feedback given by the *bishop* about the way I carry out my duties in *comparison* with other priests engaged in similar work	4	5	25	52	14	4
Feedback given by the *priest-in-charge* about the way I carry out my duties in *comparison* with other priests engaged in similar work	4	8	15	39	34	4
Feedback given by *fellow priests* about the way I carry out my duties in *comparison* with other priests engaged in similar work	5	11	33	40	11	4
Feedback given by *laypeople* about the way I carry out my duties in *comparison* with other priests engaged in similar work	10	31	30	19	10	2
Information given to me on how assessments were made by the *priest-in-charge* regarding my competence in carrying out my duties	4	3	13	40	40	4
Information given to me on what happens to the assessments regarding my competence in carrying out my duties	3	2	19	41	35	4
Recognition by the *bishop* of the efforts I make in carrying out my duties	13	31	22	29	5	2
Recognition by *priest-in-charge* of the efforts I make in carrying out my duties	9	18	23	18	32	5
Recognition by *fellow priests* of the efforts I make in carrying out my duties	10	33	29	24	4	2
Recognition by *laypeople* of the efforts I make in carrying out my duties	19	44	22	9	6	2
Reports on how I handle problems which arise in the performance of my duties	4	14	35	36	11	4

Notes

* Figures in these columns are percentage values where: 1 = a great deal; 2 = a moderate amount; 3 = very little; 4 = no communication; 5 = not applicable

M = modal values

Table 13.2 Ratings of amount of information being received about the diocese

Questions	1*	2*	3*	4*	5*	M
Information about how *diocesan* activities are funded	9	36	30	24	1	2
Information about the financial standing of the *diocese*	10	24	30	32	4	4
Information regarding the difficulties faced by the *diocese*	—	10	37	33	20	3
Information and news relating to activities and events in the *diocese*	26	42	24	6	2	2
Information about matters and affairs relating to the *parish* in which the priest worked	28	40	15	4	13	2

Notes
* Figures in these columns are percentage values where: 1 = a great deal; 2 = a moderate amount; 3 = very little; 4 = no communication; 5 = not applicable

M = modal values

amount of news and information they received concerning diocesan activities. Most respondents felt that they were given no information about financial affairs or how activities were funded, and they were also dissatisfied with the information flow regarding difficulties faced by the diocese (see Table 13.2). Research findings indicate that if such dissatisfaction persists, it will be dysfunctional both for the individual and the organisation (see Chapter 1).

3 The lack of consultation about meetings was also a cause of dissatisfaction with the majority of respondents (see Table 13.6). Meetings are a place for priests to express their ideas, as a source of information, and as a means of diocesan identification. However, the indication that there is a low level of consultation with the rank and file regarding agenda-setting could give the impression that it is seen as the bishop's meeting and is not a meeting of and for all priests to discuss matters and issues of importance to them. This result posed a challenge for the leadership within the diocese in relation to decision-making and empowerment, both of which are correlates of satisfaction and effective communication (Hargie *et al.*, 1999).

4 The majority (63 per cent) of respondents perceived the bishop of the diocese as the most influential person, while only 3 per cent thought curates had a very great influence. In fact, a substantial majority (73 per cent) of the sample indicated that curates had little or no influence at all (see Table 13.7). This perception would place curates at the bottom of the organisational pyramid, with least participation in decision-making. This again does not augur well for effective communication or satisfaction. Evidence shows that people are more satisfied when they are consulted and are allowed to participate in decisions affecting them (Hargie and Tourish, 1999b). Clearly people at the top of the hierarchy can be an important source of satisfaction. How senior staff (the bishop and his senior colleagues in this case) interact with those lower down the hierarchy (priests) is crucial in promoting maximum commitment to the

Table 13.3 Ratings of *quality* of feedback being received by priests

Questions	1*	2*	3*	4*	5*	M
Information regarding the detail of what is required of me in the performance of my duties	10	37	24	24	5	2
Feedback given by the *bishop* about the way I carry out my duties	6	26	19	36	13	4
Feedback given by the *priest-in-charge* about the way I carry out my duties	6	19	16	25	34	5
Feedback given by *fellow priests* about the way I carry out my duties	8	27	30	26	9	3
Feedback given by *laypeople* about the way I carry out my duties	17	40	26	15	2	2
Feedback given by the *bishop* about the way I carry out my duties in *comparison* with other priests engaged in similar work	3	3	24	38	32	4
Feedback given by the *priest-in-charge* about the way I carry out my duties in *comparison* with other priests engaged in similar work	5	4	14	27	50	5
Feedback given by *fellow priests* about the way I carry out my duties in *comparison* with other priests engaged in similar work	3	13	27	30	27	4
Feedback given by *laypeople* about the way I carry out my duties in *comparison* with other priests engaged in similar work	8	19	30	23	20	3
Information given to me on how assessments were made by the *priest-in-charge* regarding my competence in carrying out my duties	4	5	7	28	56	5
Information given to me on what happens to the assessments regarding my competence in carrying out my duties	4	4	6	40	46	5
Recognition by the *bishop* of the efforts I make in carrying out my duties	12	27	21	32	8	4
Recognition by *priest-in-charge* of the efforts I make in carrying out my duties	6	19	18	24	33	5
Recognition by *fellow priests* of the efforts I make in carrying out my duties	5	23	32	30	10	3
Recognition by *laypeople* of the efforts I make in carrying out my duties	14	39	26	18	3	2
Reports on how I handle problems which arise in the performance of my duties	4	23	15	35	23	4

Notes
* Figures in these columns represent percentage values where: 1 = excellent; 2 = good; 3 = indifferent; 4 = poor; 5 = not applicable

M = modal values

Table 13.4 Ratings of quality of information being received about the diocese

Questions	1*	2*	3*	4*	5*	M
Information about how *diocesan* activities are funded	9	31	13	41	6	4
Information about the financial standing of the *diocese*	10	23	17	41	9	4
Information regarding the difficulties faced by the *diocese*	5	35	21	36	3	4
Information and news relating to activities and events in the *diocese*	17	46	18	17	2	2
Information about matters and affairs relating to the *parish* in which the priest worked	14	42	13	19	12	2

Notes
* Figures in these columns represent percentage values where: 1 = excellent; 2 = good; 3 = indifferent; 4 = poor; 5 = not applicable

M = modal values

work of the organisation (the diocese), and creating a culture focused on the achievement of high quality outcomes.

5 The majority of priests saw themselves as operating within a highly bureaucratic structure. The perceptions of some 89 per cent of respondents was that the diocese was regulated by a centralised managerial structure. This perception reflected the sense of lack of participation and the perceived inability to effectively influence decision-making.

6 The extent to which a priest could go to someone in the event of his experiencing difficulties was reported as 'satisfactory' by the majority of respondents, and was viewed as a positive communication factor (see Table 13.6).

7 Lack of feedback to priests in respect of a range of aspects of communication was a major source of dissatisfaction, and this emerged as a critical communication issue needing to be addressed (see Tables 13.1–13.4). The majority of priests indicated that in relation to feedback from the bishop there was poor communication about how they performed their work in comparison to others engaged in similar work. The quantity and quality of feedback about the way assessments were made about the priest, including how he handled problems which arose in the course of his ministry, also caused some dissatisfaction. Similarly, there was a perceived need for more feedback from priests-in-charge about the way the priest discharged his duties. The communication of feedback is a key organisational process (Mead, 1990). Yet, in reviewing research in this area, Greenberg and Baron (1995) concluded: 'Unfortunately, the vast majority of employees believe that the feedback between themselves and their organizations is not as good as it should be' (pp. 358–359). One reason for this was highlighted by Downs (1988); namely, that 'there has long been a difference between management's perception of what employees need to know and what the employees say they need and want to know' (p. 31). The desire for improvements in feedback and appraisal was a key finding of the present audit.

Table 13.5 Satisfaction with working relationships

Questions	1*	2*	3*	4*	5*	M
Extent to which the problems I face are known and understood by the *bishop*	21	35	9	30	6	2
Extent to which the problems I face are known and understood by the *priest-in-charge*	13	27	9	18	33	5
Extent to which the problems I face are known and understood by *fellow priests*	23	37	21	12	7	2
Extent to which the problems I face are known and understood by *laypeople*	12	42	22	13	11	2
Extent to which the *bishop* listens and pays attention to me	26	28	21	23	2	2
Extent to which the *priest-in-charge* listens and pays attention to me	15	25	11	13	36	5
Extent of the amount of direction and advice given to me by the *bishop*	23	28	23	21	5	2
Extent of the amount of direction and advice given to me by the *priest-in-charge*	10	26	14	13	37	5
Extent of the amount of direction and advice given to me by *fellow priests*	21	42	18	10	9	2
Extent to which the *bishop* was accessible to me	55	28	4	12	1	1
Extent to which the *bishop* trusts me	46	27	12	10	5	1
Extent to which the *bishop* is open and honest with me	36	36	13	14	1	1
Extent to which the *priest-in-charge* is accessible to me	33	24	2	4	37	5
Extent to which the *priest-in-charge* trusts me	30	18	5	10	37	5
Extent to which the *priest-in-charge* is open and honest with me	23	21	10	10	36	5
Extent to which the *bishop* is receptive to new ideas and new initiatives	21	30	21	22	6	2
Extent to which the *priest-in-charge* is receptive to new ideas and new initiatives	13	27	12	12	36	5
Extent to which *diocesan* written directives and reports are clear and concise	45	30	12	12	1	1

Notes
* Figures in these columns represent percentage values where: 1 = satisfied; 2 = moderately satisfied; 3 = indifferent; 4 = dissatisfied; 5 = not applicable

M = modal values

8 A substantial number of priests expressed satisfaction with the amount and quality of feedback received horizontally from peers (see Table 13.6). This is a positive finding, since horizontal communication is crucial both to the satisfactory completion of task processes, and to the promotion of a sense of self-worth and belonging (Kreps, 1990). Its importance is such that in communication audits, managers often want this to be the major focus (Downs, 1988). This finding indicated that the diocese needs to take steps to maintain existing levels of horizontal harmony, while at the same time improving vertical communication channels.

Table 13.6 Satisfaction with horizontal communication

Questions	1*	2*	3*	4*	5*	M
Extent to which communication in the *diocese* motivates and stimulates enthusiasm among the priests	9	35	19	35	2	2
Extent to which my fellow priests in the *diocese* are good communicators in terms of written records, memos, letters, reports, etc.	18	42	27	13	—	2
Extent to which my fellow priests in the *diocese* are good communicators in terms of face-to-face contact	17	51	21	9	2	2
Extent to which I can go to someone else in the *diocese* if there is something in my work I don't know how to handle	54	36	3	4	3	1
Extent to which I have access to a priest confidant in the event of my experiencing difficulties (personal and/or work related)	67	23	4	3	3	1
Extent to which communication within the *diocese* makes me identify with the diocese	34	45	9	12	—	2
Extent to which communication within the *diocese* makes me feel a part of it	36	38	13	13	—	2
Extent to which conflicts are handled appropriately through proper communication channels	13	35	21	27	4	2
Extent to which horizontal communication with other priests in the *diocese* is accurate and free-flowing	10	50	25	15	—	2
Extent to which our *diocesan meetings* are well organised	22	39	19	18	2	2
Extent to which priests are consulted regarding agenda-setting for the *diocesan meetings*	10	22	26	37	5	4
Extent to which priests are encouraged to participate in the *diocesan meetings*	22	41	17	18	2	2
Extent to which priests have a say in the planning/structure of the *diocesan meetings* – e.g. choice of speaker, small group discussions, etc.	13	37	18	30	2	2
Extent to which *parish clergy meetings* are organised	15	30	10	23	22	2
Extent to which priests are consulted regarding agenda-setting for the *parish meetings*	13	32	13	15	27	2
Extent to which priests are encouraged to participate in the *parish clergy meetings*	23	27	13	13	24	2
Extent to which priestss have a say in the planning/structure of the *parish clergy meetings*	19	30	13	15	23	2
Extent to which informal communication between priests in the *diocese* is active	23	54	18	5	—	2
Extent to which informal communication between priests in the *diocese* is accurate	16	59	19	6	—	2

Notes
* Figures in these columns represent percentage values where: 1 = satisfied; 2 = moderately satisfied; 3 = indifferent; 4 = dissatisfied; 5 = not applicable

M = modal values

Table 13.7 Priests' perceptions of influence within the diocese

	Influence (%)					
	Very great	Great	Quite a bit	Some	Little	None
The bishop	63	21	9	7		
Auxiliary bishop	21	15	32	20	11	1
Vicars general	5	13	21	34	20	7
Vicars forane	1	1	6	33	34	24
Parish priests	6	6	17	36	24	11
Parish administrators	4	3	19	32	28	14
Curates	3	3	4	17	47	26
Deaneries	1	1	5	34	37	22
Diocesan council of priests	3	4	26	40	21	6
Ministry to priests	4	6	23	36	22	9
Laypeople	5	6	5	28	33	23

A series of ANOVA tests was conducted to test for differences across ages of respondents. These revealed highly significant differences between younger and older priests across a wide number of issues. Younger priests:

- were more dissatisfied with levels of feedback from the priest-in-charge and bishop and wanted greater availability and accessibility to these sources;
- expected to receive much more information about the work of the diocese;
- desired more input from laypeople in the diocese;
- were less satisfied with horizontal communication;
- expressed a strong wish for more involvement in all aspects of the work of the diocese.

By comparison, older priests were happier with the status quo. These findings may reflect human nature, in that as we get older we are happier with what we know and less inclined to seek change. However, they also indicate a desire amongst younger priests for greater 'democracy', and as such represent a challenge both for the diocese and the wider church.

Two open-ended questions allowed respondents freely to express their opinions about communication. Responses to these were content analysed and the main recurring themes supported the findings from the quantitative sections of the questionnaire. Just over 15 per cent of respondents expressed satisfaction with the current state of affairs in comments such as 'Information is available if I wish to get it' and 'At present I feel that communication associated with my work is OK.' The main changes which respondents wished to see were as follows:

- Twenty-two per cent of respondents wanted more contact with and feedback from the bishop. For example, one priest wanted 'More personal and less formal contact from bishop', while another expressed the view that 'The bishop needs to let priests know what he thinks of individual priests.'

- Greater consultation was a theme specifically raised by some 19 per cent of respondents. Exemplar statements included: 'We would need to be listened to more through informal means', 'The bishop must be a good listener if he is to stay in touch', and 'Honesty to face up to the real state of the diocesan church and not to what the bishop or auxiliary would like it to be.' The theme of the need for greater *listening* was, in fact, overwhelming, being mentioned in one form or another by 30 per cent of respondents. In particular, several priests felt that no one was there to listen to their views about the diocese.
- Linked to this, a related theme (cited by 18 per cent) was the desire for more meetings – the need for 'priests to meet more often', since 'people involved in the same kind of work should relate' and have a 'format to exchange ideas'.
- More input into agenda setting was desired by just under 17 per cent of respondents, especially since, as expressed by one priest, there is 'no consultation whatever in agenda for conferences or say in the planning/structure of meetings'.
- The desire for a less centralised hierarchy was raised by 12 per cent of respondents. As summarised by one priest, there was 'a need for decentralised power', another complained of 'too much needless bureaucracy', and a third wanted a 'flattened structure of decision-making'.

DISCUSSION

Priests spend a large part of their working lives interacting with fellow priests, within the diocese. In turn, the diocese is a microcosm of the Catholic Church, having a well-defined hierarchy of offices, responsibilities and authority. For the diocese to work effectively as an organisational entity, good communication between priests is essential. This audit focused on the work of one diocese in Ireland. Further work will have to be carried out in other dioceses and in other countries before any firm conclusion could be reached about communications within the Catholic Church *per se*.

The main data collection tool employed in this audit was that of a questionnaire. As with all audits which use this method, it must be borne in mind that this measured how priests *perceived* communication to be. Some of their perceptions may or may not be an accurate account of what actually happens, but it is upon perceptions that individual judgements and actions are based and so they are important determinants of behaviour. As the saying goes 'perception is everything'. The results of the audit are therefore of great value to decision-makers in the diocese. They have provided detailed feedback on a range of issues.

In particular, it is clear that priests strongly identified with the Church as an organisation and with the diocese as a locational 'branch'. This was confirmed by the high level of satisfaction expressed by respondents with regard to working relationships with their colleagues. This sense of 'belongingness' provides a firm bedrock on which to build a coherent communication strategy. Receptivity to initiatives designed to improve communications will be high. However, in considering the findings of this audit, it is worth remembering the words of Oscar Wilde that 'The truth is rarely pure, and never simple.' The challenge here was that not all priests felt the same way about communication in the diocese. The clear split between older and younger priests with regard to the need for change means that any innovations must be introduced in a sensitive fashion. While the new priests represent the future of the organisation, and their aspirations have to be recognised, the old 'hands' reflect the stability and enduring values which are also important. These differences between the old and young also mirror the views of Catholic laypeople – the 'clients' of this organisation (Lount, 1997). The Church therefore needs to tread a fine line between older (and often cherished) ways and modern necessities. Such a challenge needs carefully formulated action plans to guide change, with accompanying ongoing monitoring as they are implemented.

As academics, our main purpose in carrying out this investigation was one of fulfilling a clear research need. While the 'contract' for the audit terminated with the submission to the diocese of the completed report, the information we have to date is that the findings have not been acted upon, at least not in a 'formal' manner. In one sense this is not surprising. Change is always difficult within the work context and requires time, effort and expertise to be successfully implemented (Hargie and Tourish, 1999b). The demand for change within the Church poses particular threats (O'Brien, 1994). As a result, there is a tendency towards a more 'softly, softly' response as opposed to a 'big bang' implementation. Audits are carried out for many reasons and the results are handled in a wide variety of ways. For an organisation as old as the Church there is a natural tendency to treat established procedures and processes with reverence (Berry, 1992). Indeed, Rice (1990, p. 250), in highlighting the slowness of the authorities to change, noted that while 'The Roman Catholic Church deals in centuries . . . all Church change is speeding up, as world change is.' The pace of change in society, coupled with direct problems being faced by the Catholic Church (the celibacy debate, child abuse scandals, the ecumenical movement, attitude to contraception, etc.), means that complacency is not a solution.

The fact that priests in general wanted more information about all aspects of the work of the diocese is in itself a positive finding as well as a negative comment upon existing practices. It means that they want to be fully involved in what they see as highly important work. In organisations where dissatisfaction is rife, staff will switch off and do the minimum. There is a high NMP (not my problem) response to requests from others. This is not the case here. Priests *want* to do more and be central rather than peripheral to the core work of the diocese. Of course, if these wishes remain unfulfilled then frustration will eventually set in. If you consistently turn up with your full kit at the soccer pitch but are never invited to play, you will soon decide not to bother showing up!

A final challenge for the diocese is that of effecting change in the present system of feedback. A recurring finding across organisations is that staff lower down the hierarchy want to interface with senior managers, and especially with the chief executive (Tourish and Hargie, 1998). As a junior member of staff remarked in another audit which we carried out with a different organisation: 'It would be nice to talk to the big cheese once in a while'! Priests in this diocese echoed this common trend. They wanted to see and talk with the priest-in-charge and the bishop more frequently. Being in the presence of those of higher status and interacting with them is a valued human desire. When handled effectively such meetings can motivate and inspire staff. They also leave the impression that 'someone important cares about what I do' and hence promote bonding and foster team spirit. Yet, there is a tendency for those at the top to become bogged down with detail and forget about the people. An audit is useful in that, where this is happening, it shines the bright light of staff reactions onto the dark empty spaces where the senior managers should be treading!

While this audit was carried out with the full approval of the bishop, it was interesting that a minority of priests were opposed to the exercise. Three negative letters and two telephone calls were received by the researchers, expressing disagreement with the need for any form of audit. In addition, five unusable questionnaires were returned, some with negative comments attached. In essence, the main objection was that this type of research only served to downgrade the priesthood – to treat it as just another job and not a special 'calling'.

Overall, however, respondents were helpful in completing the questionnaires. The results have provided comprehensive and detailed information about a wide range of issues surrounding the sending and receiving of communication across all levels of the diocese. In this way, it helped to chart the topography of this particular diocese and has provided valuable data for the bishop responsible for its management.

Chapter 14

An external communication audit of a superannuation company

Charles H. Patti, Bernard McKenna,
Glen J. Thomas and William Renforth

INTRODUCTION

As CEO William Lucas and Marketing Manager Margaret Johnson were on their way to the local university to talk with staff of the business faculty, they weren't quite sure how to describe the communication challenge facing their company. They realised the importance of communicating with their customers, but felt that their industry (superannuation) presented unique problems. Their Australian company (let us call it 'SuperFund') had nearly 500,000 members and an employer membership of nearly 50,000. Each member required continual communication. William and Margaret knew that the dozens of letters, reports, brochures, publicity releases, and advertisements must be superior to those of their competitors. SuperFund had a solid reputation for financial performance, but William and Margaret began to suspect that the Fund's external communication needed to be assessed. Could the consultants help them? How?

This case describes how the management team of a large and successful superannuation fund worked with university staff to audit the effectiveness of their communication and to point the way to future improvements. The audit process developed by the university consultants is based on a number of communication theories and practices, and consists of a seven-step approach (see Figure 14.1).

KNOWING THE AUDIENCE AND COLLECTING COMMUNICATION ELEMENTS

Before beginning their assessment of SuperFund's external communications, the auditors needed to become familiar with the environment in which communication took place. They located this information through a number of sources, including a review of company documents, books, and articles about the superannuation industry, and meetings with the government's superannuation office. The primary focus of this review was to understand the context for communication.

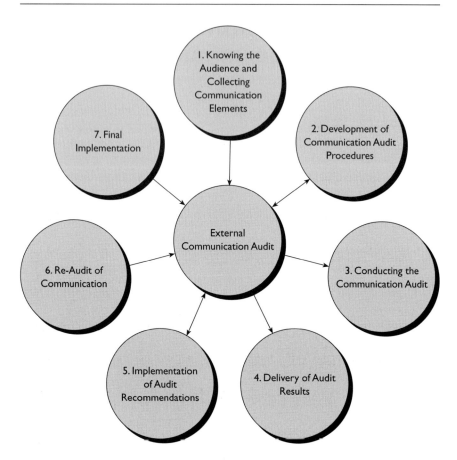

Figure 14.1 External communication audit procedure

Marketing at the Fund: an important context for communication management

The auditors initially reviewed the overall marketing and communication strategies of the Fund. The review indicated that, while the overall marketing issue was the creation of a sound marketing strategy, several supporting issues also existed. Among these were gaining an understanding of:

- member attitudes towards saving and retirement planning;
- the way current and prospective members perceive the Fund;
- how to communicate most effectively with members;
- how the Fund could be positioned most effectively;
- how to measure the effectiveness of marketing efforts.

Another indication of the importance of communication to SuperFund was the inclusion of communication tasks among their marketing objectives.

Included in the company's marketing objectives were the following statements:

- Provide first class service to both employers and employees.
- Provide timely, effective, and high quality communication to employees, employers, third party referrers, and key business influencers.
- Elevate the awareness of the Fund and promote its value.

The company was positioned as a large, state-based fund whose mission was to provide high quality superannuation at wholesale prices with personal service. This basic positioning required effective, efficient communication with a large number of employers and employees. Further, the Fund wanted to deliver a product that was rated highly on the key attributes identified by the target markets, and needed to possess the systems and procedures to respond quickly and accurately to the requirements of its clients.

Employers were considered the most important target market because they initially select the fund into which they will contribute. The Fund had successfully penetrated the small employer market: they now felt the primary opportunities for growth were among large employers (50+ employees) and new small businesses. Because new legislation allowed employees to choose among funds, they were also an increasingly important target market since they were becoming more involved in purchase decisions.

Marketing activities were the responsibility of the Marketing Manager, Margaret Johnson, who reported directly to the Fund's CEO, William Lucas. In addition to Margaret, other marketing related functions rounded out the Fund's management team. These relationships are shown in Figure 14.2. An important component of the Fund's marketing communication effort was the Call Centre. Its relationship to the marketing services support area and Fund members is shown in Figure 14.3. Key data about SuperFund's external audiences are summarised in Tables 14.1 and 14.2.

Marketing communication

Communicating the benefits of a superannuation fund is a significant part of successful marketing. By their nature, funds are a relatively complex product, requiring the communication of financial and investment information that both employees and employers see as confusing and complicated. Furthermore, industry research had shown that:

- Many members had a low level of interest in the concept of saving for retirement
- Most employees did not know the name of the superannuation fund to which they contributed

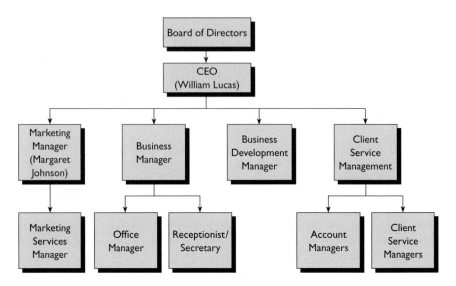

Figure 14.2 Marketing organisation within SuperFund

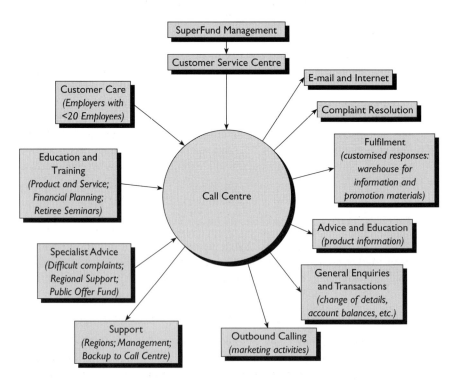

Figure 14.3 Marketing communication functions of Customer Service Centre

Table 14.1 SuperFund client data

Client	Number	Recent growth rate
Members (employees)	461,000 (260,000 are attached to an active employer)	10.6% during past 6 months
Employers	46,500	7.5% during past 6 months

Table 14.2 Other key audience data

Client data	• 0.6% of the active employers (employers with over a hundred employees) represents 35% of SuperFund members and 29% of the Fund's assets. • Employers with less than twenty employees represent 96% of the employer base, 44% of the Fund's members, and 48% of the Fund's assets. • Average number of members in the large employer group (50+ employees) is 186. • Average number of members per employer is 5.5 • Average age of active members: 35 • Member gender split: 45% female; 55% male

- A vast majority were unaware of the advent of fund choice
- Most were unaware of the benefits of transferring all superannuation money to one fund
- Many did not understand the need for fees and believed that interest earnings should cover fees

    (State Street Global Advisors Investor Education Council, 1998)

To participate in superannuation funds requires many forms of communication. There are literally dozens of letters that were integral to developing, enrolling, and maintaining members. Letters of application, acceptance, acknowledgement of contributions, financial performance reports, personal details verification, benefits payments, and other legal notices were all part of the ongoing communication between the Fund and its members. In addition to letters, the Fund used other forms of marketing communication, including financial reports, advertising, brochures, seminars, news releases, speeches, and presentations.

Collecting communication material for audit

The auditors met with Margaret Johnson to examine the range of documents that SuperFund used to communicate with their external audiences. After that meeting, the auditors suggested that Margaret supply them with copies of every form letter, and a representative sample of brochures, press releases, print

Exhibit 14.1 Example of SuperFund letter (1)

SuperFund
Ref:
Date
Address

Dear Mr X

RE: SuperFund

We have enclosed two items with this letter for your information. If you have already received an advice on these matters you will not need to take any further action.

The first item tells you about changes to insurance cover which came into effect from [*Date*]. You need only respond to us if you require more than 1 unit of cover – assuming you have not already applied to us.

The second item is a form which allows you to transfer to ARF an amount held in another fund if you wish to do so. Many SuperFund members have money in other superannuation funds and are paying fees in these funds as well.

SuperFund offers you the opportunity to transfer all your other superannuation into SuperFund. You will benefit by having all your superannuation in just one fund and will be paying only one low fee.

If you wish to transfer an amount held in another superannuation fund into SuperFund first check if any penalties will be applied by the other fund. Then just fill in and send the enclosed 'Transfer of Previous Superannuation Benefit' form to us at ARF Administration. (If you have more than one amount to transfer you will need to photocopy the form and complete one for each transfer.)

We will arrange the transfer and contact you on completion.

Yours sincerely

SuperFund

---

advertisements, speeches and display materials. Once these documents were collected, a system was devised to analyse the separate pieces of writing. This cataloguing system took the form of a table, which isolated the different aspects of each piece of communication. Each item fulfils a different function in supplying stakeholders with information. For example, letters to employers were often sent to notify the employer that they had made some form of oversight in sending money or paperwork to the Fund. Exhibits 14.1 and 14.2 are examples of SuperFund letters.

Material was classified, therefore, in terms of its function of communication to:

- Fund members;
- contributing employers;
- administrators of other funds;
- those leaving the Fund, or next of kin of deceased members;
- advertising, publicity, and promotion material.

Exhibit 14.2 Example of SuperFund letter (2)

SuperFund
Ref:
Date
Telephone:

Address

Dear Customer

RE: SuperFund

The Trustee of SuperFund has declined your recent request to transfer current account balances and to remit future contributions to an alternative fund. The Trustee has advised that the award under which the relevant members are employed stipulates that contributions can only be remitted to SuperFund. You may seek to obtain an exemption to the award from the Industrial Relations Commission, but until such time as that is granted, contributions must be remitted to SuperFund.

Our records indicate that contributions have not been made to SuperFund since [*Date*]. Please arrange for these outstanding amounts to be paid to date and for future contributions to be directed to SuperFund. At this point in time, insurance cover for your employees for death and disability has ceased due to the non payment of premiums. Insurance will re-commence on receipt of these outstanding contributions. You should advise your employees accordingly.

If you wish to discuss any of these matters, please call Alice Jones on the above telephone number.

Yours sincerely

SuperFund

DEVELOPMENT OF COMMUNICATION AUDIT PROCEDURES

Framework of analysis

Most communication audit analyses have traditionally concentrated on internal communication, rather than on the relationship between an organisation and its external clients. However, it is possible to draw some sound principles from the internal communication audit to apply to external audits. In the broadest sense, an audit should be a methodical review or examination to identify, measure, and analyse the effectiveness of an organisation's communication with its clients.

To perform this methodical review, an audit should carry out several functions (Downs, 1988):

1 It should map communication flaws as well as appropriate practices.
2 Benchmarks should be set to evaluate present and future practice.
3 It should provide innovative responses for the organisation to improve its communication.
4 The auditor needs to explain to the organisation the basis of auditing judgements by identifying the evaluation criteria.

Although the criteria may be generic, their application to a specific organisation needs to be unique.

CONDUCTING THE COMMUNICATION AUDIT

Planning and focusing the audit of the letter component was relatively painless in so far as the auditors sought specifications about the extent and depth of the audit from the external clients. Once the letters were classified, they were then subjected to a four-part analysis:

Part A: Audience and Text
Part B: Verbal Macro-Textual Features
Part C: Non-Verbal Macro-Textual Features
Part D: Verbal Micro-Textual Features

These parts are explained in Exhibit 14.3.

Part A was devoted to Audience and Text. Any form of communication has a text (usually what is said or written) and an audience (the person or people for whom this text is intended). This section identified the context in which the communication appeared, such as a single letter to a new member of the Fund, or a follow-up to a previous letter. The second component of *Part A*, readership, analysed reader apprehension, or the level of interest the reader was likely to display in the document. Readers with low apprehension are less likely to be interested and may need more encouragement to read on. This is crucial to obtaining and retaining reader attention, and also affects placement of material.

Part B analysed the Verbal Macro-Textual Features of the document. This simply considered whether the words were organised in a way that the readers could understand. A number of elements of the communication were isolated here. First, it was determined whether or not the communication employed a deductive approach. In simple terms, a deductive approach is one that provides an overview before presenting the details. For example, it is easier to correctly piece a jigsaw puzzle together when you know what the completed picture looks like. Readers are more likely to comprehend information when it is presented deductively, rather than inductively. In the analysis this was usually simply a matter of determining whether or not there was an informative subject line to the letter. Surprisingly, this was often not the case. SuperFund, in their letters to employers

Exhibit 14.3 Communication audit: textual analysis form

PART A: AUDIENCE AND TEXT

Number		Letter Type	
Referentiality/Context *single text or joint (e.g. letters and brochures); follow-ups (e.g., phone calls, visit)*			
Readership Reader Apprehension *reader interest in document negativity, hostility, indifference*			

PART B: VERBAL MACRO-TEXTUAL FEATURES

Deductive Approach Used *Subject line and opening identify the letter's purpose*	
Chunking Information *Responds to Problem* *Identifies relevant action* *(a) by reader* *(b) [to be] done by writer*	
Usability Enhancers *Reference to enclosures*	
Readability *Fog Index*	

PART C: NON-VERBAL MACRO-TEXTUAL FEATURES

Font *Size, Weight, Type*	
Layout *Justification, Tabs, Indents, and Horizontal Hierarchy*	

PART D: VERBAL MICRO-TEXTUAL FEATURES

Paragraphs *Topic Sentences* *Linkages Conjunctions, Adjuncts*	
Sentences *Length* *Clausal Structure* *Theme/Subject Usage*	
Style *Verb Active/Passive* *Verb Modality/Modulation* *Nominalisations* *Noun–Verb Ratio* *Use of Verb 'to be'* *Expletive Use (There are/It is)* *Noun clusters* *Wordiness (Superfluity, Verbosity, Redundancy, Tautology)* *Jargon, Acronyms, Colloquialisms*	
Tone *'You' orientation superior, deferential, authoritative, friendly, patronising*	
Grammar and Punctuation	

and Fund members, employed a generic subject line, such as 'SuperFund Membership Number' or similar. In many cases, this did not indicate to the reader the subject matter of the communication.

Second, the first sentence of the document is also crucial, detailing the chunking of information. This was concerned with the manner in which the communication responded to a particular problem and advised the receiver on any relevant action that needed to be taken, either by the writer or the reader. For example, if the letter asked the reader to resolve a problem, then the information should be chunked to present the problem, identify the solution, and then advise of the next action stage (e.g. return to this address).

The third aspect of *Part B* examined Usability Enhancers, such as enclosures, and whether the reader was directed towards these. While indexes provide indicative information that is easy to tabulate for the client, our method incorporates a lexico-grammatical analysis (within Part D: Verbal Micro-Textual Features) that identifies problems in more specific terms. A lexico-grammatical approach is one that looks at the word selection (the *lexis*) and at the grammar (e.g. over-use of nouns, passive voice).

Part C examined the documents from a Non-Verbal Macro-Textual perspective. This was concerned with the Font and Layout of the written material. These are important psychological elements of communication, given that readers are likely to disregard information that is presented in a 'hard to read' format. The letters were therefore analysed in terms of their degree of non-verbal reader-friendliness.

Part D of the framework isolated the 'Verbal Micro-Textual Features' of the document. Whereas the Verbal Macro-Textual Features looked at the structuring of ideas, the Micro-Textual Features examined individual words, sentences, and paragraphs. The first of these aspects, Paragraph Structure, dealt with the use of topic sentences and the links between units of information in the letters. Clumsy paragraphing is one of the characteristics of poor writing. Research has shown that there is little attention paid to paragraph structure in contemporary writing textbooks (McKenna and Thomas, 1997). Often, paragraph structuring is treated as an 'intuitive' ability that writers either possess or they do not. Sentences are also analysed in terms of their length, clausal structure, and use of marked and unmarked themes. These aspects are also important in terms of comprehension, given that readers tend to have difficulty with sentences that are longer than 20–25 words.

Analysis of the clausal structure of the sentence seeks to determine whether the main clause of the sentence is in the most prominent position (usually the start of the sentence). The use of marked and unmarked themes is concerned with the writer's use of 'signposts' at the beginning of sentences. The theme of a sentence is simply the words that appear at the start of the sentence. An unmarked theme is one where the subject is in the theme position (i.e. the front of the sentence). Marked themes do not have the subject in this position. Reader comprehension is assisted if writers (sparingly) employ words such as 'However', 'Nevertheless', 'Under these circumstances', and so forth in the theme position to mark the information that follows. In circumstances where the writer leaves the theme unmarked, the sentences were examined to see if the subject of the sentence was in the theme position.

The next section of *Part D* was devoted to Style. This section was not so much concerned with the 'elegance' of writing, but more with the way in which language was used to convey meaning. Documents were considered in the following areas:

- active versus passive constructions in sentences. The active is more direct, more forceful, tends to use fewer words and is more likely to conjure up a clear picture of what you are writing about;

- modality and modulation of verbs (qualifying statements with words like 'may', 'could', 'perhaps', 'appears', 'seems');
- nominalisations (verbs transformed into nouns, often by appending 'ion', 'ity' and 'ment' to the verb form, e.g. delegation, administration);
- ratio of nouns to verbs;
- use of the verb 'to be';
- expletives (opening sentences with 'there are' and 'it is');
- noun clusters (multiple nouns, e.g. data processing entry);
- wordiness (superfluous words, verbosity, redundant words, tautological expression);
- jargon, acronyms, colloquial usage.

Finally, the documents were analysed in relation to grammar, punctuation, and tone. A positive tone was vital in communication of this nature, as the Fund was seeking to build a rapport with clients and providers. As members were able to nominate the superannuation fund of their choice, it was imperative that the Fund cemented good relations with its existing client base.

Advertising and marketing communication analysis

In addition to the letter documents, the auditors examined a large number of advertising and marketing communication materials, including magazine advertisements, brochures, annual and interim reports, publicity releases, speeches, presentations, and display materials. The frameworks for analysis of these materials were drawn from the literature on advertising message strategy and marketing communication (e.g. Jewler, 1996; Kao, 1995; Patti and Frazer, 1988; Patti and Moriarty, 1990, Weir, 1993). Each advertising item was examined against a five-point checklist of message strategy construction (See Exhibit 14.4). Other items of marketing communication, including the advertising materials, were audited against a five-point checklist of recognised components of integrated marketing communication (Schultz, et al., 1992) (see Exhibit 14.5). These analyses allowed the auditors to evaluate SuperFund's advertising and marketing communication efforts against established principles.

DELIVERY OF AUDIT RESULTS

The auditors agreed to complete the audit within thirty days. This was a considerable task, as over 300 pieces of communication were evaluated. They did not describe their findings in terms of each piece of communication, but instead drew broad, generic conclusions concerning the nature of the Fund's communication with stakeholders. From these broad conclusions, the auditors found that there were some problems in the Fund's external communication patterns. For example, letters to stakeholders were sometimes confusing, particularly those

Exhibit 14.4 Advertising and promotion analysis checklist

Message Strategy Analysis

Message Strategy Element	Yes	No	Comments
Feature that is exclusive			
Feature that is of high relevance to target audience			
Is the message theme enduring?			
Can the message theme be copied easily by others in the marketplace?			
Is the message theme easily explained?			

1 What is the message strategy?
'Invest in SuperFund because . . .'
(Can you complete the above sentence with a few words that meet all of the criteria above?)
2 Description of the message strategy
(Provide a description of the overall, implied intent; description of how your organisation is being portrayed, i.e., industry leader, niche player, conservative. What is the point of differentiation? Is this clear in the message strategy?)
3 Description of the message tactics
(Describe and analyse the executional elements and comment on their compatibility with the strategy, i.e., use of colour, design, format, style (humour, logic, rationality, etc.).)
4 What improvements can be made?

Exhibit 14.5 Integrated marketing communication checklist

IMC Principle	Yes	No	Comments
Does communication attempt to affect behaviour of the audience?			
Are all forms of relevant contact being used?			
Does communication start with the interests of the audience?			
Does communication build synergies among all forms of communication?			
Does communication attempt to build a long-term relationship with the audience?			

directed at Fund members. Letters to those employers who contributed to the Fund on their employees' behalf were sometimes peremptory and high-handed. This suggested that the Fund was not forming the most effective communication channels with its constituents.

The auditors noted other areas for improvement as the audit progressed. These areas were primarily in communication form and content. For example, the auditors wondered whether writing a letter was the most appropriate medium when perhaps a phone call would have been quicker and less cumbersome. This was particularly the case in those instances where an error was detected in, for example, an employer's contribution to the Fund. Rather than writing to the employer to inform them of the error and request that it be corrected, the process could have been expedited by telephoning the employer. It appeared that a means of communication other than the written form would have been more timely and personal. To that end, the audit recommended that SuperFund establish a more direct and personal communication system – perhaps providing a contact name and telephone number to the stakeholder. This process would have the potential to expedite the task and to improve customer relations.

The question of customer relations was also germane to the tone of communications. Often, it was noted that letters could have been improved if their tone had been altered. One primary example was a form letter sent to the next-of-kin of Fund members who had recently died. The letter was, at best, peremptory in tone and did not adequately assess the context in which this communication took place. The audit recommended that a more sympathetic tone be employed in this (and other) documents, even if only in terms of adding a sentence to the effect of 'Please accept our sympathy for your recent loss', or similar. A simple gesture of this nature helps to build positive relations with external stakeholders. In the same vein, letters sent to administrators of other funds took a somewhat 'bossy' and demanding tone. This could work to the detriment of SuperFund, as the letter requested assistance in transferring paperwork from another superannuation fund to the company. A rule of good business communication is that requests of others should be phrased as politely as possible to increase the probability that the writer's request will be met. The audit identified a number of these instances, which suggested that SuperFund could improve communication relationship with its stakeholders.

Consistent with quality assurance measures, the consultants recommended that benchmarks of best practice be set by the company, ensuring that the Fund's external communication be as effective as possible. This should be taken in two steps: present practice and future performance. The implementation of the audit was the first step in establishing good practice. As detailed above, the audit was designed to identify those aspects of SuperFund's communication that needed improvement. After the completion of the audit, the company's management needed to ensure that the suggested improvements were made. These benchmarks could take a number of forms: for example, SuperFund's communications might be regularly audited. They may, on the other hand, elect to establish a form of a best-practice checklist and distribute this to all staff and gauge their compliance with these procedures. Such a checklist could instruct staff on agreed-upon methods of dealing with various problems when they arose. For instance, the checklist could ask staff confronted with an error in a contribution return to follow a series of steps to rectify the error in the shortest possible time.

After completing the audit, the auditors met to discuss their findings and to determine the most effective way to communicate these to SuperFund. Certainly, a written report was appropriate; however, the possibility of presenting the audit results to the entire staff of SuperFund's marketing department was also considered. Ultimately, the auditors – in discussion with William Lucas and Margaret Johnson – concluded that a written report, along with an oral presentation by the consultants, would be most appropriate. Forty days after the launch of the audit, the consultants delivered a 75-page report and presented a summary of their findings in a meeting with William and Margaret.

IMPLEMENTATION OF AUDIT RECOMMENDATIONS

Margaret Johnson and her staff implemented several of the follow-up measures recommended in the audit. Within 60 days of delivery of the initial audit, they hired a technical writer to produce two new sets of letters: one for the local office, and another set for an office in a bordering state. The auditors were then asked to review these new letters and comment on the level of improvement.

RE-AUDIT OF COMMUNICATION

The follow-up audit found that, in general, both the style and tone of the new letters had improved. The primary area of concern in the re-audited letters was in letter context. The revised letters still needed to explain why the reader was receiving the letter. They incorporated sub-headings, such as 'What this letter is about', but did not always answer the question implied by that sub-heading. In some cases, the letters also needed to explain what the recipient should do about the request. This question of context and purpose was highlighted in the first audit and appears to be one of the crucial aspects of communication with external clients and stakeholders.

Minor aspects that needed improving in the second set of letters included the tone and expression of some of the material. For example, one letter, replying to a member who had sought early release of their superannuation benefits, contained the following sentence:

> In special approved circumstances such as death, permanent incapacity, financial hardship, or on compassionate grounds, your benefit may be available earlier.

The juxtaposition of 'special approved circumstances' and the word 'death' created an unintentionally amusing sentence that may, however, cause distress to the reader. We recommended that it would be better to rephrase the sentence to read

> Your benefit may be available to you earlier in certain circumstances. These include financial hardship, compassionate grounds, permanent incapacity, or death of the contributor.

The advertising and other forms of marketing communication were not subjected to a re-audit because SuperFund was in the process of selecting a new advertising agency. Margaret and William wanted to provide the new agency with the opportunity to incorporate the recommendations of the communication audit into its development of new advertising and marketing communications materials.

FINAL IMPLEMENTATION

One way for the client to confirm the quality of a communication audit is to ask the following questions about the audit. Did the audit:

- provide valid information about the organisation based on sound research principles?
- summarise successful and unsuccessful communication activities?
- diagnose the communication situation by identifying strengths and providing strategies for overcoming problems?
- model some of the recommendations with good examples that could be replicated?
- provide benchmarks that could be applied in the future?
- provide training as part of the follow-up?

The auditors and SuperFund's management believed that the recommendations answered the above questions positively, and offered the company the opportunity to overhaul its communication strategies and tactics. The audit recommended that SuperFund not only revise the documents it sent to clients but also reconsider the very means of this communication. It further recommended that SuperFund revise its manual of procedures (or implement one), and that it employ different methods of managing communication with external bodies.

Overall, this audit resulted in a variety of recommendations designed to improve communication, all of which were implemented. In organisations, people get used to behaving the way that they always have. It becomes difficult to stand back and look at what is done with fresh eyes. The more routine the work being performed the more difficult this becomes. Form letters can look very routine indeed to those issuing them, but are often vital for those at the receiving end, and can have an enormous impact on decisions about whether to keep doing business with the company concerned. External audits of written materials are another vital means for businesses such as SuperFund to build competitive advantage into the fabric of their communications with valued customers.

Chapter 15

Auditing the annual business conference of a major beverage company

Cal W. Downs, Albert Hydeman and Allyson D. Adrian

INTRODUCTION

External audits identify areas of interdependence and collect vital information from many sources. They are crucial to business success, and to the creation of a rounded picture of the communication climate facing a given organisation. In this chapter, we provide a case study of an external audit conducted by means of deep probe interviews. Before exploring exactly what was done, it is useful to look at a rationale for external audits, which have often been neglected in favour of their internal counterparts:

1 *They complement internal audits in significant ways*
Auditors of internal communication often assume that if communication processes are working internally, then the whole company is working well and the bottom line will be productive. However, internal audits focus on the preferences, wishes, and reactions of the people inside the organisation, rather than on how interdependent agents such as clients and 'customers' react to what goes on. There is a need to extend audits to a larger group who are not on the organisation chart but who play a very significant role in determining the outcomes of business processes.

For example, we once worked with an advertising agency which started to re-engineer its structure. There was wide hope and enthusiasm that this restructuring would improve things. And internally, there was no great problem. Externally, however, a crisis emerged when clients were not pleased with the changes and threatened to take their business elsewhere if the changes were not reversed. Note that the changes had not caused any major problems internally, but they wreaked havoc with those people on the periphery.

2 *They provide a standard against which the internal operations can be assessed*
As the advertising example above demonstrates, outcomes for most organisations are determined by their intermediary clients and organisational representatives. When the effectiveness of outcomes is determined through interaction with other parties, it is vital to include those external relationships in assessments of

company processes. In other words, internal company processes do not operate in a vacuum; the external relationships provide a contextual backdrop that must be taken into account when assessing internal effectiveness.

3 *External audits measure outcomes that are significant to the organisation*
Organisations generally exist to facilitate some product or service for other people. Often the connection between the organisation and the ultimate client or customer is mediated through some other level which is attached to the organisation but which is not technically an integral part of it. The external audit is an attempt to measure outcomes as far as this middle group is concerned. How well are their needs being addressed? What problems do they see with the way the main organisation is functioning? The success of the external, interdependent agents is reciprocally related to the success of the primary organisation. For that reason, auditors must take into account the outcomes of these external mediating agencies. Acknowledging the reciprocal relationships between the parties forces auditors to investigate the complexities of organisational situations and also increases the likelihood of finding useful information that leads to relevant recommendations.

4 *External audits are a form of environmental monitoring*
Every organisation must continually make sense of what is happening around it in terms of economics, politics, society, and legalities. Subtle social changes in fads and trends often affect business. The audit also permits auditors to compare consumer attitudes towards an organisational culture with what employees think is an ideal culture. Often, employees and those on the periphery are at odds because their vested interests are different.

5 *Technology is changing the ways organisations communicate with their suppliers, vendors, business partners, and consumers*
Any such change can have important ramifications for the organisation, and managers should want to keep abreast of the impact of those changes. For example, Garbazani et al. (1996) report that organisations are increasingly called on to provide customers with access to information resources. It would seem, then, that the lines between internal and external organisation parts are growing thinner (Hargie et al., 1999). Furthermore, technologies are costly, and the audit is one method to collect information that helps measure the return on communication investment.

6 *Audits provide information not only about the focal organisation, but they also can be designed to provide sensitivity to competitive threats*
Those on the organisation's periphery are probably bombarded with information about competitors. Therefore, their comments are likely to be given from a frame of reference in which they know what the competition is offering. In other words, the focal organisation is rarely the 'only game in town'.

PRELIMINARY ISSUES

External audits, before they get off the ground, have to confront a number of preliminary issues or dilemmas. Some of the most common decisions this throws up include the following:

1 *Whether to assess via quantitative or qualitative data*
A case can be made for each, depending on what one wishes to do with the data. Many businesses prefer quantitative data. Bottom lines are determined by the numbers. Polls are taken by the numbers. People like numbers because they like what they know. Similarly, businesses are most familiar with questionnaires and interviews which sample opinions about their products and services. Consider how J.D. Power and Associates have popularised the quantitative information it gets from consumers to tell us which airline the respondents preferred in terms of satisfaction, which car is the most popular, etc. This information can be valuable and is used to create great marketing strategies. Such sampling of opinion is useful – as far as it goes. We can count how many people like the organisation, but quantitative data does not normally tell you *why* they like it. Auditors often leave the explanations behind the data to assumptions and inferential statistics.

Within the context of quantitative and qualitative data there are many different forms for collecting this information Three of the most prominent data collection methods include questionnaires, interviews, and focus groups. And there are several contrasting methodologies that can be explained for each one. The auditor makes a choice, and sometimes there is value in triangulation of the different methodologies (Downs, 1988).

One of the factors to be included in the choice is what your desired respondents will favour.

2 *Determining the people from whom to collect information*
As in any investigation, it is desirable to have (a) a representative sample so that conclusions can be generalised to the whole group, and (b) a stratified sample based on important demographic differences. However, in external audits, what constitutes the boundaries of the organisation is already less clear. It is harder to talk about getting a certain percentage of respondents or a certain type of stratification. Instead one has to identify the sources of interdependency among the primary organisation and its collaborating entities. In this chapter, we discuss these issues as they apply to conducting a qualitative audit.

3 *What skills the auditor has that can provide meaningful data*
We have chosen to demonstrate in the following case study how deep probe interviews can be used to yield promising data for external audits. In fact, it is uniquely adaptable to external audits because of the problems thrown up by the geographical distribution of respondents. For example, it may yield some of the

same data as focus groups, but it is difficult to assemble some of the respondents we would want in the same place for a focus group. But they are often easily accessible by telephone. Let us now turn to the case study itself.

INDUSTRY BACKGROUND

The beverage industry generates billions of dollars in the United States each year. The industry has seen growing competition spurred by two developments. First, until recently, there were a few central breweries that dominated sales. However, this pattern is changing and microbreweries are becoming increasingly popular and offer more competition. This marketplace has seen a proliferation of mini-brands, serving to erode marketshare dominance of all the major competitors. Second, globalisation has made it much easier to ship products across national boundaries.

The market is now highly competitive, with significant brand diversification. Acquisitions are playing a major role in building market dominance. The overall US brewing marketplace has less than five companies controlling an overwhelming majority of marketshare. An intensely competitive atmosphere requires increasingly shrewd operation, marketing, and distribution strategies. Above all, a company needs to maintain the commitment of its distributor network.

THE COMPANY

Sigma (a fictitious name) ranks in the top three beverage manufacturers and distributors in the world. An international beverage maker, it employs over six thousand employees domestically, including corporate, plant operations, field, and management staff. Additionally, there are over four hundred domestic distributors who are intensely interested in company developments.

Structurally, it has developed a somewhat decentralised corporate structure, with headquarters in the midwestern United States. Yet within its divisions it has remained very hierarchical. The primary divisions included Sales, Marketing, and Operations with product distribution through exclusive business contracts. There is also a strong Department of Corporate Communication. The primary responsibilities of the corporation included production, development, quality control, management, and distribution of various beverage brands. Additionally, the corporation developed and executed all national and international advertising.

Exclusive distribution contracts are awarded and administered by the corporation through 20 market area management offices placed locally for more direct interaction with the distributor network. For a number of years, the company has been moving towards more decentralisation, with a greater focus on local issues.

COMMUNICATION AND STRATEGY

Internal and external communication were similar to the prevalent patterns for most organisations. First, key executives had meetings and exchanged written communication with department heads within functional lines. Second, market areas' field representatives were responsible for managerial interactions between Sigma and individual distributorship leadership. Third, the primary personnel from each distributorship included the principal owner, general manager, sales manager, and operations manager; they have a communication set-up among themselves, and also with the field representatives.

One of the principal forms of communication was an annual national meeting of distributors, called the National Sales Meeting. It generally lasted two days and included a series of general sessions ending on the final evening with a large awards banquet. In the past, the content had always been a very general attempt to impart a sense of enthusiasm for the upcoming marketing campaign and the announcement of distribution promotions. The assumption was that great enthusiasm would result from a fun-filled, entertaining presentation of the general topics. In fact, their field representatives had at one stage been requesting a 'big bang' of a show, a party to celebrate a 'brand new day' that would win over the distributors to the fact that little had changed following recent management changes at Sigma. The traditions set for these meetings were very strong indeed.

But the company had experienced a change of top level leadership in critical areas. The new team valued communication and desired a more strategic approach to how it was managed. This increased awareness led to the choice of a new communication consultancy to produce a national communication event in lieu of the more entertainment-oriented type of event that been employed in the past. These new consultants had a policy of encouraging all clients to audit their audience via a standardised protocol prior to embarking on the development of new forms of national meetings.

THE AUDIT RATIONALE

It is important to note that the audit described in this chapter was not initiated as a response to a diagnosed problem. The company did not ask the consultants to 'fix' anything. There was no communication Band-Aid or surgery to be performed. Rather, they felt that they had an opportunity to improve the national event and to communicate more intelligently. The new managers appreciated the strategic role of communication, and they just wanted to adopt a 'smarter' approach.

Prior to the launch of the survey an announcement was transmitted to all distributors via the computer network which was routinely employed for the dissemination of important announcements. The bulletin gave a general overview of the rationale and proposed benefits for the audit. However, the audit was not going to be directly relevant to most of the internal personnel. Thus, the announcement was given just as a courtesy to keep them informed.

In the final analysis, this external audit was a form of environmental monitoring, based on the premise that the company needed to listen to the concerns of the distributors and then design a sales meeting which addressed those concerns.

THE AUDIT TECHNOLOGY

The basic technology used in this audit was a deep probe interview called DORA (Direct Open-end Response Analysis). Such interviews yield rich data – not about performance but about *attitudes*, *opinions*, *emotions*, and *expectations*. These are the processes that cause people to perform in the ways they do.

Initially, the business team had to be convinced of the value of this approach because most businesses, as we discussed above, are more comfortable with quantitative data. But DORA is not based on quantities. It discovers themes, feelings, and expectations.

Audit objectives

The general goals were to chart the attitudes and opinions of distributors who had attended previous meetings, and to identify their expectations of and recommendations for the next event. In the long term, it was hoped to establish trends by tracking some baseline questions. The two specific objectives were therefore to:

- assess expectations and satisfaction with regard to advertising, core brand focus, local market involvement and the Sigma management team;
- sample distributor recommendations for future National Business Conferences.

Preliminary planning

Prior to the survey, the auditors assisted the Executive Management Team to generate a list of assumptions with regard to this audience. This was performed as part of the preliminary phase of establishing their perceived objectives for the national meeting. Among the assumptions identified were the following:

1 Distributors look forward to a good show every year.
2 The meeting is considered a chance to see the new advertising.
3 The distributor audience is easily bored and does not come to the meeting for in-depth information or details.
4 Most distributors trusted the corporate leadership and were suspicious of the new executives.

Table 15.1 Interview sample population

	Large distributors	*Small distributors*	*Region*
I	27	8	California
II	68	20	Northwest and Southwest
III	33	10	Texas
IV	192	58	Midwest
V	61	18	Northeast
VI	122	37	South and Southeast

The sample

As part of the audit process, the general population pool was separated into six geographic sample sets. A random sample of 30 per cent nationally was selected. Researchers conducted interviews only with day-to-day managers of distributorships, who personally attended the National Business Conference. These samples were further subdivided, as shown in Table 15.1, between the large and small distributorships.

In a prior telephone call, an appointment was made for a call back to have the interview at a time convenient for the respondent, and they were told approximately how long the interview would take. In many cases, respondent interest led to longer interviews.

Telephone interviews

For the sake of accuracy and reliability, the interviews were conducted by previously arranged telephone conversations, and they were subject to the following controls:

- Acquisition of responses in the same time period ensured that current events which may influence attitudes were shared among the respondents. On each day of the survey, an equivalent proportion of respondents were interviewed from each of the geographical regions.
- The purpose of the survey was explained in-depth and confidentiality was assured.
- The interviewers made notations of tone and manner of the responses as well as verbatim accounts of responses. Tone is an important aspect of any message because it shades the meaning of the word. Notations were made as to whether the comment was hostile or helpful, serious or flippant. Note was also made of hesitations, long pauses, laughter, or cynicism.
- Interviewers were never allowed to use synonyms or to whitewash the language in any way. What was actually said was recorded.

THE SURVEY

Protocol

The interview protocol included specific directions to the interviewers for introducing the purpose of the interview as well as for delivery of questions, recording of responses, and ending the interviews. Particularly, interviewers were cautioned against voicing their own opinions or commenting on any answer. 'Thanks' or 'OK' were used as transitions to the next question. The objective of the protocol was to ensure that the interviews were conducted as uniformly as possible.

Questions

Thirty-four questions were ironed out with the Sigma liaison executive group to form a standardised survey interview, consisting primarily of open-ended questions. The interview guide was organised in a 'script' format with key words highlighted. When an interviewer was asked for clarity regarding an item, the interviewer could rephrase the item, making certain to include the key words.

Listed below are sample questions from the 34-question standardised interview guide:

- Why did you attend the National Business Conference last year?
- Why will you attend the meeting this year?
- What do you feel is the corporate purpose for holding a national meeting?
- What should be the corporate purpose for holding a national meeting?
- On a scale of 1–10 (with '1' representing very poor, and '10 'representing very good), how would you rate the last National Business Conference overall? Why did you give this rating?
- For you, what was the most important message of the morning General Business sessions?

Probes

In an attempt to facilitate complete answers, interviewers were given preestablished probes on their interview guides. Setting these probes required considerable planning and a thorough testing of the questions.

Pilot phase

A test phase had been conducted to monitor questioning and recording techniques for the purpose of assuring consistency. Following this pilot phase, problems with ambiguity and awkwardness were addressed prior to commencing the data collection.

THE ANALYSIS

Individual information was kept in strictest confidence, as had been promised to the respondents. The primary tool used for the analysis of responses to the deep probes was content analysis, using *ad hoc* categories or themes which were identified by the consultants. A listing of all responses for each question was printed out, or the data was transferred to 'DORA for Coding and Responses' which allowed theme development and coding on screen. The protocol called for an initial pass, theme consolidation, and then final coding.

Themes were developed by analysing responses to one question at a time, before progressing to the next question. The researcher read each response, classified the themes, and refined and modified the themes as they progressed. Once 'a pass' through all responses had been completed, the researcher made an attempt to consolidate the themes, limiting the number as much as possible without jeopardising the meaning of the responses. Then, to ensure that the theme arrangement 'worked' well, the researchers went through each response a second time, doing a manual coding of responses.

Since two researchers analysed responses to each question, the resultant themes were compared. Where major differences occurred, themes were reviewed by both researchers and the wording was refined.

Listed below are key guidelines for use in assigning themes and applying codes. It was emphasised continually that there is a difference between identification/distinction and judgement, and the auditor was to refrain from personal bias and judgement at all times.

Theme identification criteria

The following criteria were used:

- A theme is a response to the question, not mere dialogue.
- A theme is a complete thought, not necessarily a complete sentence.
- A theme can be a common thread of thought within the dialogue and may not be stated overtly.
- A single response may yield multiple themes.

Coding criteria

The researcher was required to read the complete response and ask: 'What is the most dominant point?' If the response contained multiple themes, yet no clear dominance, coding proceeded by choosing the first theme mentioned and then coding the other themes later. For example, the following themes were generated from the exemplar listed responses to the question: 'What was the most important message of the morning General Business sessions?'

Consolidation

'Probably the most significant thing in the morning was the clear statement that there will be wholesaler consolidation; in other words, an overall reduction of wholesalers in the US.'

'I would say the consolidation issues.'

'Oh, it was pretty obvious: consolidation.'

'The message on consolidation [*laughed slightly*].'

Continued focus on core brands

'Just that the . . . uh . . . core brands are picking up and are doing better, and the surprise was the depth of their interest in consolidation.'

'That we are going to focus on core brands and packages for next year.'

'It would be um . . . um . . . their um . . . commitment to the continuation of the core brand strategy . . .'

One-hour meeting

'I am not sure that an hour is really enough . . . I felt there was not the enthusiasm . . . and love and sincerity for the business coming from the top.'

'I guess the general sessions were to be one hour to maximise distributors' abilities to attend several seminars.'

'I came away feeling I was just going to have to make it on my own. Not enough time was spent . . .'

Other themes identified in response to the question were:

- Times are tough
- New distributor agreements
- There is a future for us
- New advertising
- Marketing plans

Finally, themes were then assigned to the demographic subgroups of (a) geographical region and (b) size of distributorship, so that comparisons could be established.

THE REPORT

Before any meaningful analysis could be completed, the auditors needed to understand the basic characteristics of the business and its culture, their nomenclature, and their objectives. Once the initial coding and tabulation was completed, it was useful to employ the assistance of the company's leadership to refine research insights and observed relevance of the themes.

Reports on the 34 questions generated an extensive document that followed the basic format for each question of:

(a) data on a chart;
(b) item analysis;
(c) thematic review and observations.

These were then followed by presentation of Final Observations and Conclusions.

A major thrust of this report was oriented toward the purpose of, and expectations for, the national meeting. Below, we show some of the main themes identified in response to particular interview questions:

Item analysis: Why did you attend the meeting last year?
Two main themes emerged, as Chart 15.1 shows. The fact that 22.5 per cent of the sample rated the mandatory nature of attendance as the lead reason suggested a somewhat low valuation of the potential benefits of the meeting.

The inverse correlation between the stratified samples for these top two themes was noted. It clearly indicated great interest in advertising, plans, and strategies

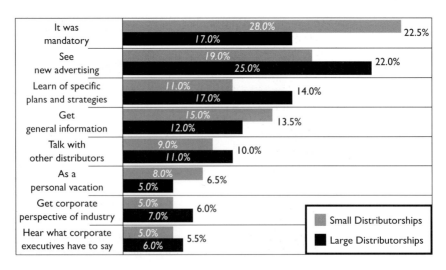

Chart 15.1 Question 1: Why did you attend the meeting last year?

by the larger, more successful distributors whereas the smaller distributors' perspectives were somewhat less optimistic.

Perhaps the most interesting of the emerging themes was the desire for interaction with other distributors. A comparison of the weight of this theme against the one referring to information from the corporate executives revealed a clear preference for information acquired from peers rather than corporate leadership.

It was important to note that data from the previous year indicating the reasons for attendance were as follows:

41%   To obtain general information
34%   It is simply a matter of business.
33%   Attendance is mandatory
14%   To meet the new management
14%   To hear future plans
11%   To see other distributors.

A review of the data revealed a shift from a mandatory, matter-of-business purpose for attending in previous years, to a far greater focus on information gathering and learning.

Item analysis: *Why will you attend the meeting this year?*
This item proved an excellent follow-up probe to the first item analysis question. Once again, two themes emerged as dominant and, as with the precedent item, there was an inverse correlation between large and smaller distributors in terms of importance (Chart 15.2).

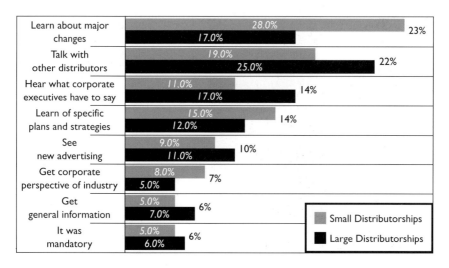

Chart 15.2 Question 2: Why will you attend the meeting this year?

The first theme (favoured by the smaller distributors) was obviously motiv-ated by the recent changes in top management. Two of the five top executives had been replaced with heretofore unknown individuals. The lower weight given this theme by the larger distributors was explained by the content of their re-sponses. These larger distributors referred to a series of smaller meetings which had been held to inform them about these new leaders.

The second theme (greatly favoured by the larger distributors) indicated an increased value for peer level interactions possible at the national meeting. Again, this, too, was more than likely a result of the changes in leadership. In terms of the larger distributors, they had met the new guys but wanted to hear their fellow distributors' opinions as well as explore the possible implications.

This probe item also showed a clear interest in more specific information regarding corporate plans and strategies. The distributors' reasons for attending this meeting versus past meetings had definitely changed, moving from moder-ate indifference to active anticipation. No longer was the mandatory aspect to the meeting so important.

In general, this population was looking to the meeting with a heightened awareness of its potential for the acquisition of information important to their business.

Item analysis: *What do you feel is the corporate purpose for holding a national meeting?*
Much like the first item analysis question, responses to this question were some-what unexpected (Chart 15.3). When first asked, many expressed a personal

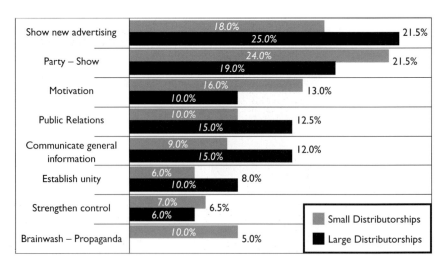

Chart 15.3 Question 3: What do you feel is the corporate purpose for holding a national meeting?

interest of their own. Virtually all respondents had to think for some time before responding, often with an answer they clearly considered a guess. Very few appeared to respond with any sense of authority.

The same curious pattern of inverse correlation between the two subgroups occurred. The large distributors perceived the unveiling of new advertising as the primary corporate purpose for the national meeting. The smaller distributors felt that the party or show was an end in itself. The smaller distributors saw a general attempt to *motivate* the masses as another main purpose for holding the national meeting, whereas the larger distributors viewed *public relations* as a general purpose.

The subordinate themes revealed some underlying attitudes which may also impact on how the meeting was perceived. Both subgroups seemed to feel that the purpose of this meeting was to exert control over the distributors. The smaller distributors went further in speculating that the leadership was interested in furthering an agenda of covert influence.

Overall, the audience seemed to consider the meeting as a 'party' or 'show' which communicated an agenda of corporate messages. These distributors considered the communication which took place at this meeting to be, for the most part, one-way. All in all, this response was not a very healthy message.

Item analysis: *What should be the corporate purpose for holding a national meeting?*
Most respondents seemed enthusiastic about the opportunity to give their opinions to this question (Chart 15.4).

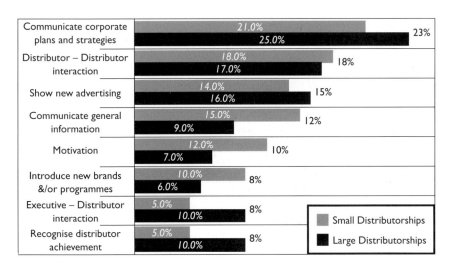

Chart 15.4 Question 4: What should be the corporate purpose for holding a national meeting?

The comparison between themes revealed some remarkable differences. The purposes cited as those *intended* by the corporation were clearly one-way and routine. The themes which emerged here as to what the purpose *should* be for the national meeting were interactive and dynamic. Several aspects of this array are really quite remarkable:

- Both subgroups seemed united in how they weighed the importance of these themes.
- These themes incorporated Advertising, Information, and Motivation.
- Approaching the meeting as a 'show' or 'party' was gone entirely. Despite the fact that a 'show' was seen as the corporate intent, it was the last approach this audience would prefer.
- This group was intensely interested in learning of the plans and strategies of the corporation.
- Distributor interaction with peers was viewed as of primary importance, to the degree that it should be an express purpose to the meeting itself.

FINAL OBSERVATIONS AND CONCLUSIONS

The pre-assessment survey provided the corporate leadership with some critical insights which allowed them to provide their distributors with a more productive meeting while avoiding some pitfalls of misunderstanding. And it was important to note how similar themes occurred in answering different questions.

From apathy to opportunity

An analysis of responses clearly indicated an enhanced interest in the upcoming meeting. The corporate leadership had believed that the distributors had always embraced these national meetings as previously designed. However, the results clearly indicated not only a history of ineffective meetings but new opportunity in the fact that this audience was keen on hearing what the new executives had to say.

The corporate assumption that the distributors trusted the former leadership was questionable. Also wrong was the assumption that the new executives would not be trusted. On the contrary, it appeared there was more receptivity than in past years as a result of the introduction of fresh blood. These executives seemed to represent a new hope for trust in the leadership. Although the jury was out, this was undoubtedly an opportunity to be seized.

Change in strategy

As a result, more time was devoted to presentations from the new executives. The agenda was changed to include more detailed information rather than just broad general comments. The leadership decided to unveil more than just the advertising but also the tactics and strategies behind the advertising and marketing. At the event, the audience responded in a very obvious manner with more spontaneous laughter and applause than any of the previous show-like meetings of the past. The increased detail prompted distributors to seek out corporate employees between sessions, engaging them in impromptu information-gathering conversations eventually leading to more business opportunities.

Venue for interaction

The leadership was aware that there was a lot of 'visiting' going on at the meetings, but they were completely surprised with the enormous value the distributors placed on simple sharing of ideas with their colleagues.

Change in strategy

Given that the informal communication channels were so highly regarded, the planners orchestrated more opportunity for the top leadership to interact with the distributors in more casual settings. Banquets became buffets and seating was made more informal. Hallway and lounge areas were furnished with comfortable seating and more time was set aside for casual interaction. A series of panel meetings rather than seminar lectures was planned for the exchange of learning between distributors. These mini-meetings not only sparked new ideas and approaches for distributors but allowed the corporate leadership to record and collect the products of these *ad hoc* 'think-tanks'.

Discovery of a 'class system'

The data had made it painfully obvious that there was a significant disparity between the large and smaller distributors. The survey revealed how corporate attempts to target their communications to the larger distributors who represented the most significant part of the business resulted in a wide difference in attitudes and beliefs and in friction between the two groups.

Change in strategy

The focus on interaction and increase of detail provided at the meeting served to empower the smaller distributors. Many commented on feeling more 'in the know' after attending the meeting.

Communication vs. show

Perhaps the most important discovery was dispelling the myth that the distributors came to the meeting to have fun, relax, and party. The traditional 'show' format was shown to be ineffective, unappreciated and a hindrance to the posit-ive possibilities for the national meeting. Rather than having a motivating effect on the audience, taking the approach of a show or party looked more like smoke and mirrors to the distributors.

Change in strategy

A more formal and dignified design was adopted. The funds formerly spent on singers, dancers and special effects was invested in state-of-the-art speaker sup-port and graphics. This allowed the executives to go into much greater detail while maintaining an effective level of understanding and retention.

The value of recognition

This was perhaps the most obvious tree overlooked as a result of focusing on the forest. These distributors worked hard to succeed, and the national meeting was the perfect place to recognise that achievement. What better way to build trust and loyalty?

Change in strategy

The meeting sessions featured documentary-style videos heralding best practice efforts of select distributors from around the country. This allowed the audience to feel a part of the main presentation and extended the value of interaction and sharing to the presentation itself. The response was overwhelming and was an obvious contributor to increased audience response and participation.

Detail not propaganda

The national meeting was now considered a communication 'event' rather than a 'show' and the focus was on communicating important and useful information. The leadership recognised the value of using this national event as a 'listening post' for new ideas and approaches to the business. The results from the meeting included more than merely furthering a national agenda. This national event now served to further develop and improve on that agenda.

THE RESULTS

The national meetings had been conducted with distributors for many years, following the same party format. It was not until an external communication audit provided detailed information to be used in designing the National Busi-ness Conference that it was transformed into an important communication event. The respondents revealed that they were tired of the 'smoke and mirrors' used in prior meetings. They complained of the grand spectacles with no substance that they were confronted with each year at the meeting. They virtually begged for just good information with great detail regarding plans and strategies, without distracting bells and whistles. They considered all the hoopla of the past as just a way to camouflage initiatives that were not necessarily in favour of the distributors.

In conjunction with the audit consultants, the executives designed a meeting that consisted of well produced speaker support and provided details of company plans. Plenty of time was set aside for two-way conversation in casual settings. A question and answer session was introduced. The results included a massive swell of support from the individual distributor principals and a reassessment and reorganisation of the field representative network, including a more direct channel to the top executives.

Another important result was that the executives were so convinced that the communication audit had benefited them they used it to plan all of their conventions. They also learned from this external audit that, regardless of how well they interacted internally at Sigma, they could not be successful unless they were successful externally with their vast network of distributors.

Part IV

Final considerations

Chapter 16

Strategy, research and pedagogy

The role of audits

Dennis Tourish and Owen Hargie

INTRODUCTION

This book has explored the contribution which audits can make to the evaluation, and then transformation, of both internal and external communications. A great deal of evidence has been presented to show that high quality communication is a crucial indicator of organisational health. Those organisations which neglect it are hampered by poor fitness levels, and bedevilled by injury problems. This hinders their ability to compete in the marketplace. A variety of methods have been proposed which will enable organisations to monitor what they do more accurately, in order to effect substantial improvements. The case study chapters in Part III testify to the opportunities for organisational development afforded by a rigorous scrutiny of current practice.

Four substantive issues remain, which we will address in this chapter. These are:

1 The nature of a communication strategy, and how audits can fit into its development.
2 How auditors can choose between the different techniques which have been discussed in this book.
3 The role of audits as a research tool.
4 The contribution of communication audits to the teaching of organisational communication.

Each of these areas is discussed below.

AUDITS AND STRATEGIC COMMUNICATION

Audits are a vital ingredient of attempts to fashion a coherent communication strategy. However, there is no obvious consensus on what the term 'communication strategy' means (Tourish, 1996). This terminological uncertainty means that there are three main traps to avoid in approaching the issue.

First, managers may anticipate that they should be able to predict all their organisation's information needs, internally and externally, over an indefinite time-frame. False conceptions (of stability, predictability and uniformity) lie behind many of the major problems which have become associated with the disappointing results of most strategic planning (Mintzberg, 1994). The word 'strategy' is often little more than a synonym for bureaucracy, and the absence of tangible outcomes. Thus, attempts to develop a strategic perspective in communications can become mired in the same bureaucratic sludge which has enveloped many corporate headquarters, exterminating all known life forms.

Second, attempts may be made to separate the communication function from the other vital roles of management, such as finance, human resources and R&D. Managers can end up paying less attention to the issue, because someone else is paying more. This distancing process is often camouflaged, albeit temporarily, by the production of thick (but slick) documents, labelled 'communication strategies'. Their primary purpose is to avoid the painful need to transform internal and external relationships. Thus, inaction is concealed behind a frantic paper chase, while the act of being busy is confused with achievement. In general, an under-focus on relationships, and an over-emphasis on the technical aspects of information transmission *('How much colour should we include in this brochure?')*, has held back the contribution of communication programmes to corporate competitiveness for many years (White and Mazur, 1995). For this reason, we would urge the wider use of the term 'communications management', rather than the ubiquitous and somewhat discredited nomenclature 'public relations'.

Third, and from the point of view of what has been defined as sense-making in organisations (Weick, 1995), many accounts of corporate decision making are retrospective constructions, which attempt to explain and justify that which has often occurred by serendipity. It goes against the grain to admit that something which turned out well could have occurred by accident, or even in spite of our best laid plans. We therefore construct myths and stories in which most successes are credited to our own brilliant insights, while corporate failures are the result of someone else's screw-ups. Success has many fathers, while failure is an orphan. We then seek reassurance about what comes next by producing detailed written 'strategies', which attempt to predict the future with the same accuracy as we can know the past. The outcome is a beautifully crafted written strategy, which nevertheless stifles initiative and bears but a feeble resemblance to emerging reality.

Tourish and Hargie (1996a) conceptualise a communication strategy in an entirely different manner. They define it as:

> A process which enables managers to evaluate the communication consequences of the decision making process, and which integrates this into the normal business planning cycle and psyche of the organisation.
>
> (Tourish and Hargie, 1996a, p. 12)

Four main consequences flow from this:

1 *Instead of attempting to force communication to the top of management's already crowded agenda, it should be linked to what is already dominating that agenda.*

As Quirke (1996, p. 71) put it, a communication strategy: 'should support the business strategy, and should help the organisation compete more effectively'. At each stage, the connection between business priorities and communication issues needs to be made explicit, concrete, and turned into objectives which can be measured.

2 *A communication strategy should be a means of transforming existing management practice, rather than an additional activity on top of everything else that managers already do.*

Responsibility for communication lies with management, rather than an isolated individual secreted in a separate office far away from where line managers do their daily work. Communication has often been neglected, while managers lavish attention on their other more favoured children. Neglect makes breakdowns inevitable. Where specialist expertise is needed, its main role should be to support line management and complement its efforts, rather than act as a substitute for it.

3 *Strategy is not an event, but a process.*

That is, a communication strategy is not something dreamt up by planners in a room; it is an ongoing activity, involving the entire organisation. Essentially, *strategy is what gets done* (Shapiro, 1998). It is what people do, rather than what anyone imagines they do, what they ought to do or what they have been told to do. Thus, a communication strategy seeks to describe the business challenges which exist, their relationship to communication variables, and the best practices the organisation is attempting to employ. A focus on changing behaviours is central to the process. Inevitably, personal example is the key to success. The leaders of the organisation must embody proactive communication in their day to day work, and model appropriate behaviours for each tier of the organisation.

When Lawrence Bossidy was appointed CEO of Allied Signals in 1991 the company was earning annual revenues of $359 million but losing money. By 1994 it was in profit and with an annual income of $708 million. A focus on communication was central to accomplishing the turnaround. Here is what Bossidy did:

> In 1991, we were haemorrhaging cash. That was the issue that needed focus. I travelled all over the company with the same message and the same

charts, over and over. Here's what I think is good about us. Here's what I'm worried about. Here's what we have to do about it . . . You can keep it simple: we're spending more than we're taking in . . . In the first 60 days, I talked to probably 5,000 employees. I would go to Los Angeles and speak to 500 people, then to Phoenix and talk to another 500. I would stand on a loading dock and talk to people and answer their questions . . . Go to the people and tell them what's wrong. And they knew. It's remarkable how many people know what's really going on in their company. I think it's important to get effective interaction with everybody in the company, and to involve everyone.

(Tichy and Charan, 1995, p. 70)

This is strategy in action. It involves influencing people by doing, rather than exhorting. As Wright (1995) pointed out, many organisations still think of communication in terms of glossy brochures and press handouts – in short, as a once-off event, which will forever remove the possibility of problems. In reality, communication is what happens to organisations while they are busy making other plans. Its occurrence is inevitable – the challenge is to manage it. Thus, an emphasis on *process* focuses attention on the ongoing management of relationships, and helps root the notion of a communication strategy in the managerial ethos of the organisation concerned.

4 *Measurement should begin with results.*

Many change initiatives fail because the process by which they are introduced is evaluated on such dimensions as satisfaction by those participating in training sessions, rather than bottom line business returns (Schaffer and Thomson, 1992). For example, public relations practitioners have tended to measure success by the amount of publicity their campaigns attract, rather than their impact on broader business outcomes (Lindenmann, 1998). We are recommending that explicit links should be made between communication and organisational outcomes by all business units. This means habituating managers and staff to address the following questions:

(a) What are the key problems that arise through poor communication? It should be noted that this is a different proposition to the identification of communication problems, important as this is. Rather, it is to suggest a focus on the deeper business problems that are caused by the organisation's communication difficulties. This ensures that the underlying thrust of a communications review *(to improve business performance)* remains in focus.
(b) Flowing from this, what are the organisation's major communication problems?
(c) What changes in behaviour are required to eliminate these problems? How specific can we be about these changes? How will we know when they have occurred?

(d) What targets can be set to eliminate the problems that arise from communication failure? What targets can be set to eliminate communication failure itself? This provides a robust framework for evaluating the new communication process. In addition, staff satisfaction with communication is important for its own sake. If existing communication practice has been thoroughly evaluated, then targets can also be set for:

- increased and sustained knowledge;
- high levels of goodwill and credibility;
- a regular flow of communication;
- accurate expectations about future milestones in organisational development (i.e. fewer toxic shocks); and
- satisfaction with levels of participation.

Ongoing audit research tracks the progress of all these factors.

Changing employee communication behaviours

It is widely argued that in order to effect deep rooted organisational change top managers must lead by doing and showing, transforming their own behaviours to model new business imperatives (e.g. Rago, 1996). Leadership is 90 per cent example. However, it is important to recognise that new behaviours, and mindsets, on the part of employees are also required. Organisations are complex, interdependent social systems. If only managers change, then nothing will change. Our own audits have found that many people are comfortable with the notion of a hierarchy, enjoy blaming managers for every real and imagined problem, avoid accepting responsibility for their own contribution to communication breakdowns, and are profoundly reluctant to contemplate changes in their own communication styles. Other researchers have highlighted the same phenomenon (e.g. Argyris, 1994). Auditors need to be on the look out for this, and show a preparedness to engage with it. Box 16.1 lists a number of suggestions, derived from a variety of research findings, which suggest some steps towards addressing the problem.

Implementing a communication strategy

Flowing from this, what concretely must managers do to develop a communication strategy? Four key stages have been identified (Tourish and Hargie, 1996a). These encompass the process for auditing communication, which we discussed in-depth in Chapter 2, and are therefore only summarised briefly here:

1 Secure senior management commitment.
2 Identify current practice.
3 Set standards to measure success.
4 Incorporate this process into the business planning cycle (and psyche) of the organisation.

Box 16.1 Transforming employees' communication behaviours

- Top managers must model the new approaches concerned, encourage others to imitate their behaviour and reward those who do.
- Training in effective communication needs to be extended into the furthermost recesses of the organisation.
- Such training should include the issue of how to give upward feedback. (Managers also need training in how to respond to criticism and ideas from the shop floor.)
- Performance review, at *all* levels, needs to take account of communication performance.
- Reward systems, again at all levels, need to do likewise.
- Targets should be set for inter-departmental co-operation. Many organisations now encourage this as part of the normal business planning cycle.
- Staff should be given the opportunity to work elsewhere in their organisations, rather than in their everyday environment. This breaks down inter-departmental barriers, and facilitates horizontal, diagonal and vertical communication.

A genuine communication strategy means involving all managers and ultimately all staff in identifying goals, standards of good practice and methods of evaluation. The starting point is the requirement that when business plans are being drawn up the communication consequences of these are considered. We return, also, to a previous point: strategy is what gets done, not what gets written in policy manuals.

It is, therefore, suggested that, at this stage, managers and staff routinely address, in a very non-routine way, the following issues:

- What are the communication or information implications of the decision making process? It is feasible to consult staff at all levels on this issue. The threats and opportunities posed by decisions should also be considered.
- What will people need to know about the implications of a given policy/decision? This could encompass publics internal and external to the organisation.
- Who is going to be responsible for transmitting the information concerned (i.e. what source of communication is most appropriate)? Communication is primarily a management responsibility, but need not and should not involve only managers.
- How will this information be communicated – face to face, through written memorandum, through group meetings (i.e. what channels of communication will be used)?
- What is the absolute essence of the information that will be required by a designated audience (i.e. what is the nature of the message that we will be disseminating)?

- What mechanisms exist to consult and involve people? How can they be strengthened?
- How can greater informality be promoted within the organisation? Specifically, how many bureaucratic procedures (the original purpose of which is long forgotten) can be eliminated this week, or better still today?
- What can we do to celebrate our achievements and honour people? One example. *Fortune* magazine has nominated Southwest Airlines as the best company to work for in America. It is also one of the most profitable. The airline publishes stories of employee accomplishments and exploits in various newsletters. One of its publications is a tabloid style magazine called *Plane Tails*, which seeks to publish 'shocking stories about sensational employees'. It also prints tributes from customers, and more 'normal' company information.
- What personal behavioural changes can managers make right away to facilitate a new pro-communications culture? How should managers be facilitated to identify their own strengths and weaknesses as communicators, motivators and, ultimately, leaders?
- How effectively is two-way communication integrated into decision-making? It is often assumed that the role of communication is to produce answers to problems which have already been solved by senior managers (Rubin, 1996). The notion is one of decision-making, followed by communication, rather than one which sees it as integral to problem-solving in a team-oriented workplace. Thus, a strategy should plan, encourage and reward participation in decision-making and problem-solving.

Within this framework, and assuming top management involvement, a basis can be laid for transforming patterns of communication, organisational structures, levels of involvement and, ultimately, key business outcomes.

WHICH AUDIT TECHNIQUE IS MOST APPROPRIATE?

Once an organisation decides to implement an audit and develop a communications strategy, the unavoidable question is raised: which method should it employ? In Chapter 2 we proposed an audit process, characteristic of good practice, and which we argued should normally be followed. Beyond this, numerous data collection techniques are available. The most important of these have been discussed, in detail, in this book. Choosing between them is no easy matter. Each audit should be tailored to the unique context in which it occurs. The challenge is to be clear about the needs of the organisation, compare those needs with the audit tools available and then select whichever approach seems most appropriate. Auditing is both a science and an art.

To assist with this analysis, Box 16.2 summarises the most widely used audit approaches, the time they take to implement, their general costs, the type of data

Box 16.2 Evaluating audit tools

Tools	Time	Costs	Data collected	Disruption
Questionnaires	30–40 minutes	Main costs are respondents' time; those responding externally may need to be paid; cost of questionnaire analysis and analytical time of auditor	Standardised; quantitative data. Some questionnaires also contain open questions, yielding qualitative data. (See Appendix)	Time spent completing questionnaires
Interviews	30–60 minutes	Interviewer time/interviewee time. (For external audits, interviewees may require fee)	Perceptions of employees/customers/suppliers. Probing permits deep coverage of topics	Time interviewees spend away from their normal tasks
Focus groups	1–2 hours	Staff time; customers (or others) may require payment	Qualitative accounts/summaries of respondents' opinions	Time participants spend away from their work
Communication diaries	Normally, at least one day and no more than a week	Used internally; expensive in terms of employee time	Identifies sources of information, channels used and communication networks	High; most respondents find it intrusive; low completion rate
ECCO	5–10 minutes	Used internally; costs limited to employee time	Identifies amount of information known; sources and channels from which it is derived	Minimal
Mystery shopper	5–30 minutes (per transaction)	Employees diverted from 'real' customers; payment of 'shopper'	Quantitative and qualitative data	Minimal, although may change behaviour of staff

Box 16.2 (cont'd)

Tools	Time	Costs	Data collected	Disruption
Video recording	Indeterminate	Costs of video equipment; some technical help may be needed	Quantitative and qualitative	Minimal; does not tend to disrupt interaction
Critical incidents/experiences	Normally, a standard part of questionnaires	No extra costs incurred; often, part of data collection technique already being employed	Lively, positive and negative examples of communication processes	Minimal
Constitutive ethnography	4–20 hours of professionals' time	Expensive; professionals may require payment, or hiring of replacements while analysis occurs	Expert insights into dynamics of communication	High; professionals taken away from normal job
Delphi	1–3 hours of participants' time	Moderate: cost of participants' time	Evaluations of communication by experts	Moderate: small numbers suffice
Direct observation	No minimum/maximum normally specified	Low. Time used is that of observer, rather than staff/customers	Data from group interaction, dyadic episodes	Minimal, providing observer succeeds in being unobtrusive

collected and the amount of disruption they cause. This offers a pen portrait of each technique contained in earlier chapters of this book. Although intended to stimulate thinking, it is not a substitute for a close analysis of the context in which the audit is being conducted. The following issues should be considered, during such a process:

1 *Does the organisation require benchmarks against which future progress can be measured?*
If so, questionnaires have many advantages (see Chapter 3). The data obtained can be readily quantified. Future audits will then show the extent to which the communication climate has improved or deteriorated. Chapter 10 provides a case study of an audit, and a follow-up, where precisely this form of evaluation occurred. Many questionnaires also contain open questions, allowing auditors the opportunity to collate illuminating anecdotes and other expressions of how people feel. The Appendix presents an example of such a questionnaire in detail. We have frequently found that a few colourful comments from audit respondents influence management thinking more than a zillion tables of hard data. (This is in line with the research evidence on the impact of statistics, discussed in Chapter 9.)

Sometimes extra effort has to be expended in interpreting such comments. For example, one audit respondent, attempting to express her appreciation of a line manager's open communication style, commented: 'My line manager always does his best to keep me informed, even when he doesn't know what's going on himself.' We think we know what she meant![1] Interviews and focus groups are much more difficult to use in benchmarking (see Chapters 4 and 5). However, if resources permit, they can be used to supplement the data obtained by the questionnaire method, cross-check its validity, and explore problems identified in more depth. Whether multiple methods are employed will often depend on such constraints as time, money and human resources.

Questionnaires are not the most useful form of data collection for all populations. Some researchers in the United States have found that Chief Executive Officers are much more willing to participate in face-to-face interviews than they are to complete questionnaires (Wasserman and Faust, 1994). Our own experience corroborates this finding. Thus, the nature of the sample population must also be considered in determining the most appropriate form of data collection.

Additionally, and perhaps surprisingly, researchers have found that postal questionnaires attract a significantly higher response rate than those distributed via e-mail (Mavis and Brocato, 1998). This may be because paper questionnaires remain on desks for longer and stay within sight. However, a wastebasket is conveniently located in the corner of every computer screen. Thus, e-mail surveys can be binned at the click of a mouse, and instantly forgotten about.

---

[1] However, forensic examination does not always yield meaning. For example, another respondent in one of our audits commented delphically: 'I never talk on the telephone, only listen.'

2 *Is the audit one of internal or external communication?*
In general, it is more difficult to use questionnaires for external audits. Internally, forums can be created where staff turn up, receive a detailed explanation of the audit process, and fill in materials under the auditors' supervision. Alternatively, they can be followed up through direct contact or by mail. However, customers have less motivation to complete questionnaires. This increases the possibility that only those with a particular axe to grind will get involved, thereby skewing the results. Several methods of dealing with this, to improve response rates, are discussed in Chapter 8. The mystery shopping technique has its origins in customer research, and allows for quantitative analysis, if this is required. In terms of evaluating direct communication with customers, in locations such as shops, this is by far the most useful approach, as discussed in Chapter 7. A number of ethical issues pertaining to this method have also been raised, which should be taken into account. Alternatively, direct observation, interviews and focus groups might be a suitable choice.

3 *Is the organisation already aware of its communication problems, and simply needs to know people's opinions in more depth?*
In this context, further quantitative data, gained from questionnaires, may be as redundant as a third leg. We have faced this situation in many of our audits. An overall picture has emerged. Managers may then wish to clarify:

- Why a particular department is more dissatisfied than others.
- Why people in one location always feel badly informed, while those elsewhere are up to speed on key issues.
- What exactly customers want to know about a given issue, or
- Why Department X is refusing to talk to Department Y, but won't make its reasons clear.

In such circumstances we have conducted follow-up focus groups and interviews to supplement quantitative data. As Downs (1988) noted, there are many advantages to using more than one method of data collection. More fine-grained analysis is one of them. The process of verifying results obtained by one means through the employment of other techniques is also sometimes known as triangulation.

4 *Has a massive crisis just occurred, requiring rapid analysis?*
We have worked with organisations which have been severely traumatised by unforeseen public relations disasters, often involving a complete breakdown in communication with customers. Invariably, the media have rushed to the scene, flashbulbs popping, and sought to pillory both the individuals involved and the wider organisation. Under such an onslaught, the careful designing of questionnaires followed by lengthy analysis is impracticable. A small number of skilfully run focus groups, or interviews, generates some rough and ready data, permitting a quick discussion of the way forward. These data are never ideal, or complete. However, a fuzzy picture is more useful than a blank screen. Once the immediate tension has eased, a more in-depth analysis can be undertaken.

5 *Does the audit need to focus closely on a small sub-set of a wider organisational system?*

We worked recently with a public sector organisation reeling from a blitz of bad publicity surrounding a particular incident. This suggested that vulnerable members of the public were ill-informed about some of its key services. Furthermore, the conduit from organisation to public was through one professional sub-section of its staff. The objective of the audit was to find out precisely what this grouping knew and didn't know about the service in question – and what it was doing to communicate relevant information to the people who needed the service. Plainly, standardised instruments (which tend to measure global aspects of communication) were of limited use in such an investigation. We therefore devised our own questionnaire, with a special emphasis on open questions, and conducted a number of focus groups and depth interviews as follow up. An 'off the shelf' approach is not always practicable. Another scenario occurs when the objective is to thoroughly audit a particular organisational system in great detail. (See Chapter 11 for an account of such a project.) Under those conditions, a wide range of audit materials can justifiably be employed, depicting communication practices from multiple perspectives.

6 *Is the audit being conducted as part of an organisational development programme, or as pure research?*

In the latter case, the primary consideration is likely to be the gathering of plentiful data, in which both depth and breadth are of crucial importance. Here, the data must answer to the most rigorous standards of academic practice, and prove capable of testing complex hypotheses. As with audits in general, the most appropriate method will depend on the research objectives which have been set. Despite the sometimes polarised nature of the debate (see Cooper and Stevenson, 1998; M. Morgan, 1998) qualitative research is now attracting considerable attention in academic circles. Increasingly, researchers employ both quantitative and qualitative methods in their work (e.g. Gable, 1994). Thus, it is entirely possible that such tools as focus groups will help to meet a number of research objectives, either on their own or in conjunction with more positivist inspired methodologies. On the other hand, Chapters 6 and 7 discuss some approaches (e.g. the Delphi technique; video recording of professional–client interaction) which are very labour intensive, and are therefore mostly employed during in-depth research investigations.

7 *Is the audit being conducted in-house, or by external consultants?*

Either way, a whole raft of issues is raised. The first step is to clarify the audit's objectives. Is benchmarking required, or is a rough picture of emerging trends sufficient? If the audit is in-house, an honest evaluation of the audit team's expertise needs to be conducted. For example, does the team have any knowledge of statistics? If not, quantitative approaches aimed at benchmarking would be ill-advised. Will it be trusted to treat questionnaires confidentially, or are leaks within the organisation the norm? Do the team members have a reputation for independence, or are they viewed as management stool pigeons? A small number of focus groups, interviews and some forms of direct observation are possible alternatives. Worries about confidentiality will remain. However, if the sample population is kept small it should be possible to provide plentiful assurances about confidentiality, and so collect at least some data. We are aware of some attempts to use questionnaires during in-house audits, which attracted pitifully low response rates and included many questionnaires only partially completed. On the other hand, if the internal audit team is well trusted, is perceived as standing apart from the top management team, and has experienced auditors as members, these problems will be much reduced and a wider range of choices will be available.

If the auditors are external, and fully conversant with the organisation's needs, then the best professional advice should be forthcoming. We recognise that the task of finding trustworthy consultants, tuned into the organisation's situation, is itself a challenge. This task is enormously simplified if the organisation has a clear view of its own needs.

In general, we believe that the balance of the argument favours involving external consultants. The main reasons for this are as follows:

- *External consultants, carefully chosen, are more likely to have the requisite expertise, and the time, to be fully and professionally engaged with the audit process.* Inevitably, internal audit teams are pulled in several directions at once. Its members still have day jobs to attend to. Frequently, it proves next to impossible to convene even something as simple as a planning meeting. They rarely have the time to consider audit data dispassionately or objectively, and often lack vital interpretative skills.
- *It is useful to seek an outside perspective on what the organisation is doing.* External auditors bring to bear experiences gained from elsewhere, including examples of best practice. As Otto von Bismarck, the famous German Chancellor, remarked in the nineteenth century: 'Only a fool learns from experience: I learn from the experience of others.'

  Internal auditors may also be handicapped by the fear of offending vital constituencies with whom they must work once the audit is completed. How, for example, do you tell your boss, on whom you depend for your bonus, that his diplomatic skills have created an internal climate reminiscent of the Cold War? Organisations should look for external consultants prepared to discuss problems such as these honestly, rather than those whose main aim is to apply liberal helpings of whitewash – while pocketing a hefty fee. A glowing report which fails to reflect reality will be of no use in effecting improvements. Such reports are often produced as a means of telling managers what they want to hear, in the hope of securing further consultancy business. Their main effect is to undermine management's credibility in the eyes of staff, who (as we discussed in Chapter 9) tend to be only too well aware that problems exist.

• *The cost of hiring external auditors has to be set against the demands on the time of internal auditors, which also costs money.* There may also be training needs for internal auditors. A related difficulty is that internal auditors rarely have the time required for comprehensive audits, and end up rushing data analysis. This is a false economy. As computer specialists often point out, 'Garbage in equals garbage out.'

RESEARCH VERSUS AUDIT

While audits can be used in research, not all audits are research. They are often simply used to evaluate the application of research findings in a given context (Malby, 1995). Their purpose is to answer questions such as: Is communication in this organisation at an acceptable level of competence? Are our customers receiving the information which they need, or not? Exploring these issues does not constitute research. Research is concerned with developing and testing hypotheses; generalising from one or more studies, to set the standards for what constitutes good practice; and contributing to the development and refinement of theories about wider social systems (Montgomery and Duck, 1991). Box 16.3

Box 16.3 Characteristics of audits and research

Audit	*Research*
Compares actual performance standards	Identifies the best approach (e.g. what communication style most helps with customer retention), and so sets the standards
Sometimes conducted by those who work within the organisation being studied	More often conducted by independent, outside researchers
Usually initiated and led by the needs of the organisation	Usually initiated by researchers, to explore wider issues
Involves access to information (e.g. employee classification system) by those normally entitled to access it	Requires access to information and databases by people who are not normally entitled to such access
Results designed to be setting-specific	Results intended to be generalisable to other settings
Uses already validated and usually well established approaches to conduct investigation	May be concerned with testing efficacy of given approach, and developing new ones
Uses already tested hypothesis to check standards, and set internal benchmarks	Develops testable hypothesis, based on audit data; and tests hypothesis based on audit data

lists the main characteristics of audit and research, indicating where they overlap and diverge. It is clear that audits have the potential to become a well respected and useful addition to the toolkit of those pursuing research into organisational studies. Here, we suggest various areas where this applies.

A wide range of research strategies and tactics are already employed in business and management research (Bryman, 1988b), which has shown great ingenuity in adapting methodologies originally developed for different purposes. Audits can be used in longitudinal or cross-sectional studies. In other words, they may be employed in an organisation(s) over a period of years, or used in a representative sample of cases to give an immediate snapshot telling researchers 'this is how it is'. They are particularly useful in the forms of research discussed below:

- *Action research.* In this, data are collected about a system, results are fed back into the system, variables are manipulated in response, and the consequences are evaluated by the collection of more data. The assumption is that new knowledge is produced, but knowledge which has concrete applications and so can be validated in action (Gummeson, 1991). In so far as communication audits enable researchers to manipulate organisational variables (e.g. information flow; channel utilisation; source frequency) they are of particular use in this form of research.
- *Case studies.* This is an umbrella term for approaches which look at a particular real life event, organisation or sub-system, and eventually seek to generalise the findings to more substantial populations (Bell, 1993). Case studies are therefore used to make causal deductions. The argument is advanced that their in-depth nature, and emphasis on situationally embedded processes, justifies such inferences (Lee, 1999). A great deal of such research, using communication audits, has now been published, and is widely referenced in this text. Several examples are also offered in Part III.
- *Focus groups.* Here, evidence is collected from specialised and carefully selected groups of individuals. Given the popularity of focus groups in communication research, they have been thoroughly discussed in Chapter 5 of this book.
- *In-depth surveys.* Typically, such surveys attempt to extract a great deal of evidence from a relatively small number of informants, normally using interviews. Such research can be conducted from within two main theoretical paradigms (Remenyi *et al.*, 1998). It can be positivist in orientation – i.e. researchers may be primarily concerned with the exploration of causal relationships by means of quantitative analysis. Accordingly, frequency counts can be employed in such techniques as content analysis. Alternatively, it may be more phenomenological in nature – i.e. researchers are primarily concerned with the deeper meanings which respondents attach to communication, or with the values which underpin their behaviours. The audit tools discussed in Part II encompass both research traditions.
- *Large scale surveys.* For example, audit questionnaires might be employed to evaluate practices across a significant number of organisations (Tourish and

Hargie, 1998). These can share a greater or lesser number of characteristics, depending upon the research objectives or hypotheses being investigated. Chapter 3 explores such issues in more detail.

• *Participant observer approach.* In this case, a researcher joins the group of individuals under discussion and engages in their activities, but maintains a primary role of observing how the group functions (Remenyi *et al.*, 1998). The mystery shopper technique is one form of this activity.

Beyond this, audits are helpful in the exploration of a wide range of research questions. Goldhaber (1993) identified six main categories under which such questions can be grouped. We discuss these below, and add our own research items to those raised by Goldhaber. We also add a seventh category of our own:

1 *Homophily studies*
These explore the extent to which various phenomena are similar or dissimilar to each other, and their connection with communication. Key research issues here would include:

• Is perceived similarity between a message source and recipient a determinant of communication needs, or likely levels of satisfaction?
• Can communication frequency be predicted by homophily?
• Are highly cohesive teams more or less likely to require high information inputs from people outside the group?

2 *Apprehension studies*
These are concerned with the interaction between levels of anxiety which people feel about where they work, or the businesses they deal with, and their corresponding feelings about communication. Thus:

• Do measures of apprehension predict frequency of interaction, its quality, and consequences?
• Can anxiety about communication be reduced, either through the process of audit, or as a result of the interventions to which it gives rise?
• Contrariwise, to what extent is communication anxiety inevitable in large organisations?
• What role does job seniority play in determining apprehension about communication?
• What is the relationship between group cohesiveness and communication anxiety? (Groups may create a strong support environment which reduces anxiety, or reinforce each member's hostility to the outside world, thereby enhancing it.)

3 *Credibility studies*
These explore the relationship between credibility and the quality of communication. Thus:

- Does information which emanates from sources with high credibility produce greater overall communication satisfaction?
- What is the relationship between interpersonal trust and the quality of information flow? (We have frequently found high levels of interpersonal trust between staff and managers, combined with strong information deficits on key issues.)
- What determines credibility in the eyes of customers, who possess limited contextual information about the source they are dealing with?

4 *Contingency theory studies*

These explore the extent to which effective communication depends on (i.e. is contingent to) such variables as age, gender, ethnicity, status, and length of employment. Thus:

- Do any of the above variables contribute to levels of satisfaction with communication?
- Do different cultures possess different communication needs?
- Can organisational culture be manipulated to resolve the problem of securing accurate upward feedback? Or is it inherently difficult to get people to speak their mind?
- Does extending communication skills training throughout an organisation increase overall levels of satisfaction with the communication process? (Some of our own audits suggest that it does, but more research is required to answer this question definitively.)

5 *Network studies*

These explore the connection between group affiliations and people's ability to sustain networks and their view of communication. Thus:

- To what extent is information about effective or ineffective communication episodes involving customers shared within local communities? Through what channels, and with what effect, is such information exchanged?
- Do people defined as isolates have a heightened perception of communication difficulties?
- Does a strong identification with a particular team, or sub-section of the workplace, enhance or reduce overall levels of company loyalty?

6 *Communication and organisational effectiveness studies*

These look at the extent to which internal and external communication impact upon organisational effectiveness. Thus:

- Does customer satisfaction with communication strengthen organisational practice, or produce complacency, inertia and lost competitive edge?
- Do employees with high satisfaction levels have lower levels of absenteeism, sickness and turnover? Are they more productive and innovative than their colleagues?

- Are low levels of communication satisfaction a cause or a consequence of organisational malaise?

7 *Communication technology change studies*
These are concerned with the impact of new technologies (as discussed in Chapter 8) on organisational functioning. Accordingly:

- What is the impact of specific new technologies on existing patterns of communication?
- Will the preference for face-to-face communication subside in virtual companies?
- Do intranet, internet and telephone technologies help organisations improve their profits? How?
- What standards and protocols can be suggested for the most effective use of such technologies?

COMMUNICATION AUDITS AS PEDAGOGY

Leipzig and More (1982) argued that communication audits bring both a theoretical and pragmatic perspective to the study of organisational communication. In other words, their use creates a testing ground for theories which purport to explain how humans interact within organisations. For this reason, many academics, ourselves included, have used audits as a standard teaching instrument for a number of years.

Three major pedagogic goals have been suggested as being served by the audit (Shelby and Reinsch, 1996):

1 It connects classroom theory to workplace practice. Given the ambitions of most students on organisational communication courses, this connection enhances motivation, participation and learning.
2 The audit requires students to practise communication skills in a real life environment. They must

- seek contact with interested organisations;
- negotiate access;
- secure the co-operation of significant gatekeepers, employees and/or customers;
- implement the audit, having selected the most appropriate technique;
- draft reports;
- make oral presentations.

The learning opportunities from such a range of activities are enormous.
3 Students are normally required to develop and then defend decision recommendations. Their diagnostic, diplomatic and rhetorical skills are sharpened.

A number of steps in integrating audits into the curriculum have been suggested (Conaway, 1994; Shelby and Reinsch, 1996). These are discussed and supplemented by us as follows.

Initiation

Here, the students are formed into audit groups, and required to identify organisations with which they want to work. Barring wholly exceptional circumstances, we insist that they look outside the university environment. This further enhances their ability to negotiate the scope of a given project, persuade people of its benefits and gain access to invaluable real world experience.

Planning

The key aim here is to ensure that projected audits are manageable in size. Small scale studies are normally all that can be realistically accomplished, given the students' limited expertise, time and other resource constraints. We encourage them to identify clearly the subset of the organisation or its external publics to be audited, and delineate the range of topics to be investigated. This analysis will also determine the audit methodology which they employ. Different groups are required to use varied methods. This ensures that whole-class learning can occur, when the feedback stage is reached at the end.

Data collection

This is the 'practice' phase of the audit, in which the methodology is implemented. Typically, we find that students have a tendency to underestimate the difficulties it will bring. Buchanan et al. (1988) discussed the special problems associated with doing research in organisations, and observed regretfully that

> the members of organisations block access to information, constrain the time allowed for interviews, lose your questionnaires, go on holiday, and join other organisations in the middle of your unfinished study. In the conflict between the desirable and the possible, the possible always wins.
>
> (Buchanan et al., 1988, p. 54)

In our experience, most students are comically unprepared for the stresses and strains of real world research, and are unduly dismayed when a wheel falls off their cart. It is also frequently necessary to restrain the over-enthusiasm of some students, who seek to employ so many methods that the organisation would find itself paralysed in an endless round of interviewing, form filling and focus groups, were it to take up their well-intentioned offers of assistance.

Analysis

This is a typical problem-solving phase, during which the data are subject to intense scrutiny. At this point, many students tend to become mesmerised with issues of statistical significance. This results from a veneration of 'hard' data, quickly acquired in a university environment, combined with a panic-stricken conviction that the subject is hideously complex, and far beyond their analytic abilities. Paralysis ensues. The problem is compounded by a tendency to over-focus on problems, rather than on also identifying strengths. As we have discussed throughout this book, a balanced approach on such issues is vital, and the need for this must be communicated to students.

Recommendations and report writing

The difficulty for students here is one shared by experienced auditors. On the one hand, recommendations should be based on best practice standards, and on relevant theory and research. On the other hand, it is also necessary to consider the existing value system of the organisation – and hence what it is capable of. In our experience, students have a tendency to rush their recommendations, by selecting a small sample from what they know of the instructing professor's work, and then trying to apply them irrespective of local circumstances. Most noticeably, they urge a vast increase in information flow (more newsletters; more videos; more team briefing; more everything), without considering the need to target specific information on particular groups through carefully selected channels. The assumption is that one colour scheme suits all houses. In short, what emerges at the end is rarely (on first attempt) calculated to meet the business needs of the organisation with which they have been working. Corrective input, and challenges to the students' perceptions, is essential.

Feedback

This takes two forms. First, we encourage students wherever possible to present their report in writing, and orally, to those they have audited. This lends further 'edge' to the assignment. Second, we require them to present it orally to their colleagues. This ensures that the pros and cons of different methodologies are widely aired, stimulating learning and taking advantage of the competitive instincts of the students, who want to impress their colleagues.

Throughout, clear protocols and guidelines are essential. Students need to be advised of what is expected from them in terms of final reports, presentations, and use of methods. We endorse the view of Shelby and Reinsch (1996), who pointed out that

> the instructor must be willing and able to tolerate ambiguity, fend off anxious questions for which there are not single right answers, require

students to assume direction and responsibility for their own audits, and know when and when not to intervene . . . the instructor must value process above product, while insisting on products that a working professional may read and will find potentially useful.

(Shelby and Reinsch, 1996, p. 107)

Audits as a pedagogic tool offer an invaluable means of exploring many wider issues in organisational communication – e.g. the role of hierarchy, democracy, power and organisational citizenship. Additionally, they equip students with 'hard' real world skills which they can use to sell themselves at interviews. Overall, with some encouragement and assistance, most students respond well to the challenge of utilising communication audits, and derive significant benefits from the process.

CONCLUSION

The central purpose of this book has been to explore research, theory and practice in the field of communication audits. Practitioners, researchers and students of organisational communication can all benefit from a wider use of the audit approach. We have therefore proposed an action framework which integrates audits into the process of developing communication strategies in organisations. We have also illustrated their wider use as research and pedagogic instruments. Earlier chapters in this book outlined many audit tools, and we have made suggestions here designed to help auditors chose from among them.

The main lessons which we think stand out are as follows:

1 *Transforming communication requires time and resources.* There is little point in paying lip service to the need for a positive communication climate, unless this is accepted. No one can compete in a race without making an effort, and being prepared to turn up for regular training sessions.
2 *People generally welcome the opportunity to discuss their own communicative performance.* They also learn, and their performance improves, when this is contrasted with best practice models derived from elsewhere.
3 *A communication strategy should focus overwhelmingly on changing the behaviours of key people.* Mostly, and contrary to popular opinion, it is the deed which is father to the thought, rather than the other way round. A communication strategy should therefore seek to change *behaviour,* in the expectation that *relationships* and *attitudes* will follow.
4 *Feedback is the key.* Open communication without feedback is like a ladder without rungs. It will never move organisations from where they are to where the marketplace tells them they need to be.
5 *Persistence and fresh vision are vital.* There are no 'final solutions.' Keeping the channels of communication in good repair is like painting the Golden Gate Bridge. No matter how much you have done, you have only ever just started.

6 *Measurement is indispensable.* Measure attitudes, measure performance, measure outcomes. Then devise relevant rewards – and measure their impact.

Communication is increasingly recognised as a crucial variable in determining organisational success, and as a vital issue requiring further research. How people interact with each other remains one of the most fascinating and elusive topics to attract study. We discussed a number of research issues earlier in this chapter where audits can be of particular help. As this suggests, there is still so much about which we know so little. The voyage of discovery has barely begun. The methods and tools discussed in this book will facilitate the work of researchers and practitioners prepared to explore the exciting world of human communication, in the still largely unfamiliar territory of organisational life.

Communication Audit Questionnaire

The International Communication Association developed an audit questionnaire in the 1970s, widely piloted in the United States. This questionnaire is discussed in Chapter 3, and alluded to at other points of this book (see, for example, Chapter 10). It is generally regarded as a milestone in the development of organisational communication research instruments. Further work has now been conducted by the editors of this book, using the ICA questionnaire as a basic template, to check its reliability and validity as we enter the new millennium.

As a result, the ICA instrument has been substantially revised. A number of new items have been added at various points, and old ones omitted. For example, when investigating channels the original instrument asked respondents to identify how much information they received about their organisation through various national media. By the same token, given the period during which the instrument was devised, it did not itemise e-mail or the intranet generally. The present questionnaire updates the original in these respects. We have also added more qualitative sections (including our most recent Section 12). The intention is to produce an instrument which continues to yield meaningful quantitative data, while also providing auditors with more of the insights and benefits normally obtained from focus groups and interviews.

We have identified other areas in which the original ICA questionnaire can now be shortened. For example, the original contained many more sections which asked for critical incidents concerning each of the dimensions of communication explored. We have reduced this to one critical incident, designed to secure examples from respondents of an incident which most typifies communication for them in their organisation. In addition, the explanatory guide for respondents which opens the questionnaire describes what follows as a 'staff survey'. Since the 1970s, audits have been extended into many areas of organisational life, and have come to acquire judgemental connotations for many people. In our experience, describing the process in terms of a staff survey carries a reduced feeling of threat and improves response rates.

Having conducted extensive work with the revised instrument a sample of 500 cases was analysed to determine the internal reliability of the items within each section of the questionnaire and also to ascertain the degree of relevance of each item to the overall theme as represented by the section topic. Internal reliability scores for each section were consistently high, with an overall Cronbach's alpha value = 0.84.

STAFF SURVEY

This Questionnaire has been designed in order to find out your views about the effectiveness of communication within [name organisation]. It therefore contains a number of questions relating to the sending and receiving of communication. The purpose of this survey is to allow you to openly and honestly tell us how you feel about the way people communicate with you within the [name organisation].

The Questionnaire is completely confidential, so do not write your name on it. However, to help us carry out a full analysis of the results we would ask you to provide some background information by answering the questions on the next two pages.

For most of the remainder of the questions you are asked simply to select and circle a number which best reflects your opinion regarding a particular issue. Please answer all of the questions.

Finally, there is one open question at the beginning and three at the end of the Questionnaire. These allow you: firstly, to identify strengths and weaknesses in communication; secondly, to describe an actual example of communication within [name organisation]; thirdly to consider the challenges which you think lie ahead; and finally to make suggestions for future communication improvements.

Source: G. Goldhaber, *Organisational Communication, 6/e* (1993), WCB Brown and Benchmark. Reproduced with permission of The McGraw-Hill Companies.

BACKGROUND INFORMATION

This questionnaire is anonymous so please do not write your name on it. However, the following information is necessary to help us analyse the findings in more detail. Please circle the relevant number in each case.

What is your gender?

1. Female
2. Male

What is your age?

1. Under 20 years old
2. 21 to 30 years old
3. 31 to 40 years old
4. 41 to 50 years old
5. Over 50 years old

Do you work:

1. Full-time
2. Part-time
3. Temporary full-time
4. Temporary part-time
5. Job-share

How long have you been employed here?

1. Less than 1 year
2. 1 to 5 years
3. 6 to 10 years
4. 11 to 15 years
5. More than 15 years

How long have you held your present position?

1. Less than 1 year
2. 1 to 5 years
3. 6 to 10 years
4. 11 to 15 years
5. More than 15 years

What is your present level of managerial responsibility?

1. I don't supervise anyone
2. First-line manager
3. Middle manager
4. Senior manager
5. Other (please specify)_____

Where are you employed?

_____

What professional group do you belong to?

1. [List
2. the
3. various
4. professional groups
5. found within
6. the organisation
7. being audited]
8. Other (please specify)_____

How much special training specifically to improve your communication skills have you had?

1. No training at all
2. Little training (attended one seminar/workshop/course)
3. Some training (attended a few seminars/workshops/courses)
4. Extensive training (attended a large number of seminars/workshops/courses)

Section 1: Strengths and weaknesses in communication

List below what for you are the three main strengths in the way people in [name organisation] communicate with you:

1. _____

_____

_____

2. _____

_____

_____

3. _____

_____

_____

List below what for you are the three main weaknesses in the way people in [name organisation] communicate with you:

1. _____

_____

_____

2. _____

_____

_____

3. _____

_____

_____

SECTION 2: How do you feel about the amount of information you are receiving?

KEY FOR SCORING ITEMS:

VL = VERY LITTLE; L = LITTLE; S = SOME; G = GREAT;
VG = VERY GREAT

For each area listed below please *circle* the number which best represents the amount of information you are receiving now and the amount you feel you need to receive to do your job most effectively.

Topic Area	This is the amount of information I receive now					This is the amount of information I need to receive				
	VL	L	S	G	VG	VL	L	S	G	VG
My performance in my job	1	2	3	4	5	1	2	3	4	5
What is expected from me in my job	1	2	3	4	5	1	2	3	4	5
Pay, benefits and conditions	1	2	3	4	5	1	2	3	4	5
Things that go wrong in my organisation	1	2	3	4	5	1	2	3	4	5
Performance appraisal systems	1	2	3	4	5	1	2	3	4	5
How problems which I report in my job are dealt with	1	2	3	4	5	1	2	3	4	5
How decisions that affect my job are reached	1	2	3	4	5	1	2	3	4	5
Promotion opportunities	1	2	3	4	5	1	2	3	4	5
Staff development opportunities	1	2	3	4	5	1	2	3	4	5
How my job contributes to the organisation	1	2	3	4	5	1	2	3	4	5
Specific problems faced by the organisation	1	2	3	4	5	1	2	3	4	5
Major management decisions	1	2	3	4	5	1	2	3	4	5
Important new service/ production developments	1	2	3	4	5	1	2	3	4	5
Improvements in services/ production, or how services/ production are delivered	1	2	3	4	5	1	2	3	4	5
The goals of the organisation	1	2	3	4	5	1	2	3	4	5
The total range of services offered by my organisation	1	2	3	4	5	1	2	3	4	5

SECTION 3: How do you feel about the amount of information you are receiving from the following sources?

KEY FOR SCORING ITEMS:

VL = VERY LITTLE; L = LITTLE; S = SOME; G = GREAT;
VG = VERY GREAT

For each person or source listed below, circle the number that accurately indicates the amount of information you *are* receiving and the amount of information you feel you *need* to receive to be able to your job well.

Source	This is the amount of information I receive now					This is the amount of information I need to receive				
	VL	L	S	G	VG	VL	L	S	G	VG
Staff who are accountable directly to me	1	2	3	4	5	1	2	3	4	5
Immediate work colleagues	1	2	3	4	5	1	2	3	4	5
Colleagues in other departments	1	2	3	4	5	1	2	3	4	5
People in other departments who provide services for your area	1	2	3	4	5	1	2	3	4	5
Immediate line manager	1	2	3	4	5	1	2	3	4	5
Middle managers	1	2	3	4	5	1	2	3	4	5
Senior managers	1	2	3	4	5	1	2	3	4	5
Team briefings	1	2	3	4	5	1	2	3	4	5
Special talks given by middle managers	1	2	3	4	5	1	2	3	4	5
Special talks given by senior managers	1	2	3	4	5	1	2	3	4	5
The grapevine (by random word of mouth)	1	2	3	4	5	1	2	3	4	5

SECTION 4: How much information are you receiving through these channels?

KEY FOR SCORING ITEMS:

VL = VERY LITTLE; L = LITTLE; S = SOME; G = GREAT;
VG = VERY GREAT

The following questions indicate a variety of *channels* through which information is sent to employees. Please circle the responses which accurately represent the amount of information you *are* receiving through that channel now and the amount of information you *need* to receive to do your job most effectively.

Channel	This is the amount of information I receive now					This is the amount of information I need to receive				
	VL	L	S	G	VG	VL	L	S	G	VG
Face-to-face contact between myself and my managers	1	2	3	4	5	1	2	3	4	5
Face-to-face contact among people in my work area	1	2	3	4	5	1	2	3	4	5
Telephone calls from my managers	1	2	3	4	5	1	2	3	4	5
Written communications from my managers (memos, letters, etc.)	1	2	3	4	5	1	2	3	4	5
Policy statements	1	2	3	4	5	1	2	3	4	5
Notice Boards	1	2	3	4	5	1	2	3	4	5
Internal publications (magazine, newsletter, etc.)	1	2	3	4	5	1	2	3	4	5
Internal audio-visual material (videos, films, slides, etc.)	1	2	3	4	5	1	2	3	4	5
With your pay slips	1	2	3	4	5	1	2	3	4	5
E-mail	1	2	3	4	5	1	2	3	4	5
Intranet	1	2	3	4	5	1	2	3	4	5

SECTION 5: How do you feel about the amount of information you are sending?

KEY FOR SCORING ITEMS:

VL = VERY LITTLE; L = LITTLE; S = SOME; G = GREAT;
VG = VERY GREAT

For each topic listed below please circle the number which accurately represents the amount of information you are sending now and the amount you feel you need to send to do your job most effectively.

Topic Area	This is the amount of information I send now					This is the amount of information I need to send				
	VL	L	S	G	VG	VL	L	S	G	VG
Reporting my successes and achievements	1	2	3	4	5	1	2	3	4	5
Reporting problems in my work	1	2	3	4	5	1	2	3	4	5
Expressing my opinions about my job	1	2	3	4	5	1	2	3	4	5
Asking for information essential for my work	1	2	3	4	5	1	2	3	4	5
Giving my opinions about the performance of my immediate manager	1	2	3	4	5	1	2	3	4	5
Requesting clearer work instructions	1	2	3	4	5	1	2	3	4	5
Reporting mistakes or failures that occur in my work area	1	2	3	4	5	1	2	3	4	5

SECTION 6: How do you feel about the action taken on information you are sending?

KEY FOR SCORING ITEMS:

VL = VERY LITTLE; L = LITTLE; S = SOME; G = GREAT;
VG = VERY GREAT

Indicate the amount of *action* that is taken on information you send to the people listed below. Please also indicate the amount of action that you feel *needs* to be taken on this information.

Target People	This is the amount of action taken now					This is the amount of of action needed				
	VL	L	S	G	VG	VL	L	S	G	VG
Staff who are accountable directly to me	1	2	3	4	5	1	2	3	4	5
Immediate work colleagues	1	2	3	4	5	1	2	3	4	5
Colleagues in other departments	1	2	3	4	5	1	2	3	4	5
People in other departments who provide services for your area	1	2	3	4	5	1	2	3	4	5
Immediate line manager	1	2	3	4	5	1	2	3	4	5
Middle managers	1	2	3	4	5	1	2	3	4	5
Senior managers	1	2	3	4	5	1	2	3	4	5

Section 7: How quickly do you get information from the following sources?

KEY FOR SCORING ITEMS:

N = NEVER ON TIME; R = RARELY ON TIME; SOT = SOMETIMES ON TIME; MOT = MOSTLY ON TIME; A = ALWAYS ON TIME

Indicate, by circling the appropriate number, the extent to which information from each of the following is usually *timely* (i.e. you get information when you most need it).

Source	N	R	SOT	MOT	A
Staff who are accountable directly to me	1	2	3	4	5
Immediate work colleagues	1	2	3	4	5
Colleagues in other departments	1	2	3	4	5
People in other departments who provide services for your area	1	2	3	4	5
Immediate line manager	1	2	3	4	5
Middle managers	1	2	3	4	5
Senior managers	1	2	3	4	5

SECTION 8: Working relationships

KEY FOR SCORING ITEMS:

VL = VERY LITTLE; L = LITTLE; S = SOMETIMES; O = OFTEN;
A = ALWAYS

In terms of people in [name organisation], please circle the number which accurately describes how much you trust each of the following in terms of working together.

I trust the following:	VL	L	S	O	A
Staff who are accountable directly to me	1	2	3	4	5
Immediate work colleagues	1	2	3	4	5
Colleagues in other departments	1	2	3	4	5
Immediate line manager	1	2	3	4	5
Middle managers	1	2	3	4	5
Senior managers	1	2	3	4	5

SECTION 9: How much information do you receive on important issues* facing your organisation?

KEY FOR SCORING ITEMS:

VL = VERY LITTLE; L = LITTLE; S = SOME; G = GREAT;
VG = VERY GREAT

There are a number of important issues facing your organisation on which you may be receiving information. For each issue, please circle the number which most accurately indicates how much information you are *receiving now* and the amount of information you feel you *need to receive*.

Topic Area	This is the amount of information I receive now					This is the amount of information I need to receive				
	VL	L	S	G	VG	VL	L	S	G	VG
The current financial climate	1	2	3	4	5	1	2	3	4	5
The impact of everything that is happening on jobs	1	2	3	4	5	1	2	3	4	5
How other bodies buy our services	1	2	3	4	5	1	2	3	4	5
Compulsory Competitive Tendering	1	2	3	4	5	1	2	3	4	5
Training and development opportunities	1	2	3	4	5	1	2	3	4	5
The structure of the organisation	1	2	3	4	5	1	2	3	4	5

SECTION 10: How much information do you send on
important issues* facing your organisation?

KEY FOR SCORING ITEMS:

VL = VERY LITTLE; L = LITTLE; S = SOME; G = GREAT;
VG = VERY GREAT

There are a number of important issues facing your organisation on which you
may be sending information. For each issue, please circle the number which
most accurately indicates how much information you are *sending now* and the
amount of information you feel you *need to send.*

	This is the amount of information I send now					This is the amount of information I need to send				
Topic Area	VL	L	S	G	VG	VL	L	S	G	VG
The current financial climate	1	2	3	4	5	1	2	3	4	5
The impact of everything that is happening on jobs	1	2	3	4	5	1	2	3	4	5
How other bodies buy our services	1	2	3	4	5	1	2	3	4	5
Compulsory Competitive Tendering	1	2	3	4	5	1	2	3	4	5
Training and development opportunities	1	2	3	4	5	1	2	3	4	5
The structure of the organisation	1	2	3	4	5	1	2	3	4	5

Section 11: Communication experience

It would be helpful if you could describe below *one* communication experience in your organisation. This experience should be one which for you is most typical of communication within your organisation. Please answer the questions below and then give a summary of the experience.

To whom does this experience primarily relate? (circle one)

1. Person accountable to me
2. Immediate colleague
3. Immediate line manager
4. Middle manager
5. Senior manager
6. Person in a department which provides services for me

Was the communication (circle one)

1. Effective   2. Ineffective

Describe the communicative experience, what led up to it, what the other person(s) involved did that made her/him an ineffective or effective communicator, and the consequences of what the person did.

_____

_____

_____

_____

_____

_____

_____

_____

_____

_____

_____

_____

_____

SECTION 12: The challenges ahead

1. What do you think is the greatest challenge which faces this organisation during the coming year?

2. What is your own biggest priority in the workplace during the next twelve months?

3. What do you think your managers most expect from you in terms of performance and priorities right now?

Section 13: Suggestions for making communication better

List below three changes in the way people communicate with you which would make communication better in [name organisation]. Be as specific as possible.

1. _____

_____

_____

_____

_____

2. _____

_____

_____

_____

_____

3. _____

_____

_____

_____

_____

THANK YOU FOR COMPLETING THIS OUESTIONNAIRE

*Explanatory note on Sections 9 and 10

Obviously, the issues of most importance at any given time vary from organisation to organisation. We recommend that the senior management group be facilitated by the audit team to identify the top half dozen or so issues which they believe to be of most importance at the time of the audit, and that these be included here. In Sections 9 and 10 we give an example of some issues from a recent audit conducted by us.

References

Abernathy, D. (1998) Intranets: are we there yet? *Training and Development*, 52, 78–79.

Adams, N., Bell, J., Saunders, C. and Whittington, D. (1994) *Communication Skills in Physiotherapist–Patient Interactions*, Jordanstown: University of Ulster.

Agar, M. and McDonald, J. (1995) Focus groups and ethnography. *Human Organization*, 54, 78–86.

Albrecht, T., Burleson, B. and Goldsmith, D. (1994) Supportive communication. In M. Knapp and G. Miller (eds) *Handbook of Interpersonal Communication* (2nd edition), London: Sage.

Allen, M. and Preiss, W. (1998) *Persuasion: Advances Through Meta-Analysis*, London: Sage.

Allen, N.J. and Meyer, J.R. (1990) The measurement and antecedents of affective, continuance and normative commitment to the organisation. *Journal of Occupational Psychology*, 63, 1–18.

Amernic, J. (1992) A case study of corporate financial reporting: Massey-Ferguson's visible accounting decisions 1970–87. *Critical Perspectives on Accounting*, 3, 1–43.

Anderson, C. (1995) The accidental superhighway: a survey of the Internet. *The Economist*, 1 July.

Anderson, L. and Wilson, S. (1997) Critical incident technique. In D. Whetzel and G. Wheaton (eds) *Applied Measurement Methods in Industrial Psychology*. Palo Alto: Davies-Black.

Anderson, N., Hardy, G. and West, M. (1992) Management team innovation. *Management Decision*, 30, 17–21.

Angle, H. and Perry, J. (1981) An empirical assessment of organizational commitment and organizational effectiveness. *Administrative Science Quarterly*, 21, 1–14.

Argyle, M. (1987) *The Psychology of Happiness*. London: Routledge.

Argyle, M. (1994) *The Psychology of Social Class*. London: Routledge.

Argyris, C. (1994) Good communication that blocks learning. *Harvard Business Review*, 72, 77–87.

Argyris, C. (1998) Empowerment: the emperor's new clothes. *Harvard Business Review*, 76, 98–105.

Arnold, W. (1993) The leader's role in implementing quality improvement: walking the talk. *Quality Review Bulletin*, March, 79–82.

Arnott, M. (1987) Effective employee communication. In N. Hart (ed.) *Effective Corporate Relations*. London: McGraw-Hill.

Ashford, S. and Tsui, A. (1991) Self-regulation for managerial effectiveness: the role of active feedback setting. *Academy of Management Journal*, 34, 251–280.

Ashley, M. (1992) The validity of sociometric status. *Educational Research*, 34, 149–154.

Audit Commission (1993) *What Seems to be the Matter: Communication Between Hospitals and Patients*. London: HMSO.

Audit Commission (1994a) *Is Anybody There? Improving Performance in Answering Letters and Telephones*. London: HMSO.

Audit Commission (1994b) *Trusting in the Future: Towards an Audit Agenda for NHS Providers*. London: HMSO.

Badaracco, C. (1988) The politics of communication audits. *Public Relations Quarterly*, Fall, 27–31.

Baig, E. (1994) Ready steady – go on-line. *Business Week/The Information Revolution* (Special Issue), 18 May, 124–133.

Baker, R. (1999) The role of clinical audit in changing performance. In R. Baker, H. Hearnshaw and N. Robertson (eds) *Implementing Change With Clinical Audit*. Chichester: Wiley.

Baker, R., Hearnshaw, H. and Robertson, N. (eds) (1999) *Implementing Change with Clinical Audit*. Chichester: Wiley.

Banach, B. (1998) The best interests of the child: decision-making factors. *Families in Society*, 79, 331–340.

Banister, P., Burman, E., Parker, I., Taylor, M. and Tindall, C. (1994) *Qualitative Methods in Psychology*. Buckingham: Open University Press.

Barrington, G. (1992) Evaluation skills nobody taught me. In A. Vaux, M. Stockdale and M. Schwerin (eds) *Independent Consulting for Evaluators*. Newbury Park, Calif.: Sage.

Barry, B. and Bateman, T. (1992) Perceptions of influence in managerial dyads: the role of hierarchy, media and tactics. *Human Relations*, 45, 555–574.

Bass, L. and Stein, C. (1997) Comparing the structure and stability of network ties using the Social Support Questionnaire and the Social Network List. *Journal of Social and Personal Relationships*, 14, 123–132.

Beck, L., Trombetta, W. and Share, S. (1986) Using focus group sessions before decisions are made. *North Carolina Medical Journal*, 47, 73–74.

Bedien, A. (1980) *Organizations: Theory and Analysis*, Hinsdale, Ill.: The Dryden Press.

Bejou, D., Edvardsson, B. and Rakowski, J. (1996) A critical incident approach to examining the effects of service failures on customer relationships: the case of Swedish and US airlines. *Journal of Travel Research*, 35, 35–40.

Bell, J. (1993) *Doing Your Research Project: A Guide For First-time Researchers in Education and Social Science* (2nd edition). Milton Keynes: Open University Press.

Benn, T. (1992) *The End of an Era: Diaries, 1980–1990* (R. Winstone, ed.). London: Hutchinson.

Berger, B. (1994) Revolution at Whirlpool, *Internal Communication Focus*, November, 8–11.

Berger, C. (1987) Communicating under uncertainty. In M. Roloff and G. Millar (eds) *Interpersonal Processes: New Directions in Communications Research*. London: Sage.

Berry, J. (1992) *Lead Us Not Into Temptation: Catholic Priests and the Sexual Abuse of Children*. New York: Doubleday.

Biere, A. (1998) Solving mystery shopping. *Bank Marketing*, 30, 30–34.

Bland, M. and Jackson, P. (1990) *Effective Employee Communications*. London: Kogan Page.

Blundel, R. (1998) *Effective Business Communication*. London: Prentice-Hall.

Booth, A. (1986) *Communications Audits: A UK Survey*. Leicester: Taylor Graham.

Booth, A. (1988) *The Communications Audit*. Cambridge: Gower.

Bostrom, R.N. (1997) The process of listening. In O.D.W. Hargie (ed.) *The Handbook of Communication Skills* (2nd edition). London: Routledge.

Bowen, D., Gilliland, S. and Folger, R. (1999) HRM and service fairness: how being fair with employees spills over to customers. *Organizational Dynamics*, 27, 7–23.

Bowman, J. and Branchaw, B. (1983) *Business Report Writing*, Chicago: Holt-Saunders.

Breakwell, G.M. and Wood, P. (1995) Diary techniques. In G.M. Breakwell, S. Hammond and C. Fife-Shaw (eds) *Research Methods in Psychology*, London: Sage.

Brenner, M. (1981) Skills in the research interview. In M. Argyle (ed.) *Social Skills and Work*. London: Methuen.

Brewer, A. (1996) Developing commitment between managers and employees. *Journal of Managerial Psychology*, 11, 24–34.

Briner, R. (1998) Feeling and smiling. *The Psychologist*, 12, 16–19.

Brown, R. and Newman, D. (1983) An investigation of the effects of different data presentation formats and order of arguments in a simulated adversary evaluation. *Educational Evaluation and Policy Analysis*, 4, 197–203.

Bryman, A. (1988a) *Quantity and Quality in Social Research*, London: Unwin Hyman.

Bryman, A. (ed.) (1988b) *Doing Research in Organisations*. London: Routledge.

Buchanan, D. and Huczynski, A. (1997) *Organizational Behaviour* (3rd edition), London: Prentice-Hall.

Buchanan, D., Boddy, D. and McCalman, J. (1988) Getting in, getting on, getting out and getting back. In A. Bryman (ed.) *Doing Research in Organisations*. London: Routledge.

Buckingham, L. and Cowe, R. (1999) We'd rather not go to the shops. *The Guardian*, 3 April, 26.

Bukowski, W. and Cillessen, A. (eds) (1998) *Sociometry Then and Now: Building on Six Decades of Measuring Children's Experiences with the Peer Group*. San Francisco: Jossey-Bass.

Burnett, R. (1991) Accounts and narratives. In B. Montgomery and S. Duck (eds) *Studying Interpersonal Interaction*. London: Guilford Press.

Burnside, A. (1994) In-store spies snuff out poor service. *Marketing*, 28 April, 32–33.

Cairncross, F. (1998) *The Death of Distance: How The Communications Revolution Will Change Our Lives*. London: Orion Business Books.

Calder, B. (1980) Focus group interviews and qualitative research in organizations. In E. Lawer, D. Nadler and C. Cammann (eds) *Organizational Assessment: Perspectives on the Measurement of Organizational Behavior and the Quality of Work Life*. New York: Wiley.

Campbell, M. (1982) The business communications audit: evaluating and improving business communications. *Montana Business Quarterly*, 20, 15–18.

Campion, M.A., Palmer, D.K. and Campion, J.E. (1997) A review of structure in the selection interview. *Personnel Psychology*, 50, 655–702.

Carey, M. (1995) Issues and applications of focus groups: introduction. *Journal of Qualitative Health Research*, 5, 413.

Cascio, W. (1982) *Costing Human Resources: The Financial Impact of Behavior in Organizations*. Boston: Kent.

Caves, R. (1988) Consultative methods for extracting expert knowledge about professional competence. In R. Ellis (ed.) *Professional Competence and Quality Assurance in the Caring Professions*. London: Croom Helm.

Caywood, C. (1998) Taking an outside-in approach. *Strategic Communication Management*, February–March, 21.

Chamine, S. (1998) Making your intranet an effective HR tool. *Human Resources Focus*, 75, 11–12.

Charns, M. and Tewksbury, L. (1993) *Collaborative Management in Health Care: Implementing the Integrative Organization*. San Francisco: Jossey-Bass.

Cheek, J., O'Brien, B., Ballantyne, A. and Pincombe, J. (1997) Using critical incident technique to inform aged and extended care nursing. *Western Journal of Nursing Research*, 19, 667–682.

Cheney, G., Straub, J., Speirs-Glebe, L., Stohl, C., DeGooyer, D., Whalen, S., Garvin-Doxas, K. and Carlone, D. (1998) Democracy, participation, and communication at work: a multidisciplinary perspective. In M. Roloff and G. Paulson (eds) *Communication Yearbook* (Vol. 21). New York: Sage.

Chisnall, P. (1997) *Marketing Research* (5th edition). Maidenhead: McGraw-Hill.

Cialdini, R. (1993) *Influence: Science and Practice* (3rd edition). New York: HarperCollins.

Clair, R.P. (1994) Resistance and oppression as a self-contained opposite: an organizational communication analysis of one man's story of sexual harassment. *Western Journal of Communication*, 58, 235–262.

Clampitt, P. (1991) *Communicating for Managerial Effectiveness*. Newbury Park, Calif.: Sage Publications.

Clampitt, P. and Berk, L. (1996) Strategically communicating organisational change. *Journal of Communication Management*, 1, 15–28.

Clampitt, P. and Downs, C. (1993) Employee perceptions of the relationship between communication and productivity: a field study. *Journal of Business Communication*, 30, 5–28.

Clampitt, P. and Girard, D. (1987) Time for reflection: a factor analytic study of the communication satisfaction instrument. Paper presented at the ICA Convention.

Clampitt, P. and Girard, D. (1993) Communication satisfaction: a useful construct? *New Jersey Journal of Communication*, 1, 84–102.

Clayton, M. (1997) Delphi: a technique to harness expert opinion for critical decision-making tasks in education. *Educational Psychology*, 17, 373–386.

Cobb, R. (1997) Isn't it just common sense? *Marketing*, 31 July, S16–18.

Cohen, J. (1960) A coefficient of agreement for nominal scales. *Educational and Psychological Measurement*, 20, 37–46.

Cohen, L. and Manion, L. (1980) *Research Methods in Education*. London: Croom Helm.

Coles, M. (1999) E-mail gossip lands companies in court. *The Sunday Times (Appointments Section)*, 28 February, 22.

Collins, M. (1997) Interviewer variability: a review of the problem. *Journal of the Market Research Society*, 39, 69–84.

Colville, I., Waterman, R. and Weick, K. (1999) Organizing and the search for excellence: making sense of the times in theory and practice. *Organization*, 6, 129–148.

Conaway, R. (1994) The communication audit as a class project. *The Bulletin of Association for Business Communication*, 57, 39–43.

Congor, J. (1998) The necessary art of persuasion. *Harvard Business Review*, 76, 85–95.

Consumers' Association (1991) Pharmacists. How reliable are they? *Which? Way to Health*, December, 191–194.

Cook, P. (1991) Communicating bad news to employees. *Compensation and Benefits Review*, 23, 13–20.

Cooper, N. and Stevenson, C. (1998) 'New science' and psychology. *The Psychologist*, October, 484–485.

Cortese, A. (1997) A way out of the web maze. *Business Week*, 17 February.

Cox, A. and Thompson, I. (1998) On the appropriateness of benchmarking. *Journal of General Management*, 23, 1–20.

Cox, K., Bergen, A. and Norman, I. (1993) Exploring consumer views of care provided by the Macmillan nurse using the critical incident technique. *Journal of Advanced Nursing*, 18, 408–415.

Coyne, J. and Calarco, M. (1995) Effects of the experience of depression: application of focus group and survey methodologies. *Psychiatry – Interpersonal and Biological Processes*, 58, 149–163.

Cramp, B. (1994) Industrious espionage. *Marketing*, 18 August, 17–18.

Crampton, S., Hodge, J. and Mishra, J. (1998) The informal communication network: factors influencing grapevine activity. *Public Personnel Management*, 27, 569–584.

Crino, M.D. and White, M.C. (1981) Satisfaction in communication: an examination of the Downs–Hazen measure. *Psychological Reports*, 49, 831–838.

Cronin, M. (1998) Ford's intranet success. *Fortune*, 137, 158.

Dalkey, N. and Helmer, O. (1963) An experimental application of the Delphi method to the use of experts. *Management Science*, 9, 458–467.

Davidson, P., Merritt-Gray, M., Buchanan, J. and Noel, J. (1997) Voices from practice: mental health nurses identify research priorities. *Archives of Psychiatric Nursing*, 11, 340–345.

Davis, K. (1953) A method of studying communication patterns in organizations. *Personnel Psychology*, 6, 301–312.

Dawes, R. (1994) *House of Cards: Psychology and Psychotherapy Built on Myth*. New York: Free Press.

Dawson, J. and Hillier, J. (1995) Competitor mystery shopping: methodological considerations and implications for the MRS Code of Conduct. *Journal of the Market Research Society*, 37, 417–427.

Dawson-Sheperd, A. and White, J. (1994) Communication: why UK managers are shooting themselves in the foot. *Business News*, May, 6.

Day, J., Dean, A. and Reynolds, P. (1998) Relationship marketing: its key role in entrepreuneurship. *Long Range Planning*, 31, 828–837.

Deetz, S. (1995) *Transforming Communication, Transforming Business: Building Responsive and Responsible Workplaces*. Cresskill, NJ: Hampton Press.

Dennis, H. (1975) The construction of a managerial communication climate inventory for use in complex organizations. Paper at the annual convention of the International Communication Association, Chicago.

Denzin, N. and Lincoln, Y. (1998) Introduction: entering the field of qualitative research. In N. Denzin and Y. Lincoln (eds) *Collecting and Interpreting Qualitative Material*. Thousand Oaks, Calif.: Sage.

de Ruyter, K. (1996) Focus versus nominal group interviews. *Marketing Intelligence and Planning*, 14, 44–51.

DeWine, S. and James, A. (1988) Examining the communication audit: assessment and modification. *Management Communication Quarterly*, 2, 144–168.

DeWine, S., James, A.C. and Walance, W. (1985) Validation of organizational communication audit instruments. Paper presented at the International Communication Association convention, Honolulu.

Dickson, D., Hargie, O. and Morrow, N. (1997) *Communication Skills Training for Health Professionals* (2nd edition). London: Chapman and Hall.

Dickson, D., Saunders, C. and Stringer, M. (1993) *Rewarding People: The Skill of Responding Positively*. London: Routledge.

Dillon, J. (1997) Questioning. In O.D.W. Hargie (ed.) *The Handbook of Communication Skills* (2nd edition). London: Routledge.

Donohue, W. and Kolt, R. (1992) *Managing Interpersonal Conflict*. London: Sage.

Doucouliagos, C. (1995) Worker participation and productivity in labor-managed and participatory capitalist forms: a meta-analysis. *Industrial and Labor Relations Review*, 49, 58–77.

Dowling, G. (1994) *Corporate Reputations*. London: Kogan Page.

Downs, C. (1988) *Communication Audits*. Glenview, Ill.: Scott, Foresman.

Downs, C. and Hazen, M.D. (1977) A factor analytic study of communication satisfaction. *Journal of Business Communication* 14, 63–73.

Downs, C., Clampitt, P. and Laird, A. (1981) Critique of the ICA communication audit. Paper presented to the International Communication Association, Minneapolis, May.

Downs, C., DeWine, S. and Greenbaum, H. (1994) Measures of organizational communication. In R. Rubin, P. Palmgreen and H. Sypher (eds) *Communication Research Measures: A Sourcebook*. New York: Guilford Press.

Dowrick, P. (1991) *Practical Guide to Using Video in the Behavioral Sciences*. New York: Wiley.

Duck, S. (1991) Diaries and logs. In B. Montgomery and S. Duck (eds) *Studying Interpersonal Interaction*. New York: Guilford Press.

Dunn, P.J. (1990) *Priesthood: A Re-examination of the Roman Catholic Theology of the Presbyterate*. New York: Alban House.

Dunn, W. and Hamilton, D. (1986) The critical incident technique: a brief guide. *Medical Teacher*, 8, 207–215.

Eden, D. (1993) Interpersonal expectations in organisations. In P. Blanck (ed.) *Interpersonal Expectations: Theory, Research and Applications*. Cambridge: Cambridge University Press.

Edwards, J., Thomas, M., Rosenfeld, P. and Booth-Kewley, S. (1997) *How to Conduct Organizational Surveys: A Step-by-step Guide*, London: Sage.

Egan, A., Jones, S., Luloff, A. and Finley, J. (1995) Value of using multiple methods: an illustration using survey, focus group and Delphi techniques. *Society and Natural Resources*, 8, 457–465.

Ellis, D., Barker, R., Potter, S. and Pridgeon, C. (1993) Information audits, communication audits and information mapping. *International Journal of Information Management*, 13, 134–151.

Emmanuel, M. (1985) Auditing communication practices. In C. Reuss and R. DiSilvas (eds) *Inside Organisational Communication* (2nd edition). New York: Longman.

Emory, C. and Cooper, D. (1991) *Business Research Methods*. Burr Ridge, Ill.: Irwin.

Ericsson, K. and Smith, J. (eds) (1991) *Toward a General Theory of Expertise*. Cambridge: Cambridge University Press.

Ettorre, B. (1997) How to get the unvarnished truth. *HR Focus*, 74, 1–3.

Falcione, R., Sussman, L. and Herden, R. (1987) Communication climate in organizations. In F. Jablin, L. Putnam, L. Roberts and L. Porter (eds) *Handbook of Organizational Communication*. Newbury Park, Calif.: Sage.

Fink, A. (1995) *The Survey Kit*. Thousand Oaks, Calif.: Sage.

Flanagan, J.C. (1948) Contributions of research in the Armed Forces to personnel psychology. *Personnel Psychology*, 1, 52–53.

Flanagan, J.C. (1954) The critical incident technique. *Psychological Bulletin*, 5, 327–358.

Fletcher, B (1995) Not just a room with a view. *Marketing*, 23 March, 27–29.

Fletcher, J. (1992) Ethical issues in the selection interview. *Journal of Business Ethics*, 11, 361–367.

Fly, B., van Bark, W., Weinman, L., Kitchener, K. and Lang, P. (1997) Ethical transgressions of psychology graduate students: critical incidents with implications for training. *Professional Psychology: Research and Practice*, 28, 492–495.

Flynn, G. (1998) Why employees are so angry. *Workforce*, September, 26–32.

Fontana, A. and Frey, J. (1998) Interviewing: the art of science. In N. Denzin and Y. Lincoln (eds) *Collecting and Interpreting Qualitative Data*. Thousand Oaks, Calif.: Sage.

Ford, M. (1999) *Surveillance and Privacy at Work*. London: Institute of Employment Rights.

Fowler, F.J. and Mangione, T.W. (1990) *Standardized Survey Interviewing: Minimizing Interviewer-related Type Error*. Applied Social Research Methods Series Volume 18. Newbury Park, Calif.: Sage.

Francis, L. and Jones, S. (1996) *Psychological Perspectives on Christian Ministry*. Leominster: Gracewing Fowler Wright Books.

Frank, A. and Brownell, J. (1989) *Organisational Communication and Behaviour*. New York: Holt, Rinehart and Winston.

Frey, J.H. (1989) *Survey Research by Telephone* (2nd edition), Newbury Park, Calif.: Sage.

Gaber, I. (1996) Hocus-pocus polling: you can get any result you want from a focus group. That doesn't mean it will be right. *New Statesman*, 125, 20–22.

Gable, G. (1994) Integrating case study and survey research methods: an example in information systems. *European Journal of Information Systems*, 3, 112–126.

Gabriel, Y. (1998) The use of stories. In G. Symon and C. Cassell (eds) *Qualitative Methods and Analysis in Organizational Research. A Practical Guide*. London: Sage.

Gadher, D. (1999) Smile, you're on 300 candid cameras. *The Sunday Times*, 14 February, 5.

Gaiser, T. (1997) Conducting on-line focus groups: a methodological discussion. *Social Science Computer Review*, 15, 143–144.

Garbazani, A., Haas, A. and O'Brien, M. (1996) Trends in the corporate network: a user survey. *Telecommunications*, December.

Gaska, A. and Frey, D. (1996) Occupation-determined role relationships. In A. Auhagen and M. von Salisch (eds) *The Diversity of Human Relationships*. Cambridge: Cambridge University Press.

Ghoshal, S., Korine, H. and Szulanski, G. (1994) Interunit communication in multinational corporations. *Management Science*, 40, 96–110.

Gildea, J. and Rosenberg, K. (1979) Auditing organizational communications: is there life beyond print-outs? *University of Michigan Business Review*, 41, 7–12.

Gladstone, B. (1998) The medium is the message: when old paradigm meets new technology. *Journal of General Management*, 24, 51–58.

Goldhaber, G. (1976) The ICA communication audit: rationale and development. Paper presented at the Academy of Management convention, Kansas City.

Goldhaber, G. (1993) *Organizational Communication* (6th edition). Madison, Wis.: WCB Brown and Benchmark.

Goldhaber, G. and Krivonos, P. (1977) The ICA communication audit: process, status, and critique. *Journal of Business Communication*, 15, 41–64.

Goldhaber, G.M. and Rogers, D.P. (1979) *Auditing Organizational Communication Systems: The ICA Communication Audit*, Dubuque, Ia: Kendall/Hunt.

Goldman, E. and McDonald, S. (1987) *The Group Depth Interview: Principles and Practice*. Englewood Cliffs, NJ.: Prentice-Hall.

Goldsmith, W. and Clutterbuck, D. (1997) *The Winning Streak Mark II*. London: Orion Business Books.

Gorden, R.L. (1987) *Interviewing: Strategies, Techniques and Tactics* (4th edition). Homewood, Ill.: Dorsey Press.

Gray, P. (1997) How to become intranet savvy. *HR Magazine*, 42, 66–71.

Green, S.M. (1992) Total systems intervention: organizational communication in North Yorkshire Police. *Systems Practice*, 5, 585–599.

Greenbaum, H. and White, N. (1976) Biofeedback at the organisational level: the communication audit. *Journal of Business Communication*, 13, 3–15.

Greenbaum, H., Clampitt, P. and Willihnganz, S. (1988) Organizational communication: an examination of four instruments. *Management Communication Quarterly*, 2, 245–282.

Greenbaum, T. (1987) *The Practical Handbook and Guide to Focus Group Research*. Lexington, Mass.: Lexington Books.

Greenbaum, T. (1991) Outside moderators maximise focus group results. *Public Relations Journal*, 47, 31–33.

Greenbaum, T. (1993) Don't lose focus! Tips for effective focus groups. *Bank Marketing*, 25, 38–40.

Greenbaum, T. (1994) Focus group research: a useful tool. *HR Focus*, 71, 3.

Greenbaum, T. (1998) *The Handbook for Focus Group Research*. Thousand Oaks, Calif.: Sage.

Greenberg, J. and Baron, R.B. (1995) *Behavior in Organizations: Understanding and Managing the Human Side of Work* (5th edition). Englewood Cliffs, N.J.: Prentice-Hall.

Greengard, S. (1998) Achieving greater intranet efficiency. *Workforce*, 77, 72–76.

Grove, S. and Fisk, R. (1997) The impact of other customers on service experiences: a critical incident examination of 'getting along'. *Journal of Retailing*, 73, 63–85.

Gummeson, E. (1991) *Qualitative Methods in Management Research*. London: Sage.

Gumpert, G. and Drucker, S. (1998) The demise of privacy in a private world: from front porches to chat rooms. *Communication Theory*, 8, 408–425.

Hague, P. and Jackson, P. (1995) *Do Your Own Market Research* (2nd edition). London: Kogan Page.

Hallowell, E. (1999) The human moment at work. *Harvard Business Review*, 77, 58–70.

Hamm, S. and Stephanek, M. (1999) From reengineering to e-engineering. *Business Week*, 22 March, EB14.

Hanson, G. (1986) Determinants of firm performance: an integration of economic and organizational factors. Unpublished doctoral dissertation, University of Michigan Business School.

Hargie, O.D.W. (1997) Interpersonal communication: a theoretical framework. In O.D.W. Hargie (ed.) *The Handbook of Communication Skills* (2nd edition). London: Routledge.

Hargie, O. and Tourish, D. (1993) Assessing the effectiveness of communication in organisations: the communication audit approach. *Health Services Management Research*, 6, 276–285.

Hargie, O. and Tourish, D. (1994) Communication skills training: management manipulation or personal development? *Human Relations*, 47, 1377–1389.

Hargie, O. and Tourish, D. (1996a) Auditing communication practices to improve the management of human resources: a regional study. *Health Services Management Research*, 9, 209–222.

Hargie, O. and Tourish, D. (1996b) Auditing internal communication to build business success. *Internal Communication Focus*, November, 10–14.

Hargie, O. and Tourish, D. (1999a) The psychology of interpersonal skill. In A. Memon and R. Bull (eds) *Handbook of the Psychology of Interviewing*. Chichester: Wiley.

Hargie, O. and Tourish, D. (1999b) Internal communications and the management of change. In R. Baker, H. Hearnshaw and N. Robertson (eds) *Implementing Change with Clinical Audit*. Chichester: Wiley.

Hargie, O., Dickson, D. and Tourish, D. (1999) *Communication in Management*. Aldershot: Gower.

Hargie, O.D.W., Morrow, N.C. and Woodman, C. (1992) Consumer perceptions of and attitudes to community pharmacy services. *Pharmaceutical Journal*, 249, 688–691.

Hargie, O., Morrow, N. and Woodman, C. (1993) *Looking into Community Pharmacy: Identifying Effective Communication Skills in Pharmacist–Patient Consultations*, Jordanstown: University of Ulster.

Hargie, O., Saunders, C. and Dickson, D. (1994) *Social Skills in Interpersonal Communication* (3rd edition). London: Routledge.

Hargie, O.D.W., Dickson, D., Boohan, M. and Hughes, K. (1998) A survey of communication skills training in UK schools of medicine: present practices and prospective proposals. *Medical Education*, 32, 25–34.

Harrison, S., Hunter, D. and Pollitt, C. (1990) *The Dynamics of British Health Policy*. London: Unwin Hyman.

Hart, G. (1996) Making the grapevine bear fruit: developing communication competence. *Journal of Communication Management*, 1, 95–101.

Hartline, M. and Ferrell, O. (1996) The management of customer-contact service employees. *Journal of Marketing*, 60, 7–26.

Haywood, R. (1991) *All About Public Relations* (2nd edition). London: McGraw-Hill.

Hecht, M.L. (1978) Measures of communication satisfaction. *Human Communication Research*, 4, 350–368.

Helmer, O. and Rescher, N. (1959) On the epistemology of the inexact sciences. *Management Science*, 6, 25–52.

Hennink, M. and Diamond, I. (1999) Using focus groups in social research. In A. Memon and R. Bull (eds) *Handbook of the Psychology of Interviewing*. Chichester: John Wiley.

Henwood, K. and Pidgeon, N. (1995) Grounded theory and psychological research. *The Psychologist*, 8, 115–118.

Hibbs, J. (1999) E-mail puts diplomatic relations on fast track. *Daily Telegraph*, 15 March, 6.

Hilpern, K. (1999) Heat of the moment. *Independent on Sunday*, 14 March, 11.

HMSO (1996) *The National Health Service: A Service with Ambitions*. London: HMSO.

Hofstede, G. (1998) Attitudes, values and organizational culture: disentangling the concepts. *Organization Studies*, 19, 477–492.

Holbert, N. and Speece, M. (1993) *Practical Market Research: An Integrated Global Perspective*. London: Prentice-Hall.

Hopfl, H. (1992) The making of the corporate acolyte: some thoughts on charismatic leadership and the reality of organizational commitment. *Journal of Management Studies*, 29, 23–33.

Hougaard, S. and Duus, H. (1999) Competing in the digital age. *Journal of General Management*, 24, 67–69.

Houtkoop-Steenstra, H. (1996) Probing behaviour of interviewers in the standardised semi-open research interview. *Quality and Quantity*, 30, 205–230.

Houtz, J. and Weinerman, I. (1997) Teachers' perceptions of effective preparation to teach. *Psychological Reports*, 80, 966–961.

Hurst, B. (1991) *The Handbook of Communication Skills*. London: Kogan Page.

Hutton, J. (1996) Making the connection between public relations and marketing. *Journal of Communication Management*, 1, 37–48.

Integralis Survey (1999) E-mail gossips cost businesses millions. *Belfast Telegraph*, 16 March, 8.

Irwin, A. (1998) Calls to mobile phones 'a rip off'. *Daily Telegraph*, 6 March, 6.

Irwin, A. (1999) 'Brain strain' risk for telephone staff. *Daily Telegraph*, 6 January, 6.

Jacobs, M., Jacobs, A., Feldman, G. and Cavior, N. (1973) The 'credibility gap': delivery of positive and negative emotional and behavioural feedback in groups. *Journal of Consulting and Clinical Psychology*, 41, 215–223.

Jagoda, A. and de Villepin, M. (1993) *Mobile Communications*. Chichester: Wiley.

Jeffery, G., Hache, G. and Lehr, R. (1995) A group-based Delphi application: defining rural career counselling needs. *Measurement and Evaluation in Counseling and Development*, 28, 45–60.

Jenkins, D. (1996) A reflecting team approach to family therapy: A delphi study. *Journal of Marital and Family Therapy*, 22, 219–238.

Jennings, C., McCarthy, W. and Undy, R. (1990) *Employee Relations Audits*. London: Routledge.

Jewler, A.J. (1996). *Creative Strategy in Advertising*. Belmont, Calif.: Wadsworth.

Johnson, H. (1993) Training 101: another look at employee surveys. *Training and Development*, July, 15–18.

Johnston, R. (1995) The determinants of service quality: satisfiers and dissatisfiers. *International Journal of Service Industry Management*, 6, 53–71.

Jones. E. (1990) *Interpersonal Perception*. New York: Freeman.

Jones, H. (1998) Lost focus. *Campaign*, 4 September, 43.

Jones, T. (1997) Create the write impression. *Special Supplement: Communicating With Your Customer. The Times*, 18 February, 8.

Kanter, R. (1983) *The Change Masters: Innovation and Entrepreuneurship in the American Corporation*. New York: Simon and Schuster.

Kanter, R. (1988) Three tiers for innovation research. *Communication Research*, 15, 509–523.

Kanter, R. (1991) Change-master skills: what it takes to be creative. In J. Henry and D. Walker (eds) *Managing Innovation*. London: Sage.

Kao, J. (1995). *Managing Creativity*. Englewood Cliffs, NJ.: Prentice-Hall.

Karger, T. (1987) Focus groups are for focusing, and for little else. *Marketing News*, 28 August, 52–55.

Keaveney, S. (1995) Customer switching behavior in service industries: an exploratory study. *Journal of Marketing*, 59, 71–82.

Kehoe, L. (1996) Big rise in hacker break-ins. *The Financial Times*, 3 July (Information technology review section).

Kennedy, D. (1998) Millions call for privacy. *The Times* (London), 14 February, 10.

Kent, G., Wills, G., Faulkner, A., Parry, G. *et al.* (1996) Patient reactions to met and unmet psychological need: a critical incident analysis. *Patient Education and Counseling*, 28, 187–190.

Kent, K. (1996) Communication as a core management discipline. *Journal of Communication Management*, 1, 29–36.

Kiesler, S. (1986) Thinking ahead. *Harvard Business Review*, 64, 46–60.

King, N. (1994) The qualitative research interview. In C. Cassell and G. Symon (eds) *Qualitative Methods in Organizational Research. A Practical Guide*. London: Sage.

King, N. (1998) Template analysis. In G. Symon and C. Cassell (eds) *Qualitative Methods and Analysis in Organizational Research. A Practical Guide*. London: Sage.

King, N., Bailey, J. and Newton, P. (1994) Analysing general practitioners' referral decisions. 1 Developing an analytical framework. *Family Practice*, 11, 3–8.

Kippendorf, K. (1980) *Content Analysis: An Introduction to its Methodology*. Beverly Hills, Calif.: Sage.

Knodel, J. (1993) The design and analysis of focus group studies: a practical approach. In D. Morgan (ed.) *Successful Focus Groups: Advancing the State of the Art*. Newburns Park, Calif.: Sage.

Knodel, J., Havanon, N. and Pramualratana, A. (1984) Fertility transition in Thailand: a qualitative analysis. *Population and Development Review*, 10, 297–328.

Koehly, L. and Shivey, V. (1998) Social network analysis: a new methodology for counseling research. *Journal of Counseling Psychology*, 45, 3–17.

Kopec, J. (1982) The communication audit. *Public Relations Journal*, 39, 24–27.

Kotter, J. (1982) *The General Managers*. New York: Free Press.

Kramlinger, T. (1998) How to deliver a change message. *Training and Development*, April, 44–47.

Kreps, G.L. (1990) *Organizational Communication*. London: Longman.

Krueger, R. (1986) Focus group interviewing: a helpful technique for agricultural education. *The Visitor*, 73, 1–4.

Krueger, R. (1988) *Focus Groups: A Practical Guide for Applied Research* (1st edition). Newbury Park, Calif.: Sage.

Krueger, R. (1994) *Focus Groups: A Practical Guide for Applied Research* (2nd edition). Thousand Oaks, Calif.: Sage.

Krueger, R. (1998a) *Developing Questions for Focus Groups*. Thousand Oaks, Calif.: Sage.

Krueger, R. (1998b) *Moderating Focus Groups*. Thousand Oaks, Calif.: Sage.

Krueger, R. (1998c) *Analyzing and Reporting Focus Group Results*. Thousand Oaks, Calif.: Sage.

Lammers, J. (1994) The organizational climate of hospitals: sectional and national differences. Paper presented at the Annual International Communication Association Conference, Sydney, Australia.

Lanigan, D. (1997) The focus group groupies. *Campaign*, 26 September, 36–37.

Lauer, L. (1996) Are you using the power of assessments and audits? *Nonprofit World*, 14, 43–47.

Lee, T. (1999) *Using Qualitative Methods in Organizational Research*. Thousand Oaks, Calif.: Sage.

Leeds, B. (1992) Mystery shopping offers clues to quality service. *Bank Marketing*, 24, 24–26.

Leeds, B. (1995) Mystery shopping: from novelty to necessity. *Bank Marketing*, 27, 17–21.

Leipzig, J. and More, E. (1982) Organisational communication: a review and analysis of three current approaches to the field. *Journal of Business Communication*, 19, 78–89.

Lewis, D. (1992) Communicating organisational culture. *Australian Journal of Communication*, 19, 47–57.

Lewis, D. (1997) *Shaming, Blaming and Flaming: Corporate Miscommunication on the Information Age*. Bracknell: Novell.

Lewis, L. and Seibold, D. (1998) Reconceptualising organisational change implementation as a communication problem: a review of literature and research agenda. In M. Roloff and G. Paulson (eds) *Communication Yearbook* (Vol. 21). New York: Sage.

Lindenmann, W. (1998) Only PR outcomes count – that is the real bottom line. *Journal of Communication Management*, 3, 66–73.

Linstone, H. and Turoff, M. (1975) *The Delphi Method: Techniques and Applications*. Reading, Mass.: Addison-Wesley.

Lockshin, L. and McDougall, G. (1998) Service problems and recovery strategies: an examination of the critical incident technique in a business-to-business market. *International Journal of Retail and Distribution Management*, 26, 429–438.

Lount, M. (1997) Interpersonal communication processes in the pastoral ministry of Catholic clergy. Unpublished D.Phil. thesis, University of Ulster, Magee College, Londonderry.

Lount, M. and Hargie, O. (1997) The priest as counsellor: an investigation of critical incidents in the pastoral work of Catholic priests. *Counselling Psychology Quarterly*, 10, 259–271.

Lount, M. and Hargie, O. (1998) Preparation for the priesthood: a training need analysis. *Journal of Vocational Education and Training*, 50, 61–77.

Lucius, R. and Kuhnert, K. (1997) Using sociometry to predict team performance in the work place. *Journal of Psychology*, 131, 21–32.

Lunt, P. and Livingstone, S. (1996) Rethinking the focus group in media and communication research. *Journal of Communication*, 46, 79–98.

Luthans, F. and Larsen, J. (1986) How managers really communicate. *Human Relations*, 39, 161–178.

Lydecker, T. (1986) Focus group dynamics. *Associate Management*, 38, 73–78.

Mabrito, M. (1997) Writing on the front line: a study of workplace writing. *Business Communication Quarterly*, 60, 58–70.

MacErlean, N. (1997) How to deal with rudeness on the telephone. *The Observer* (London), 31 October.

Macht, J. (1998) The new market research. *Inc.*, 20, 86–93.

McKeans, P. (1990) GM division builds a classic system to share internal information. *Public Relations Journal*, 46, 24–41.

McKenna, H. (1994) The Delphi technique: a worthwhile research approach for nursing? *Journal of Advanced Nursing*, 19, 1221–1225.

McKenna, B. and Thomas, G. (1997). A survey of recent technical writing textbooks. *Journal of Technical Writing and Communication*, 27(4), 441–452.

Malby, R. (1995a) Getting started on audit. In R. Malby (ed.) *Clinical Audit for Nurses and Therapists*. London: Scutari Press.

Malby, R. (1995b) The whys and wherefores of audit. In R. Malby (ed.) *Clinical Audit for Nurses and Therapists*. London: Scutari Press.

Management Decisions Systems (1993) *Employee Surveys: Current and Future Practices*. Darien, Conn.: MDS.

Management Development Group (1992) *Reviewing Communication: A Guide for Co-ordinators*. Edinburgh: MDG.

Manfredi, C., Lacey, L., Warnecke, R. and Balch, G. (1997) Method effects in survey and focus group findings: understanding smoking cessation in low-SES African American women. *Health Education and Behaviour*, 24, 786–800.

Marinker, M. (1986) Performance review and professional values. In D. Pendleton, T. Schofield and M. Marinker (eds) *In Pursuit of Quality: Approaches to Performance Review in General Practice*. Exeter, Devon: Royal College of General Practitioners.

Markar, T. and Mahadeshwar, S. (1998) Audit on communication between general practitioners and psychiatrists following an initial outpatient assessment of patients with learning disabilities. *British Journal of Developmental Disabilities*, 44, 38–41.

Market Research Society (1997) *Best Practice in Mystery Customer Research*. London: MRS.

Mason, J. (1996) *Qualitative Researching*. London: Sage.

Mavis, B. and Brocato, J. (1998) Postal surveys versus electronic mail surveys: the tortoise and the hare revisited. *Evaluation and the Health Professions*, 21, 395–408.

Mead, R. (1990) *Cross-cultural Management Comunication*. Chichester: Wiley.

Meehan, H. (1979) *Learning Lessons: Social Organization in the Classroom*. Cambridge, Mass.: Harvard University Press.

Merton, R. (1987) The focussed interview and focus groups: continuities and discontinuities. *Public Opinion Quarterly*, 51, 550–566.

Merton, R., Fiske, M. and Kendall, P. (1990) *The Focused Interview*. New York: Free Press.

Messe, L., Kerr, N. and Sattler, D. (1992) 'But some animals are more equal than others': the supervisor as a privileged status in group contexts. In S. Worchel, W. Wood and J. Simpson (eds) *Group Process and Productivity*. London: Sage.

Meyer, H. (1997) Health care Mata Hari. *Hospitals and Health Networks*, 71, 46–48.

Meyer, J. and Allen, N. (1997) *Commitment in the Workplace*. London: Sage.

Miles, L. (1993) Rise of the mystery shopper. *Marketing*, July, 19–20.

Millar, R. and Gallagher, M. (1997) The selection interview. In O. Hargie (ed.) *The Handbook of Communication Skills* (2nd edition). London: Routledge.

Millar, R., Crute, V. and Hargie, O. (1992) *Professional Interviewing*. London: Routledge.

Miller, K., Hartman-Ellis, B., Zook, E. and Lyles, J. (1990) An integrated model of communication, stress and burnout in the workplace. *Communication Research*, 17, 300–326.

Miller, R. (1998) Undercover shopping. *Marketing*, May, 27–29.

Millward, L. (1995) Focus groups. In G. Breakwell, S. Hammond and C. Fife-Schaw (eds) *Research Methods in Psychology*. London: Sage.

Milne, S. (1999) Call to regulate growth in workplace 'spying'. *Guardian*, 18 February, 9.

Mintzberg, H. (1973) *The Nature of Managerial Work*. New York: Harper and Row.

Mintzberg, H. (1989) *Mintzberg on Management*. New York: The Free Press.

Mintzberg, H. (1993) The pitfalls of strategic planning. *California Management Review*, 5, 42–47.

Mintzberg, H. (1994) *The Rise and Fall of Strategic Planning*. New York: Prentice-Hall.

Mintzberg, H. (1996) Musings on management. *Harvard Business Review*, 74, 61–67.

Montgomery, B. and Duck, S. (eds) (1991) *Studying Interpersonal Interaction*. London: Guildford Press.

Moorhead, G. and Griffin, R. (1986) *Organisational Behaviour*. London: Houghton Mifflin.

Moreno, J. (1953) *Who Shall Survive? Foundations of Sociometry, Group Psychotherapy and Sociodrama*. New York: Beacon House.

Morgan, D. (1997) *Focus Groups and Qualitative Research* (2nd edition). Thousand Oaks, Calif.: Sage.

Morgan, D. (1998) *The Focus Group Guidebook*. Thousand Oaks, Calif.: Sage.

Morgan, D. and Krueger, R. (1993) When to use focus groups and why. In D. Morgan (ed.) *Successful Focus Groups: Advancing the State of the Art*. Newbury Park, Calif.: Sage.

Morgan, D. and Scannell, A. (1998) *Planning Focus Groups*, Thousand Oaks, Calif.: Sage.

Morgan, M. (1998) Qualitative research . . . science or pseudo-science? *The Psychologist*, October, 481–483.

Morris, G. and LoVerde, M. (1993) Consortium surveys. In P. Rosenfeld, J. Edwards and M. Thomas (eds) *Improving Organisational Surveys: New Directions, Methods and Applications*. Newbury Park, Calif.: Sage.

Morris, J., Cascio, W. and Young, C. (1999) Downsizing after all these years: questions and answers about who did it, how many did it, and who benefited from it. *Organizational Dynamics*, 27, 78–87.

Morris, T., Lydka, H. and O'Creevy, M. (1993) Can commitment be managed? A longitudinal analysis of employee commitment and human resource policies. *Human Resource Management Journal*, 3, 21–42.

Morrison, L., Colman, A. and Preston, C. (1997) Mystery customer research: cognitive processes affecting accuracy. *Journal of the Market Research Society*, 39, 349–361.

Morrow, N. and Hargie, O. (1996) Influencing and persuading skills at the interprofessional interface: training for action. *Journal of Continuing Education in the Health Professions*, 16, 94–102.

Morwitz, V., Steckel, J. and Gupta, A. (1997) When do purchase intentions predict sales? *Marketing Science Institute*, Working Paper Report No. 97–112, 1–38.

Mugford, M., Banfield, P. and O'Hanlon, M. (1991) Effects of feedback of information on clinical practice: a review. *British Medical Journal*, 303, 398–402.

Muncer, S.J. and Gillen, K. (1997) Network analysis and lay interpretation: some issues of consensus and representation. *British Journal of Social Psychology*, 36, 537–551.

Murray, H. (1989) Training in giving and receiving criticism. *Training and Development*, January, 19–20.

Myers, D. (1996) *Social Psychology*. New York: McGraw-Hill.

NHS Management Executive (1995) *Setting Standards for NHS Communications: Consultation Document*. London: NHS Management Executive.

Norton, R.W. (1980) Nonmetric multidimensional scaling in communication research: smallest space analysis. In P. Monge and N. Cappella (eds) *Multivariate Techniques in Human Communication Research*. New York: Academic Press.

O'Brien, J. (1994) *Seeds of a New Church*. Blackrock: Columba Press.

O'Connell, D. and Kowal, S. (1995) Basic principles of transcription. In J. Smith, R. Harre and L. van Langenhove (eds) *Rethinking Methods in Psychology*. London: Sage.

O'Keefe, D. (1990) *Persuasion: Theory and Research*. Newbury Park, Calif.: Sage.

O'Muircheartaigh, C. and Campanelli, P. (1998) The relative impact of interviewer effects and sample design effects on survey precision. *Journal of the Royal Statistical Society*, 161, 63–77.

Oakley, A. (1981) Interviewing women: a contradiction in terms. In H. Roberts (ed.) *Doing Feminist Research*. Boston: Routledge and Kegan Paul.

Odiorne, G. (1954) An application of the communications audit. *Personnel Psychology*, 7, 235–243.

Odom, M. (1993) Kissing up really works on boss. *San Diego Union-Tribune*, 12 August, E12.

O'Donnell, J. (1988) Focus groups: a habit-forming evaluation technique. *Training and Development Journal*, 42, 71–73.

Office for Public Management (1994) *The Medium and the Message: A Survey of Communication Objectives and Practices in the NHS*. London: Office for Public Management.

Office of Population Censuses and Surveys (1992) *General Household Survey*. London: OPCS.

Oliver, A. and Ebers, M. (1998) Networking network studies: an analysis of conceptual configurations in the study of inter-organisational relationships. *Organization Studies*, 19, 549–583.

Osbourne, K.B. (1988) *Priesthood: A History of Ordained Ministry in the Roman Catholic Church*. New York: Paulist Press.

Padfield, A. and Procter, I. (1996) The effect of interviewer's gender on the interviewing process: a comparative enquiry. *Sociology*, 30, 355–366.

Padget, P. (1983) *Communications and Reports*. London: Cassell.

Patti, C.H. and Frazer, C. (1988). *Advertising: A Decision-making Approach*. Hinsdale, Ill.: Dryden Press.

Patti, C.H. and Moriarty, S. (1990). *The Making of Effective Advertising*. Englewood Cliffs, NJ.: Prentice-Hall.

Payne, J. (1996) Developing and implementing strategies for communicating bad news. *Journal of Communication Management*, 1, 80–88.

Payne, S. (1999) Interview in qualitative research. In A. Memon and R. Bull (eds) *Handbook of the Psychology of Interviewing*. Chichester: Wiley.

Pearson, A. (1991) Managing innovation: an uncertainty reduction process. In J. Henry and D. Walker (eds) *Managing Innovation*. London: Sage.

Perloff, R. (1993) *The Dynamics of Persuasion*, Hillsdale, N.J.: Lawrence Erlbaum.

Peterson, C., Maier, S. and Seligman, M. (1993) *Learned Helplessness: A Theory for the Age of Personal Control*. Oxford: Oxford University Press.

Petit, J., Goris, J. and Vaught, B. (1997) An examination of organizational communication as a moderator of the relationship between job performance and job satisfaction. *Journal of Business Communication*, 34, 81–98.

Pettigrew, A., Ferlie, E. and McKee, L. (1992) Shaping strategic change: the case of the NHS. *Public Money and Management*, 12, 27–32.

Pfeffer, J. (1992) *Managing With Power*. Cambridge, Mass.: Harvard Business School Press.

Pfeffer, J. (1996) When it comes to 'best practices' – why do smart organisations do dumb things? *Organizational Dynamics*, 25, 33–44.

Pfeffer, J. (1998) *The Human Equation*. Boston, Mass.: Harvard Business School Press.

Pfeffer, J. and Cialdini, R. (1998) Illusions of influence. In R. Kramer and M. Neale (eds) *Power and Influence in Organisations*. London: Sage.

Phelps, L.D. and duFrene, D.D. (1989) Improving organizational communication through trust. *Journal of Technical Writing and Communication*, 19, 267–276.

Pincus, J.D. (1986) Communication satisfaction, job satisfaction, and job performance. *Human Communication Research*, 12, 395–419.

Pollner, M. (1998) The effects of interviewer gender in mental health interviews. *Journal of Nervous and Mental Disease*, 186, 369–373.

Porter, D.T. (1988) Diagnosing communication networks. In C. Downs (ed.) *Communication Audits*. New York: HarperCollins.

Povey, T., Dunbar P. and Kendall, H. (1990) Pharmacist perceptions of the factors important to consumer loyalty. *Pharmaceutical Journal*, 245, R18.

Pratkanis, A. and Aronson, E. (1992) *Age of Propaganda: The Everyday Use and Abuse of Persuasion*. New York: Freeman.

Pryce-Jones, M. (1993) Critical incident technique as a method of assessing patient satisfaction. In R. Fitzpatrick and A. Hopkins (eds) *Measurement of Patients' Satisfaction with their Care*. London: Royal College of Physicians.

Quible, Z. (1998) A focus on focus groups. *Business Communication Quarterly*, 61, 28–38.

Quirke, B. (1995) Internal communication. In N. Hart (ed.) *Strategic Public Relations*. Basingstoke: Macmillan.

Quirke, B. (1996) Putting communication on management's agenda. *Journal of Communication Management*, 1, 67–79.

Rackham, N. and Carlisle, J. (1978) The effective negotiator – Part 1. *Journal of European Industrial Training*, 2(6), 6–10.

Rago, W. (1996) Struggles in transformation: a study in TQM, leadership and organisational culture in a government agency. *Public Administration Review*, 56, 227–234.

Ransom, S., Bryman, A. and Hinings, B. (1977) *Clergy, Ministers and Priests*. London: Routledge and Kegan Paul.

Rauch, W. (1979) The decision Delphi. *Technological Forecasting and Social Change*, 15, 159–169.

Rawlins, W. (1998) Theorizing public and private domains and practices of communication. *Communication Theory*, 8, 369–380.

Reardon, K. (1991) *Persuasion in Practice*. Newbury Park, Calif.: Sage.

Redding, W. (1972) *Communication Within the Organization: An Interpretive Review of Theory and Research*. New York: Industrial Communication Council.

Reichfield, F. (1996a) Learning from customer defections. *Harvard Business Review*, 74, 56–61.

Reichfield, F. (1996b) *The Loyalty Effect*. Boston, Mass.: Harvard Business School Press.

Reid, N. (1988) The Delphi technique: its contribution to the evaluation of professional practice. In R. Ellis (ed.) *Professional Competence and Quality Assurance in the Caring Professions*. London: Croom Helm.

Reid, W., Pease, J. and Taylor, R. (1990) The Delphi technique as an aid to organization development activities. *Organization Development Journal*, 8, 37–42.

Remenyi, D., Williams, B., Money, A. and Swartz, E. (1998) *Doing Research in Business and Management: An Introduction to Process and Method*, London: Sage.

Renkema, J. and Hoeken, H. (1998) The influence of negative newspaper publicity on corporate image in the Netherlands. *Journal of Business Communication*, 35, 521–535.

Rice, D. (1990) *Shattered Vows: Exodus from the Priesthood*. Belfast: Blackstaff Press.

Roberts, K.H. and O'Reilly, C.A. (1973) Measuring organizational communication. *Journal of Applied Psychology*, 59, 321–326.

Roberts-Gray, C. (1992) Preparing resorts and presentations that strengthen the link between research and action. In A. Vaux, M. Stockdale and M. Schwerin (eds) *Independent Consulting for Evaluators*. Newbury Park, Calif.: Sage.

Ronan, W. and Latham, G. (1974) The reliability and validity of the critical incident technique: a closer look. *Studies in Personnel Psychology*, 6, 53–64.

Rosenfeld, P., Giacalone, R. and Riordan, C. (1995) *Impression Management in Organizations*. Routledge: London.

Rosenhan, D. (1973) On being sane in insane places. *Science*, 179, 250–258.

Rossiter, J. and Perry, L. (1987) *Advertising and Promotion Management*. New York: McGraw-Hill.

Rubin, J. (1996) New corporate practice, new classroom pedagogy: toward a redefinition of management communication. *Business Communication Quarterly*, 59, 7–19.

Rubin, R., Palmgreen, P. and Sypher, H. (eds) (1994) *Communication Research Measures: A Sourcebook*. New York: Guilford Press.

Rucci, A., Kirn, S. and Quinn, R. (1998) The employee–customer–profit chain at Sears. *Harvard Business Review*, 76, 82–98.

Ryder, I. (1998) Moments of truth management. *Strategic Communication Management*, February–March, 16–21.

Sarangi, S. (1994) Accounting for mismatches in intercultural selection interviews. *Multilingua*, 13, 163–194.

Saunders, C. (1986) Opening and closing. In O. Hargie (ed.) *A Handbook of Communication Skills* (1st edition). London: Croom Helm.

Saunders, C. and Caves, R. (1986) An empirical approach to the identification of communication skills with reference to speech therapy. *Journal of Further and Higher Education*, 10, 29–44.

Saunders, C. and Saunders, E.D. (1993a) Expert teachers' perceptions of university teaching: the identification of teaching skills. In R. Ellis (ed.) *Quality Assurance for University Teaching*, Buckingham: Open University Press.

Saunders, C. and Saunders, E.D. (1993b) *Expert Teachers' Perceptions of University Teaching: The Identification of Teaching Skills*. Jordanstown: University of Ulster.

Scarpello, V. and Vandenberg, R. (1991) Some issues to consider when surveying employee opinions. In W. Jones, B. Steffy and D. Bray (eds) *Applying Psychology in Business: The Handbook for Managers and Human Resource Professionals*. Lexington, Mass.: Lexington Books.

Schaffer, R. and Thomson, H. (1992) Successful change programmes begin with results. *Harvard Business Review*, 70, 80–89.

Schofield, T. and Pendleton, D. (1986) What sort of doctor? In D. Pendleton, T. Schofield and M. Marinker (eds) *In Pursuit of Quality: Approaches to Performance Review in General Practice*. Exeter, Devon: Royal College of General Practitioners.

Schrage, M. (1999) The nightmare of networks: when best practices meet the intranet, innovation takes a holiday. *Fortune*, 139, 198.

Schultz, D.E., Tannenbaum, S.T. and Lauterborn, R. (1992). *Integrated Marketing Communications: Pulling It Together and Making It Work*. Lincolnwood, Ill.: NTC Publishing.

Scott, J. (1991) *Social Network Analysis: A Handbook*. London: Sage.

Scott, M. (1996) Can consumers change corporations? *Executive Female*, 19, 42–46.

Seidman, I.E. (1991) *Interviewing as Qualitative Research. A Guide for Researchers in Education and the Social Sciences*. New York: Teachers College Press.

Selltiz, C., Wrightsman, L. and Cook, S. (1976) *Research Methods in Social Relations*. New York: Holt, Rinehart and Winston.

Semler, R. (1989) Managing without managers. *Harvard Business Review*, 67, 76–85.

Semler, R. (1993) *Maverick*. London: Century.

Shapiro, E. (1995) *Fad Surfing in the Boardroom*. London: HarperCollins.

Shapiro, E. (1998) *The Seven Deadly Sins of Business*. Oxford: Capstone.

Shapiro, J. (1999) Implementing change with audit: the role of management. In R. Baker, H. Hearnshaw and N. Robertson (eds) *Implementing Change with Clinical Audit*. Chichester: Wiley.

Shelby, A. and Reinsch, N. (1996) The communication audit: a framework for teaching management communication. *Business Communication Quarterly*, 59, 95–108.

Sheridan, J., White, J. and Fairchild, T. (1992) Ineffective staff, ineffective supervision, or ineffective administration? Why some nursing homes fail to provide adequate care. *The Gerontologist*, 32, 334–341.

Short, J., Williams, E. and Christie, B. (1976) *The Social Psychology of Telecommunications*. London: John Wiley.

Sias, P.M. and Cahill, D.J. (1998) From coworkers to friends: the development of peer friendships in the workplace. *Western Journal of Communication*, 62, 273–299.

Sim, J. (1998) Collecting and analysing qualitative data: issues raised by the focus group. *Journal of Advanced Nursing*, 28, 345–352.

Sims, H. and Lorenzi, P. (1992) *The New Leadership Paradigm: Social Learning and Cognition in Organisations*. London: Sage.

Sinickas, A. (1998) Communication measurement. *Strategic Communication Management*, 2, 8–9.

Skinner, B.F. (1954) The science of learning and the art of teaching. *Harvard Educational Review*, 24, 86–97.

Skipper, M. (1992) Communication processes and their effectiveness in the management and treatment of dysphagia. Unpublished D. Phil. thesis, Jordanstown, University of Ulster.

Smeltzer, L. (1993) Emerging questions and research paradigms in business communication research. *Journal of Business Communication*, 30, 181–198.

Smith, A. (1991) *Innovative Employee Communication: New Approaches to Improving Trust, Teamwork and Performance*. Englewood Cliffs, N.J.: Prentice-Hall.

Smith, F., Salkind M. and Jolly, B. (1990) Community pharmacy: a method of assessing quality of care. *Social Science and Medicine*, 31, 603–607.

Smith, J., Harre, R. and van Langenhove, L. (1995) Idiography and the case study. In J. Smith, R. Harre and L. van Langenhove (eds) *Rethinking Psychology*. London: Sage.

Smith, M. and Robertson, I.T. (1993) *The Theory and Practice of Systematic Personnel Selection* (2nd edition). London: Macmillan.

Snyder, R. and Morris, J. (1984) Organisational communication and performance. *Journal of Applied Psychology*, 69, 461–465.

Spurgeon, P. and Barwell, F. (1991) *Implementing Change in the NHS*. London: Chapman and Hall.

Stackman, R. and Pinder, C. (1999) Context and sex effects on personal work networks. *Journal of Social and Personal Relationships*, 16, 39–64.

Stallworth, Y. and Roberts-Gray, C. (1987) The craft of evaluation: reporting to the busy decision maker. *Evaluation Review*, 13, 91–103.

Stanton, M. (1981) How to audit communications. *Management Today*, November, 69–73.

State Street Global Advisors Investor Education Council (1998). Retirement Confidence Survey, Boston, Mass.: SSGA.

Stewart, C.J. and Cash, W.B. (1988) *Interviewing: Principles and Practices*. Dubuque, Iowa: W.C. Brown.

Stewart, D. and Shamdasani, P. (1990) *Focus Groups: Theory and Practice*, Newbury Park, Calif.: Sage.

Stewart, R. (1967) *Managers And Their Jobs*. New York: Macmillan.

Stewart, T. (1999) The status of communication today. *Strategic Communication Management*, 3, 22–25.

Stone, B. (1995) Strategic marketing and communications audits. *Marketing Health Services*, 15, 54–56.

Strenski, J. (1978) The communications audit: primary PR measurement tool. *Public Relations Quarterly*, Winter, 17–18.

Strenski, J. (1984) The communications audit: basic to business development. *Public Relations Quarterly*, Spring, 14–17.

Sutherland, S. (1992) *Irrationality*. London: Constable.

Szybillo, J. and Berger, R. (1979) What advertising agencies think of focus groups. *Journal of Advertising Research*, 19, 29–33.

Taaffe, J. (1996) Europe races towards intranets. *Computerworld*, 23 December, 76.

Tang, T. and Ibrahim, A. (1998) Antecedents of organisational citizenship behaviour revisited: public personnel in the United States and in the Middle East. *Public Personnel Management*, 27, 529–549.

Thach, E. and Murphy, K. (1995) Competencies for distance education professionals. *Educational Technology Research and Development*, 43, 57–79.

Thompson, G. (1996) Communication assets in the information age: the impact of communications technology on corporate communications. *Corporate Communications: An International Journal*, 1, 8–10.

Tichy, N. and Charan, R. (1995) The CEO as coach: an interview with Allied Signal's Lawrence Bossidy. *Harvard Business Review*, March–April, 68–79.

Tittmar, H. (1978) Seasonal fluctuation in condom retrieval. *IRCS Medical Science*, 6, 135.

Tjosvold, D. (1991) *Team Organisation: An Enduring Competitive Advantage*. New York: John Wiley.

Tourish, B. and Tourish, D. (1997) Auditing internal communications in local authority leisure facilities: a case study from a leisure complex. *Managing Leisure: An International Journal*, 2(3), 155–173.

Tourish, D. (1996) Internal communication and the NHS: the results of a fieldwork analysis, and implications for corporate practice. Unpublished D. Phil. thesis, University of Ulster.

Tourish, D. (1997) Transforming internal corporate communications: the power of symbolic gestures, and barriers to change. *Corporate Communications: An International Journal*, 2(3), 109–116.

Tourish, D. (1998) 'The god that failed': replacing visionary leadership with open communication. *Australian Journal of Communication*, 25, 99–114.

Tourish, D. and Hargie, O. (1996a) Internal communication: key steps in evaluating and improving performance. *Corporate Communications*, 1, 11–16.

Tourish, D. and Hargie, O. (1996b) Communication audits and the management of change: a case study from an NHS trust. *Health Services Management Research*, 9, 125–135.

Tourish, D. and Hargie, O. (1996c) Communication in the NHS: using qualitative approaches to analyse effectiveness. *Journal of Management in Medicine*, 10, 38–54.

Tourish, D. and Hargie, O. (1998) Communication between managers and staff in the NHS: trends and prospects. *British Journal of Management*, 9, 53–71.

Tourish, D. and Mulholland, J. (1997) Communication between nurses and nurse managers: a case study from an NHS Trust. *Journal of Nursing Management*, 5, 25–36.

Tourish, D. and Tourish, B. (1996) Assessing staff–management relationships in local authority leisure facilities: the communication audit approach. *Managing Leisure: An International Journal*, 1, 91–104.

Towers-Perrin (1993) *Improving Business Performance Through Your People*. San Francisco: Towers Perrin.

Tracy, K. and Tracy, S. (1998) Rudeness at 911. *Human Communication Research*, 25, 225–251.

Treadwell, D. and Harrison, T. (1994) Conceptualizing and assessing organizational image: model images, commitment and communication. *Communication Monographs*, 61, 63–85.

Tsui, A., Ashford, S., St. Clair, L. and Xin, K. (1995) Dealing with discrepant expectations: response strategies and managerial effectiveness. *Academy of Management Journal*, 38, 1515–1543.

Tufte, E. (1983) *The Visual Display of Quantitative Information*. Cheshire, Conn.: Graphics Press.

Turk, C. (1985) *Effective Speaking*. London: Spon.

Turnbull, P. and Wass, V. (1998) Marksist management: sophisticated human relations in a high street retail store. *Industrial Relations Journal*, 29, 99–111.

Turner, L. (1997) Participation, democracy and efficiency in the US workplace. *Industrial Relations Journal*, 28, 309–313.

Utley, A. (1997) Abusive e-mails ignite work fury. *The Times Higher Education Supplement*, 30 May, 1.

van de Gaag, A. and Reid, D. (1998) *Clinical Guidelines by Consensus for Speech and Language Therapists*. London: Royal College of Speech and Language Therapists.

Van Tilburg, T. (1998) Interviewer effects in the measurement of personal network size: a nonexperimental study. *Sociological Methods and Research*, 26, 300–328.

Varney, G. (1990) A study of the core literature in organization development. *Organization Development Journal*, 8, 59–66.

Vaughn, S., Schumm, J. and Sinagub, J. (1996) *Focus Group Interviews in Education and Psychology*, Thousand Oaks, Calif.: Sage.

von Eye, A. (1990) *Introduction to Configural Frequency Analysis*. Cambridge: Cambridge University Press.

Walker, R. (ed.) (1985) *Applied Qualitative Research*. Aldershot: Gower.

Wasserman, S. and Faust, K. (1994) *Social Network Analysis*. Cambridge: Cambridge University Press.

Webb, M. and Palmer, G. (1998) Evading surveillance and making time: an ethnographic view of the Japanese factory floor in Britain. *British Journal of Industrial Relations*, 36, 611–627.

Weber, M. (1947) *The Theory of Social and Economic Organization*. New York: Oxford.

Weick, K. (1995) *Sensemaking in Organisations*. London: Sage.

Weinberger, M., Ferguson, J., Westmoreland, G., Mamlin, L., Segar, D., Eckert, G., Greene, J., Martin, D. and Tierney, W. (1998) Can raters consistently evaluate the content of focus groups? *Social Science and Medicine*, 46, 929–933.

Weinshall, T. (1979) *Managerial Communication: Concepts, Approaches and Techniques*. London: Academic Press.

Weir, W. (1993). *How to Create Interest-evoking, Sales-inducing, Non-irritating Advertising*, Norwood, Australia.: Haworth Press.

Welch, J. (1996) Intranet boom needs careful management. *People Management*, 2, 10–11.

Wells, B. and Spinks, N. (1996) The good, the bad, the persuasive strategies for business managers. *Corporate Communications: An International Journal*, 1, 22–31.

Wells, J. (1996) Not exactly a picture of health. *Health Service Journal*, 10, 20–22.

Wetlaufer, S. (1999) Driving change: an interview with Ford Motor Company's Jacques Nasser. *Harvard Business Review*, March–April, 76–88.

Whetten, D. and Cameron, K. (1991) *Developing Management Skills* (2nd edition). London: HarperCollins.

White, G. and Thomson, A. (1995) Anonymized focus groups as a research tool for health professionals. *Qualitative Health Research*, 5, 256–261.

White, J. and Mazur, L. (1995) *Strategic Communications Management: Making Public Relations Work*. Wokingham: Addison-Wesley.

Wiio, O.A. (1975) *Systems of Information, Communication, and Organization*. Helsinki: Helsinki Research Institute for Business Economics.

Wiio, O.A. (1977) *Organizational Communication and its Development*. Helsinki: Viestintainstituuti (Institute for Human Communication).

Wilmot, R. and McClelland, V. (1990) How to run a reality check. *Training*, May, 66–72.

Wilson, A. (1998) The use of mystery shopping in the measurement of service delivery. *Service Industries Journal*, 18, 148–163.

Wilson, A. and Gutmann, J. (1998) Public transport: the role of mystery shopping in investment decisions. *Journal of the Market Research Society*, 40, 285–293.

Wilson, M., Robinson, E. and Ellis, A. (1989) Studying communication between community pharmacists and their customers. *Counselling Psychology Quarterly*, 2, 367–380.

Wright, D. (1995) The role of corporate public relations executives in the future of employee communications. *Public Relations Review*, 21, 181–198.

Wynne, B. (1990) Internal communications. *Training and Development*, 8, 28–30.

Zack, M.H. and McKenney, J.L. (1995) Social context and interaction in ongoing computer-supported management groups. *Organization Science*, 6, 394–422.

Zimmerman, S., Sypher, B. and Haas, J. (1996) A communication metamyth in the workplace: the assumption that none is better. *Journal of Business Communication*, 33, 185–204.

Zorn, T. (1995) Bosses and buddies: constructing and performing simultaneously hierarchical and close friendship relationships. In J. Wood and S. Duck (eds) *Under-studied Relationships*. London: Sage.

Subject index

Author index